Connectivity, Imperialism, and the Han Iron Industry

This book examines the rise of the iron industry during the Warring States and Western Han periods (ca. 400 BCE–9 CE) in ancient China, which is characterized not only by various technological innovations but also as a remarkable phenomenon, leading to the widespread distribution of iron implements and the emergence of massive ironworks that were rarely seen in later periods.

With *Connectivity, Imperialism, and the Han Iron Industry*, Lam Wengcheong combines archaeological and historical analyses to piece together fragmentary evidence and to refocus our gaze onto the economic and political mechanism that gave birth to an iron industry unique in the ancient world. Guiding readers through the macroscopic social settings of the iron industry and distribution patterns of iron implements to the microscopic organization of workplace and workers' foodways, Lam explores how iron production and transportation processes intersected with the transformation of the Han capital region in the Guanzhong basin. Using various lines of evidence of iron production in Guanzhong and its connection with other production centers, this book shows how the production and transportation of iron at various scales played a significant role in generating the "connectivity" between various parts of the Western Han empire, and casts new light on the workings of the economic system in imperial China.

Connectivity, Imperialism, and the Han Iron Industry will appeal to anyone interested in Chinese archaeology, the history of the Han empire, and the history of science and engineering in ancient China, as well as to scholars working on the comparative study of ancient imperialism, market exchange, and economic history.

Wengcheong Lam is Assistant Professor in the Department of Anthropology and Department of History at the Chinese University of Hong Kong. His work focuses on the economic system, development of metal techniques, and exchange network in early ancient China.

Routledge Studies in Chinese Archaeology
Series editor: Rowan K. Flad

The Routledge Series in Chinese Archaeology contains theoretically informed studies of Chinese archaeological material. The books in the series contribute both to our understanding of China's past through an archaeological lens and to the broader theoretical discourse on anthropological and historical topics. Engaging with the overlapping fields of East Asian archaeology, anthropology, history and art history, books in this series provide scholarly studies of new research and syntheses that contribute to specialist discourse in these disciplines and intervene in scholarship that transcends the Chinese context.

Connectivity, Imperialism, and the Han Iron Industry
Wengcheong Lam

Weapons in Late Shang (c. 1250–1050 BCE) China
Beyond Typology and Ritual
Qin Cao

For more information about this series, please visit: Routledge Studies in Chinese Archaeology: Routledge Studies in Chinese Archaeology – Book Series – Routledge & CRC Press

Connectivity, Imperialism, and the Han Iron Industry

Wengcheong Lam

Routledge
Taylor & Francis Group

LONDON AND NEW YORK

First published 2023
by Routledge
4 Park Square, Milton Park, Abingdon, Oxon OX14 4RN

and by Routledge
605 Third Avenue, New York, NY 10158

Routledge is an imprint of the Taylor & Francis Group, an informa business

British Library Cataloguing-in-Publication Data
A catalogue record for this book is available from the British Library

Library of Congress Cataloging-in-Publication Data
A catalog record has been requested for this book

ISBN: 978-1-032-19447-9 (hbk)
ISBN: 978-1-032-19448-6 (pbk)
ISBN: 978-1-003-25922-0 (ebk)

DOI: 10.4324/9781003259220

Typeset in Times New Roman
by codeMantra

Printed in the United Kingdom
by Henry Ling Limited

In memory of Professor Liu Xu 刘绪 (1949–2021)
With my deepest respect and gratitude for all his teaching

Contents

List of figure   ix
List of tables   xiv
Chronological table and important historical events
   mentioned in texts   xv
Equivalents for weights and measures during the Han period   xvi
Acknowledgments   xvii

Introduction   **1**
   1 Imperialism and connectivity 1
   2 Imperial transformation and the role of the capital region 7
   3 Iron industry and its significance to social relations 12
   4 Chapter structure 18

PART I

1   The rise of iron and imperial state power   29
   1 Iron as an emblem of prestige 32
   2 The coming of the large-scale cast iron manufacturing 38
   3 Ambiguous emergence of iron technology in the Qin state 44

**2   The rise of the capital region and the management of craft
industry during the Han dynasty**   57
   1 The imperial capital and its hinterland 59
   2 The imperial management of craft industries 70
   3 Craft industries in the capital region: ceramic, bronze, and iron 76

3   Iron making in the center of the Han state   87
   *1 Iron making techniques and the operational chain in the
     Han period 89*

   2 *Industrial clusters in the broader Central Plains region 96*
   3 *Iron-making in the Han capital region 107*

PART II

4 Organization and labor division of ironworks   119
   1 *Understanding the social organization of workers in "silent" records 120*
   2 *Making for the masses: the emergence of concentrated workshops predating the Han period 128*
   3 *The organization and nature of labor at ironworks in Guanzhong: a microscopic viewpoint 138*

5 Food and economic embeddedness of iron production communities   152
   1 *Food supply system and economic embeddedness 153*
   2 *Deep economic embeddedness in Warring States' metropolitan areas 161*
   3 *Food supply and the embeddedness of iron production in the capital region 169*

6 Market integration and the distribution system for iron goods   182
   1 *Conceptualizing regional integration and market exchange in ancient China 184*
   2 *Dendritic distribution of metal in the Warring States period 194*
   3 *Appearance of an integrated market in the Han capital 202*

Conclusion: management of iron and the *shihuo* system   **216**

   Glossary   228
   Bibliography   239
   Index   299

Figures

I.1 Major traffic routes and ruling towns of the Han empire
(after Tan 1967:Fig 1–4)   2
I.2 The geography of the Guanzhong basin and pathways
connecting to Chang'an (after Xin 1988:Fig 1)   8
1.1 Distribution map of early iron objects in Xinjiang,
bimetallic weapons, early cast iron objects in the Central
Plains, and cemeteries that are mentioned in the chapter   34
1.2 Selective bimetallic weapons and tools in the Spring-and-
Autumn period (a–b: redrawn from Henan & Sanmenxia
1999:Fig 105.3; c: redrawn from Zhang et al. 2020:Fig 3; d:
redrawn from Chen et al. 2009:Fig 3; e: redrawn from Han
1998:Fig 1.4; f: redrawn from Tian & Lei 1993:Fig 7.1)   35
1.3 Percentage of tombs including major types of iron wares in
the three regions during the Warring States period. Please
note that the data for the Chu state only come from the
Changsha and Yiyang areas, not including the Jiangling area   43
1.4 Migration route of the Qin state (after Liang 2020:Fig 1)   44
1.5 Layout of the Yongcheng capital (after Tian 2018:Fig 1;
source of the background map: Google Map)   45
1.6 Layout of the Xianyang capital (after Xu & Su 2016:Fig 1;
Xu 2021:Fig 1; Zhongguo Shehui 2010:Fig 1-1)   47
1.7 Representative iron implements found in the Qin state
during the Warring States period (after Lam et al. 2017a:Fig 4, 6)   49
2.1 Layout of Chang'an city and distribution of manufacturing
remains inside (after Bai 2011:Fig 2; Zhang 2016:Fig 58)   58
2.2 Distribution of various gardens, pavilions, and palaces
inside Shanglin yuan that were mentioned in transmitted
texts (after Yu & Li 2012:Fig 1; source of the background
DEM: USGS SRTM Void Filled Dataset)   63
2.3 Distribution of cemeteries in the suburbs of Chang'an   64
2.4 Distribution of mausoleum towns and Chang'an (redrawn
from Zhang 2016:Fig 145)   65

2.5   Canal systems in the Guanzhong basin (after Li 2004:Fig 2-3, Fig 3-3, Fig 3-6, Fig 3-8, Fig 3-10)   67
2.6   Distribution of iron ores surrounding the Guanzhong basin and craft production centers inside   69
2.7   Location of the Han cemetery, ironworks, and settlements of various periods identified through a survey in the Taicheng site complex (after Shaanxi Yanjiuyuan 2018a:Fig 3; also note that the survey results did not show large-scale residential sites in contemporary with the ironworks)   81
3.1   Operational chain of iron manufacture and techniques in ancient China   96
3.2   Locations of iron offices mentioned in *Hanshu* and *Hou Hanshu*   97
3.3   Locations of ironworks that were archaeologically found in the broader Central Plains region   98
3.4   The layout of the Guxingzhen ironworks and reconstruction of one of the blast furnaces (a: Layout of Guxingzhen ironworks, after Zhengzhou 1978:Fig 2; b: the reconstructed profile of the blast furnace no. 1 employed in Guxing, redrawn from Wagner 2001:Fig 11; c: the reconstructed working scene, redrawn from Wagner 2001:Fig 12)   100
3.5   Layout of Linzi walled city and location of various craft workshops (redrawn from Zhongguo Shehui et al. 2020:Fig 5-1)   104
3.6   Plan of various excavated features at Taicheng and manufacturing remains found in the ironworks (a: after Shaanxi Yanjiuyuan 2018a:Fig 5; b: plowshare core, redrawn from Shaanxi Yanjiuyuan 2018a:Fig 15-2; c: plowshare mold, redrawn from Shaanxi Yanjiuyuan 2018a:Fig 79-2; d: hoe-head mold, redrawn from Shaanxi Yanjiuyuan 2018a:Fig 42-2; e: hoe-head mold, redrawn from Shaanxi Yanjiuyuan 2018a:Fig 76-4; f–k: iron pieces, redrawn from Shaanxi Yanjiuyuan 2018a:Fig 33)   109
3.7   Process flow diagram showing the reconstructed production system at Taicheng   111
4.1   Plan showing the organization of the modern ironworks in Huize (after Yang et al. 2010:Fig 32)   125
4.2   Location of the Niucun bronze foundry and molds/models for bronze manufacturing (a: location of various loci at the Niucun site complex, after Shanxi 1993:Fig 3; Shanxi 2012:Fig 2. The triangle represents another bronze foundry contemporary with the one at Niucun; b: example of a "pattern block" from locus II, redrawn from Shanxi 1993: c–e: examples of molds and models for casting various appendages; c: redrawn from Shanxi 1996:Fig 54; d: redrawn from Shanxi 1996:Fig 220; e: redrawn from Shanxi 1993:Fig 139)   129

4.3 Distribution of various types of remains and features in locus XXII and the two main types of casting molds from the locus (a: layout of locus XXII, Late Spring-and-Autumn period, after Shanxi 1993:Fig 19; b & c: molds for casting chisel/axe and *kongshoubu*, b: redrawn from Shanxi 1993:Fig 39-7, c: redrawn from Shanxi 1993:Fig 46-1) 133

4.4 Plan of the Zheng-Han Gucheng (Xinzheng) and location of the Zhonghang ironworks (redrawn from Ma 1999:Fig 2; Wang 2010:Appendix 2) 134

4.5 Distribution of various types of remains and features at Zhonghang ironworks and the two main types of casting molds for making iron implements from the ironworks (a: layout of the Zhonghang ironworks, after Henan 2006:Fig 491; b & c: molds for casting *jue* axe and *chu* hoe-heads, b: redrawn from Henan 2006:Fig 503-1, c: redrawn from Henan 2006:Fig 505-12) 136

4.6 Plans of large-scale ironworks in the Taishan cluster during the Han period (a: Dongpingling, after Shandong et al. 2019:Fig 3; b: Linzi, Kanjiazhai locus bI; after Zhongguo Shehui et al. 2020:Fig 3-8) 142

4.7 Plan showing the internal organization of the Taicheng ironworks (after Shaanxi Yanjiuyuan 2018a:Fig 5) 144

4.8 Photographs of joining markers and spacers on casting molds (a: two types of joining markers on the top edge of hoe-head molds; b: two types of spacers on plowshare cores, photographed by the author) 145

4.9 Hypothetical scheme showing the connection between workers taking charge of different stages of production at Taicheng (this scheme shows that the production of the same type of molds might have been conducted by different groups of workers. Molds of the same type but with different colors represent those products with different joining markers. Meanwhile, molds were not randomly passed down to casting workers. Each group or team of casting workers seemed to have had a connection with a specific group of mold workers. The assemblages of casting molds used by different groups of casting workers might, therefore, be different) 147

5.1 Recovery rates of cattle elements from Zhonghang and Taicheng 164

5.2 Illustrations that show the elements with the two highest recovery rates among the cattle skeletons in the Zhonghang and Taicheng assemblages (redrawn from König & Liebich 2020:Fig 1.28) 165

5.3 Recovery rates of pig elements from Zhonghang and Taicheng 165

5.4   Illustrations that show the elements with the two highest
      recovery rates among the pig skeletons in the Zhonghang
      and Taicheng assemblages (redrawn from König & Liebich
      2020:Fig 1.27)   166
5.5   Kill-off patterns of cattle (a), dogs (b), and pigs (c) based on
      epiphyseal fusion at Zhonghang (mos = months) (age stages
      and grouping of cattle bones fusing are following Brunson
      et al. 2016; Silver 1969; age stages and fusing of dog bones
      are following Silver 1969). The estimated pig age of each
      stage is based on Grant (1982) and Zeder et al. (2015)   167
5.6   Eruption and wear stage of teeth in pig tooth-rows and
      loose teeth (mandible) at Zhonghang (a) and Taicheng (b).
      Mos = months. The estimated age of each stage is based
      on Grant (1982) and adjusted based on the Bronze Age pig
      assemblages at Yinxu by Li (2011)   168
5.7   Recovery rates of dog elements from Taicheng   172
5.8   Illustrations that show the elements with the two highest
      recovery rates among the dog skeletons in Taicheng
      (redrawn from König & Liebich 2020:Fig 1.26)   172
5.9   Kill-off patterns of cattle (a) and dogs (b) based on
      epiphyseal fusion at Taicheng (mos = months) (age stages
      and grouping of cattle bones fusing are following Brunson
      et al. 2016; Silver 1969; age stages and fusing of dog bones
      are following Silver 1969)   174
6.1   Schematics for three market-exchange models: dendritic
      (left); administrative-integrated (center); fully-integrated
      (right). Key: circle drawn with a solid black line represents
      the market area covered by the capital (largest solid black
      dot at the center of the circle); circles drawn with dashed
      lines represent market areas covered by administrative
      centers (black dots) other than the capital; medium size dots
      represent major (first-rank) centers; small dots represent
      minor or second-rank centers; straight lines between solid
      black dots represent market connections between centers
      (redrawn from Minc 2006:Fig 1; Smith 1976a:Fig 4)   190
6.2   Distribution of Warring States cemeteries of the Qin State
      in the Guanzhong basin, including parts of cemeteries
      dating to the Spring-and-Autumn and Qin unification periods   195
6.3   Percentage of tombs containing iron items at eight burial
      groups in Guanzhong from the Warring States through Qin
      periods   198
6.4   Graph showing a correlation between distance to Xianyang
      city and percentage of tombs containing two types of metal
      goods at eight burial groups from the Middle Warring
      States through Qin unification periods (ca. 350–206 BCE)

(a: iron objects; b: bronze objects; X-axis: distance from an
area to Xianyang city calculated by the average distance
between the cemeteries in the area to the capital; Y-axis:
percentage of tombs containing any one of four types of
iron objects in the area)   200

6.5   Percentage of tombs containing bronze items at eight burial
groups in Guanzhong during the Warring States through
Qin periods   201

6.6   Map of Western Han cemeteries in the Guanzhong basin   203

6.7   Percentage of tombs containing iron items at nine burial
groups in Guanzhong during the Western Han period   205

6.8   Graph showing a correlation between distance to Chang'an
city and percentage of tombs containing two types of metal
goods at nine burial groups during the Western Han period
(a: iron objects; b: bronze objects)   206

6.9   Percentage of tombs containing bronze items at nine burial
groups in Guanzhong during the Western Han period   208

Tables

I.1 Summary of Carrier's framework that conceptualizes the elements of commodity economy in 17th-century Britain   16

2.1 General structure of the Han central government (according to Loewe 2006)   72

3.1 Definition of basic technical terminologies   89

4.1 Definitions of the four parameters (upper) and eight types of specialization in Costin's framework (lower) (based on Costin 1991:11, 13, 15, 16; 2007:152)   122

4.2 Counts of assembling markers on hoe-head molds   144

4.3 Counts of assembling markers on plowshare molds   145

4.4 Counts of different types of spacers on plowshare cores   146

5.1 Types of economic embeddedness and corresponding types of workshop organization   157

5.2 Price of livestock mentioned in textual records (unit: *qian*)   161

5.3 Taxonomic representation at the Zhonghang and Taicheng ironworks   163

6.1 Types of market exchange and indicators for three exchange models   189

6.2 Tombs found at eight burial groups dating to the Warring States-Qin periods   196

6.3 Ranking of various burial groups at various centers during the Warring States-Qin periods   197

6.4 Comparison of percentages of iron and bronze objects found in Warring States-Qin tombs from capital, first-rank, and second-rank settlements   201

6.5 Numbers of tombs found in nine burial groups dating to the Western Han period   202

6.6 Ranking of Burial Groups at Various Centers during the Western Han period   204

6.7 Comparison of percentages of iron and bronze objects found in Western Han tombs from capital, first-rank, and second-rank settlements   207

Chronological table and important historical events mentioned in texts

Shang Period 1600–1046 BCE

    Late Shang (Yinxu) 1200–1046 BCE

Western Zhou 1046–771 BCE
Spring-and-Autumn Period 771–454 BCE
Warring States Period 454–221 BCE

    The division of the Jin state into the Han, Zhao, and Wei states 403 BCE
    The annexation of the Zheng state by the Han state 375 BCE
    Han state 403–230 BCE
    Zhao state 403–226 BCE
    Wei state 403–225 BCE
    The annexation of the Chu state by the Qin state 223 BCE

Qin Empire 221–207 BCE
Chu-Han War 207–202 BCE
Western Han 202 BCE–6 CE

    Gozu Emperor Gozu (ruling 202–195 BCE)
    Huidi Emperor Hui (ruling 195–188 BCE)
    Empress Lü (ruling 195–180 BCE)
    Wendi Emperor Wen (ruling 180–157 BCE)
    Jingdi Emperor Jing (ruling 157–141 BCE)
    Wudi Emperor Wu (ruling 141–87 BCE)
    Full implementation of the salt and iron monopoly policies (117 BCE)
    Zhaodi Emperor Zhao (ruling 87–74 BCE)
    Xuandi Emperor Xuan (ruling 74–48 BCE)
    Yuandi Emperor Yuan (ruling 48–33 BCE)
    Chengdi Emperor Cheng (ruling 33–7 BCE)
    Aidi Emperor Ai (ruling 7–1 BCE)
    Pingdi Emperor Ping (ruling 1 BCE–6 CE)

Xin Mang Period 9–23 CE
Eastern Han 25–220 CE

Equivalents for weights and measures during the Han period

Weight

1 *jin* 斤 = 248 g
1 *shi* 石 (weight unit) = 29.76 kg

Length

1 *li* 里 (distance unit) = 415.8 m

Capacity

1 *shi* 石 (volume unit) = 20,215 ml
1 *dou* 斗 = 1/10 *shi* ≈ 2,021 ml
1 *sheng* 升 = 1/10 *dou* ≈ 202 ml
1 *zhong* 鍾 = 6 *shi* (*hu* 斛) and 4 *dou* ≈ 129.4 liter.

Area

1 *mu* 畝 = 461 m^2
(Sources: Barbieri-Low, Anthony J., and Yates, Robin D. S. 2015 *Law, State, and Society in Early Imperial China: A Study with Critical Edition and Translation of the Legal Texts from Zhangjiashan Tomb no. 247, Section 1.4.* Leiden: Brill. Wu, Zhaoyang 吴朝阳, and Jin, Wen 晋文 2013 秦亩产新考——兼析传世文献中的相关亩产记载 (A new investigation on per mu yield of millet of Qin dynasty and an analysis of per mu yield of millet appeared in historical literature). 中国经济史研究 [*Researches in Chinese Economic History*] 2013(4):38–44, 64.)

Acknowledgments

This book grew out of my doctoral dissertation. First and foremost, I am grateful to my advisor Professor Rowan Flad for guiding me through all sorts of difficulties and unceasingly giving me insightful and creative comments on this work. It has been a privilege to be his student. I also want to express my appreciation to my other committee members: Professor Chen Jianli 陈建立, C.C. Lamberg-Karlovsky, Richard Meadow, and Michael Puett for providing invaluable advice and comments on early drafts of the dissertation. I am particularly thankful to Professor Chen Jianli for not only introducing the world of iron metallurgy to me but also providing various fieldwork and lab-work opportunities through which I have profited greatly.

At CUHK where I have held the joint teaching position since 2015, I am most grateful to Professor Gordon Mathew, Andrew Kinips, Lai Ming Chiu 黎明钊, and Poo Mu-chou 蒲慕洲 for their support and mentoring. I am also very thankful to other colleagues in the two departments for creating a wonderful and intellectual atmosphere that benefits my writing in various ways.

Previous versions of some materials in several chapters appeared in the following publication: chapter 1 in *The Oxford Handbook of Early China*, edited by Elizabeth Childs-Johnson (pp. 596–614, Oxford University Press); chapter 3, in "An iron production and exchange system at the center of the Western Han empire: scientific study of iron products and manufacturing remains from the Taicheng site complex" (*Journal of Archaeological Science* 100:88–101); chapters 4 and 5, in "Economic embeddedness and small-scale iron production in the capital region of the Han Empire: the perspective from faunal remains" (*Archaeological Research in Asia* 17:117–132); chapter 6, in "Integration and regional market system in the early Chinese empires: a case study of the distribution of iron and bronze objects in the Wei River valley" (*Asian Perspectives* 59(1):117–158). All such material has been substantially revised to reflect the latest scholarship. I wish to express my heartful gratitude to the comments that I have received from various editors before.

Various parts of the present book were built upon the fieldwork at the Taicheng site in Shaanxi between 2011 and 2013, and several field trips at metal production sites in Henan, Shandong, and other places in China, particularly in Hunan and Guangdong, from 2009 onward. I am incredibly grateful to Chong Jianrong 种建荣, my collaborator in the field project in Shaanxi. I want to extend my thanks for his unfailing help and advice. Thanks are also due to Sun Zhouyong 孙周勇, Tian Yaqi 田亚歧, Wang Zhankui 王占奎, Yang Qihuang 杨歧黄, Zhang Pengcheng 张鹏程, Zhao Fengyang 赵凤燕, and Zhao Yipeng 赵艺蓬 who supported me in various ways throughout the field project. Other members of the Taicheng excavation team were also critical to the completeness of the project by helping me finish most of the tedious and mechanical measuring. I have also benefited from the assistance of many other colleagues in Shaanxi that I cannot list here.

I would also like to thank Chang Huaiying 常怀颖, Gao Xiangping 郜向平, Ma Sai 马赛, Xie Su 谢肃, Wang Hui 王辉, Yu Wei 于薇, and Yu Wenjing 余雯晶. The time spent with them during our summer surveys and discussions about the entanglements between archaeology and history since 2009 inspired me in many ways and helped me understand the complexity of the world of Han material culture. My special thanks go to teachers at Peking University: Professor Cui Jianfeng 崔剑锋, Lei Xingshan 雷兴山, Sun Qingwei 孙庆伟, and particularly, late Professor Liu Xu 刘绪. I am thankful to friends and colleagues who commented on various parts of this book during the preparation process or contributed to projects beyond Shaanxi that eventually made this book possible: Francis Allard, Mick Atha, Bai Yunxiang 白云翔, Nathaniel Erb-Satullo, Huang Mingchong 黄铭崇, Lisa Kealhofer, Li Xiuzhen Janice 李秀珍, Li Zhipeng 李志鹏, Liu Siran 刘思然, Lv Liangbo 吕良波, Luo Shengqiang 罗胜强, Ma Xiaolin 马萧林, Mo Linheng 莫林衡, Wong Wai-yee Sharon, Alice Yao, You Yifei 游逸飞, Zhang Ji 张吉, Zhang Qianglu 张强禄, Zhang Zhouyu 张周瑜, and many other scholars and friends.

I am greatly grateful for the funding support of RGC GFR (#14621718). The Faculty of Arts at CUHK also provided financial support (Direct grant #4051151) for the research and publication of this book. I am grateful to my research assistants and graduate students: Tse Ngaying 谢雅妍, Sammie Wu 胡心儿, and Zou Yuqi 邹钰淇, for generating figures and organizing the bibliography for the manuscript. I also owe my gratitude to Neil O'Reilly for his critical contributions to this project and for carefully reading the early version of this manuscript. My other graduate students, Chen Yutong 陈虞通, Xiao Yuqi 肖毓绮, and Zhang Zhao 张钊, also helped with the preparation process. David Wilmshurst, my indefatigable editor for this book manuscript, has always challenged me to clarify and pushed me to dig deeper into my inquiries.

Finally, I cannot begin to express my feelings of gratitude to my wife, Liao Mingying 廖明英, who fully supported me through all manner of trial and tribulations; to my sons, Immanuel and Theodore, and to my sister, parents, and parent-in-law. I would never have completed this book without the help and support of my family.

Introduction

1 Imperialism and connectivity

In a synthetic work about the social lives in the Han period, Lao Kan (1907–2003), one of the most prominent historians in the study of excavated documents of the Han period, provides a vivid portrayal of a scene of heavy traffic in the northwestern frontiers of the Han empire. As he notes:

> On the pathway to Juyan were incessant streams of carriages, cattle, and horses travelling. Some of them belonged to the government, while others were privately owned. Those belonging to the government included *zhuanche, zhuanma,* and carriage fleets transporting necessities from inland. Those belonging to private owners had to show the permits for passage......The necessities from inland include cloth, silk, and clothes. Grains transported from nearby counties (from inland if the supply was not enough) include millets, wheat, *mi* millet, and *kuangmai.* Those necessities would eventually be transported to the storage points inside Juyan county or barriers, and then to other storage points.[1]

This reconstruction is based on the extraction of voluminous unearthed documents from Juyan, a military center that the Han state set up in present-day Ejin Banner, Inner Mongolia, against its nomadic Xiongnu enemies, who posed a threat from the Eurasian steppes to the Han state throughout its history. As Juyun was at least 1,500 km from the capital at Chang'an (Figure I.1), the transportation of weapons, cloth, grain, and other daily necessities (e.g., iron daily-use tools) from the capital to soldiers guarding the frontiers at Juyan or other garrisons nearby would take at least 60 days,[2] longer still if it started from further inland to the east of the capital.

Today, the town of Juyan and its defensive work are covered by a desert stretching as far as the eye can see. During the Han period, there would have been occasional villages along this long supply route, making the replenishing of supplies possible during the journey. Overland transportation to such distant centers was known to be both time-consuming and costly.[3] In order to maintain the outpost to protect the corridor and keep the communication

DOI: 10.4324/9781003259220-1

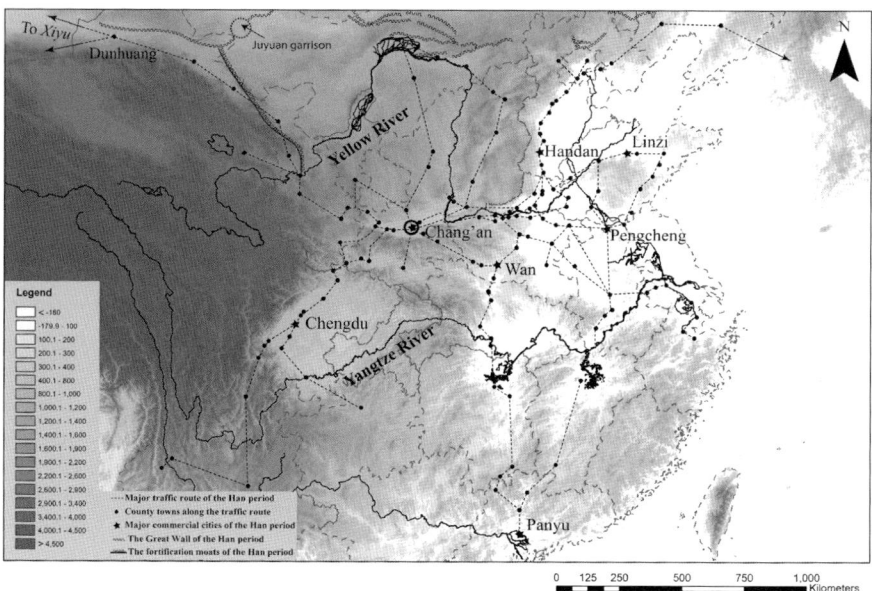

Figure I.1 Major traffic routes and ruling towns of the Han empire (after Tan 1967:Fig 1–4).[4]

lines between Xiyu (Western Regions) and attacks from nomadic Xiongnu open, however, the Han state had no choice but to do its utmost to em-ploy the state power—which also imposed a burden upon its people—to transport supplies to its frontier fortresses, which started northeast China, and ran through the Gobi desert, to Dunhuang and Xiyu in present-day Xinjiang.[5]

Building upon the foundations laid by the Qin state, the Western Han dynasty (206 BCE–25 CE, including the Xin Mang period) improved the transport system by building an imperial road network from the capital to the most important frontier centers, to strengthen its control over its far-flung empire. Through the state-supported mailing and transportation sys-tem, imperial orders could be delivered from Chang'an to the frontiers at the rate of about 70 km per day, a relatively fast speed in ancient times (Zhang 2007).[6] In an emergency, messages could be delivered even faster.[7] Besides issuing administrative information and imperial edicts, the Han state also constructed storage facilities that eased the movement of physical goods, such as grain and weaponry, from production centers located to the east of Guanzhong to the capital region or further west. Most importantly, the imperial system mobilized convict and conscript labor throughout its terri-tories. The garrison in Juyan was mostly recruited from military conscript labor, primarily from present-day Henan province to the east of the capital

region (Chen 1986:17), whose able-bodied men were each required to perform a year's service as frontier guards. The movement of population and
resources was thus a critical strategy used by the Han state to consolidate its
power (Chang 2007; Chen 1980; Korolkov & Hein 2020; Yao 2020).

The expansion of both the transportation network and bureaucratic system, also known as the *jun-xian* (commandery-county) system, all over the
Han territories undoubtedly intensified the exchange of information and
ideas as well as the transportation of goods manufactured by different production centers. Thanks to the recent discovery of a rich trove of government documents written on bamboo strips in garrisons on the northwestern
frontiers and in governmental centers at southern peripheries, scholars
have been able to clarify the organization of local institutions at various
levels. We now know the administrative duties of commandery governors
and county-level officials, and how the basic administrative units, *li* wards,
worked.[8] We now also have a better understanding of how the central court
issued documents, and how local county governments submitted census sta-
tistics and doubtful cases in which decisions were difficult to make for jurid-
ical review to a higher authority (Barbieri-low & Yates 2015:171).[9]

While this text-based analysis provides indispensable data for understanding the integration of various parts into the political infrastructure, in
the "Great Unity"[10] that was presented in material records such as the widespread use of Han-style roof-tiles in ruling towns at peripheries, we see how
the Han empire encountered various challenges. These challenges were due
to physical obstacles and barriers as well as responses to the Han expansion
ranging from resistance to collaboration,[11] differences that are unsurprising
given the huge varieties of ecological, environmental, and cultural zones
covered by the imperial entity. The uneven distribution of resources that
were required by the state, and uneven demand for supplies, also led to the
adoption of various ruling strategies within the vast imperial territories,
strategies that depended on local circumstances. But how was the ruling
apparatus designed and adjusted in order to connect the various regions
into a whole? Any explanation is hampered by the uneven distribution of
excavated textual records in the Han period. Most surviving records have
been found either near the northwestern frontiers (dating from the Middle
Western Han to Early Eastern Han) or near the southern frontiers (Linxiang
county in present-day Hunan, dating primarily to the Easter Han), respectively. While the body of records is by no means small, information on the
transportation of goods from various origins, their cost, and other marketplace transaction records is often too fragmented to give a complete picture
of the movement and marketplace exchange of goods between various parts
of the empire.[12] Since the transportation and communication system was
managed primarily by officials rather than private commercial concerns,
Han-era records detailing travel distances and costs are also relatively rare,
making it difficult to employ a quantitative approach to illustrate how goods
were transported.[13] An investigation based purely on textual evidence would

give a partial and biased picture of the operation of the Han imperial system and its profound impacts on various societies.

Besides studying surviving texts, scholars have also been interested in the extensive spread of stylistically homogeneous material culture during the Han period, for the purpose of understanding the expansion of the Han state. Han-style architectural ceramics and artifacts such as Han-style black-and-red lacquerware with geometric designs, bronze mirrors with running curves (*lianhu jing*), and pommel-ring knives have been widely found at various parts of peripheries, offering support for the thesis of a "Great Unity" of the Han political entity. These items have been found not only in the interior of China but also in northern Vietnam, the Hexi corridor, and the Korean Peninsula, which attest to the high degree of integration of these regions within the Han empire. Meanwhile, standardized sets of funeral ceramics, including *ding* tripods, *hu* vessels, *jing* wells, *cang* storage houses, and *zao* stoves, were widely used in medium- to small-scale burials throughout the Han territories (e.g., Jiang 2016; Psarras 2015; Song 2016). Clearly, the spread of homogenous artifacts throughout the Han dominions implies a degree of integration and suggests that the Han state was as capable of spreading its ideas outwards from the Central Plains to the empire's peripheries as it was at orchestrating the large-scale migration of people.

While the extensive spread of Han-style artifacts can scarcely be denied, it has been suggested recently that the research interest in the "homogenization" of Han-style materials should be moved further in order to reconsider the mechanisms of heightened connectivity which resulted in "processes and effects akin to those of modern globalization" (Shelach-Lavi 2016). Unfortunately, there has been little study of how these mechanisms worked in practice. The archaeology data of the Han empire have not yet been adequately studied from the viewpoint of imperial expansion (c.f., Allard 2006; Yao 2016), with the result that the specific patterns of Han imperialism remain poorly understood. While the "Sinicization" techniques practiced by the Han empire have often been examined,[14] more studies are needed to understand the mechanisms which produced this impression of a homogenous Han society.[15] Archaeology can help in this process, but excavated materials tend to be very uneven within the territories of the Han state. The palaces where the elites lived and administrative centers often survive, as do the utensils and agricultural implements which were used inside in daily lives. The humble dwellings of the lower classes, however, have mostly perished and are not well represented in current datasets. Because of this limitation, archaeology alone cannot answer all the questions raised above, and we need to turn to other approaches to supplement the information which it provides.

One fruitful method is the comparative approach. The Han empire has often been compared with its Western counterpart, the Roman empire, and to a certain extent such comparisons are legitimate and useful. In the exploration of the expansion of the Roman empire and associated transformation of local communities (i.e., Romanization), for instance, the integration process was often attributed to military force, warfare, and large-scale relocation of populations, which would eventually foster the widespread distribution of ideas and material culture (e.g., coins and *terra sigillata*), a process some-times known as the "globalization" of Roman culture (Hingley 2005; Pitts & Versluys 2014). In addition, the integration of market systems into a network in which prices would be rationally determined has often been claimed as a driving factor in the Roman case of connectivity (Erdkamp 2005:24). While long-distance exchange is a very early phenomenon in human history, the successful development of transportation systems which connected various regions stretching across broad territories often is attributable to the emer-gence of a dominant empire. Improvements in transportation infrastruc-ture, which stimulated trade and enabled resources to be distributed more efficiently, went hand in hand with imperial expansion (Morley 2010:86). In daily lives, the improved transportation and communication also connected increasing numbers of people—as consumers, producers, and suppliers of raw materials—with markets (Erdkamp 2005:27–28), which eventually led to the appearance of regional labor division of craft production and crop production.

As Bleda Düring noted in a recent study of imperialism as practiced in the Middle Assyrian empire, empires should be understood as the com-bined effort of various strategies that "more or less successfully overcome logistical challenges of distance as well as local resistance and obstruction" (Düring 2020:9). This could happen in many ways, given that empires were necessarily large and controlled multiple ethnic groups. In reality, the ways in which different subjugated parts were connected with one another varied considerably. For example, Neville Morley argued, even with the integrated market system, that Romans were unable to "compress" time and space to the same extent as their modern "globalizing" counterparts, to create a fully well-connected web for the movement of goods, raw materials, and infor-mation throughout its territories (Morley 2014). Other scholars have also queried the simplistic assumption that integration of markets always devel-oped in the same way. By examining the networks through which trade ac-tivities and the movement of goods were conducted, Roman historian Peter Bang argues that the Roman imperial network never completely integrated the various market systems that existed around the Mediterranean Sea (Bang 2006; c.f., Horden & Purcell 2000). Nor did all regions benefit equally from the development of the expansive trading networks. Centers that were advantageously situated along major traffic lanes stood to gain from the development of a "global network", but there were large hinterlands and pe-ripheral areas which often remained underdeveloped (Erdkamp 2005:196).

In order to better understand the factors underlying the expansion and consolidation process of the Han empire, this book argues that the archaeo-logical phenomenon "connectivity" should be subjected to detailed interro-gation. By drawing insights from recent theoretical trends of "network-based approaches" in archaeology (Brughmans 2013:634), connectivity is considered here as interactions at the border of zones around sites and connection of various parts caused by the political and economic system. Underneath this phenomenon are various changes such as the integration of the market system, the expansion of distribution network, the widespread use of new techniques, changes in the production system, transformations of religious practices, and the penetration of the administrative system alongside the consolidation of the state system.

Instead of merely identifying the geographical connections between sites, however, archaeological studies should endeavor to illustrate the structure of the network and measure how interaction changed over time. It is helpful to look beyond the superficial homogenous imperial images[16] cultivated by ancient rulers and to consider an ancient empire as a series of overlapping networks in political and socio-economic domains, and to find ways of going beyond what our surviving texts already tell us. I believe that "connectivity" offers a promising line of perspective. To fully exploit the theoretical potential, we need to analyze in depth the ways in which goods were manufactured, exchanged, and distributed. Also, we must be careful not to assume a homogenous imperial process. Rather, connectivity should be viewed as a dynamic process that reshaped and altered social relations and tradition (Naerebout 2013:270; Witcher 2017), but only to a certain extent: the pre-existing social structures in each ruling region simultaneously dictated a degree of divergence from the old ways. Meanwhile, the connection generated by the empire would manifest itself and impact individuals at various scales.

While comparisons between Han and Roman imperialism can be instructive, we should bear in mind that, unlike Rome, the Han state was never truly expansionist, and never pursued "an empire without limits" (*imperium sine fine*).[17] With minor exceptions, the Han territories reached their furthest extent of its *jun-xian* administrative system shortly after the creation of the Han empire, during an approximate 30-year period in Wudi (Emperor Wu, ruling from 141 to 87 BCE)'s reign. Instead of concentrating primarily on military expansion, the Han emperors built roads and mobilized the empire's material resources in order to shore up their frontier defenses. While most ancient empires adopted similar strategies to enhance the transportation infrastructure, how those strategies were employed and their collective results would present regional variations, contingent on the political infrastructure and social tradition in local communities. In the case of the Han empire, rich archaeological data have been accumulated in recent decades. Together with other unearthed textual records, these precious testimonies can provide vital political, military, and economic information, and help us see how "connectivity" worked in practice. But methodologically, it is essential to first clarify appropriate indicators in archaeological remains to evaluate "connectivity", and practical frameworks that allow us to piece together various strands of evidence leading to a clearer depiction of what these connections looked like in practice.

2 Imperial transformation and the role of the capital region

Connectivity studies focus on the mechanisms that tied empires tog
and their consequences. Recent studies of ancient empires have already
taken a particular interest in the imperial peripheries, where the presence of
the state and the response by local leaders at peripheries often took dramatically different forms. Rejecting the traditional view of "Romanization",
which assumes that the Romans forcibly changed indigenous societies to
make them appear more Roman, for instance, several recent studies of
Rome have stressed instead how imperial expansion took many forms in
peripheral societies, and how the Romans often collaborated with local
elites to support the expansion and economic growth of their empire.[18] The
expansion of an empire was also not always a top-down process. Instead,
it had to align with the interests of a small number of elite recipients "with
sufficient promise of opportunity such that a wider section of society saw
possibilities" (Pitts 2017).

While the peripheral perspective can provide indispensable evidence for
understanding specific connectivity that took place on the ground, I argue
that the imperial process should be viewed as one in which both the imperial
core and its peripheries interacted and transformed due to the integrated
relationship. In this light, the focus on the core region, especially in the case
of the Han empire, could also provide information as essential as that from
the "periphery perspective" in terms of the stimulus for connectivity. Even
though it is necessary to incorporate the experience in peripheries in order
to generate the full image of regional connectivity, the importance of the
capital core should not be therefore overlooked in the investigation of the
transformation caused by the complicated process of the development of
imperial rule.

Following the definition usually adopted by archaeologists to address regional settlement patterns (Fish & Kowalewski 1990), I define a "region" as
an independent topo-geographical unit, which may include various topographic zones bounded by certain geomorphological features such as river
valleys or mountains, and which has been described as having distinctive
cultural traditions in historical documents. The capital region of the Qin
and Han states, which was known as the Guanzhong basin, was such a geographical unit. It was bounded to the west by the Qian and Yong Rivers, in
present-day Fengxiang, and to the east by the Yellow River and Hua Mountains. Geologically, this river basin appears to be a narrow strip bounded by
the plateau, mountains, and the Yellow River, and extends from west to east
about 300 km, making the region well protected from attack from the east.
Archaeological evidence attested that the capital region probably had much
the same cultural tradition as that evidenced in other regions from the early
Bronze Age onwards (Liang 2008, 2020).[19] The unique topographic and geographic setting of the Qin-Han capital region made it fundamental for illustrating the operation of these two massive empires. The contemporary

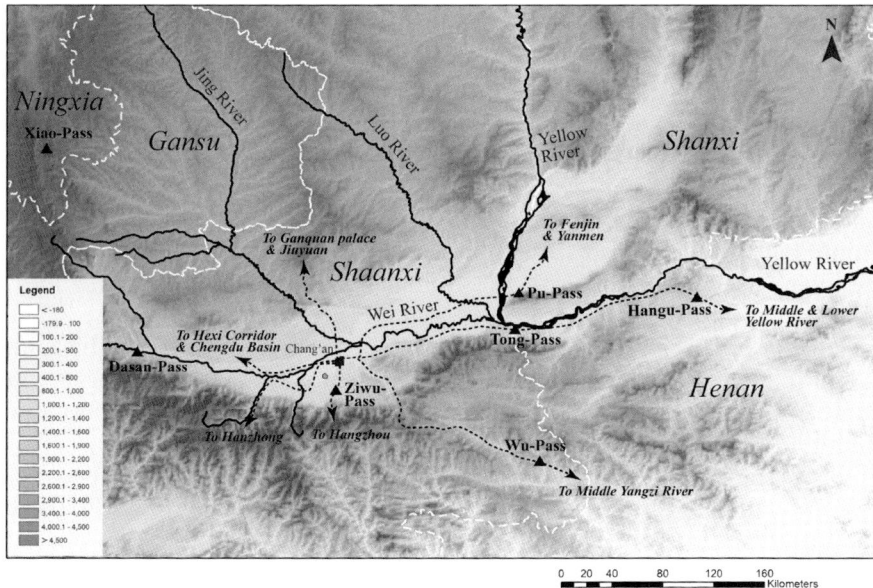

Figure I.2 The geography of the Guanzhong basin and pathways connecting to Chang'an (after Xin 1988:Fig 1).

texts describe that the strategic dominance of Guanzhong enabled the Han state to "grip the throat" and "strike the back"[20] of those eastern territories. Taking the military advantage[21] of Guanzhong over the other portions of the empire, the Han empire also employed Guanzhong-central policies, such as controlling traffic into and out of Guanzhong, and transporting resources to the capital (Liang 2013; Yang J. 2010), so as to maintain control by the core over Guandong,[22] namely the areas to the east of Hangu[23] originally controlled by its rivals (e.g., Hsing 2011[1983]; Hu 2015; Xin 2008) (Figure I.2).

Since the Han empire made a huge effort to gain its control over the northern (i.e., Hetao region) and northwestern frontiers (i.e., Hexi corridor) in order to defend against Xiongnu ethnic groups and their allies, one can also easily tell the strategic position in which the Guanzhong basin was situated. To maintain the fortification system and various expenses required to support frontier troops, weaponry, crops, and other daily necessities had to be drawn from other parts of the empire, especially to the east and south of the capital region. Regardless of their origin, these supplies had to be first transported through Guanzhong, rendering the capital region a supply center for the military campaign and maintenance of the frontiers like a hub in the center of a network.

To facilitate the transportation and delivery of information after the unification war, Qin Shihuang (the first Qin emperor; ruling 247–210 BCE) established the *chidao* road system in 220 BCE by joining the pre-existing roads inside the Qin and other territorial states into a national network (Wang Z. 2018:46). By doing so, he was the creator of a national road network centered on Guanzhong. Later in 212 BCE, Qin Shihuang also issued the command to construct the *zhidao* highway network, which stretched for more than 1,800 km from Yunyang in northern Guanzhong to Jiuyuan on the northern frontiers (Ma et al. 2018; Wang Z. 2018). While most of the roads that originally made up these two highway systems have been destroyed, some sections still survive and provide a testimony to "connectivity" between the capital core and various parts of the empire (Figure I.2). The Han state inherited the *chidao* and *zhidao* systems from the Qin state, and repaired and expanded roads leading to the eastern part of the empire and the northern and northwestern frontiers. As a result, Guanzhong eventually became the focal point for a network of roads which bound the empire to- gether (Tan 1967; Xin 1988). Chang'an, a trading city located in the center of the Guanzhong basin, was ideally placed to become the imperial capital (Li 1957:200; Shi 1991).[24] *Shiji* Chapter 129 mentions:

> ....In accord with (Qin preference to rule from within the Passes) the Han made its capital at Chang'an. From various imperial tombs in the four directions [to the capital, on road like] spokes of a [wheel into] the hub, came [the people] from these different directions, gathering together [in the capital]. The [amount of] land was small, and the population was crowded. Therefore, the people became more and more frivolous and crafty, and engaged in secondary (occupations, that is, trading and crafts).[25]

Chang'an's rise is clearly attributed to its role as the transportation hub of the entire Guanzhong basin, which allowed goods from various parts of the empire to be bought and sold there (Nylan 2015; Wang S. 1999). The officials, members of the royal family, and intellectuals attracted to the capital, as well as labor and others coerced to resettle in towns in the capital core[26] also made the Chang'an area one of the most densely populated cities in the ancient world (Chen 2016; Ge 1986). Its strategic location allowed the Han state to impose control and to monitor the movement of people through the pathways and transportation networks from the east to the further west (Liang 2016; Xin 2010; Yang J. 2010), an important strategy employed by the Han state to maintain social stability.

Besides its geographical setting, the reason that the capital region provides the core foundation for understanding how connectivity worked again lies in the imbalanced focus inherited in archaeological data. Archaeological works in commanderies outside the capital region often give disproportionate attention to mortuary data, as burials were often more widely encountered in survey and salvage archaeological projects. In addition, most of the ruling towns were overlaid by modern towns or destroyed in historical periods; only those walled towns in northern or northwestern frontiers were relatively well preserved with clear outlines that could still be easily identified via pedestrian survey.[27] More importantly, current studies of settlement patterns indicate that political subjects in counties often lived beyond the town walls, in villages or rural areas (Han & Zhang 2015; Hsing 2009). Even fewer examples of this kind of settlement have been excavated or studied.[28] When taken together with the voluminous archaeological excavation data obtained from surveys and excavations of Chang'an's immediate hinterland, the material evidence in the capital region presents a fine-grained image of Han society at a resolution which no other regions can match. If the expansion and consolidation of the Han empire led to an increase in interregional interaction and associated changes, a phenomenon that has been coined as "ancient globalization" (Jennings 2011:13), their impacts should have been experienced both in the capital region and at the peripheries. By systematically scrutinizing the representation of "connectivity" in archaeological evidence in the capital region, we can illustrate how the Han's imperial power spread out from the Guanzhong basin, transforming social relationships elsewhere. This will also provide a comparative reference for characterizing changes in other regions.

In other ancient empires, imperial progress often brought changes to the capital. Again, the case of Rome provides a useful comparative example. Studies of the regions surrounding Rome have demonstrated that rural settlement patterns and population density, farming lands, the location of marketplace for exchange and distribution of various craft production centers all changed significantly during the later decades of the Roman Republic and the early Imperial period (2nd century BCE–2nd century CE), when the capital region gradually became a metropolitan center.[29] The expansion of frontiers and the development of infrastructural networks unquestionably led to an influx of exotic goods into the capital for elite consumption, causing the assemblage of daily goods to become much more diverse. By then, the capital was the home not only of the Roman elites but also of merchants, intellectuals, and other migrants coerced by the state. Meanwhile, the migration to Rome also led to a great extent of depopulation of the countryside evidenced by the settlement patterns in archaeological records (Patterson 2006:69).

Those changes evidenced in archaeological patterns also show the transformation of social lives alongside the alternation of connectivity. For instance, urbanization transformed the layout of cities, making domestic spaces increasingly important (Patterson 2006:182). The exportation of wine boosted trading activities and caused the facility for firing ceramic amphora to become more widespread in broader rural areas beyond Rome. The huge consumption of crops also led to the increase of marketplaces in major traffic nodes (Morley 2010:81). Farmers in market villas produced a full range of crops in hinterlands and urban centers alongside the intensification of production (ibid:88). This suggests that the emergence of a relatively well-connected core that linked residents and farmers in the capital center to the economic system at the peripheries also generated forces and responses that transformed the local economic structure within the region.

In the Han empire, its capital region emerged as a relatively well-connected core, because of the communication infrastructure mentioned in texts. But in comparison with Rome, the aspects of towns and villages beyond the capital city remained to be insufficiently investigated on a granular scale. While archaeological fieldwork in previous decades has generated a considerable number of site reports regarding the infrastructure of Chang'an city,[30] surrounding mausoleum towns adjacent to Chang'an (Xianyangshi Wenwu 2010), as well as royal palaces and imperial storage facilities inside or adjacent to the capital (Zhongguo Shehui 1996a, 2003, 2005; Zhongguo Shehui & Riben 2007; Zhongguo Shehui & Xi'anshi Yanjiuyuan 2018; Zhongguo Shehui Chang'an & Xi'anshi Yanjiuyuan 2017)—all of which collectively already offer an image of settlement pattern on a resolution much higher than that in other regions—the details of archaeological data are not yet refined enough to allow us to pinpoint what changes, if any, occurred in the rural area of Chang'an and other lower rank urban centers in the capital region during the period when the Han state was consolidating its rule in the Guanzhong basin and various territories. Archaeological excavations have been mostly confined to the administrative offices or palaces in ruling towns and tombs surrounding settlements instead of the discovery of household and implements more relevant to the daily lives of ordinary people, with the result that we still know very little about life in the smaller towns. During the transformation from a territorial state (Qin state) to a mega-scale imperial entity (Han empire), how did peasants respond to the fluctuation of supplies and availability of daily necessities? How did urban life change during Chang'an's transformation into a metropolitan center? Constrained by the lack of textual evidence that directly demonstrates the manufacture date of artifacts, the study of settlement patterns corresponding to the location of towns (e.g., Chen 2016; Xu 2013) often falls short of identifying refined stages of development in the overall history from the Qin to the Han state represented by material culture.

The incompleteness of available archaeological data does not mean that the silent witness of material culture should be underrated. By looking at the "trajectories" of objects—the patterns of production, exchange, and consumption that were derived partially from the nature of objects themselves—as proposed in recent studies focusing on Roman material culture (Pitts 2017; van Oyen 2015), archaeological inquiry can potentially explain how social relations were reproduced, in addition to the changes in daily practice mediated through the new social structure imposed by the Qin and Han states. Connectivity could be conceived as a series of relations involved in producing, exchanging, and using of objects at different levels of the imperial infrastructure. These relations can often be captured by archeological materials, as changes in connectivity often intersect with different stages of the social life of craft products. In this sense, craft products, even those used in mundane life, should be viewed as a medium through which the empire was able to restructure the relations between different communities in daily routines, along with changes in ruling policies and resulted connectivity. The importation of mundane objects manufactured elsewhere and their use in daily life might even have woven the social lives of individuals at peripheries into the pan-cultural sphere and economic system defined by the state, and thus evoked a different sense of the understanding of the imperial order, as argued by Gardner's study of Roman coins in the context of Roman colonies (Gardner 2012).

In comparison with the transformation evidenced in peripheries of various regions, the driving force generated in the capital region of the Han empire by the movement and mobilization of goods should be no less significant in understanding connectivity. While intensified connectivity would have different effects in various domains, I suggest that the transformation processes reflected by the craft industry in the capital region are a productive line of enquiry in archaeological research, especially in the case of the Han empire. The empirical transformation in economic domains provides an approach to articulate changes instigated by the Han empire and driving factors that caused the expansion of imperial networks. Under imperial rule, changes in craft industries, especially those that were caused by the imperial transformation, shed light on the endeavor by the state of integrating various parts and the new relations generated during the production and consumption processes that underpinned the consolidation of political entities.

As explained above, evidence showing increases in connectivity is not rare in cases of ancient empires. Instead, a more meaningful issue to pursue is to identify the extent to which the formation of the empire altered the pre-existing economic and political networks and transformed the daily lives of political subjects so that they could be integrated, to a greater or lesser extent, into the new system that was being reshaped by the political infrastructure, military presence, and market system. Since changes in the Han capital region might have generated centripetal forces through which various regions were further integrated into the imperial system, a better understanding of the patterns evidenced in the craft industry in the capital region, in turn, provides an important reference for examining related processes in the rest of the empire. In other words, mundane items can be used to illuminate the imperial process towards a more centralized system that otherwise cannot be gleaned from macroscopic settlement pattern data.

3 Iron industry and its significance to social relations

This book builds on a relational approach to look at evidence of craft specialization by situating the production, exchange, and distribution within the imperial process in the capital region in order to understand the contribution of the craft production to the connectivity and the consolidation of the imperial entity. Addressing the production procedures of daily-use implements, forces generated by demands in daily lives, and the transportation of goods is the first step to explore archaeologically the actual structure of imperial economies working in the capital region and transformation caused by those strategies strengthening the ruling of the state. But instead of summarizing various types of manufactured products at the price of sidetracking the focus of connectivity, this book will investigate specifically the changes in relations involved in the iron industry. Scrutinizing how the iron production process and transportation intersected with the transformation of the capital region offers a helpful perspective for illuminating the "connectivity" operated between various parts of the Western Han empire.

In ancient China, the iron techniques in use belonged to the tradition of cast iron, known as the type of iron that was melted and cast, usually with about 4 percent of carbon (Wagner 1993:336). The initial development of ironworking was derived from the so-called bloomery iron[31] around the middle of the 8th century BCE. Cast iron technology was then gradually established and replaced bloomery iron in the Central Plains and in the peripheral states (Lam 2014) between the 7th to 5th century BCE, and during the Qin and Han periods reached a scale and level of development unmatched elsewhere in the pre-industrial world. By the beginning of the Warring States period, cast iron technology had already emerged as an alternative to bronze, and was beginning to be employed in the large-scale manufacture of agricultural tools and other daily-use implements (Bai 2005:116; Lam 2014; Lam et al. 2017a; Wagner 2008:140). For early Chinese empires, casting iron agricultural implements and manufacturing cast iron tools were probably one of the most important domains in the craft industry, and the scale of mass production during the Qin-Han periods evidenced by archaeological records was even unseen in later historical periods.

Cast iron manufacturing has long been viewed as closely intertwined with state management, given the high requirement of labor force and fuel to generate the heat needed during the production process (Wagner 2001). The Qin and Han states were both interested in the management of craft industries and in the income generated by taxing those who were allowed to mine iron ore and cast implements. Thanks to its sophisticated bureaucratic system at a scale rarely seen in the ancient world,[32] the two dynasties were able to impose tight control over the iron industry. This probably explains the controversial decision taken by the Han emperor Wudi to take over the production and selling of iron and salt and declare them as state-owned enterprises in 117 BCE.[33] His aim was clearly to exploiting profits from natural resources to replenish a treasury exhausted by constant warfare and flooding in eastern territories. Meanwhile, those who manufactured strategic necessities without state permission would be severely punished. Some other products, such as mirrors and lacquerware might have also come under the control of the state administration,[34] even though the evidence of this is less explicit than it is for the monopolies of iron and salt—another lucrative and tightly controlled industry[35]—that were promulgated in official documents.

Given the state's obsession with managing resources, the iron economies, which comprised various component production and distribution parts of the iron industry, was one critical section that generated a major revenue stream for the state, even though the prices of most iron implements were relatively low and affordable by most ordinary people. At the same time, the waste and lack of flexibility associated with centralized production were quickly acknowledged and criticized in contemporary political discourses. One major criticism of the state monopoly in *Yantielun*, a book compiled in about 44 BCE to record the debate[36] (81 BCE) between Confucian scholars (*wenxue* Literati and *xianliang* Worthies) and Yushi dafu (Imperial Counsellor) Sang Hongyang (ca. 152–80 BCE) focusing on whether the Han state should continue the monopolies after the policies were introduced almost 30 years, lies in the deteriorating quality of iron implements and overproduction. Consequently, relatively expensive yet poor quality products inevitably hurt agricultural production among ordinary people.

With this in mind, this book aims to illustrate how social relations changed alongside the transformation of connectivity in both the capital and the regions supplying iron to the centers. While the current chronology might not be sufficiently granular to pinpoint specific effects caused by the monopoly policies, an understanding of the organization of the iron industry and the social context in which production took place, in addition to the temporal changes of the craft specialization system from the Warring States to the Han period, is essential to assess the development of connectivity over the course of history.

In order to explore various domains related to craft production records and the social interaction involved in the entire biography of iron objects, I find James Carrier's anthropological discussion about the emergence of commodity economies (1995) particularly insightful for disentangling the social relations involved in the imperial process in the capital region surrounding the production and consumption of iron. Carrier's argument that commodity economies could be used to illustrate not only the phenomenon of large-scale manufacturing and marketplace exchange but also the transformation of social relations at various scales indicates how a sensitive study of the iron industry can yield insights hitherto overlooked.

Carrier's work attempted to fully reveal the two forms of exchange, gifts and commodities within the long tradition of economic anthropology starting from Mauss's (1990[1954]). The two categories of transactions that anthropologists often employ to understand the nature of economic phenomena involve varied relations between transactors, based on the assumption that objects of these two types carry very different values. To put the discussion in a succinct way, commodities exchange involves a transaction of the so-called "alienable objects", which refers to the type of goods that

were transported out of producers' hands without their control, and that
were procured by consumers who were not concerned with the identity of
producers. Since objects are only treated as bearers of abstract value, the
transaction does not "speak of any past or future relationships between
transactors" (Carrier 1995:21). The purchase of groceries at a supermarket is
an example of commodity transactions. In contrast, gift exchange involves
an exchange of inalienable things, and the transaction itself aims to maintain an existing social relationship between individuals who are in a state of
reciprocal dependence (Gregory 1982:12, 19; 1997). Meanwhile, the concern
in the gift exchange is with the "creation and recreation of people as social
identities, defined by their identifiable relationships with other individuals
and groups in the society" (Carrier 1995:21). In other words, gift-giving,
such as inviting friends for a meal or giving them a Christmas present, has
to build upon the deep relational web of obligation, trust, and prestige that
is already established, whereas commodities are characterized by their exchange value, and only involve "shallow", impersonal relations between
buyers and sellers in the marketplace.[37]

As more recent scholarship in economic anthropology has pointed out,
we should not oversimplify to assume that commodity exchange does not involve any interpersonal relationship (e.g., trust) (Feinman & Garraty 2010).
Nor should we exclude the rational calculation of exchange value in the case
of gift exchange. Nonetheless, Carrier insightfully points out that the production system of commodities allowing the transactions to extend beyond
transactors who know each other must occur in certain social settings different from those involved in the production of "gifts". Adopting a historical
approach to illustrate this idea, Carrier shows that the commodity exchange
took its dominant place in the British economic systems after the 17th century along with the emergence of market exchange and the new web of social
relations. Before the 17th century, the production of daily-use goods, such as
cotton textiles, often was conducted in the household-level working setting.
Since workers were usually apprentices for the owners or family members,
they could use the tools and raw materials controlled by themselves. Also,
the trade often took place between people who were known or linked to each
other in the same community. Therefore, the obligation and social relations
involved made the production more or less align with the broad definition
of "gift exchange". Alongside the progress of the industrial revolution, however, the orientation towards commodity-driven production transformed
the working environment, steering family businesses to become concentrated, full-time specialization in a factory-like setting, in which workers
usually focused on and specialized in only one discrete step in a sequence.
As a result, workers in a factory setting as hired laborers no longer controlled the goods that they produced, or even the tools that they used. The
transformation thus resulted in "alienation" between producers, the products that they made, and customers. Based on these transformations, Carrier further conceptualized the opposition of gifts and commodities as a

Table I.1 Summary of Carrier's framework that conceptualizes the elements of commodity economy in 17th-century Britain

Aspects	Details of transformation in the late 17th century
Location	Moving to a central place; separation of industrial areas from residential ones
Tools	Workers are less likely to have their own tools
Identity	Workers were treated as impersonal laborers
Organization	Increased division of labor; breaking down of production into more and simpler steps; each step was routinized
Exchange	Marketplace exchange took over; buying transactions became impersonalized

spectrum of various social aspects, including the production location, ownership of tools, workers' identity, organization, and the market exchange of final products; all of them witnessed substantial changes in economic spheres in Britain during the 17th and 18th century (Table I.1).

In the Han period, iron implements were indisputably commodities,[38] even though the industry was entirely taken over by the state during Wudi's reign. Previous studies already underscored that a growing population, urbanization, and the development of intensive farming during the Han period tremendously stimulated the growth of manufacturing and increased the scale and efficiency in iron production, much like the transition to commodity-driven production described above. In this sense, the framework about the evolution of the opposition proposed by Carrier would be a source of inspiration for archaeological research on the intensification in craft production and concomitant changes in social relations at various social levels. I suggest that the question of connectivity, especially in the case of looking at a specific region, represented by changes in iron production, should be explored along several lines of inquiry: (1) whether manufacturing areas were located in a central place (i.e., a concentrated factory) distinct from a household setting, and how different production centers interacted with each other; (2) whether manufacturing became more intensive and, if so, whether workers had to spend more to procure what they could no longer make for themselves; (3) whether there was a high degree of labor division and an assembly-line-style breakdown of production processes, and whether workers were converted to routine operations (i.e., the techniques were standardized to increase efficiency); and (4) whether the transportation and distribution of final products occurred through a market system because commoditization always de-emphasizes the significance of personal relationship between buyers and vendors.

When looking at theoretical discourses of gifts and commodities, one must recognize that the dichotomy of gifts and commodities at best represents two types of ideal transactions. The borrowing of such a framework does not assume that the iron industry in the capital region necessarily changed from a small-scale industry run by family workshops towards a factory-like production system. Instead, such a framework should be viewed as a tool for shedding heuristic light on the relationship along with the appearance of mass production evidenced by archaeological records. Through scrutinizing various lines of evidence related to iron production, including workshop organization, food supply system to ironworks, distribution system of iron implements, and inter-regional interaction of iron production system, this study tries to understand the relationship between workers themselves, between workers and their neighbors or customers, and between individuals involved in the production and distribution and the state. Since commodities were produced principally for exchange through the market system, they must involve specific social conditions or mechanisms resulting in the production of large-scale and standardized goods (Appadurai 1986:42), so that the circulation of goods could go beyond the direct link between producers and consumers. This aspect predetermines commodities to be manufactured in a specific setting of production organization and the relationship between producers and those who sponsor or manage the production. All these dimensions encapsulate the concerns that were advocated above of re-centering on the transformation of social relations changed by the new type of connectivity during the imperial process.

Summarizing the discussion, the intrinsic nature of commodities lies in certain principles governing their production (including the organization of production, skills, labor, and standardization), consumption, and distribution. All these factors would result in these products becoming impersonalized or alienated from producers and consumers. Meanwhile, changes of parameters in the web of social relations, including the demand, political control by the state, and development of the transportation network and techniques, would, in turn, alter those principles in production as well as social relations, generating different types of distribution patterns and connectivity. Therefore, several parameters, including the organization of workers and their labor division at production sites, relations between local community and producers, and market exchange of products, are put forward, and elaborated below, together with macroscopic changes in the Central Plains region, to characterize various transformations that caused the changes of connectivity in the region.

Through the lens proposed by Carrier for understanding the new social relations in capitalist commodities, this book argues that the production, transportation, and distribution of iron products in the capital region allow us to better understand how communities, production centers, and markets were interwoven via the progress of the social life of iron. We need to ground our understanding of connectivity in the recognition that the widespread distribution of iron implements involves a two-way process, given the complex techniques and resources required for cast iron manufacturing. On the one hand, the intensification of social demands due to agriculture and warfare, and the control of potential instability caused by iron production would alter the production system in various ways such as the increase in the number of production centers, the centralization of ironworks and intensification of specialization, or the standardization of products and streamlined production procedures. The approaches selected to address new issues would be contingent on the state management, the development of transportation techniques and market system, and even the ideological design of the capital to maintain its dominant role. On the other hand, the ways through which the production system was transformed in the capital might alter the supply of raw materials and final products from other production regions, generating different types of interregional and intraregional connectivity. I attempt to bridge two domains that are often examined separately, and explore the intersection between imperial changes and various domains of the iron industry that generated new social relations at different scales. In order to examine changes that occurred in the capital region, this book combines multiple strands of evidence related to the manufacturing and distribution of iron. Below I explain how each strand of evidence will be addressed in each chapter, and how various aspects would be synthesized eventually to shed light on the underlying process of transformation initiated by the Han empire.

4 Chapter structure

Focusing on the changes of social relations involved in iron production and consumption, this book casts light on various aspects of the iron industry that occurred in the Han capital region, with an aim to understand how the connectivity was presented, altered, and transformed in the background of the imperial process. The aim of this book is to shift the focus to unfold the kaleidoscopic facets of the Han's economic system from the perspective of iron commodities in daily lives. Through studying various aspects of the iron industry in the capital region, I shed insight on the interaction of the economic system between the capital region and beyond that facilitated the state to consolidate its power and connectivity in its various parts.

As explained earlier, the framework of integration not only focuses on the establishment of long-distance interregional exchange but also on how the imperial process altered and reshaped the economic, symbolic, and ritual aspects at various scales. Only through situating the discussion with a *longue durée* perspective can archaeological study fulfill its potential to illustrate such chronological transformations. Chapter 1 first describes the origin and development of the iron industry during the first millennium BCE and examines the role of the Qin state in the transmission and early development of iron technology in early China. During the Shang and Zhou eras, the central court controlled the production of prestige items as well as daily necessities via the management of labor and artisans who were often members of the same lineage and inherited the skills from generation to generation (Barbieri-Low 2007:41–42; Lin 2014; Satō 1962:25–29). Following such tradition, the initial development of the iron industry often appeared to be associated with the centralized government, while private production managed by merchants might have co-existed in some Central Plains states. Even though the early iron technology and the assemblage of iron objects from the Qin state shared considerable similarities with other territorial states, I argue that the regional variations during the transition to large-scale cast iron manufacturing should not be overlooked. Contrary to received wisdom, my analysis of surviving iron implements from the Jin, Chu, and Qin states presented in Chapter 1 suggests that the Qin's iron industry was less advanced than those of other territorial states during the Warring States period. Nor did the Qin state use its iron industry to manufacture weapons, unlike some of its contemporaries. One reason might lie in the relatively underdeveloped market system in the Qin state during most of the Warring States period. The development of the iron industry in the Qin state might have predetermined the trajectory of the iron industry in later periods, in which the iron industry in the capital region stands in a striking contrast with that in other regions.

Since the Qin state, the Qin unified empire, and the Western Han empire were all centered in the Guanzhong region, the cultural and political landscapes of the capital could also lay down the foundation for studying the integration of the Han empire and associated changes in daily lives. For addressing the issues of integration at various scales, Chapter 2 first provides a detailed description of the social setting and topo-geography of the Han capital region and an account of the development of imperial management over iron in its well-controlled surroundings. A detailed description is presented to explain how the administrative system changed and adjusted to manage various businesses related to iron production. The infrastructure provided the framework for understanding the implementation of monopoly policies during Wudi's reign. I will also discuss recent advances in our knowledge of various types of craft production in the region in order to understand the overall impacts of the new market exchange and transportation system imposed by the Han state. While the demand for iron implements fueled by the development of agriculture in the region would have been strong, I argue that iron production and other craft industries for producing mundane objects were fairly small-scale, both in Chang'an itself and in its hinterland. By contrast, the iron industry in the capital cities of the eastern territorial states during the preceding Warring States period was on a much larger scale, and this trend continued in the Han period. Even though the Guanzhong basin eventually became the core for bronze minting and bronze ritual objects controlled by the state workshop, the sparseness of the evidence for iron manufacturing in Guanzhong may indicate that the interregional transportation network was a key factor in the economic development of the Han's capital.

In Chapter 3, I look at two specific issues related to the beginning of the iron industry: iron manufacturing techniques and the procurement of raw materials. After outlining the basic techniques and operational chains employed in iron production during the Han period, I discuss the implications of the recent discoveries of ironworks to the east of Guanzhong. I argue that the distribution of ironworks currently known suggests a "clustering" pattern whereby the Han state centralized the large-scale iron production in iron-rich regions in order to supply resources and raw materials to other regions (including the capital region) via the state-managed transportation system. I also consider the implications of an ironworks named Taicheng, which was the only well-published and excavated ironworks in the capital region so far. The study of the Taicheng ironworks suggests that, in comparison with other known ironworks in the Guandong region, small-scale iron manufacture relied heavily on the importation of both raw materials and semi-products in sharp contrast to the other ironworks in urban centers beyond Guanzhong that manufactured both raw materials and a wide array of final products. In addition, the study of iron products from the cemetery nearby Taicheng ironworks suggests that these products were unlikely to be manufactured by small-scale iron production centers. In line with the suggestion proposed in Chapter 2, the small-scale ironworks in county-level settlements in Guanzhong must have relied on the development of exchange and distribution networks for various types of materials, which linked up various aspects of economic lives in the Han period.

With the explanation of historical background and social setting of the iron industry established, the second part of the book focuses on more microscopic aspects of iron production by centering on the case of Taicheng as well as the distribution system of iron in the capital region. Chapter 4 focuses on the organization of labor represented through the intra-site distribution of remains. Three cases will be selected for the purpose of comparison: Niucun, Zhonghang, and Taicheng, in order to articulate chronological transitions through time. The first two cases are associated with large-scale manufacturing centers during the Eastern Zhou period, while Taicheng was a small-scale ironworks in a county-level settlement during the Han era. For ironworks pre-dating the Han time, the assemblage of products demonstrated a trend towards labor division, as these production complexes often include multiple locations specializing in different ranges of products. This chapter will further explore the collaboration demonstrated via the intra-site distribution of manufacturing remains, which I will coin "horizontal collaboration" of multiple labor cells. In the Taicheng case, the intra-site analysis of remains from Taicheng also shows a complex collaboration of labor units focusing on the same stage of production as well as sequential stages along the production line. Based on the centralized supervision potential required for such complex collaboration, this chapter also argues that the Han state played an active role in expanding the iron manufacturing system with a complex collaboration system to the broader areas in the capital region, as a strategy to supplement the supplies of ironware that were largely consumed. Since this chapter and the subsequent two chapters will focus on different specific aspects of material evidence, frameworks and related discussion in the literature will be discussed to explain how aspects of various types of organization and market integration can be conceptualized in archaeological records.

In order to further understand the intensity issue of craft specialization, Chapter 5 examines the meat procurement pattern of ironworks. In this chapter, I introduce relevant cases of workshops pre-dating the Western Han, in order to identify whether any changes in the reliance of local communities, via the perspective of meat consumption patterns, could be identified in the case of ironworks in the capital region. Based on the concept of economic embeddedness, i.e., a specialized exchange network through which full-time production units rely on their patrons or other local specialists to procure raw materials and food market exchange, I argue that three types of hypothetical embeddedness would be employed to evaluate the archaeological cases of different ironworks or other metal production centers. By looking at the taxa assemblage, element assemblage, and age profile of animals at Zhonghang and Taicheng, I argue that the small-scale ironworks relied heavily on urban-meat supply and "deep economic embeddedness". This supports my earlier argument that the Taicheng ironworks, and probably other ironworks in Guanzhong as well, were organized as full-time production factories. In addition, the ironworks in the Han period relied on potentially wild animal resources (e.g., deer) even less than the case of the Warring-States ironworks, suggesting that the Han example shows a stronger intensity of the way through which workers engaged in production. In other words, the expansion of the iron production network in the capital region was attributable to the development of a meat marketing system that permitted labor specialization: some laborers worked full-time to produce iron, while others worked full-time to supply them with food. Surviving faunal remains together with textual records shed light on the potential involvement of the state in the supply and subsidy of food to workers in the iron production centers.

Chapter 6 considers regional transportation patterns and focuses on the contribution of market exchange to the distribution and transportation of metal goods. Emphasis is placed on the part played by market forces in integrating and connecting communities on a regional level. The structuring principles of ancient markets, the forces driving change in market systems, and the underlying mechanisms of administrative control over the movement of material culture are all explored. These factors have not been comprehensively addressed in previous studies but were essential to market exchange in the Qin and Han periods. An analysis of distribution patterns of everyday iron and bronze items from burial sites within the capital region of the Qin and Western Han empires reveals a major shift in the development of the market system and sub-regional integration between the Late Warring States (and Qin unification) and Western Han periods. The region gradually became more integrated, though it was still dominated by major

rative centers, especially Chang'an. An interregional exchange net-
veloped, and small-scale production systems in lower-rank settle-
:panded. It is clear that the administration of the Han state was
~ involved in the process of increasing regional integration.

Through the detailed analysis of the iron industry, this book addresses
several issues related to connectivity in the capital region. How did iron
manufacturing change alongside the development of the connectivity between the Guanzhong basin and other regions? How was labor in these production centers organized, and did the organization patterns present change
in response to the development of a new imperial financial system? How
was the ironworks embedded within the food supply system, and to what
extent the types of embeddedness changed over time? Last but not least, how
did the market exchange manifest itself in the economic system that witnessed
an increase in connectivity? I argue that the integration of lower-level administrative centers as well as the connection to the long-distance exchange
network was a key aspect, albeit neglected in previous studies, in articulating the issue of connectivity in the case of the Han imperialism. To a great
extent, such transformation in the iron industry would be viewed as part of
a long-term imperial project of consolidating the state power, even before
the official implementation of monopoly policies. Through looking at the
manufacture, supply, and circulation of iron implements in the core, I seek
to show how craft production was organized and knitted various dimensions
of social lives together. Finally, I hope to shed more light on certain wider
questions: how the core interacted with the other parts of the empire; how
the Han-style material culture spread to the various parts of the Han empire;
and, most importantly, how the study of the iron industry on a regional basis
illuminates unique aspects of the Chinese economic system.

Notes

1 Lao (1993:17).
2 The normal transportation speed of official documents in the Han period was
about 60 *li* (1 *li* is equivalent to 415.8 m) per day, according to Lao (1986:20).
3 According to *Shiji* 30.1421, the transportation of grain over one-thousand *li*
would cost more than 30 *zhong* for one *shi* (1 *zhong* is equivalent to 6.4 *shi*), suggesting that overland transportation of grain was hugely expensive.
4 Except those explained individually in the caption, all maps in this book were
drawn by the author in ArcGIS using a dataset from Harvard's China Historical
GIS (https://sites.fas.harvard.edu/~chgis/data/chgis/v6).
5 For the location and identification of Han Great Wall as well as fortification systems in the northern and northwestern frontiers, see Huang (2013); Hsing (2020);
Ren et al. (2017); Wei (2020); Wu (2005).
6 For comparison, the traveling speed of state post or private couriers for fast
carriage in the Roman world was about 67 km/day. See the explanation for the
ORBIS: The Stanford Geospatial Network Model of the Roman World project
(https://orbis.stanford.edu/).
7 *Hanshu* 69.2983 mentioned that Zhao Chongguo, who was appointed Hou
Jiangjun (General of the Rear), sent out an urgent mail from Jincheng to

Chang'an to explain his strategy of allying with lesser Qiang tribes, Han and Teng, to against the more powerful unit, Xianling, instead of a strong action against the formers. The approval from the central court was then received seven days later. Even with present-day highway, the distance between Jincheng (present-day Lianzhou) to Chang'an is about 630 km. In other words, the document was delivered at a rate of at least 180 km per day. For relevant records about Zhao Chongguo, see Loewe (2000:702); for a general introduction of the mailing and transportation system, see Lao (1947); Fujita (2016); Hsing (2009); Zhang (2007).

8 For the overall introduction about the administrative system and discussion about related unearthed documents, see Ikeda (2017); Loewe (2004, 2006); Zou (2008).

9 Also see Kim and Lai (2018) for a synthetic review of the legal system during the Han period.

10 Pines argued that the imperial unification of the Qin state and unified political system of the Han dynasty was attributed to the paradigm of the "Great Unity" that emerged during the Warring States period as a response to the disintegration of social order by contemporary thinkers (see Pines 2000; for a comparative study in Chinese literature, see Bu 2018). For a critical review of the Great Unity paradigm in the archaeological research of prehistoric China, see Li X. (2020).

11 See Di Cosmo (2009) and Wang (2021) for discussions about Han's ruling strategies in various peripheries.

12 One exception is the recent publication of bamboo slips from Wuyi Guangchang, which provided some valuable cases about the transportation of textiles and grains from various locations to Linxiang in present-day Changsha. For the reconstruction of the trade route, see Zhang (2019).

13 For an example of calculating the distance and the time spent on the traveling between different cities in the Roman case, see Scheidel (2014).

14 For an archaeological approach of studying "Sinicization" through burial datasets, see Jiang (2016). Di Cosmo (2009) also examined the same issue, but primarily through the lens of textual analysis.

15 For instance, Nam Kim challenged the traditional view that attributed various changes in northern Vietnam during the last century BCE to the incorporation by a dominant and powerful Sinitic force. Instead, his case study of the Cổ Loa excellently demonstrated that the use of ideological symbols associated with material culture or techniques from the north might have been strategically used by local leaders as a new means to consolidate their power (see Kim 2018).

16 See Mattingly (2011:4–13) for a useful discussion about the modern term "imperialism" and its etymology "imperium Romanum". Here I follow Mattingly's definition that views an empire as the geopolitical manifestation of relationships of control imposed by a state from the core, which is often found to be metropolitan-controlled territory, on the sovereignty of others in peripheral territories. Imperialism, therefore, can be defined as "the process and attitudes by which an empire is established and maintained" (Mattingly 2011:6).

17 Similar observation can be seen and has been discussed in Mustchler and Mittag (2008:422–425).

18 One of the most important works in this regard is *Becoming Roman: The Origins of Provincial Civilization in Gaul* by Woolf (1998). For a more updated discussion of Romanization and issues related to this concept in the literature of Roman imperialism, see Mattingly (2011).

19 Similar account can also be found in texts dating to the Han period (see *Hanshu* 40.2032–2033 and *Shiji* 129.3261).

20 *Shiji* 99.2716.

21 A similar opinion can also be seen in *Shiji* 55.2044 (transl. Watson 1993[1961]:108–109)

> the three sides of [the Guanzhong] were circumscribed by a natural boundary. There is only one side to control over eastern Kings. If they were subordinated, food from all over the world could be transported to the capital through the road pathway and water channels of the Yellow River and Wei River. If there was rebellion, armies and military supplies could be moved eastward along the Rivers.

22 According to Hsing (2011[1983]), this term also refers to areas on different scales. One refers to the area covering all other six states during the Warring States period, while the other one, which was formed during the Han period, refers specifically to the eastern part of the empire except the northern frontiers and the area to the south of the Hui River.

23 It is important to note that the Hangu Pass was originally in the Sanmenxia area and relocated to present-day Xin'an during Wudi's reign in order to strengthen the control over Luoyang (for the discussion about the purpose of relocation, or the so-called "guangguan" in texts, see Hu 2015; Xin 2008; for the archaeological excavation of the Hangu gate, see Luoyangshi 2000).

24 *Hanshu* 24b.1280.

25 *Shiji* 129.3261; transl. Swann (1950:438).

26 In order to strengthen the core and weaken the peripheries, the Han state relocated a great population to the Guanzhong, especially those affiliated with local power and royal families in various conquered states. See *Shiji* 99.2720 and more specific discussion in Shang (2008). For a detailed discussion of the strategies of relocation, see Barbieri-Low (2021). This issue will also be explained in greater detail in Chapter 2.

27 For a synthetic research on the settlement patterns and the layout of walled-towns in the northern frontiers, see Wang (2014); Xu (2013).

28 In archaeology, the study and investigation of Sanyangzhuang provided the most extensive study of the residential area of ordinary people. For a general summary of the site and country settlement in the Han period, see Kidder et al. (2012); Poo (2018).

29 For instance, see various examples related to craft production and farming techniques in de Haas and Tol (2017).

30 For a basic summary of the structure of Chang'an, see Liu and Li (2005). For a more updated introduction about the Chang'an city, see Liu Z. (2016, 2017, 2018); Xu L. (2021).

31 Bloomery iron refers to the type of iron that was smelted by reduction of the ore to solid iron at a low temperature in a small-scale hearth or a shaft furnace, which is often called a bloomery. Final products usually are wrought iron (iron with carbon content in the range 0.1–0.3 percent) (Wagner 1993:274; 2008:89).

32 For the comparison of the Han and Roman bureaucratic systems, see Scheidel (2015). In addition, it has been recognized that iron production in Rome occurred primarily in thousands of tiny units scattering in villages, which stands in sharp contrast with the large-scale factories in Han China (Wagner 2001:c7).

33 *Hanshu* 24a.1165; *Shiji* 30.1429. For a useful reference of the background information and translation of some of the most important chapters, see Gale (1967); Loewe (1974).

34 For the bronze mirror industry, see Bai (2020); for changes of the lacquerware industry, see Bai (2014).

35 For a discussion about the salt monopoly policy, see Kageyama (1984); Luo and Luo (1995a, 1995b, 1996); Vogel (1993).

36 The agenda of the main organizer, Huo Guang, remains to be a debatable issue. Previous scholarship has often claimed that Huo Guang might have incited those Confucian scholars to strike Sang Hongyang in order to further centralize his power (e.g., see Jin 2011). Yet, more recent studies (Lin 2018) cast doubt on this idea, since Huo Guang already controlled supreme power in the central court by then. For an extensive review of related literature, see Sterckx (2020). It is also important to note that, while both sides debated on whether the Han state should allow for a more autarkic management, the argument for "the need for the state to control the flow of both people and goods" was embraced by both parties.

37 As pointed out by one of the reviews of Carrier's work (Fine 1997), the opposition between gift and commodity might not always be decisive and appropriate. The gift relationship can be subordinate to the commodity relationship that is itself social in nature. Here I see these concepts as two ideal types of production and exchange processes that are involved with different types of social relationships.

38 In fact, the ideas surrounding the Han commodity economy used to be a hotly debated issue. The arguments could come down to three camps. The first group (e.g., Fu 1982), which includes devotees of the Marxist five stages of development, tended to view commodity economy in the Han period as still not fully developed, and the entire social-economic system as still dominated by natural economies (i.e., the production usually is related to self-support). Consequently, the economic system during the Qin-Han periods still belonged to the so-called "feudalist economy" (Li 2001) based upon the agriculture production and the relationship between landlord and peasants. The opposite side of the debate (Deng 1994; Gao 2008; Leng 2002a, 2002b; Zhang 2003), however, views the elements in the commodity economy as more fully developed given the wide range of products (i.e., exotic goods) traded through the market system, even though they often held the same prior view of the "five-stage development". Having recognized the issues on both sides, more recent scholarship often took a "middleground" standpoint and tried to use a compromised framework to reconcile the debates of the two sides. Huang (2003, 2005), for instance, views that market or commercial economies (products only used for exchange) were relatively developed in the Han period, but emphasizes that this did not mean commodity economies controlled by market rules were established. Especially, in terms of the macro-scale environment, a uniformed and national market did not form during this period, and the development of each region was not balanced. While it still remains unclear how the Han state was integrated via the economic system, the development of commodity economies in the Han period was viewed as an unquestionable issue in recent discussions about the Han economic systems (e.g., von Glahn 2016).

Part I

1 The rise of iron and imperial state power[1]

The date of the origin of iron technology in ancient China is much disputed. While some Chinese characters that are suspiciously related to iron appeared in sporadic texts from the Eastern Zhou period,[2] the debatable etymological meaning and ambiguous contexts of those terms often make it difficult to decide when and where iron metallurgy began. The chapter "Shitie" in the Odes of Qin, *The Book of Poetry*, indicates exactly this difficulty. The poem says:

> Our ruler to the hunt proceeds;
> And black as iron are his steeds.
> That heed the charioteer's command,
> Who holds the six reins in his hand.
> His favorites follow to the chase,
> Rejoicing in his special grace.[3]

In the verses quoted above describing the imposing appearance of Qin chariot warriors, one character pronounced as "tie" (驖) is often translated as iron-color or black color, as it is phonologically related to the Chinese term for iron, *tie* (鐵). Several scholars have argued that iron might have existed in the Qin state in this period, and so the derivative character that was etymologically related was created to describe those "iron-color" horses (e.g., Tang 1993; Zhang & Tang 2017). But a counter-argument could be similarly made. The Chinese character of iron would have been borrowed from the character with the etymological origin that was used to depict dark or a specific color, similar to the color of iron viewed in the ancient poet's eyes (Wagner 2008:83).

Given the difficulty of deciding what "tie" meant in early textual records, scholars of early iron technology have turned instead to material records. A recent study of iron technology in the Eastern Mediterranean and Anatolia shows that iron started to be worked there on a large scale as early as the 12th century BCE (Erb-Satullo 2019), far earlier than in other parts of the Eurasian continent. Using the latest radiocarbon dating results, scholars working in China generally agree that the earliest examples of worked iron

DOI: 10.4324/9781003259220-3

in Xinjiang date either from the 10th or 9th century BCE (e.g., Guo 2009).[4] While any conclusion must be tentative, it seems likely that the knowledge of iron working was imported into China from the West (e.g., Chen J. 2014, 2020). Several other technologies, including copper metallurgy, cattle, and sheep/goat husbandry, and wheat farming, were transmitted to ancient China along the Silk Road in the late Neolithic period, or about the third millennium BCE (Flad 2018).[5] Iron products and knowledge of how to make them probably also arrived in China by this means, well before silk and other textiles became major commodities. On this view, it is likely that artisans in the early Qin state, which was located in the Longdong region (i.e., eastern Gansu)—the eastern end of the ancient Silk Road—were among the first communities in China to experiment with iron technology, engendering the early appearance of the character etymologically related to "iron" in the Qin state. If so, the favorable geographical location of the Qin state, situated at the intersection of the east-west communication pathway, probably influenced the later development of the iron industry.

Soon after its initial domestication, the early iron working in ancient China developed into cast iron production, which was a trajectory different from the tradition evidenced in other parts of the Old world such as West Asia. Since casting iron required a larger consumption of fuel, ore, and labor force than the previous copper-based technology, one may argue that the Qin political infrastructure, which was capable of mobilizing a large labor force for projects such as mausoleums and the Great Wall (Barbieri-Low 2021), probably stimulated the transition towards cast iron production. The Qin's bureaucratic system would also help to manage and connect the production centers in the capital region and other regions. To explore the social meaning of iron in the Han period, this chapter will first review the development of the iron industry in the Qin state during the second half of the first millennium BCE and will consider in greater detail various aspects of cast iron production among contemporary territorial states.

In archaeological literature, iron has often been seen simply in terms of being more "advanced" technology compared to bronze and other types of materials that ancient people used to make tools (e.g., Childe 1944).[6] While this conventional idea does not always hold true, especially during the initial development of iron metallurgy,[7] the manufacturing of iron, particularly cast iron, involved not only the technological ability to operate a furnace at high temperatures (usually above 1,300°C) but also a supporting organization and social conditions that allowed production or technological changes to take place. The background to the rise of iron technology must be illuminated in order to understand how and why iron played a central role involved in imperial governance along with the expansion of the Han empire. This chapter will therefore first look at social conditions during the first millennium BCE, during which the transitions to iron manufacturing and the spread of iron tools took place.

The importance of cast iron technology in various social domains, such as in stimulating the manufacture of more useful agricultural tools, has been extensively discussed (e.g., Bai 2005; Hsu 1980; Yang K. 2003:42–57, 2004). But the developmental process of iron technology in ancient China has not yet been scrutinized in detail, especially taking into consideration the relationship between its rise and changes in state power. As a result, two critical aspects have long been under-addressed. First, where did local iron technology first emerge? And how did the transition to cast iron-based industry and associated steel-making techniques take place? Although some Chinese scholars have suggested that the area of the Chu state in the middle Yangtze River valley was the first center of cast iron technology (Huang 1976; Yang Q. 2004), Donald Wagner, a respected scholar of the history of iron metallurgy in ancient China, argued that the technology was innovated in the lower Yangtze River valley (1993, 2008), rather than, as usually considered, in the Central Plains. Whichever standpoint is correct, no one has yet critically considered the argument from a long-term perspective by integrating the technology in the region to the later overall development of the iron industry during the Han period.

The second critical issue is how the production of iron was organized in the various divided vassal states during the Warring States period, and how far this technology contributed to the social development of these entities. It is generally agreed that the widespread appearance of iron objects in tombs from the Warring States period implies the underlying existence of a large-scale cast iron industry (e.g., Barnard & Satō 1975; Lei 1980; Li 1975; Satō 1962:378–399; Yang K. 2004). Nonetheless, previous studies have not fully addressed how the industry was organized in each of these individual states. It has also been assumed that iron technology developed in much the same way from state to state. Some scholars even have suggested that iron technology, or the organization of iron production, might have been an important factor in the unification of the Qin state (e.g., Trousdale 1977; Wagner 2008:146–147),[8] but no comparisons between the Qin and other states have yet been made.

Since numerous excavation reports of sites dating from the Warring States period have been published in recent decades, it is timely to revisit the nature of technological change and social development of iron in ancient China. Therefore, this chapter attempts to review iron technology in ancient China and offer some new insights. I initially review recent studies related to iron metallurgy (e.g., Han 1998; Han & Duan 2009; Han & Chen 2013; Han & Ke 2007) during the first half of the first millennium BCE. Then I explore the different types of iron objects made and the different technologies used in China's three main states: Jin (or the three Jin states: Han, Zhao, and Wei), Chu, and Qin. More information has been published on these three states than on other contemporary states such as Qi and Yan.[9] Finally, I bring together multiple lines of evidence to illustrate an image of the iron industry, which is different from that depicted in previous literature. During the Early

.stern Zhou period, the use of iron in the manufacturing of weapons was ...dely practiced in the north but not in the south, indicating potential technological transmission from Central Asia or the Eurasian steppes (Wagner 1993; Bronson 1999). While the artisans in the Qin state might have played a critical role in experimenting with early iron working, cast iron technology quickly developed in both the Jin and Chu states, but not in the Qin state, shortly after its initial spread. In this light, it seems likely that the iron industry was underdeveloped in the Qin state, at least during the major period of the Warring States.

It is noteworthy that the Warring States period also saw momentous social changes, and is often viewed as one of the greatest transformational eras in Chinese history. Besides escalations in warfare (e.g., Lewis 1999; Yang K. 2004:89–187), a large and rapid increase in population, a new land system that granted each household a piece of land in the Qin (and Jin) states,[10] and a stimulus of agricultural production (Hsu 1980; Liu X. 2017) all occurred within this period of about 200 years. These changes would have collectively prompted the development of the iron industry, given the large scale of products manufactured and the improved efficiency obtained by converting iron to steel (iron with carbon content in the range of 0.5-1%). Presumably, the pressure of developing agriculture might have been similarly experienced across the various territorial states. It has thus been argued that the cast iron transition developed at the same pace in all three states. But a close examination of records shows that the assemblages of iron products between these states were rather different. The varying pace of development between the three territorial states should not be neglected, as it may have foreshadowed the patterns of the development of the iron industry in the Han period. Even though the package of iron-making techniques employed by these states was generally similar and belonged to the cast iron tradition, I argue that the social setting in which the iron production took place and the organization of labor differenced. A regional perspective is thus essential to illustrate the trajectory of the iron industry during the Warring States period.

1 Iron as an emblem of prestige

In ancient China, iron manufacturing often employed the so-called cast iron technique, which refers to the type of iron that was smelted and cast in a liquid state, usually with about 4 percent of carbon (Wagner 1993:336). In Chapter 3, the specific techniques and related terminologies will be explained more comprehensively. Since the rise of iron technology in the pre-Qin period created the conditions for the development of the iron industry during the subsequent Han period, it is desirable at this stage to provide an explanatory sketch of the difference between cast iron and its counterpart, bloomery iron. Cast iron refers to the smelting or melting of iron to its liquid stage for casting and requires the control of a high temperature and strong reducing atmosphere inside the furnace. In contrast, bloomery iron refers to reducing iron ores in a relatively low temperature and weak-reducing environment. The final products of the later technique were sponge-shaped mixtures of metallic iron and other waste debris since slag was not completely separated from the metallic iron during the bloomery process. While the high temperature involved in cast iron smelting could efficiently remove impurities, its products were in fact an iron-carbon alloy, which is extremely hard and lacks flexibility. Annealing (i.e., heat treatment) and decarburizing are necessary in order to make cast iron tools practical (i.e., to convert cast iron into steel, or to make it "soft") in production.[11] In contrast, bloomery iron is relatively soft; ironsmiths need to carburize bloomery iron to steel during the hammering and forging process to harden it and shape the bloom into the required shape. Given the relatively lower thresholds for techniques involved, almost all early experiments with iron in ancient societies started with the manufacture of bloomery iron (Rehren et al. 2013). China was no exception to this trend.

The social conditions under which these two types of iron were made were often very different. The production of cast iron requires considerable investment in facilities (e.g., furnaces, air supply system, and fining system to convert cast iron into steel), an abundant workforce, and the availability of large quantities of fuel to generate the high temperature and reduce environment to melt iron and produce free-flowing slag (Wagner 1993:48). Given the cost of assembling the facilities, workforce, and raw materials, a developed transportation network and copious market are needed for manufacturing to become economical. Otherwise, overstocking would create unnecessary waste. In contrast, a bloomery furnace produces small amounts of iron in a single smelting operation and requires less heat and fuel. Bloomery iron production would have been a better choice in areas where production was constrained by a limited workforce, limited supplies of fuel, or under-developed communication routes. The point has already been made (Wagner 2008:-144–146, 210–220) that in the ancient world manufacturing iron, particularly cast iron, required not only large amounts of fuel and raw materials but also a complex system for organizing a large labor force, which is applicable to understanding ancient Chinese society and production. The rise of cast iron technology must be understood within its social context.

To contextualize iron technology in its historical background, I will first clarify how early iron-smelting technology was developed in ancient China. The earliest iron products from ancient China discovered so far are two iron pieces (one iron bar and one iron lump) from the Mogou cemetery in Gansu province associated with the Siwa culture (Chen et al. 2012), dating to about the 14th century BCE (Figure 1.1). Metallurgical analysis of these two iron pieces has shown that they are bloomery iron products. The discovery of these early iron pieces from Mogou supports the theory (e.g., Tang 1993; Zhao 2012) that early iron technology (i.e., bloomery iron) was the result of cultural exchange or interaction with Central or West Asia, rather than a local invention (cf. Bai 2005:42–43). However, since only a handful of early

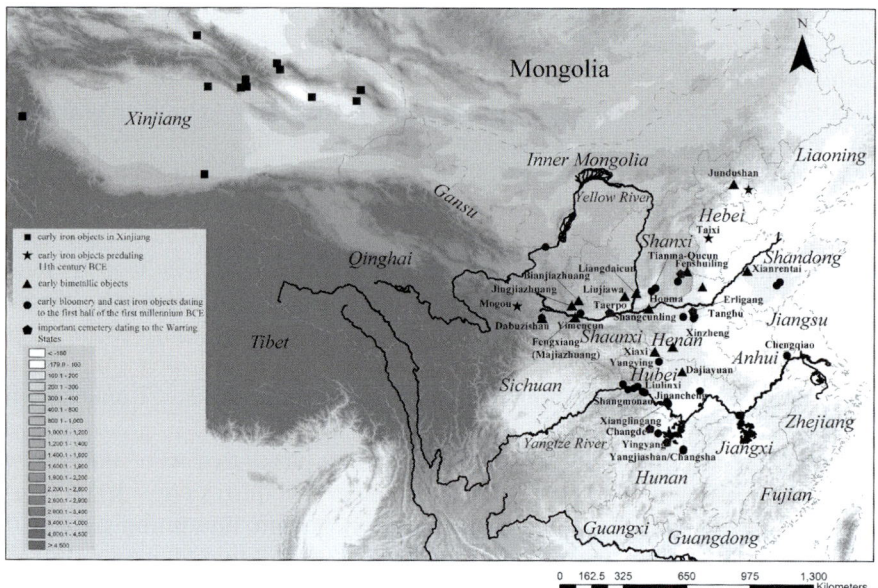

Figure 1.1 Distribution map of early iron objects in Xinjiang, bimetallic weapons, early cast iron objects in the Central Plains, and cemeteries that are mentioned in the chapter.

iron objects securely dating from the 10th and 9th century BCE have been found in Xinjiang, and elsewhere in western China (Chen J. 2014:220; 2020), we still cannot say how iron technology was spread from Xinjiang through the Hexi Corridor to the Central Plains[12]—the middle Yellow River valley and southeastern edge of the Loess Plateau—and how it led to the manufacturing of bimetallic weapons (i.e., the materials for making different parts of a weapon include two types of metal) dating to the Shang dynasty, as represented by the two *yue* axes from the Taixi site (Hebei 1985) and Liujiahe site (Zhang & Zhang 1990), both are in Hebei.[13] Nonetheless, the edge of these two examples was made from meteoric iron, not smelted iron (Li 1976) (Figure 1.1).[14]

The widespread adoption and employment of iron technology in craft production is more clearly evident during the 8th and 7th century BCE, which saw the transition between the Western Zhou and Eastern Zhou dynasties. Bloomery iron and meteoric iron were used in considerable quantities for manufacturing elite, such as *ge* dagger-axes and daggers (Figure 1.2), carried by noblemen as prestige symbols. Iron was used for making the blade part of most of these items. The evidence for the use of smelted iron has been found in a number of elite funeral contexts[15] during this period, including Jingjiazhuang (Liu & Zhu 1981) and Dabuzishan (Chen and Ma 2009; Liang 2020) in Gansu; Bianjiazhuang (Shaanxi

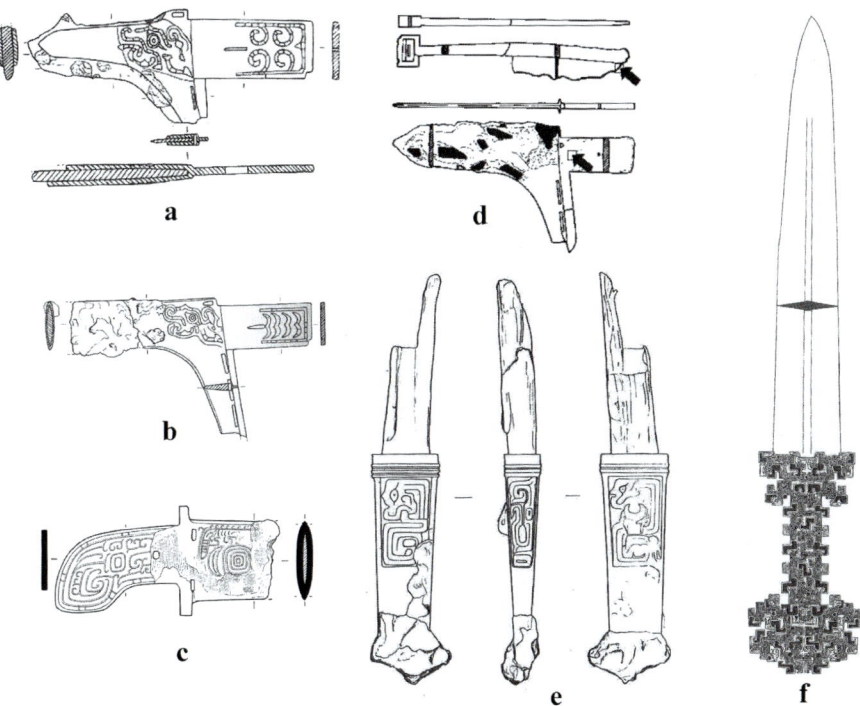

Figure 1.2 Selective bimetallic weapons and tools in the Spring-and-Autumn period (a–b: redrawn from Henan & Sanmenxia 1999:Fig 105.3; c: redrawn from Zhang et al. 2020:Fig 3; d: redrawn from Chen et al. 2009:Fig 3; e: redrawn from Han 1998:Fig 1.4; f: redrawn from Tian & Lei 1993:Fig 7.1).

Yanjiusuo & Baojishi 1988), Yimencun (Tian & Lei 1993), and Liangdaicun (Chen et al. 2009) in Shaanxi; Shangcunling (Henan & Sanmenxia 1999) in Henan; Jundushan (He et al. 2004) in Hebei; and Xianrentai (Shandong Daxue 1998) in Shandong (Figure 1.1); most of them are in the Qin territory and the Central Plains. Individuals associated with these discoveries were mostly of elite class, and these discoveries could be classified into two groups. Dabuzishan, Shangcunling, Liangdaicun, and Xianrentai belonged to the cemeteries of vassal states affiliated with the Zhou system in which marquis-level tombs have been identified. In the other group, Jingjiazhuang, Bianjiazhuang, Yimencun, and Jundushan—the first three locations are all within the Qin state—the tomb occupants were non-Sinitic members, probably associated with the *rong* barbarian groups.[16] This suggests that artisans serving the elites in the Qin state played a critical role in the transmission of early iron metallurgy.

The origin of the sudden widespread adoption of smelted iron employed in the manufacturing of weapons remains unclear. While iron smelting techniques might have been actually invented by local bronze specialists (e.g., Bai 2005), scholars increasingly prefer an explanation involving external transmission along the early Silk Road, given the discoveries of considerable quantities of early smelted iron objects have been found in various locations in the region.[17] Scholars often claimed those early worked iron as the "archaeological signal" of the spread of iron technology transmitted from the Eurasian steppes or Central Asia, probably caused by the migration of early pastoral-nomadic groups (e.g., Wagner 1993). However, the sparseness of iron artifacts identified in the region, together with the lack of solid evidence of smelting or iron working until the second half of the first millennium BCE (Chen J. 2020; Guo 2009), suggests that those early iron objects might have been brought in by exchange instead of being local iron products. Even though the initial smelting of bloomery iron in Xinjiang might have occurred under the influence of interregional connection, the transmission process did not immediately cause the adoption of the new technique by artisans along the continental traffic route, or at the least left little in the way of evidence that could be found archaeologically.

In southern China (i.e., Yangtze River valley), very few bimetallic weapons have been found. The best evidence of early iron working to date came from an iron dagger, which was mounted on a jade shaft, found in tomb No. 10 at Xiasi (Henan Wenwu et al. 1991) in present-day Henan, an elite cemetery associated with the Chu state belonging to the Wei lineage. Yet, the cemetery was located on the edge of the Central Plains, not too distant from other discoveries of early iron weapons. Also, this piece might represent the late arrival of the bimetallic tradition in the manufacture of elite weapons to the south of the Central Plains, since this tomb is usually dated to the Late Spring-and-Autumn period. The concentration of early iron objects in the western part of the Central Plains extending towards the Hexi Corridor (Figure 1.1) appears to support the hypothesis that the invention of early iron technology was stimulated by external influences, probably from West Asia.

The social status of owners of those early iron objects also indicates an interesting pattern. Except for the case of Jundushan, which was clearly associated with a non-Sinitic low-status occupant,[18] all other tombs were occupied by noblemen associated with the Zhou system and contained large amounts of bronze vessels and other prestige goods such as jade. Metallurgical analyses demonstrate that most of these items used either bloomery iron or meteoric iron (Chen 2014; Wang et al. 2019), and no pattern was present between the smelting technique employed and the types of goods. Even though the provenance of these objects has not been addressed, their wide distribution implies that iron was regarded by elites as a prestigious token in most of the Eastern Zhou states in the Central Plains and the Qin state. The Early and Middle Spring-and-Autumn period might also have experienced the stage of experimenting with iron-smelting techniques in ancient China. According to the context of these early iron objects, the development of bloomery iron in ancient China therefore embodies the historian of science Cyril S. Smith (1903–1992)'s observation (1970) that the use of new materials in human history was usually not triggered by practical need but rather by the interests of art. The invention of ironcasting was perhaps one of the indirect results of elite patronage in the craft industry.

From the 7th to 5th century BCE, cast iron technology was also gradually established in the Central Plains as well as in the Yangtze River valley alongside the widespread use of bloomery iron in the manufacture of prestige weaponry (Han & Chen 2013; Lam 2014). The early evidence of cast iron production comes from the Tianma-Qucun (Beida Shangzhou & Shanxi 2000) site in Houma, Shanxi. Two fragments of cast iron have been unearthed from residential contexts dating to the Early Spring-and-Autumn period. Nonetheless, the shape of these objects is so irregular that metallurgists are more favorable to view them as the by-products of the smelting  process of bloomery iron (Han & Chen 2013). In Henan province, a number of cast iron tools were reported from the excavation of cemeteries and residential sites predating the 5th century BCE (Li 1975), which are often considered as the signal of initial large-scale manufacturing of cast iron implements in the Central Plains. It is also important to note that two cases of early evidence showing the emergence of cast iron production during the Late Spring-and-Autumn period were found in the Qin state (Lam 2014). One is an iron *cha*-spade found in one of the sacrificial pits in the courtyard of the no. 2 palace at Majiazhuang, and the other one includes a handful of *cha*-spades found during the excavation of Duke Jing's Mausoleum of the Qin State (Han & Jiao 1988). Both cases are located in Yongcheng, the capital of the Qin state from the 7th to 4th century BCE. Some scholars have claimed that these discoveries imply an early development of cast iron production in the Qin state (Bai 2005:27; Zhang & Tang 2017), as tools of this type were usually cast objects. Nonetheless, it remains unclear whether these tools came from an *in situ* context based on the descriptions in preliminary reports. Given the relatively few discoveries of cast iron remains on  residential sites of the Qin state, even in the Warring State period as I will demonstrate later, I consider the early discoveries more likely to be intrusions from a later historical period.

Grounded on bloomery iron, the earliest iron industry in ancient China was employed primarily in the manufacturing of elite weapons, which appears to have been different from the industry in the later period after the 5th century BCE. During the initial adoption stage, a considerable number of discoveries (e.g., Jinjiazhuang, Dabuzishan, Yimencun, and Bianjiazhuang) were found inside the Qin state, or among ethnic groups associated with the Qin state. Nonetheless, such early adoption should not be assumed as the direct result of cast iron manufacturing in the subsequent period, as the heterogeneity of regional patterns of the cast iron industry, especially the development trajectory in southern China, has long been overlooked.

2 The coming of the large-scale cast iron manufacturing

Soon after the gradual establishment of cast iron technology in the Central Plains from the 7th to 5th centuries BCE (Han & Chen 2013; Lam 2014), iron quickly replaced other major types of tool manufacturing materials in some territorial states. The widespread adoption also laid down the foundation for iron to eventually become an essential commodity in the financial system of the Han empire (206 BCE–202 CE). But since southern China witnessed a relatively early arrival of the cast iron industry, probably no later than that in the Central Plains, in the manufacturing of various agricultural tools in comparison with the three Jin states, the coming of cast iron in the south will be first examined below.

Agricultural implements[19] and remains related to early cast iron products have been found in a number of locations in the middle Yangtze River and Han River valleys, notably Shangmonao (Hubei 2000), Liulinxi (Guowuyuan & Guojia 2003), Dajiayuan (Hubei & Xiaogan 2006), Xianglinggang (Jingmen 1990), and Yangying (Hubei & Laohekou 2003)[20] (Figure 1.1). All these locations are considered to date to the Late or even the Middle Spring-and-Autumn period.[21] Only samples from Yangying have been subject to systematic metallurgical analysis (Chen 2014), which shows that all objects are cast iron. A more significant discovery of early cast iron comes from further south. One iron sword that was made by the so-called "decarburization of cast iron"[22] and a cast iron cauldron were unearthed from a small-scale Chu tomb without any bronze ritual vessels in Changsha dating to the Late Spring-and-Autumn period (Changsha 1978).[23] Similar objects have not been found in any contemporary contexts. The discoveries of iron tools in various residential sites also suggest that cast iron might have become rather widespread in the Chu region by the end of the Spring-and-Autumn period.

Other early cast iron objects have also been found in the lower Yangtze River valley. Two lumps of iron and an iron bar were discovered in two burials dating to the Late Spring-and-Autumn period, respectively, at the Chengqiao site in Jiangsu. One of them is cast iron, whereas the other one, based on metallurgical analysis, has been reported to be bloomery iron (Jiangsu & Nanjing 1965; Nanjing 1974). As already mentioned, the distribution pattern, together with the widespread adoption of bronze in the manufacturing of agricultural tools, a pattern also existed in the Jin state, has led some scholars to suggest that cast iron technology might have first been invented in this part of China which is not richly endowed with copper, as an alternative material to supplement the huge demand in metal production (Wagner 2008:105–112). Nonetheless, the scarcity of cast iron implements from proto-porcelain production site and cemeteries in this region (Zhejiang 2009; Zhejiang & Deqing 2011) puts this hypothesis in doubt. No matter which region was the first to invent the iron-casting technique, the widespread evidence of cast iron production is unquestionable during the

Late Spring-and-Autumn period, or before the middle of the 5th century BCE, especially in regions near the Yangtze River valley.

The appearance of agricultural implements on a large scale might be closely allied with the technique of annealing, which also appeared in the Chu region relatively early. Annealing is one of the essential fabrication techniques that were used to enhance the physical properties of cast iron tools by heating iron implements at a relatively low temperature for a long time to reduce carbon content. The annealing technique enables brittle cast iron to be transformed into a practical material for making weaponry or tools. By the dawn of the Qin unification (221 BCE), the rapid increase in the use of iron resulted in the innovation of various fabrication techniques in different territorial states (Han & Duan 2009; Han & Ke 2007:604), which I will consider further later. The use of an early annealing technique has also been reported in Yangying, in addition to two pieces of evidence from burial sites in the Central Plains, one at Tanghu in the Zheng state (Li 1975) and the other in Luoyang within the territory controlled by the Eastern Zhou royal family. The sword from the Chu tomb at Yangjiashan previously has also been claimed to be made of decarburized cast iron (Changsha 1978), and may offer the earliest evidence for the use of cast iron in the manufacture of weaponry. These objects consist of the assemblage of early evidence showing annealing identified so far. Given the various locations reported as having cast iron wares, it is possible that the new technique appeared simultaneously in multiple centers or states covering both the Central Plains and the Yangtze River valley, while the latter region seems to yield more evidence and thus represent a more dynamic development. During the Warring States period, many iron objects, which are either agricultural implements or weapons, had been processed by annealing (e.g., see the results in Li X. 2006; Rong et al. 2013), suggesting a wide adoption of the technique during the second half of the first millennium BCE.

Based on the evidence published thus far, the technical transition to iron-casting seems to have been achieved in less than 400 years, from the 7th century BCE when early cast iron initially appeared, to the 4th century BCE when large-scale manufacturing is robustly attested. Reliable archaeological evidence from both the Central Plains and Yangtze River valley suggests that the techniques of decarburizing and annealing appeared no later than the Late Spring-and-Autumn period, which, together with other pre-existing skills such as casting-mold technique and the management of large-scale labor, might lay down an essential technical foundation for the widespread distribution of iron technology and the start of the massive production of iron objects in most divided states during the Warring States period. The turn to cast iron production might have been triggered by the huge demand for bronze agricultural tools by initially serving as a supplementary source (Lam 2014), focused predominantly on commoners' needs and fueled the production of daily-use goods, especially those consumed on a very large scale such as digging tools or agricultural implements.

As mentioned earlier, it has been claimed for a long time (e.g., Yang K. 2004) that the development of iron and steel technology proceeded along similar lines in different states. After the invention and widespread use of cast iron technology, it was generally considered that these territorial states adopted the technology at more or less the same time, and that there was little difference in their ability to manufacture advanced steel agricultural implements. Based on archaeological data, I suggest on the contrary that there was more heterogeneity in terms of regional development among these states, as the following interregional comparison reveals. With the understanding of the basic development of iron technology, I now turn to explore regional developments and variations represented in the Jin and Chu regions to compare with the Qin discussed above. During the past few decades, large numbers of archaeological reports of cemeteries dating to the Eastern Zhou period have been published, which provide useful datasets for comparative study. This growing dataset allows me not only to draw more solid conclusions through interregional comparison but also to reevaluate the surviving textual records with the help of new material evidence.[24]

Jin states

As other scholars have demonstrated (Han & Duan 2009), Jin states (i.e., Han, Zhou, Wei) comprised a relatively well-studied region for cast iron technology and its iron industry. The most useful statistical figures for comparisons have been given by Han and Duan (2009). In their systematic study of iron technology of the Jin state, they recorded a total of 751 iron artifacts from more than 1,000 graves of commoners. Relatively few iron weapons have been found (about 50 pieces), and most iron objects were either belthooks (more than 60 percent of the 751 artifacts recorded) or agricultural implements including axes, shovels, sickles, and pickaxes. Their metallurgical analysis showed that 90 percent of 60 selected iron samples were cast from the liquid state, including 22 white iron samples softened by annealing. In other words, most of these iron tools were made of cast iron. Iron tools have also been frequently identified in workshop contexts. From the Niucun foundry (Shanxi 1993) in the Houma capital of the Jin state that I will introduce in detail in Chapter 4, for instance, two pieces of iron, probably belonging to iron knives, were found in a stratum dating to the Early Warring States period or even earlier. From a ceramic workshop in the capital of the Han state dating to the Middle and Late Warring States periods, one sickle and nine knives were discovered alongside manufacturing debris of daily-use and architectural ceramics (Henan Wenwu 1991b). As Han and Duan argue through the metallurgical study (2009), the high quality and large scale of production may have made a crucial contribution to the widespread use of iron tools in daily life during the Warring States period.

Information from the burial sites at Fenshuiling (Shanxi et al. 2010) in Changzi (Figure 1.1) belonging to the Han state[25] gives a more granular idea of the scale of the iron industry during this period. From a total of 165 tombs dating primarily to the Early and Middle Warring States period, 29 iron implements have been found, including five belt-hooks, 16 axes, and four spades; some tools might have been remains after the tomb was constructed instead of being purposely included as burial goods. Further information about the use of iron in burial contexts from the Warring States period has been provided by the Erligang (Henan Wenhuaju 1959) cemetery in present-day Zhengzhou city, which was also controlled by the Han state. A total of 52 iron belt-hooks, two knives, three hoe-heads, two *cha* spades, and seven *jue* axes have been found in the cemetery including 212 tombs, most of which date to the Late Warring States period. This assemblage approximates the dataset from the Fenshuiling cemetery; yet iron objects are more frequently included in the former case (at least 24 percent of tombs included at least one iron object), probably due to the further development of the iron industry in the later period presented by the majority of tombs at Erligang.

Besides iron tools in workshops, large-scale ironworks specializing in manufacturing agricultural tools have been widely found within the walled capitals and towns of the Jin states, including Zheng-Han Gucheng (the capital of the Zheng and later Han state, present-day Xinzheng) (Henan 2006), Yangcheng (Henan Wenwu & Zhongguo 1992), and Yuwangcheng (Zhang & Huang 1993). One representative example is the Zhonghang ironworks, which was located inside the capital of the Zheng and Han states. The assemblage of products, manufacturing techniques, as well as the production organization will be further explained elsewhere in this book. The large corpus of casting molds and plentiful finds of manufacturing waste prove that iron was produced there on a large scale. It should be noted that the assemblage of iron implements in these residential sites was largely different from that found in tombs mentioned earlier. In the assemblage of burial goods, iron belt-hooks were often the most common implements found from the Warring States period, while relatively few iron tools have been discovered. In addition, iron weaponry rarely appears in Jin-era finds in archaeological contexts. Even in the Fenshuiling cemetery, which included at least 25 elite tombs with bronze vessels of various types, hardly any iron weapons were found. From almost all the highest-ranking tombs that were identified so far, iron objects were primarily related to agricultural implements. Bronze weaponry, in contrast, occurs quite often in elite male tombs; at least 15 bronze daggers have been found, indicating that the manufacture of iron weapons might not have been equally advanced in the three Jin states.

Chu state

Although the discovery of early steel products in the Changsha area, the southern territory of the Chu state, has attracted considerable discussion (Huang 1976), surprisingly few iron products have been discovered from tombs within the capital core of Chu territory, known as the Jiangling area in present-day Jingzhou. As Wagner (2008:106–107) and Bai (2005:378) pointed out, only one iron axe and one spade have been identified from the Yutaishan (Hubei Jingdi 1984) cemetery. As one of the largest cemeteries excavated so far, Yutaishan included 500-plus tombs dating from the Middle Spring-and-Autumn to the Middle Warring States period. Similarly, iron objects were rarely found at the Jiudian cemetery (Hubei 1995), another large commoner cemetery contemporary to Yutaishan adjacent to the Chu capital, Jinancheng. More than 590 tombs have been excavated, but only seven iron objects—one decarburized steel sword,[26] one iron axe, one knife, and four objects whose purpose remains unknown—have been discovered in only seven tombs. Even in elite tombs such as Tianxingguan tomb Nos. 1 (Hubei Jingdi 1982) and 2 (Hubei Jingzhou 2003), Baoshan Tomb No. 2 (Hubei Jingsha 1991), and Zuozhong Tomb No. 1 (Hubei et al. 2006), iron objects were very few, with just several simple forms of tools. The pattern in the assemblage presents a remarkable difference compared to the scenario in the Jin states, which at least includes some iron body ornaments such as belt-hooks. What is more intriguing is the fact that no evidence of large-scale iron foundries has been identified within Jinancheng dating from the Late Spring-and-Autumn[27] to the Middle Warring States period. The organization of the iron industry in the Chu state seems therefore much less present than in the Jin states. However, some iron implements including spades, sickles, chisels, axes, and other tools have been often found in residential contexts (e.g., gates and houses) inside Jinancheng (Hubei Bowuguan 1982a, 1982b) and surrounding areas (Hubei Wenwuju & Hubei Nanshuibeidao 2018). Although it is curious that a cast iron foundry has not yet been discovered, cast iron production was likely to have been sizable.

The relatively common discovery of iron objects from tombs in the southern territory of the Chu state contrasts remarkably with the situation in the capital core. As previously explained, Changsha (Changsha1978) is one of the areas[28] yielding early steel[29] weaponry in ancient China. In addition, iron weapons have frequently been found in commoner's cemeteries[30] in this region. In the Greater Changsha area, for instance, site reports have been made of 2,048 tombs dating primarily to the Warring States period. So far, 135 iron tools and 39 iron weapons have been discovered in these tombs. Meanwhile, bronze weaponry still played an essential role: 960 bronze weapons (or parts thereof) have been found in various cemeteries dating from the Warring States period.

To the west of Changsha, iron objects have also been frequently discovered in tombs dating from the Early and Middle Warring States period in the Yiyang area (Yiyang & Yiyangshi 2008) (Figure 1.1) in the Yuan River valley, a major river system running through the western part of Hunan. According to the site reports, 126 iron implements, including 23 swords and various types of tools, have been found in 89 tombs. Interestingly, few iron belt-hooks featured among these finds. Two iron sword samples have been analyzed and identified as cast iron.[31] Although iron weapons were not as

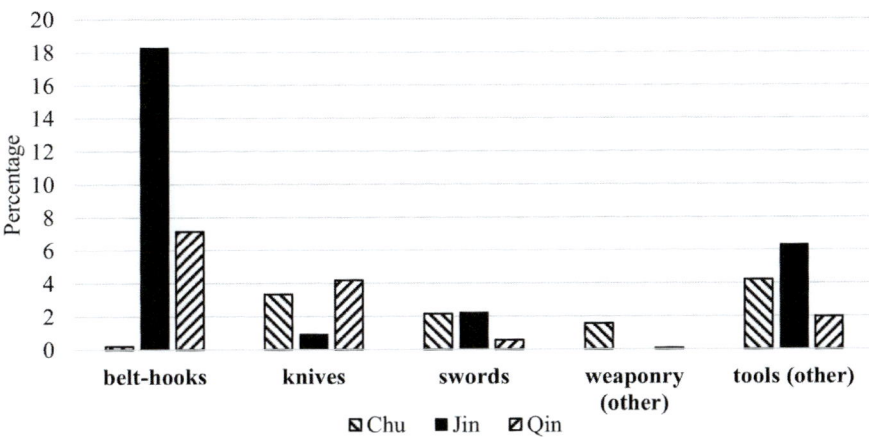

Figure 1.3 Percentage of tombs including major types of iron wares in the three regions during the Warring States period. Please note that the data for the Chu state only come from the Changsha and Yiyang areas, not including the Jiangling area.

common as their bronze counterparts (99 bronze swords have been found in more than 650 burials), more iron weapons have been found here than in the Chu core or in the territories of other contemporary states (Figure 1.3).

The reason for these regional differences is not yet clear, but the abundance of iron objects found in the northern Hunan region, together with the discovery of early cast iron from sites within the Chu territories (e.g., Yangying), undermines previous claims that the iron industry in the Chu state was underdeveloped or operated on a small scale (Wagner 2008:126–128). By looking at the discovery of iron objects, the arrival of new technology (cast iron and decarburized weaponry) in the Chu state appeared to be slightly earlier, or at least no later than some other territorial states. In addition, the large-scale production of iron weapons appeared to undoubtedly occur in the southern frontier of the Chu state during the Warring States period, as a good number of these weapons were accessible to commoners in the Chu state but have rarely if ever been found in other places. Especially, if the Jinancheng capital was constructed later than what was proposed before in the Early Warring States period (Yin 2019), the scarcity of iron implements in burials in the capital area perhaps was more likely due to other cultural preferences or political restriction on using iron objects for funeral rites rather than the shortage of iron supply. The iron industry Chu state also appeared to focus more on manufacturing iron weapons, indicating that the widespread adoption of iron in the Chu state might have been driven by various factors instead of primarily driven by agricultural production as cases of the Jin states presented.

3 Ambiguous emergence of iron technology in the Qin state

In comparison with the discoveries of iron implements from the Central Plains and the Chu state, the types and quantities of iron products found from the Qin state during the Warring States period presented certain discrepancies. Such differences reflect that the development of the iron industry might have followed a trajectory different from the two other comparative states. To better provide the background for explaining the observed patterns, I will also sketch out the layout of capitals and craft production centers inside during the Warring States and unification periods.

Following the migration of the Qin state into the Wei River valley from the Longdong region in 677 BCE (Figure 1.4), Yongcheng (Figure 1.5) served as the capital for more than 300 years until 383 BCE, and provided the most important set of materials for understanding the Qin state before the Warring States era. The capital was not only politically significant, but also became a ritual center for holding sacrificial ceremonies, as evidenced by the recent discovery of the large corpus of sacrificial pits at the Xuechi site nearby Yongcheng (Shaanxi Yanjiuyuan et al. 2020). Even after the capital

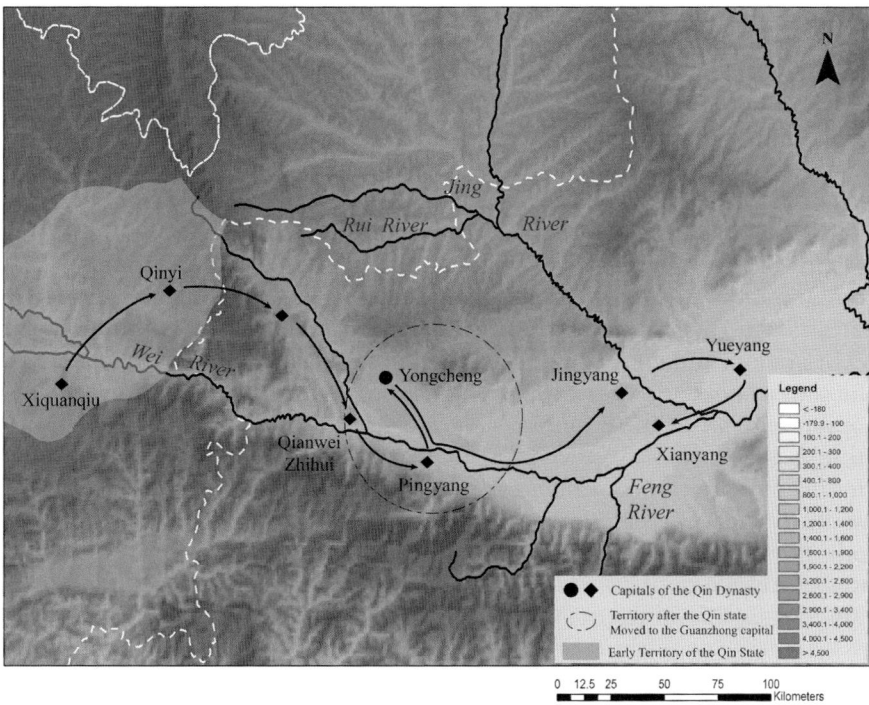

Figure 1.4 Migration route of the Qin state (after Liang 2020:Fig 1).

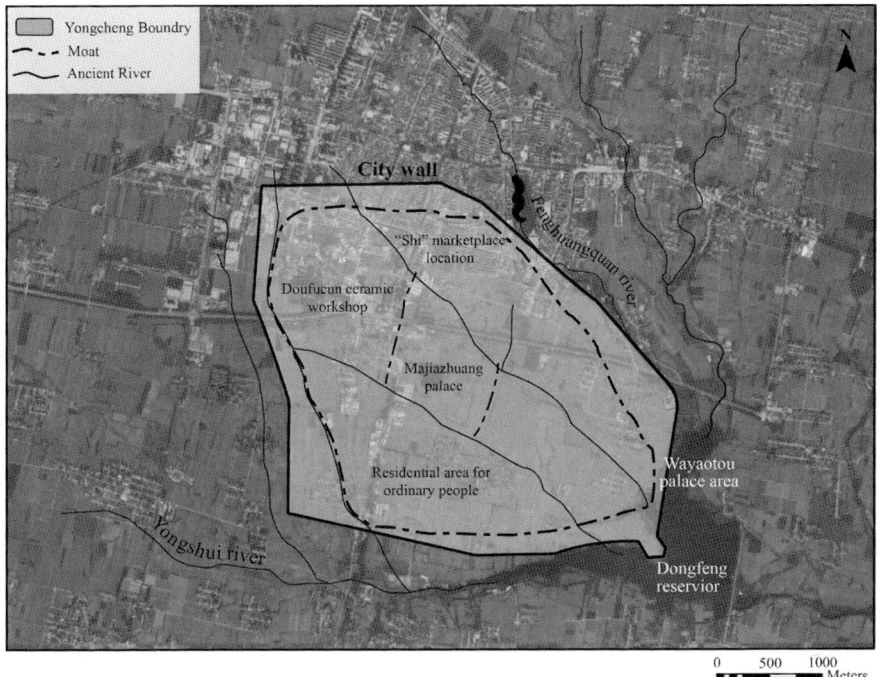

Figure 1.5 Layout of the Yongcheng capital (after Tian 2018:Fig 1; source of the background map: Google Map).

was moved to Yueyang and then Xianyang, Yongcheng remained an important ritual center up to the Western Han period.[32]

Thanks to decades of archaeological fieldwork and settlement pattern surveys, the basic layout of Yongcheng has been known in considerable detail (Tian 2013, 2018). Enclosed by several river tributaries, the walled town, with its distinctive trapezoid shape, covered an area of about 10 km² (Figure 1.5). If various cemeteries and mausoleums to the south of the capital are included, the total area of the entire site complex was more than 30 km². Internally, the walled capital was divided into four sections, including three areas in which palaces or temples have been identified, and one section reserved for craft specialization. One of the suspicious cast iron tools from the Qin state came from a sacrificial pit at Majiazhuang No. 1 palace in the palace area in the center of Yongcheng. To the northwestern part of the walled capital there was a workshop area, a pattern that widely existed in contemporary capital towns. The craft production center included at least one ceramic workshop and one bronze foundry, but to date, only the ceramic workshop located at Doufucun has been systematically reported (Shaanxi Yanjiuyuan et al. 2013).

The Doufucun ceramic workshop in Yongcheng was in operation from around 650 to 350 BCE, and supposedly witnessed the critical transformation to cast iron production. Whereas evidence from other ceramic centers in the Jin states is plentiful, little solid evidence for this cast iron transition can be found in the material records from Doufucun. Manufacturing remains and production tools for various types of daily vessels and architectural ceramics (tiles and tile-ends with decorative animal motifs) have been found at the site, and a number of bronze tools (e.g., knives) have also been reported. However, no iron implements have been found in the Warring States and the Spring-and-Autumn strata. The organized layout of facilities of various stages in the production process, including kilns and storage pits of clay, and the network of waterpipes that run through the workshop indicate that its layout had been systematically planned and that it was intended to serve the Qin state on a long-term basis. However, no iron implements have been found that date from the three centuries during which the workshop was functioning. This fact requires explanation. One plausible theory is that manufacturing of cast iron tools in the Qin state, at least as late as the 4th century BCE, was far less developed than in the Jin states. The widespread adoption of cast iron tools in the Qin state therefore took place much later than has often been claimed. If so, this undermines the contention, based on the discoveries from Majiazhuang, that the cast iron industry appeared in the Qin state at a much earlier period (e.g., Bai 2005).

Due to mounting westward military pressure from the Wei state, Duke Xian of Qin (ruling 384–362 BCE) boldly moved his capital to Yueyang in 383 BCE (Figure 1.4), close to the front line in the fluctuating wars between the two states. In 350 BCE, Duke Xiao (ruling 361–338 BCE) moved the capital back to Xianyang, since its favorable site across the routes from the eastern to western Guanzhong was of strategic significance. The current reconstructed layout of Xianyang differs from those of other contemporary walled capitals in Guandong (i.e., regions to the east of Guanzhong separated by the Hangu Pass) in a number of aspects (Figure 1.6). First of all, no enclosing walls have yet been found. Second, the urban center was separated into two halves by the present-day Wei River.[33] Palace areas were located in the northern part of the district currently known as Niejiagou, but it is not clear whether there are inner enclosure walls, generally referred to as *gongcheng* in the literature, surrounding the palatial areas, which was widely seen in other contemporary walled capitals.[34] More research is needed to resolve this question.

Craft production remains have been identified at a number of locations in Xianyang. Iron slag and manufacturing remains have been reported to the northwest of the ruins of the palace, suggesting that ironworks attached to the state might have existed (Xu 2003). But its scale was likely small, since previous archaeological surveys have not found any pattern of casting molds of agricultural tools or manufacturing waste. Recent discoveries have also identified a facility for storing armor and a bone workshop

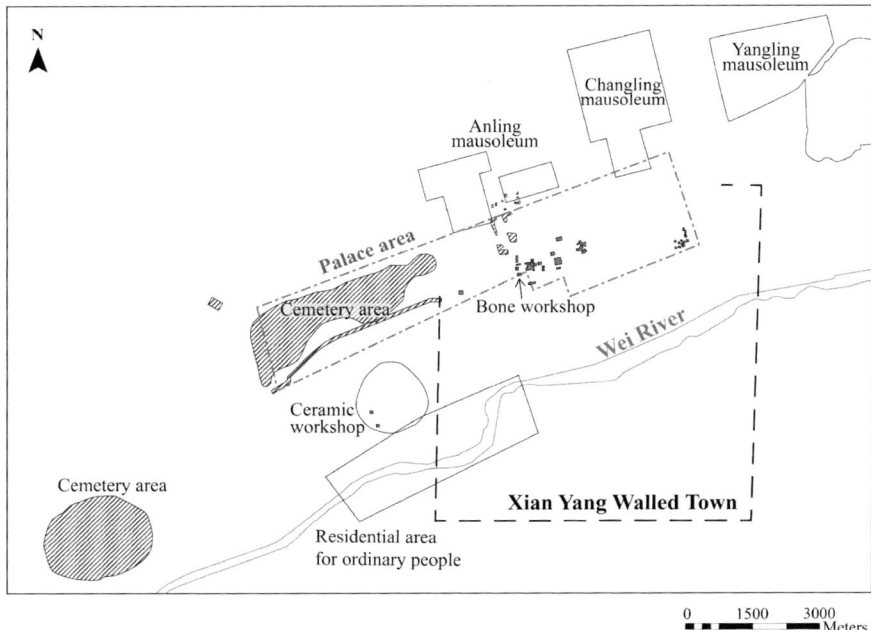

Figure 1.6 Layout of the Xianyang capital (after Xu & Su 2016:Fig 1; Xu 2021:Fig 1; Zhongguo Shehui 2010:Fig 1-1).

near the palace complexes (Shaanxi Yanjiuyuan et al. 2019). All those craft production centers within the palace area might have been attached to the state, supplying products primarily for the royal family. To the south of palace area on the northern bank of the Wei River in present-day Maojiatan, an extensive ceramic workshop has been identified. Organized wells and a drainage system have also been found within the workshop area (Shaanxi Yanjiusuo 2004b). Besides ceramic manufacturing tools and debris, scrap bronzes, probably for remelting, were found from a hoard inside the workshop area. The large corpus of ceramic inscriptions found on vessels and architectural ceramics, which often include the names of potters and the *li* ward, the basic administrative unit of the Qin-Han period in which they dwelled, suggests that at least 100 potters worked within this concentrated area (Lam 2019; Yuan & Liu 2009). A bronze foundry might also have existed within this limited area. Again, however, no iron implements have yet been reported. While archaeological discoveries are largely a matter of luck, the absence of iron implements within the locations already intensively studied suggests that most of the production tools used were not made of iron.

Xianyang was a metropolitan center during the second half of the first millennium BCE, and a huge population lived in the city and in its immediate hinterland. Previous studies have estimated that between 250,000 and

320,000 individuals might have lived within the Xianyang area (Wang X. 1999) before the unification, not including the additional 120,000 households (equivalent to 600,000 residents) originally from the Qi and Chu states relocated by Qin Shihuang later. The large size of the population is hinted at by the discovery of cemeteries for ordinary people in the western part of Xianyang and to the south of the Wei River valley, a site later occupied by the vast city of Chang'an in the Han dynasty. Numerous site reports on Qin tombs near Xianyang, most of them dating to the Late Warring States and Qin unification period, have been published in previous decades (e.g., Xianyangshi Wenwu 1998, 2005; Shaanxi Yanjiusuo 2004b, 2006c; Shaanxi Yanjiuyuan 2008a, 2018b, 2018c).[35] These discoveries not only give a good sense of the Qin's burial and funeral practices (Teng 2002, 2013) but also provide information on the use of iron in burial goods. In order to compare with the scenario in the Jin and Chu states, I collected published data that include enough for statistical analysis and date to the Warring States and Qin unification period—which now covers more than 1,700 tombs[36]—to understand how iron objects were adopted in assemblages and how those reflect social change. This dataset, which consists primarily of belt-hooks, knives, and digging tools, is fairly similar to that recorded for the Jin tombs (Figure 1.7). As the cast iron objects (e.g., belt-hooks and digging tools) produced by the Qin and Jin states were much the same in terms of their types, the Qin ironworks probably used similar techniques and manufactured a similar assemblage of iron products. But the total quantity of iron objects was much smaller than those attested in the three Jin states.

Upon closer scrutiny, the types of iron implements and the frequency of certain types of iron implements included in Qin tombs present certain patterns. For instance, the percentages of tombs including these major types of iron implements are lower in comparison with the Jin states and Chu states (Figure 1.3). In addition, iron weapons were not commonly found in burials. About 13 iron swords, for instance, have so far been identified from various locations.[37] By comparison with the total number of burials identified, the number of iron weapons still appears to be disproportionally small, unlike the scenario of the Chu state. In most cases, commoners' tombs still did not contain substantial numbers or various types of iron products.[38] Agricultural implements were identified in tombs, but they were primarily spades and, more often than not, were found in refilled soil, indicating that they were likely left-over remains after a tomb's construction. Burying iron digging tools or wood-working implements seems to be a rare practice in Qin tombs.

In order to enhance the understanding of the statistical survey of the Fenshuiling and Erligang cemeteries, I select data from the Ta'erpo cemetery (Xianyangshi Wenwu 1998) to compare with the Jin dataset. This cemetery is one of the well-published commoner cemeteries within the area of Xianyang. More importantly, as I will demonstrate in Chapter 6, tombs in cemeteries adjacent to Xianyang usually present a higher frequency of including

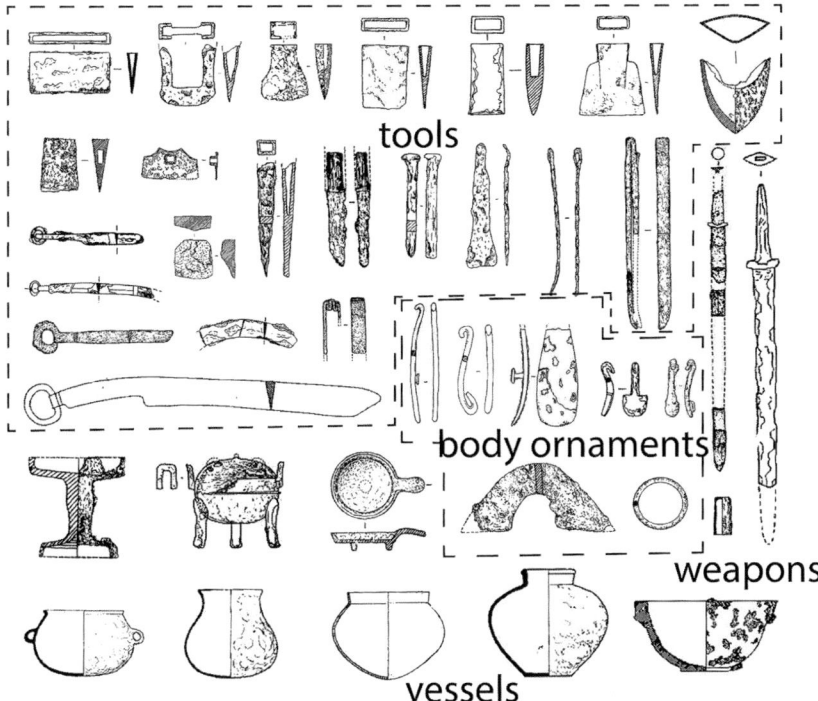

Figure 1.7 Representative iron implements found in the Qin state during the Warring States period (after Lam et al. 2017a:Fig 4, 6).

iron implements compared to those in cemeteries more distant from the
capital. Since this cemetery also includes a total of 391 tombs, this dataset
should be representative of the assemblage of iron objects found in funeral
contexts in the Qin state during the Late Warring States period. From all
burials at Ta'erpo, 67 belt-hooks, 40 knives, and ten other types of tools were
found. For those burials with iron objects, each one usually contained one
knife or one belt-hook. While iron knives appeared to be frequently found
in the assemblage and were well represented in the assemblage, the percentage of tombs with iron belt-hooks (17 percent) is still lower than that in the
contemporary Erligang cemetery in Zhengzhou (24 percent).

Even though the total number of iron implements and the frequency in
burial contexts did not show a sharp contrast between the patterns in the
Jin or Chu sites, there was a wider discrepancy presented by the scenario in
the residential context as illustrated above. First of all, the scale of the ironworks inside the Qin palace area remains unclear. Numerous manufacturing
remains have been found in the capitals of the three eastern states, including
not only slag but also casting molds, tuyeres, and furnace fragments. Significantly, no iron implements have yet been reported from the residential

refuse pits within the area of ceramic workshops, similar to the situation represented by the Doufucun workshop in Yongcheng. The only exception is a newly reported bone workshop within the palace area, in which a considerable number of iron tools, including chisels, knives, and scrapers, have been identified (Shaanxi Yanjiuyuan et al. 2019). Judging from their stratigraphy, however, this assemblage of iron products dates to the Qin unification period, or to the very end of the Qin state. Similar to this discovery, a workshop producing stone armor associated with the Qin Shihuang mausoleum (Shaanxi Yanjiusuo & Qinshihuang 2007)—which also post-dates the Qin unification—was reported to yield considerable amounts of iron tools. While large-scale ceramic and bone manufacturing were an integrated part of the Xianyang capital, ironworks, which were often identified in the capital centers associated with the Jin states or other territorial states, were curiously small-scale in the case of the Qin state. Nor does the discovery of iron implements from residential contexts clearly indicate that iron tools were widely employed in various production activities before the Qin unification period, as the data from other territorial states often demonstrate.

Besides the ambiguous scale of the industry manufacturing daily-use projects such as agricultural tools, the scale of iron weaponry manufacturing was surprisingly limited. In burial contexts, Qin tombs rarely contained iron weapons. In comparison with the total numbers of tombs reported so far, the amounts of iron weaponry identified are disproportionally small. In particular, even in the well-known Terra-Cotta Warriors Pits in Qin Shihuang mausoleum from which hundreds of thousands of bronze daggers, *ge* dagger-axes, crossbows, and arrowheads were identified, no iron weaponry has yet been reported (Shaanxi Yanjiusuo & Qinshihuang 2007).[39] In the Chu state, the large-scale manufacturing of iron weaponry took place during or even before the Middle Warring States, but the corresponding industry in the Qin state appeared to be mysteriously absent in archaeological records. It is noteworthy that iron weaponry might not necessarily be superior to its bronze counterparts with careful control of the ratios of different alloys (Wagner 1993:144). Instead, a more plausible reason may lie in the fact that iron would provide an alternative option for using more readily available resources for large-scale manufacturing. No matter which factor drove the manufacturing of iron weaponry during the Warring States period, there is little evidence that the production of iron weapons in the Qin state was conducted on a large scale.

Archaeological data are always subject to various biases, particularly when using excavated data to analyze historical changes in technology.[40] But the investigation of iron technology through regional comparison reveals several critical aspects in the development as well as the organization of the iron industry in the Qin state. Archaeological evidence of regional discrepancies clearly challenges the simplistic assumption that there was a linear development of iron technology during the second half of the first millennium BCE. In this regard, the study of the iron industry and its differences in the economic and political structures of states durin tumultuous Eastern Zhou period provides an important context for the development of the craft industry in the subsequent Han period.

Cast iron technology was probably inspired by the metallurgical proces smelting bloomery iron, as several previous studies have suggested (Wagner 2008:113). But for the Central Plains states and the Qin state, the socio-economic significance of this technology lies not so much in the production of weapons as in the production of utilitarian and agricultural implements (Lam 2014). In the Central Plains, no evidence has so far been found to document the use of this technology for weapon production (cf. Wang & Liang 2000:246). Except for the Yan state,[41] which, strictly speaking, did not belong to the Central Plains, limited iron weapons have been discovered. The Qin state probably followed this major trend. Once cast iron technology was invented, the knowledge and techniques of smelting and casting were rapidly adopted across different states. At the same time, regional differences in the iron industry were represented not only in terms of scale but also in terms of the types of products made, depending on their particular circumstances. Various lines of evidence indicated that the iron industry in the Qin state was less developed than that of its regional counterparts, at least before the unification in 221 BCE. It may be too early to say how far these regional differences influenced economic or military power. Yet, the trajectory of a less-developed iron industry that was shaped by the long-term historical process might not be substantially altered in the short term, even though considerable changes around the time of the unification, such as coerced relocation of craftsmen from Guandong to the capital region, were introduced. The discrepancy might also have extended to the later Han period, determining the pattern of development of regional labor division in this later period.

Why was the Qin state less developed than its counterparts in this respect? A lack of resources and the dominance of the pre-existing bronze technology might have played a part. Besides the potential lack of technological expertise, the Qin state was less commercially developed, so that the stimulus for the adoption of a new technology was probably lacking. The development of extensive trade networks has often been seen as an important characteristic of the Warring States period, but this view cannot be overstated in the case of the Qin state. According to Emura (1995, 2000, 2011), there was considerable regional variation in urban development, and he compared this pattern to a "mosaic". He also noted that the peripheral location of the Qin state was one of the reasons why it lagged behind its counterparts in terms of its overall market or commercial development. Crucially, formal markets and a coinage system were only established in the Qin state by Duke Xian around 378 BCE and 336 BCE, respectively,[42] at least 100 years later than their appearance in the three Jin states. The Lord Shang's reforms (358 and 350 BCE),[43] which created the impetus for Qin unification by promoting agricultural development, might also have depressed commercial activities to a certain extent.[44]

Historical texts provide essential background for interpreting the subsequent changes of the iron industry observable in material records. After the unification, the Qin state relocated many of its new subjects to the capital region, as a way of dissipating local discontent in the newly conquered territories. The amount of labor mobilized by the exploitative Qin state to the capital region for the construction of the mausoleum was unprecedented. Besides marshaling labor from various conquered territorial states to build mausoleums, the Qin state also levied craftsmen to make the life-sized terracotta soldiers and extravagant bronze figurines which accompanied the emperor Qin Shihuang on his journey to the afterlife. According to ceramic inscriptions, the construction of *Yuchi* (fish pond) and ceramic production in Liyi often involved potters from various parts of Guanzhong who were relocated to production centers close to the mausoleum (Yuan & Liu 2009). It is reasonable to believe that craftsmen who specialized in metal, jade, and other high-elite items were also relocated to Guanzhong during the period of Qin expansion towards the end of the Warring States period. Other workers with specialized skills in iron smelting and casting might also have been the targets for exploitation, given the large-scale construction project and manufacturing of burial goods evidenced by the Qin Shihuang's mausoleum. The importation of so many skilled ironsmiths from the conquered territories probably stimulated the development of Qin's undeveloped iron industry, since these iron masters would have brought with them new skills and knowledge, and tools for manufacturing and agricultural production from other regions to the Xianyang capital.

While regional differences must be recognized, the exchange or transition of techniques between the Qin and other newly conquered regions might have occurred simultaneously in a way that might not be easily understood within our current chronological framework. If the Chu state had an advanced iron industry as I argue here, the occupation of the Chu capital (Jinancheng, present-day Hubei) in 278 BCE would have offered a good  opportunity for the Qin state to procure new techniques and resources well before the final incorporation of the Chu state in 223 BCE. As I will discuss later in the book, the documents recovered from Shuihudi (present-day Yunmeng, Hubei) and Liye (present-day Zhangjiajie, Hunan) where the Qin state established its new administrative system on the newly conquered lands prove that the local county governments managed iron mining and even manufacturing (Tang 2019). In other words, the Qin state was clearly aware of the importance of iron in the broader southern frontiers in the period immediately following unification. If the iron industry was already established in newly conquered lands, it would have been an obvious step to integrate it into the administrative framework. The takeover of the region would also have provided the opportunity for relocating many of its ironsmiths to the capital. While the iron industry in the Qin state was relatively underdeveloped, the Qin state would have addressed the issue via various approaches such as re-utilizing and integrating various pre-existing production systems.

Instead of setting up large-scale ironworks in the capital region, a policy often adopted by the three Jin states, the Qin state adopted other strategies to foster its imperial pretensions, some of which would also have continued through the Han period.

As attested by archaeological evidence, cast iron technology gradually established in the Qin state as well as other territorial states during the second half of the first millennium BCE. Yet, multiple strands of evidence seem to collectively suggest an underdeveloped pattern in the iron industry in the Qin region. The peripheral location of the Qin compared to the other states in the Central Plains and the delayed development of commercial economies might have played a role in hindering the production of iron in the Qin state on a scale as massive as the Qin's contemporaries. Alongside the development of Qin's unification wars, it became reasonable for the Qin state to exploit the more developed iron industry in other regions after they were integrated into the imperial system. Besides the initial centralization of management of the iron industry into the central court and local governments' hands, other strategies might have included the transportation of products and relocation of craftsmen to the capital region to meet the demands rapidly spurred by the population pressure. It is also plausible that the interregional connection between Guanzhong and other regions with rich iron ore during the Han period, as I will explain in Chapters 2 and 3, might have had a historical root tracing back to the less developed pattern in the headquarters of the preceding Qin empire.

Notes

1 This chapter has been revised and expanded for publication based on some material in a previous book chapter (Lam 2021).
2 According to Wagner (2008:83–87), most related textual records are relatively late dating to the end of the 5th century BCE. Huang (1976) was also very critical to most of the early textual records that were claimed to be related to iron during the pre-Qin period.
3 *Maoshi Zhengyi* 6.3.411; transl. Legge (1876:158).
4 For the location of early iron objects in Xinjiang, see Figure 1.1.
5 For detailed discussion of the transmission of copper metallurgy, see Chen et al. (2018, 2019); for detailed discussion of the adoption of sheep/goat and cattle husbandry, see Yang et al. (2019); Vaiglova et al. (2021); for detailed discussion of the dispersal of wheat farming and other potential routes, see Betts et al. (2014); Liu et al. (2017).
6 One example can be found in Wertime & Muhly edited volume, *The Coming of the Age of Iron* (Wertime & Muhly 1980). In this significant work addressing the origin of iron metallurgy through a comparative perspective, most of the contributed articles agree that the ability of smelting and working on iron represented a major determinant of technology.
7 A number of studies already pointed out that early iron objects might not be as good as their bronze contemporaries in terms of the physical properties; see Maddin et al. (1977). Waldbaum (1999), for instance, argued that the widespread adoption to iron smelting in the Near East was probably due to the shortage of tin and using of iron as substitute material of bronze (for a different idea, also

see Zaccagnini 1990). Instead of looking at property advantage and resource availability, more recent scholarship (e.g., Yahalom-Mack & Eliyahu-Behar 2015; Erb-Satullo 2019) often focuses on changes of the social setting such as the emergence of new urban centers and a centralized political entity that could better control all production steps and associated manpower on a local level.

8 For criticism of this idea, see Keightley (1976); Barnard (1978–1979).

9 For the general introduction about the discoveries of iron implements in the Qi and Yan states, see Lam and Chen (2017).

10 For useful discussions about the land system, also known as the *shoutian* system, see Zhang (2013:166–224); Zang (2017).

11 For detailed definition of the terminologies, see Table 3.1 in Chapter 3.

12 It is possible that iron spread from Central Asia to the Hexi Corridor then west into Xinjian and East to the rest of China, like other technologies that may have entered Gansu from the north rather than Xinjiang; see Jaang (2015). Similarly, recent study of chariot technology has demonstrated that the transmission to Anyang was along the northern steppe route (starting from southern Urals, through southern Siberia, Mongolia, then along the Taihang Mountains down to Anyang), rather than the southern historical Silk Road (Wu 2011).

13 Two bimetallic weapons in the Freer Gallery of Art that were claimed to be yielded from Xunxian, Henan, should also date to the Shang period, roughly post-dating the two weapons from Taixi and Liujiahe; see Gettens et al. (1971); Zhang T. et al. (2020).

14 By definition, meteoric iron artifacts mean employing the techniques of cold-forging or heat-forging to produce edges that were made from meteoric iron, which could then be cast into other bronze weapons. Since meteoritic iron is relatively rare, these weapons must have been luxury items during the Shang period. Nonetheless, the connection between the production of meteoric iron weapons and later man-made iron technique (through smelting iron ore to produce bloomery or cast iron iron) appeared in the Late Western Zhou period is highly debatable. Some scholars, such as Wagner, even suggested that the meteoric iron production seemed irrelevant to later developments of iron smelting technology (Wanger 2008:99-101).

15 All these products were made of either bloomery iron or meteoric iron, and most of them were fitted with bronze handles.

16 For the discussion of the identities of the three burials, see Zhao (1997); Liang (2020:102–103).

17 The date of most early iron objects in Xinjiang is highly debatable, since the burial contexts in which iron objects were found were not usually subject to systematic radio-carbon dating. For the most updated and comprehensive review, see Chen J. (2020).

18 Bimetallic weapons have also been found in the vicinity of the "crescent shaped cultural communication belt", as Tong (1990) called it, which stretched from Guyuan, Ningxia to Kunming, Yunnan. These examples will not be discussed here, because it is not clear whether they have any connection with the core areas that concern us.

19 Although some scholars (e.g., Yang K. 2004) believed that some items might have been made of bloomery iron, the result of metallurgical analysis has not been fully published, and it is not yet clear whether these southern states employed bloomery iron production technology.

20 According to published site reports, (cast) iron agricultural implements have also been found at Bojiawang (Hubei 2011) in Danjiangkou, Zhangjiaping (Hubei & Hubei 2010) in Yunxi, and Xiangzikou (Hubei & Guangshui 2008) in Suizhou. However, these finds are difficult to date, and they are usually attributed roughly to the Late Spring-and-Autumn and Early Warring States periods.

21 Of these sites, only Yangying has AMS-C14 data, which shows that iron objects were made between 518 and 350 BCE (after calibration, 2σ) (Chen 2014:223). It is possible that the date based on ceramic typology might be too early, and the typology of the Yangying site may need to be revisited after the full publication of the site report.

22 Decarburization of cast iron means the object was made of cast iron and then heat-treated to reduce the carbon content. For a detailed definition, see Chapter 3.

23 For a critical re-evaluation of the date of Chu tombs in Changsha, see Wu (2008).

24 Chu and Han (one of the three Jin states) have often been depicted as major iron manufacturing centers with advanced techniques in the manufacturing of iron weaponry. These texts include *Xunzi* chapter 15 *"Yibing"* (*Xunzi Jijie* 10.15.282) and *Shiji* 79. For a detailed discussion about warfare during the Warring States period, see Lewis (1999).

25 According to the site report, the cemetery first belonged to the Zhou state, but by 358 BCE the area was occupied by the Han state.

26 This iron sword was identified as "zhugangjian" ("cast-steel sword") with large ferrite grains and widmanstatten structure. But I think this term should refer to "decarburized steel" instead of "cast-steel", according to the microstructure described.

27 While the original report suggested that the earliest phase of Jinancheng date to the Middle Spring-and-Autumn period, more recent studies of the walled capital and other walled towns place the initial phase of the walled town much later; see Yin (2019).

28 The date of those early iron finished goods found in present-day Hunan has been widely debated (see Wu 2008). Some scholars working in Hunan province (Gao 2012:35–36, 265–278), however, reconfirmed the dates of these pre-Warring States' iron and steel discoveries and emphasized the development of the iron industry in the production of agricultural implements and weaponry. Here I agree with the conclusion of early dating.

29 Based on the brief description about the metallographic structure of the object, I suspect that this sword might have been made of steel decarburized from cast iron, since the brittle structure of cast iron is not ideal for making combat weapons.

30 Commoner cemeteries here refer to the burial grounds containing mostly commoner tombs. Nonetheless, this type of cemetery sometimes included tombs with bronze ritual vessels.

31 The report mentioned they were cast iron, but I suspect they might have been incompletely decarburized steel.

32 For the discussion about the relationship between the Xuechi site and "Yongzhi" ritual center, see Xin (2018). The role of Yong for holding national sacrificial ceremonies was replaced by the southern suburbs of Chang'an during the ritual reform in the Late Western Han period. For the discussion about the imperial sacrificial system, see Tian (2015).

33 According to the discoveries of ancient bridges of the Han period on the Wei River, the ancient course of the Wei River should be immediately adjacent to Chang'an, much further south to the present-day Wei River. For the discoveries of ancient bridges, see Shaanxi Yanjiuyuan et al. (2014); The location of these bridges can also be found in Figure 2.3.

34 For the most extensive research on the walled-towns during the Warring States period, see Xu (2017).

35 For a synthetic summery of the distribution of these cemeteries in the suburbs of Xianyang, see Xiao et al. (2017).

36 Chapter 6 will provide a general discussion about the burial dataset.

37 These locations include Fengxiang Gaozhuang, Xianyang Taerpo, Xi'an Youji-azhuang, Xi'an northern suburbs, Lintong Xinfeng, Dali Chaoyi, and Yangling Xibei Nongye Xueyuan.
38 For a more elaboration about the general characteristics of those burials and the statistical analysis, see Chapter 6.
39 Similar pattern has also been noted in the systematic study of bronze weapons inside the Terra-cotta Warriors Pits; see Li X. (2020b:141–142).
40 It is necessary to take the preservation biases into consideration. For instance, since the preservation of iron objects in burial contexts was often not as ideal as that of bronze implements, the condition of iron implements found archaeology would undoubtedly have an impact on the statistical results presented above.
41 From the Wuyangtai location at Yanxiadu (Hebei 1996), a substantial amount of iron weaponry was discovered; some items were subject to metallurgical analysis and belong to bloomery iron. The site report even mentions that iron armies were commonly found at the Gaomocun and Langjingcun locations. In addition, fragments of iron armors and 51 pieces of iron weapons were discovered in a mass grave (tomb No. 44) (Beijing Gangtie 1975).
42 *Shiji* 6.289.
43 *Shangjunshu Zhuyi* 1.2.9. "Kenling". For the introduction of the background and translation, see Pines (2017).
44 While it is widely known that the Lord Shang's reforms emphasized on exalting agriculture and repressing trade, commercial activities were widely found among unearthed textual records during the Qin period. Therefore, the role of commercial exchange should not be over underestimated in the Qin state. The political rhetoric of promoting agriculture and suppressing merchants would rather serve as a mechanism that facilitated rulers to "manage every single of farmer's life" (see Sterckx 2015, 2020 and references therein).

2 The rise of the capital region and the management of craft industry during the Han dynasty

The Han empire and its Qin predecessor sited their capitals in the Wei River valley in Shaanxi, also known as the Guanzhong basin. In contemporary texts, the capital region was called *sanfu*. It included the three commanderies (Fufeng, Pingyin, and Jingzhao) and encompassed 72 counties.[1] By centralizing treasures, population, and military force from all over the state, the capital Chang'an in the center of the Guanzhong basin, became not only the political core but also the cosmopolitan hub of the entire Han state for more than 200 years.[2] The city of Chang'an covered an area of 36 km^2 and was larger than any city previously seen in China (Figure 2.1). Several other towns with large populations ringed Chang'an, forming a cluster of high-ranking urban centers unmatched anywhere else in contemporary China. The dominance of the capital region also lay in its capacity for agricultural production. The region has long been viewed as the breadbasket of the Han period and is known to have been the cradle of new farming techniques, such as the *daitian* method. Building upon its geographical and agricultural advantages, the dominance of the capital region over other territories laid the foundation for Han's rule.

A study of its social setting of the capital region thus provides essential information for understanding craft industries. This social setting[3] includes the management system of natural features (e.g., mountains, rivers, and terraces) and man-made features (e.g., towns, roads, storage facilities, and canals) which enabled the Han and the Qin states to manage the production and distribution of final goods. This chapter will address two related issues: how the capital evolved in the Han state; and how the craft industry in general, and the iron industry specifically, was structured and reshaped as the capital grew. For this purpose, I will present a range of evidence bearing on the long process of capital transformation.

In the first part of this chapter, I will describe the region in which the capitals of Yongcheng, Xianyang, and Chang'an were situated, with particular emphasis on the natural environment and man-made facilities constructed by the Han state. The second part of the chapter will summarize the imperial management of craft production at various levels mentioned in traditional

DOI: 10.4324/9781003259220-4

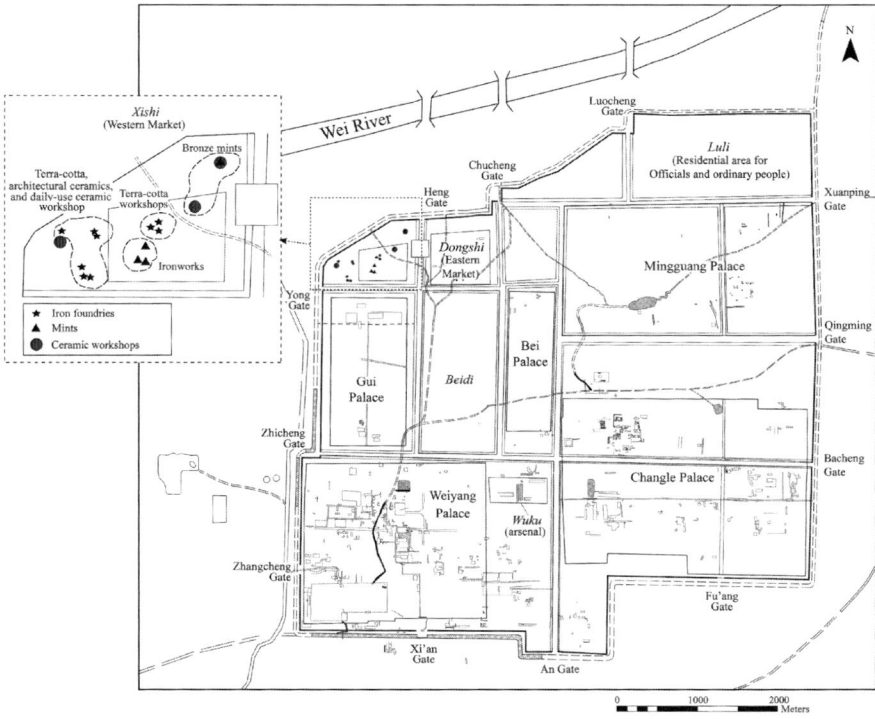

Figure 2.1 Layout of Chang'an city and distribution of manufacturing remains in-side (after Bai 2011:Fig 2; Zhang 2016:Fig 58).

texts. Unsurprisingly, limited textual records are available detailing the daily operation of craft production, probably because the low-status labor-ers did not interest the men who compiled the official historical records. Yet these pieces of information in the second part still provide an indispensa-ble perspective for contextualizing the administrative management of craft production. The third part of the chapter attempts to scrutinize discoveries associated with various types of craft production in the Han capital region. The development of the imperial capital prompted the demand and supply of various products, including both mundane and elite items. As mentioned in Chapter 1, few ironworks have been discovered inside the Qin capital. How did the emerging Han state respond to such limitations? This chapter argues that a detailed study of the evidence documenting various types of craft industries challenges the conventional assumption that the needs of the metropolis often led to the intensification of craft specialization. The synthesized archaeological and related textual evidence therefore can cast light on the strategies for managing the craft industries during the great transformation of the capital region.

1 The imperial capital and its hinterland

The Guanzhong basin played an important role in the rise of the Qin Dynasty. During the war between the Han forces led by Liu Bang (256–195 BCE) and Western Chu forces led by Xiang Yu (232–202 BCE) after the overthrow of the Qin regime, the Han dynasty first sited its capital at Yueyang but soon moved to Chang'an in 206 BCE due to its strategic location. Before the relocation took place, there was a debate on whether the new dynasty should site its capital in Guanzhong or move to Luoyang, a area which had enjoyed enormous prestige since at least the Western Zhou period.[4] In *Shiji* Chapter 99, Liu Jing proposed to Liu Bang that the Han dynasty should fix its capital in Guanzhong, as the old Qin land had certain strategic advantages over Luoyang. His argument, in fact, captured certain essential advantages of Guanzhong. He argued,

> ......the area of Qin, surrounded by mountains and girdled by the Yellow River........enjoys the advantages of its vast and fertile fields and possesses a veritable storehouse created by nature. If Your Majesty will enter the [Hangu] Pass and make your capital there, then, although there should be an uprising east of the [Yaoshan] mountains, you can still keep complete control of the old land of Qin. Now when you fight with a man, you have to grip his throat and strike him in the back before you can be sure of your victory.[5]

The strategic importance of Guanzhong lay firstly in its geographical location. The Wei River basin is a narrow strip bounded by the Qinling Mountains to the south and the Shaanbei plateau to the north.[6] As its name implies, Guanzhong means the region "within the passes". There are four important checkpoints controlling the entrance into the basin, namely the Hangu Pass to the east, the Wu Pass to the South, the Pu Pass to the North, and the Dasan Pass to the West (Wang 2007). All these passes are situated on a plain that was circumscribed by mountains on multiple sides, with one passage passing through the fortress installation (Barbieri-Low & Yates 2015:1114) (Figure I.2). The topography of these mountain pass fortresses together with the natural barriers to the north and the south of the basin sheltered this region from external attack. The natural setting of the basin was thus a strategic asset both for the Qin state, the Qin empire after unification, and eventually for the Western Han empire in its campaign to control or conquer the eastern territories.[7]

During the Western Han period, the favorable geographical location of Guanzhong was essential to its stability. Its strategic location played a particularly important role during the Rebellion of the Seven States led by the Wu-Chu states (kingdoms) (154 BCE), one critical crisis during the early phase of the Han empire. Whereas the Han state imposed the commandery-county system in well-controlled regions (i.e., Guanzhong basin, western Henan, southern Shanxi, western part of Hubei, and the Chengdu plain) from the beginning of the Western Han period, the rest of the eastern and southern territories were bestowed as fiefs on non-relative generals and emperors' male relatives. However, these local kingdoms were notorious for not being controlled by the Han state until Jingdi's reign (157–141 BCE), as the local lords could appoint their own officials and kept most income back from the central government. Eventually, the policies implemented by Jingdi to weaken these kingdoms and centralize the state authority triggered the rebellion of seven kingdoms led by Wu and Chu. The topography of the Guanzhong basin, however, protected the capital region away from the great rebellion in eastern territories. The successful control of Xinyang, the eastern gateway of the pathway entering Guanzhong, by the Han force has long been viewed as a key factor in the suppression of the rebels.[8] Since the Guanzhong basin also lies in one of the strategic pathways entering the Hexi Corridor from eastern China, its location together with resources centralized inside also made the basin a transportation hub and the base for the Han's military success against Xiongnu at a later period, maintaining the garrison systems alongside the long extending frontiers.

The basin was also an important center of food production, which supported the growth of the Han state and the dominance of the capital over other regions (Ji 1981[1936]). The Wei River and the Jing and Lou tributaries brought rich loess sediment from the north and contributed to the formation of a rich alluvial plain and flat landform, mostly distributed along the river valleys or between the river systems in the region. The moving of rivers also cut the riverbanks and created numerous terraces and small plateaus. Such topography characterized the western part of the Guanzhong basin and was an ideal environment for the development of intensive farming during the Qin-Han periods (Wang Y. 2004; Xu 2011). Meanwhile, the Qinling Mountains in the south generated many small tributary systems intersecting the present-day southern, western, and eastern Xi'an area, providing not only natural protection but also a water supply for the urban population and a drainage system connecting gardens and royal palaces inside the capital Chang'an.

To the east of Chang'an, the alluvial soil brought by the Wei and its tributaries significantly slowed the current of the Wei River. The natural landscape was characterized by alluvial plains but filled with swamps and ponds, resulting in the occurrence of salty soil which persists to the present day. During its eastward expansion after 350 BCE, the Qin state started to construct a large-scale canal system, the Zhengguo Canal, to connect the Jing and Luo Rivers. Small irrigation networks were then extended from this main canal to water the infertile land on both sides of the canal. The topography and natural geography in the western part of Guanzhong and the engineering system in eastern Guanzhong created by the Qin state collectively made the basin well known for its "rich soil and watered lands for a thousand *li*",[9] and eventually the breadbasket during the Han period.

During the Western Han period, a new farming technique, known as the *daitian* method,[10] emerged and was probably first developed in Guanzhong. The big leap in farming techniques evidenced during the Qin and Western Han periods had various causes, including a particularly favorable climate. Palaeoclimate studies have shown that, around the second half of the first millennium BCE, Guanzhong experienced a relatively warm climate, with temperatures about the same as they are now, ranging from 6°C to 13°C. Only after Wudi's reign did the environment and temperature become drier and colder (Ge 2011; Ge et al. 2006; Zhu et al. 1998).[11] Several texts mentioned that the Guanzhong basin was covered by vegetation and even bamboo forests during the Early Western Han period,[12] and it was clearly more fertile than at any period in its history. The favorable environment might have further accelerated the rapid agricultural boom in the Guanzhong basin and supported the formation of early empires.

A large influx of population was certainly another factor which stimulated the growth of agriculture around the capital. During the Qin period, a large population was brought into the Guanzhong basin from Guandong. The Western Han rulers also relocated many influential families, especially those of powerful merchants, to mausoleum towns or settlements surrounding Chang'an. Taking into account servants, merchants, officials, elites, and royal families, the entire regional population might have already reached the level of 500,000 in the Early Western Han period (Ge 1986:24). Right before the end of the Western Han period, the population living inside the capital region exceeded 2.5 million (Ge 1986:24). As previous studies of the Han demography have also pointed out (Ge 1986; Shang 2008; Wang Y. 2004), the population density in the entire Guanzhong basin, especially in the habitable flat land, was about 1,000 people per km^2 just before the end of the Western Han empire, making Guanzhong the region with the highest population density in the entire empire.

Chang'an also owed its prosperity to its leading political role and unique strategic location as the transportation center within the imperial traffic network. As alluded to earlier, Qin Shihuang had already constructed *zhidao* and *chidao* during the unification period and made Xianyang a pivotal point in the national transportation system.[13] Since Chang'an was located immediately to the south of Xianyang across the Wei River, it inherited the strategic role of its predecessor in the communication system connecting to various parts of the empire. First of all, Chang'an was the hub of east-west routes, namely Weibei pathway, Hangu pathway, and Puguan pathway in the Han period (Figure I.2). The former connected Chang'an to the Hexi Corridor via the Wei River valley, whereas the latter two pathways connected Chang'an to the middle and lower Yellow River valley and the Taihang Mountain regions, respectively. Meanwhile, Chang'an was located at the entrance of the Wuguan pathway and Ziwu pathway, which served as the major arteries joining Chang'an with the Nanyang basin and

Hanzhong basin (Xin 1988, 1989a). Resources from the Yangtze River valley and the Chengdu plains further south were directly transported to Chang'an through these valleys. Finally, the Han state continued to use the *zhidao* system constructed by Qin Shihuang to send troops and resources to the Hetao region on the northern frontiers. In this imperial infrastructure, resources from distant areas would be transported to the headquarters,[14] and then to other territories (Xin 1988). Situated at the junction of these major pathways that connected to different parts of the empire, the strategic location of the capital allowed the central government to control the movement of people and information transported through the networks (Xin 2010).

The Han empire was thus able to construct Chang'an as a metropolitan center on a massive scale. Covering about 36 km^2, Chang'an was much larger than any walled capital preceding the Han period. Internally, the urban center was divided into 11 sections by a grid of roads (Figure 2.1). Inside the walled city, all sections or palace complexes were connected via drainage networks to either the ponds or tributaries surrounding Chang'an, joining various parts of Chang'an together as a whole.[15] The main section, the Weiyang palace complex, covered 5 km^2, which is equal to one-sixth of the entire Chang'an, and included the emperor's residential palaces, areas for official departments, an arsenal site (Wuku), and the Dongdi residential area for the high elites (Zhongguo Shehui 1996a; Zhongguo Shehui & Riben 2007). To the east of Weiyang palace was the Changle palace for the empress. While residential sections for non-royal members such as merchants and officials, which were structured in the way of *li* ward (i.e., an enclosed block in which residential areas were geometrically divided) (Zhang 2015), also existed inside Chang'an, two-thirds of the site was in fact occupied by temples, royal storage facilities, and royal palaces, which made Chang'an unlike other urban centers in early China even in comparison with the Qin state (Liu 2000; Pirazzoli-t'Serstevens 2010). Outside the enclosed area were various detached palaces (e.g., Jianzhang palace) and an area of royal gardens that were generally known as Shanglin yuan, which extended more than 300 *li* (equal to about 124 km) into the hinterland and served as a royal hunting Park (Liu 1995; Liu & Li 2006) (Figure 2.2). In one sense, Chang'an walled city is best considered as a complex of royal palaces and administrative centers that was built on a massive scale. Its major purpose was to serve the royal and imperial families as well as the central administrative system.[16] Its role, in other words, resembled the function of the Forbidden City in Beijing at a much later date.

The internal layout of the city also served to advertise various ranks in the social hierarchy. A close look at the reconstructed layout of Chang'an will identify a road,   running east-west from the Bacheng gate on the east wall and the Zhicheng gate on the west wall. Extending more than 2,900 m with 62 m in the widest part (Zhongguo Shehui Chang'an 2018), this road divided the entire Chang'an city into the northern and southern parts. Scholars have long believed that Chang'an had been built around a north-south axis (e.g.,

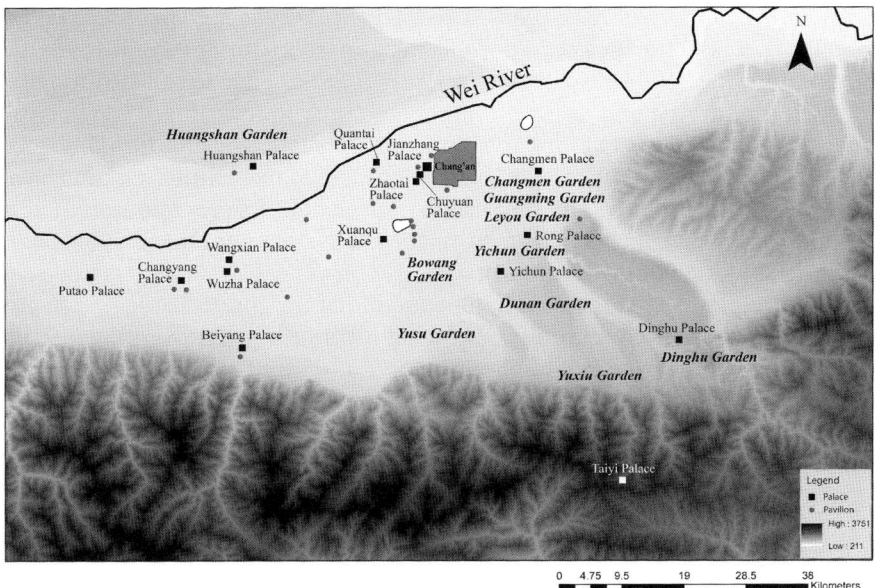

Figure 2.2 Distribution of various gardens, pavilions, and palaces inside Shanglin yuan that were mentioned in transmitted texts (after Yu & Li 2012:Fig 1; source of the background DEM: USGS SRTM Void Filled Dataset).

Qin et al. 1995), but recent studies suggest that the city's north-south orientation may only date from the Late Western Han period, and was a feature of Wang Mang's ritual reform and construction of the Mingtang ritual halls in the southern suburbs (Duan 2017; Liu 2011:46–47). Previously, the city seems to have been oriented from east to west,[17] and this east-west axis delineated hierarchical division. The southern part, which contained the Changle and Weiyang palaces, was preserved solely for emperors and empresses. In contrast, the northern part, which included the palaces of Gui, Bei, and Mingguang was reserved for concubines, court ladies, and their servants, marketplaces, and craft production area (e.g., Xishi and Dongshi), as well as the residential area (*lüli*) for elite members registered under Chang'an and officials. Members in all these sections in the northern part were inferior to the emperor.

Intriguingly, the northeastern corner, or the so-called *lüli* area, was the only section where ordinary people and even officials would densely dwell inside. To the east of the *lüli* area were the so-called Dongshi (eastern marketplace) and Xishi (western marketplace), in which craft production centers as well as locations for exchange and transaction were located (Figure 2.1). Given the importance of commercial exchange, there were nine marketplaces, including Xishi and Dongshi, either inside or close to Chang'an reported by surviving texts (Qian 2020). But the total area of Xishi, Dongshi (including the craft production section) was disproportionally small in comparison with the sections preserved for the royal palaces. Also, the limited area of *lüli* in the northeastern corner was apparently unable to host a large population. For this reason, it seems likely that the majority of commoners registered under Chang'an, including merchants, lower-rank officials, artisans, and Confucian scholars, lived outside the walled town, probably near the Xishi or Dongshi (Wang 2007). Unfortunately, residential remains have rarely been reported in the hinterland,[18] even though numerous cemeteries and tombs have been excavated in the eastern and southern suburbs of Chang'an (Hou 2004) (Figure 2.3).

The hinterland of Chang'an also included the nearby mausoleums to the north and south of the capital. Following a tradition that originated from the Warring States period, each emperor was buried inside an independent mausoleum park together with his empress, as an important way to demonstrate his supreme power (Zhao 2006). To be buried inside an imperial mausoleum and to accompany the emperor after death was viewed as a prestigious honor[19] in the Han period, and only high elites or prestige officials with prominent reputations or military merits were allowed this privilege. In total, 11 mausoleum parks were constructed during the Western Han period: nine on the northern bank of the Wei River, and two

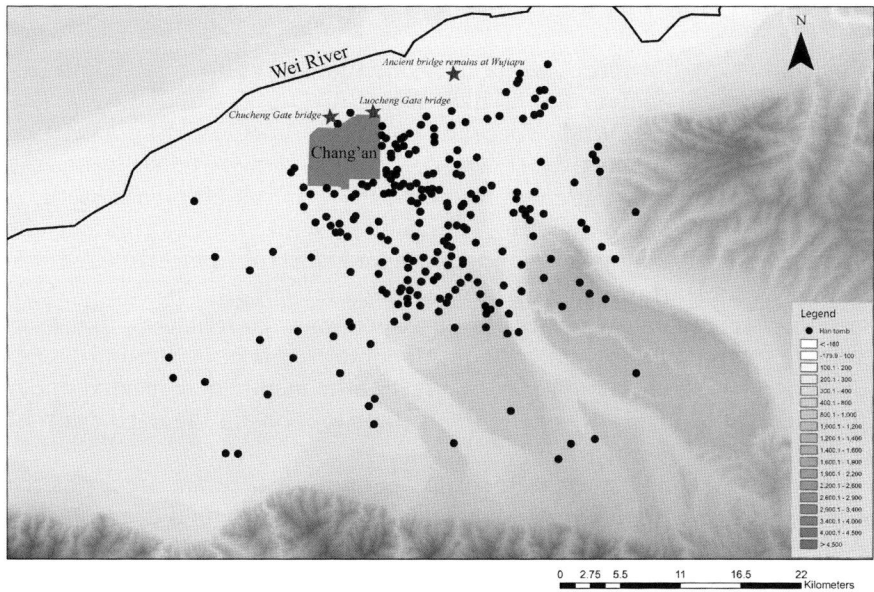

Figure 2.3 Distribution of cemeteries in the suburbs of Chang'an.

Source: Xi'anshi and Zhengzhou (2004:Fig 1); Shaanxi Yanjiuyuan et al. (2014:Fig 1); the star symbol represents the location of ancient bridges outside city gates that were confirmed through archaeological work, indicating the course of ancient Wei River in the Han period.

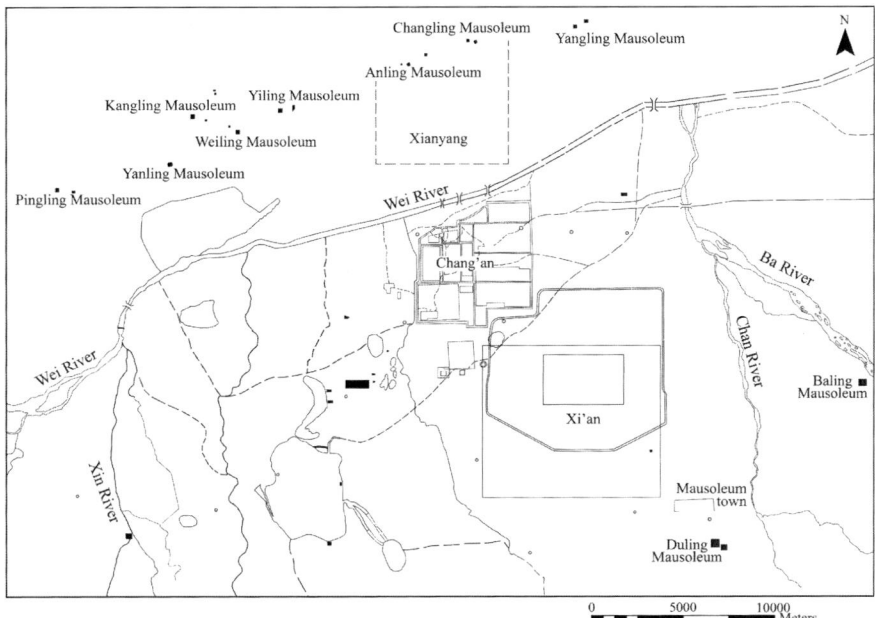

Figure 2.4 Distribution of mausoleum towns and Chang'an (redrawn from Zhang 2016:Fig 145).

some distance to the south of Chang'an, in the foothills of the Zhongnan Mountains (Figure 2.4). Although it is not clear why there were two groups of mausoleums (Shen 2001; Yang 2009), the mausoleum parks on the northern bank of the Wei River were aligned along an axis that ran parallel to the Wei River, which might have expressed the auspicious wish for the long continuation of the royal court symbolized by the perpetual flowing of the Wei River (Yang 2009).

Archaeological investigations in recent decades (Jiao 2013; Jiao & Ma 2011; Ma 2011; Yang & Wang 2014)[20] have shown that each mausoleum park contained the tumuli and tombs of emperors and empresses, which were enclosed within walls, together with outside storage pits (*wai cangguo*), attendant burials, and associated mausoleum towns.[21] Substantial amounts of food, animal sacrifices, and exotic goods (Shaanxi Yanjiuyuan 2008b) were often buried in the outside storage pits (Jiao 2006, 2013) associated with the tumuli. Meanwhile, sacrificial rituals had to be organized annually in temples for each emperor. To support the sacrificial rituals on such a large scale, a considerable population[22] was relocated to the towns associated with each mausoleum. One of them, Maoling, even hosted 277,277 registered people within the mausoleum town area in 2 CE.[23] If this figure can be trusted, its population was higher than that of the city of Chang'an itself. In a broader sense, the population of the mausoleum towns is better seen as part of the populations of the greater Chang'an area.

The system of mausoleum towns was established to resettle influential local families from the Guandong area, probably along with their bound servants and slaves. These mausoleum towns, nonetheless, are much smaller than Chang'an: the largest one, Yangling mausoleum town, covers only around 5.5 km^2. According to the survey and mapping results, most of these mausoleum towns mentioned above were enclosed by walls. Road systems and architectural complexes have also been identified. Surprisingly, very few kilns or ceramic production facilities have been discovered inside these mausoleum towns, and most of them were used for firing roof tiles and other architectural ceramics (Xianyangshi Wenwu 2010; Xi'anshi Yanjiuyuan & Beijing Lianhe 2020). Traces of iron or bronze manufacturing have also seldom been identified in the voluminous preliminary reports. At this stage, the evidence is insufficient to determine whether large-scale craft production took place in these satellite centers. Instead of producing craft products, these new settlements seem to have focused exclusively on consumption. Together with Chang'an, these mausoleum towns consisted of a network of satellite cities with the highest density of population in the entire empire, which would have had strong demand for goods and daily necessities to support various activities, from sacrificial rituals and feasting to daily food preparation.

Since a large proportion of the population in the capital area (including those in urban mausoleum towns) did not engage in any farming, it is not hard to understand why the Han state managed to build transportation canals and other irrigation systems to make intensive agricultural production possible and acquire enough food to support daily consumption on a large scale. In the eastern part of the basin characterized by larger terraces, three major canal systems, including the Bai Canal, the Liufu Canal, and the Longshou Canal, were constructed during Wudi's reign (Figure 2.5).[24] These state projects were designed to further transform the entire eastern part of Guanzhong into the breadbasket for the empire. Since this region was characterized by low-lying alluvial land and high underground water level (Li 2004:155–156), the canal network that joined the different river tributaries together improved the irrigation of the adjacent land and mitigated the problems of soil salinization and alkalization. In western Guanzhong, the Chengguo Canal was constructed on the northern bank of the Wei River also during Wudi's reign, albeit on a smaller scale, to enhance agricultural production (Li 2004:102–106). The canals and irrigation network in the basin fueled and stimulated the development of agriculture, making Guanzhong the staple food production center for the Han empire. Given the large population and the need to maintain the food supply, agricultural tools made of iron (or steel) were important resources influencing "the life and death of farmers" during the Han period.[25] The advanced and intensified agricultural industry must also rely on a large supply of iron tools, whether they were locally produced or procured from production centers beyond the capital region.

Although an improved irrigation system spurred agricultural development, the regional yield might not have been insufficient enough to support the large population concentrated in and around Chang'an, as previous studies noted (Peng 2010; Wang 2009).[26] Meanwhile, the needs of the frontier garrisons placed an additional burden on the food supply system in the capital region. Moving grain and other necessities from various parts of the empire to the capital became essential to supporting the prosperity of the capital region and the frontier regions. However, the Wei River was not naturally suitable to serve as a large-scale transportation channel. The volume of water was not stable throughout the year, especially during the winter, making the transportation of staple foods and necessities from the lower reaches of the Wei River to the capital very difficult. The various turnings of the lower Wei River channel also significantly increased the time and costs of moving resources through shipping. In order to facilitate the transportation of considerable amounts of stable goods from the eastern part of the empire, Wudi ordered the construction of the Cao Canal (Figure 2.5), from Chang'an to present-day Huaxian, to link the tributaries of the Wei with the Yellow River.[27] This canal also linked several imperial warehouses

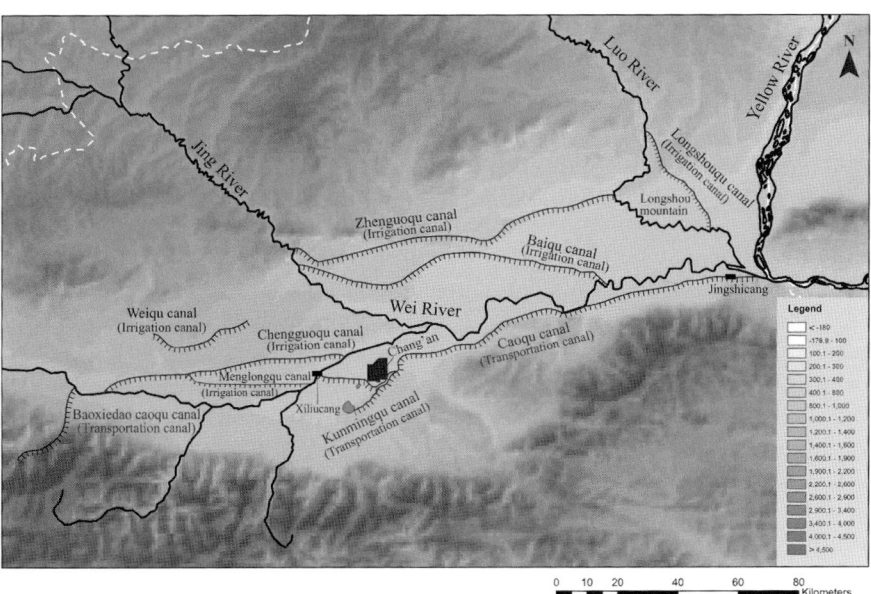

Figure 2.5 Canal systems in the Guanzhong basin (after Li 2004:Fig 2-3, Fig 3-3, Fig 3-6, Fig 3-8, Fig 3-10).

associated with the capital (e.g., Taicang) (Xin 1989b), so that grain would be conveniently stored there for urban consumption.

In addition to canals, storage facilities also played an important part in the operation of the imperial transportation system. Besides the imperial warehouse mentioned above, several large-scale storage facilities were built along the Wei River. In Huaxian, the Han state set up the Jingshicang (capital warehouse) (Shaanxi Yanjiusuo 1990) next to the point where the Wei River merged with the Yellow River (Figure 2.5). Taking advantage of its geographical advantage, the capital warehouse could facilitate the collection of grain produced from the eastern part of the basin, during the time when the water level of the Wei River was too low for shipping grain further west to the capital. To the west of Chang'an, the Han state also set up the Xiliucang (Xiliu warehouse)[28] to collect agricultural produce from the area covered by the Chengguo canal in the western part of Guanzhong (Xin 2010) (Figure 2.5). The discovery of warehouses in Baoji indicates that the canal network extended further to the west. At Sunjianantou, adjacent to the Qian River, a docking site and an associated storage facility have been discovered (Shaanxi Yanjiusuo et al. 2005; Shaanxi Yanjiuyuan et al. 2015), probably for the transportation of grain to the garrisons in the Hexi Corridor. Clearly, these large storage houses at both ends of the Wei River valley were constructed to facilitate the transportation of grain, supply the large population in the capital area, and provision the garrisons along northwest and northern frontiers. Along with road networks, the engineered canal systems and storage facilities well connected the capital region to other parts of the imperial territories, enabling the movement and transportation of staple grain on a large scale to Guanzhong.

Other necessities and raw materials in addition to grain were needed in the Guanzhong basin. Although it supported a thriving farming industry, the Guanzhong basin had few mineral resources. Modern surveys (Shaanxi Difangzhi 1993; Zhongguo Kuangcang 1996:142–143) show that most iron ores are only small or medium scale deposits (Figure 2.6). According to modern geological surveys, large-scale iron deposits are particularly scarce within the Wei River valley. Some iron ore deposits have been reported in the Qinling Mountains to the south and on the margins of the Guanzhong basin (e.g., in present-day Hancheng) (Shaanxi Difangzhi 1993), but they are mostly of insufficient quality to support the demands for production, and their small scale makes them unprofitable to exploit, even with modern mining techniques. For other natural minerals, while copper was available along the edges of the Qinling Mountains,[29] its yield was probably insufficient to support the large quantities of coins produced in the basin after the minting was centralized in the central court.[30] Raw mineral resources had to be transported to the heartland of the empire from smelting sites, probably in the form of ingots in order to fully support production and consumption. Meanwhile, since the central court controlled the manufacturing of luxury goods through state-supported workshops, most of which were supposed to

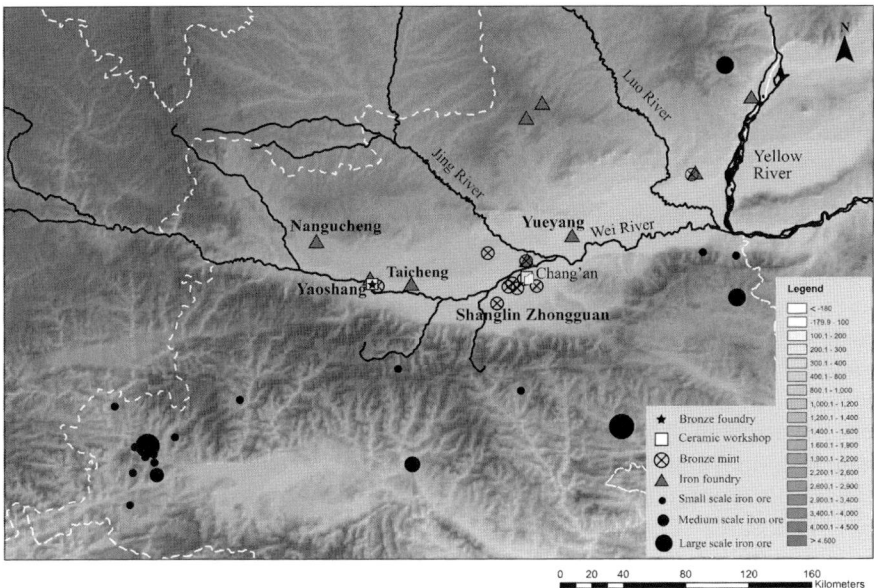

Figure 2.6 Distribution of iron ores surrounding the Guanzhong basin and craft production centers inside.
Source: Bai (2005: Appendix 1); Shaanxi Difangzhi (1993); Xu L. (2020).

be located adjacent to Chang'an, other raw materials such as silk, jade, gold, and silver, had to be imported from sources outside the basin, in addition to the large amount of staple grain from the eastern territories transported to the center of the empire via the river network.

The Guanzhong basin therefore became the transportation hub of the entire empire. Given the importance of Chang'an in the commodity exchange and trading markets, the capital was conceptualized in contemporary texts not only as an imperial metropolis but also as the focal point of the transportation system during the Han period.[31] *Shiji* Chapter 129 mentions:

> ....(In accord with Qin preference to rule from within the Passes) the Han made its capital at Chang'an. From various mausoleum towns in the four directions [to the capital, on road like] spokes of a [wheel into] the hub, came [the people] from these different directions, gathering together [in the capital]. The [amount of] land was small, and the population was crowded. Therefore, the people became more and more frivolous and crafty, and engaged in secondary (occupations, that is, trading and crafts).[32]

Sima Qian, the grand historian, here provided an important observation about the economic role of the capital and its social setting. As mentioned in the passage, the development of Chang'an as the capital attracted the population from various directions to concentrate there. Grain and raw materials would have been needed, and thus transported on a massive scale from different directions, particularly from eastern territories, to the capital along the Wei River, Cao Canal, and the land routes annually up until the end of the Western Han state. The rise of Chang'an and those mausoleum towns nearby was undoubtedly attributable to the developed transportation system linking Chang'an to other regional centers. Meanwhile, as the capital region was the breadbasket for the empire, large-scale agricultural production would also have stimulated the demand for iron agricultural tools and other production tools. But how did the iron industry and other craft industries inside the capital region work together with the rise of the imperial network that extended to all directions? In the Han period, government involvement, both direct and indirect, was one defining feature in the structure of craft industries. While the management system often left tenuous and fragmentary archaeological records, textual evidence can provide important background for understanding the state management of the infrastructure of craft production. The relevant textual evidence is therefore examined here before we look at the archaeological evidence for iron manufacturing and other industries in the capital region.

2 The imperial management of craft industries

A brief look at the organization of the central government demonstrates its involvement in various craft industries. The basic structure of the administrative system has been thoroughly studied by previous scholars (Bielenstein 1980; Loewe 2004, 2006). Inheriting the legacy of the Qin state, the central government of the Han state was designed to manage miscellaneous affairs of the entire empire, including palace security, judicial affairs, state-sponsored rituals, the management of grain in imperial storage houses, and the collection of census data from all commanderies. In the central administrative system, Jiuqing (nine superintendents) oversaw various aspects of daily administration under the coordination of Sangong (three excellencies) (Table 2.1). Of these superintendents, the Shaofu (minor treasury) managed the production of items consumed by elite households including the manufacturing of textiles (primarily silk), bronze vessels, bronze weapons, jade, lacquerware, ceramic figurines destined for elite tombs, and even the building of palaces. Some of these products were produced inside the capital area, but most were manufactured by workshops in various commanderies, including Shu, Guanghan, Henan, Nanyang, and Yingchuan. The Shaofu institute also handled tax incomes generated from mountains (e.g., mining), seas (fishing), rivers, and resources in ponds, to support the high cost of manufacturing prestigious goods (Lin 2008; Ma 1983:97–113; Yamada 1993:419–425).

Besides serving elite members and controlling natural resources, the central court also managed the production of daily use goods (e.g., metal daily goods and lacquerware), of which iron was the most important (Lu 2018; Sahara 2002[1994]). Textual evidence demonstrates that control of the iron industry was already a bureaucratic responsibility before the establishment of the Han state. Sima Chang, the great-grandfather of the famous historian Sima Qian, was in charge of "iron office"[33] during the unification period in the Qin state. A position with the same title is known to have overseen a commandery-level monopoly during the emperor Han Wudi's reign. A clay seal inscribed *"tie guan cheng yin"* (chief iron office of the Qin state) has been discovered near Xianyang, indicating that the "Tieguan" department handling matters involving the iron industry probably already existed by this point (Tang 2019). It is also noteworthy that the management of daily use goods was not unique in the Qin state, especially in those other states with a developed iron industry. In the Qi state, for instance, seals with "iron office" inscriptions have been reported in archaeological records (Chen 1980:107–108).[34] In the Zhao state, two merchants (Mr. Zhuo and Guo Zhong) were mentioned specifically in *Shiji* as magnates[35] who had become wealthy through iron mining (and probably casting), and were then relocated to other regions, such as Chengdu, by the Qin state. It is reasonable to suggest that the Zhao court probably had an official institute managing the prosperous iron industry, similar to that evidenced in the Qin state.

The Chu state might also have had departments overseeing the production of iron for the central court, although no direct evidence of their existence has yet emerged. As I briefly introduced earlier, documents found near the southern frontiers of the Qin state at Shuihudi (Yunmeng in Hubei province), which date around 217 BCE, mention officials entitled Zuo caitie and You caitie in charge of iron mining.[36] Tieguan also appeared in Liye Qin bamboo slips (Qin unification period)[37] from present-day Zhangjiajie, Hunan, which was claimed to be the subordinate official in the Dongtian commandery to take charge of the issue of iron production. Some studies (e.g., Tang 2019) consider the term Tieguan as an indicator of the management system of the iron industry in the Qin infrastructure. However, the records claiming that the Qin state was the first to invent the administrative system over iron must be treated with caution. If the iron industry was relatively developed in the Chu state (Chapter 1) during the Warring States period, it is possible that a primitive iron management system might have existed in the Chu local administration, which might partly have been taken over by the incoming Qin government after its annexation.

The management of daily use goods of the Western Han was primarily inherited from the Qin state. One substantial change occurred during Wudi's reign when the administration of the iron industry became part of the duties (Tieshi) of the superintendent of agriculture and was "detached" from Shaofu. Unlike those of other superintendents, the Dasinong's (superintendent of agriculture) duties were more directly relevant to the public administration and ordinary people. While the title Dasinong literally means the "supervisor of agriculture", his subordinate officials

Table 2.1 General structure of the Han central government (according to Loewe 2006).

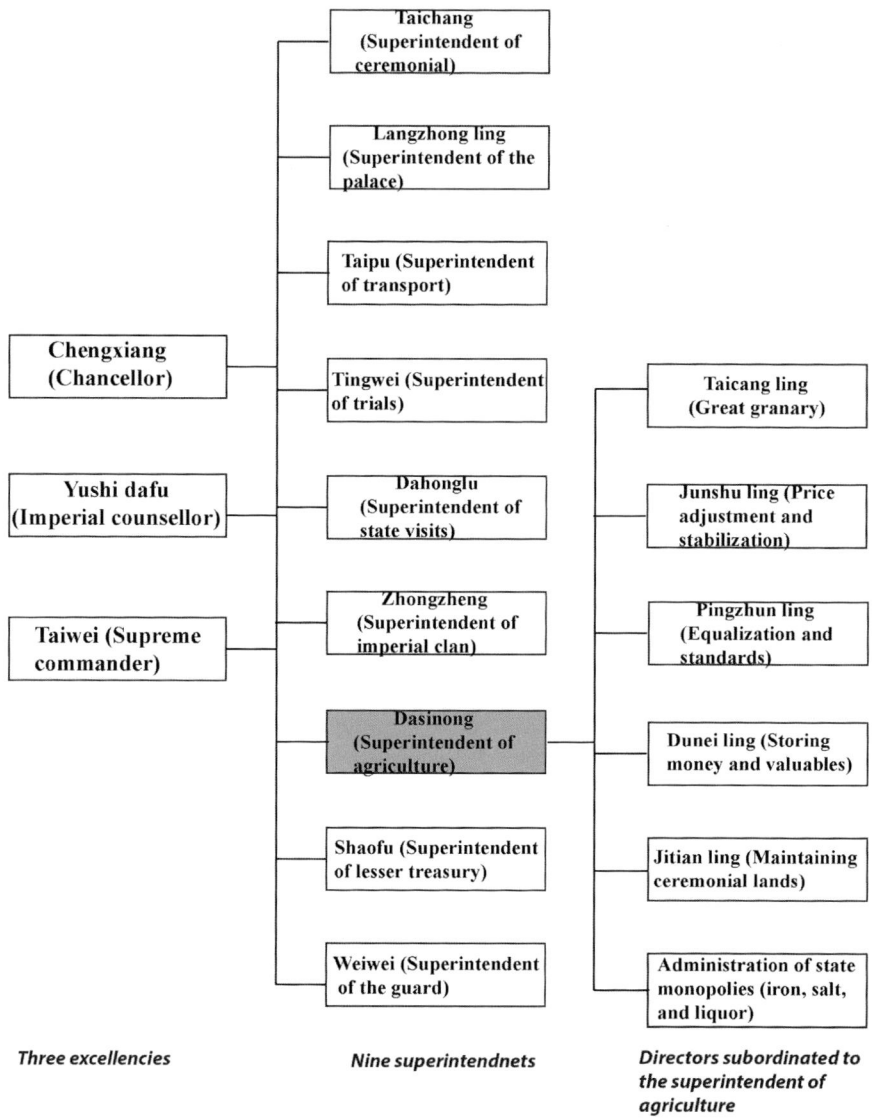

managed various duties ranging from the collection of taxes to transporting them to the capital; all those duties were well beyond the literal meaning of this title.[38] After its transfer to the Dasinong, the administration of iron might have included the coordination of iron production and movement of resources between different commanderies through the regional branch offices named Duguan,[39] in addition to the taxation of iron ores or products that already existed. The bureaucratic system of the Han period might also have provided the essential foundation for achieving coordination between various iron offices or between workshops underneath the same iron office.

In the Qin and Han system, local officials were involved in the management of various industries supplying mundane goods. According to previous studies on the Statutes on Stables and Parks[40] and Statutes on Currencies[41] in Shuihudi bamboo slips from Hubei, the local governor Xianling (county magistrate) at the basic administrative unit, *xian* county, managed a quite remarkable number of iron (or bronze) agricultural implements or tools which could be lent to farmers (Guo 2011; Loewe 2006:47; Zhou 1999). They were branded with specific markers, and if they rusted, the Xianling was required to sell them so as to recoup their value in cash during the seventh month of each year.[42] Presumably, the Xianling also needed to purchase new ones to replace rusted items. Given the duties mentioned before, the Xianling might have been the major seller as well as the buyer of certain types of craft products (tools and probably vessels) in the market. The system of lending agricultural tools to farmers, especially large-size tools such as plowshares too expensive for most farmers to purchase, continued in the Han period. Selling or buying iron goods thus played an essential part in the administration of these local officials during the Han time, which eventually became more standardized and entirely controlled in the hands of Tieguan after the implementation of iron monopoly.

Related to craft industries, control over the transportation of iron and the taxation of iron (and other minerals) manufacturing were other essential parts of the local administration from the Qin to the Early Western Han. The *Ernian lüling* texts found in Zhangjiashan Tomb no. 247, Hubei, dating to the second year of Empress Lü (186 BCE) records:

> An imperial decision instructs the Chief Prosecutor: 'Let all the passes be ordered that: the taking out of privately owned metal objects or iron is prohibited. Should there be one who enters with metal objects, the pass [officials] are to carefully record [the objects] in a register. When [the person] attempts to exit [the pass, the objects] are again to be enumerated [and checked against the register]; then send him or her out.'[43]

In other words, private trading and transportation of finished iron goods between different regions were prohibited, unless the individual was given an authorization permit. The sale or trading of iron objects and weapons to foreign groups outside the state was prohibited. While this statute was initially targeted against kingdoms in eastern territories, the control over the cross-regional movement of iron might not have lifted entirely after the implementation of the monopoly. Meanwhile, local officials were responsible for collecting taxes set at one-fifth of the income of those who mined iron and a further one-fifth of their income if they cast iron objects,[44] according to the textual records from Zhangjiashan. For officials in areas where iron and mineral ores were mined privately, taxing miners and casters was one administrative duty and source of financial income. Logistically, local officials needed to maintain a roster to keep track of those who mined iron ores and produced cast iron objects. Local officials also needed to inspect on a regular basis the volume of ores mined and products manufactured to calculate the taxes.

While the iron monopoly seems to have been first invented by the Han state, the practice of centralizing resources was deeply rooted in the ideology of ancient China, under which all natural resources under heaven, including iron ore, were claimed by the Emperor as his own "properties". In this light, the taxes collected from the craft industry and natural resources in the Qin and early Western Han government system were sent to the Shaofu to support the expenses of the Emperor and his royal family,[45] instead of being spent on administration and military campaigns. Only during the reign of Wudi did intensive warfare force the Han government to devote the revenues generated by some natural resources to military expenditure. Besides the financial drain caused by the military campaigns against Xiongnu during Wudi's reign,[46] state finances deteriorated even further when merchants took advantage of the opportunity to accumulate goods and manipulated the prices of goods in the market. In order to cover the shortfall in imperial revenue, the Han state put into place the monopolies of iron and salt in 117 BCE initially proposed by Dongguo Xianyang and Kong Jin,[47] who were originally big iron and salt merchants but eventually became officials taking charge of Dasinong.

The monopolies focused on several key components: iron, salt, and minting. They also included liquor and the setting up of an equable market,[48] or *junshu* (Table 2.1). To implement the monopolies, the government first banned the private production of iron, salt, and coins, which had been allowed before the sixth year of Yuanshou (117 BCE),[49] since some merchants, especially ironmasters, made excessive fortunes through iron mining and smelting. One well-known example is a wealthy merchant named Mr. Zhuo, who was deported with his wife as captives from the Zhao state to Sichuan by the Qin state. Through begging and bribing officials, he was then sent to Linqiong where iron was known to be abundant. Eventually, he became so rich by mining and smelting iron that he possessed 1,000 slaves.[50] The lineage of Kong Jin, the merchant-turned official, built up their fortunes in a similar way. One of his ancestors was removed from the Wei state by Qin to Nanyang, and eventually acquired vast wealth through iron smelting and mining.[51] After the implementation of the policy during Wudi's reign, however, the duties and privileges of iron production were centralized in the hands of the Tieguan office, as the position was set up at the commandery level under the supervision of the commandery chief to manage the production, and perhaps even the transportation of iron. "Iron offices" and "salt offices" were established in counties where raw materials for iron mining or salt production were available,[52] so as to take charge of production and expand the duties of county-level officials in managing natural resources. For counties without rich iron resources, Xiaotieguan (small iron offices) were set up to take charge of selling or recycling scrap iron. Parallel to the control of iron and salt, minting—the workshops for which were located near the capital—was centralized in the hands of Shuiheng duwei (Commander of water and parks). Even though iron, salt, and other resources already constituted a major part of the imperial finances before the implementation of these policies, the involvement of the state had probably limited to the form of taxing or indirect control. It was after the implementation of the new policies that the private sector might have eventually been eliminated, and that the degree to which resources and economic activities were exploited by the central court became intensified, being entirely under the control of the state.

In short, through prohibiting the participation of private merchants and replacing them in the industries, the new policies attempted to centralize and maximize the revenues from the important industries of iron, salt, and minting. Some other industries, such as lacquerware, were also in the hands of the state[53] after those industries were incorporated into the new centralization system. Since one of the Dasinong chiefs, Kong Jin, might have worked with the Han central government by changing his business into a state-owned industry, it is likely that some existing iron workshops continued to operate in the later period. Meanwhile, the monopoly would have spurred the emergence of new ironworks in regions especially rich in iron ore but not exploited before.

The economic benefits to the state of the monopoly policies were considerable, as texts make clear.[54] Yet, the over centralized state economies also hurt the economic system in certain domains. One big issue related to the iron industry was the overstocking of finished products. As *wenxue* in the *Discourse on salt and iron* stated,

> when the magistrates establish monopolies and standardize, then iron implements lose their suitability, and the farming population loses their convenient use. When the tools are not suited to their use, the farmer is exhausted in the fields, and grass and weeds are not kept down.[55]

Since the output of state-owned ironworks often failed to meet local needs, a good portion of final products might have thus become overstock products, causing large quantities of waste. In some cases, officials even produced poor quality iron tools merely in order to meet production quotas, and farmers were coerced to buy those products. In addition, as products produced by centralized ironworks in the monopolized system might only respond to the administrative order, the large-scale state-sponsored iron industry came at the price of quality and adaptability to the local environment. While the monopoly of iron came with various problems, the excessive wealth centralized by this policy probably made it last until the end of the Western

Han period.[56] During the Eastern Han period, it is debated whether the monopoly was reimplemented. Private production in general was allowed, particularly after the second year of Zhanghe in Zhangdi's reign (88 CE),[57] as the central government lifted the monopoly. However, the system of using iron offices to collect taxes from iron miners or casters, or even to centralize iron production in some locations, likely persisted throughout the Eastern Han period (Gao 1986).[58]

Summarizing the Han political system involved in craft industries, it seems clear that the Western Han government controlled or managed the majority of craft products, including both prestigious and utilitarian goods, in many direct and indirect ways. In studying the operation of workshops and the distribution of goods, the roles of the Han state need to be taken fully into consideration. While it is obvious that the implementation of monopoly necessarily involved state control, the previous role of local and central government in the production of daily use goods, such as iron, should not be underestimated. Meanwhile, collecting taxes from craft industries was part of the duties of the local administration throughout the Han period.[59] In this light, the monopoly policies accentuated the presence of state involvement in, instead of imposing a new management over, craft industries of iron and salt. The implementation of the monopoly was thus merely a further step that extended an extreme trend. The observation that the attachment to the state was one characteristic of craft industries also reinforced my argument that craft production centers were often an integrated part in the capital cities in the Qin and other territorial states during the Warring States period.

Through piecing together various textual evidence, we generate an image that the Han administrative system played an important role in the management of the craft industry, no matter whether the goods were for elite consumption or daily utilization by commoners. Since the management of the iron industry was an important administrative responsibility, one may also postulate that the Han state allocated resources to spur the development of the supply system,[60] such as establishing large scale ironworks, in order to provide sufficient goods to residents in the capital core and to overcome the pre-existing underdevelopment pattern. Archaeological evidence, however, provides a perspective different from such an idea. In the last section of this chapter, I will focus on the archaeological discoveries illuminating the various craft industries in the capital region during the Western Han period, before giving a full account of the iron industry in the next chapter. The introduction can further provide the social setting for contextualizing the iron industries within the regional economic system as a whole.

3 Craft industries in the capital region: ceramic, bronze, and iron

Following the social trend during the Warring States period, the centers for craft production appeared to be an important component in Yongcheng and Xianyang. In comparison with its predecessor, however, one dramatic change in the craft industry evidenced by the layout of Chang'an was its relatively small section for craft production in the northwestern corner of the capital city (Zhongguo Shehui 1995, 1997). In the northwestern corner of Chang'an, or the craft production area, at least three types of workshops— iron, pottery, and bronze minting[61]—co-existed within an area of less than 150,000 m^2, and each cluster of production facilities did not show a clear, separating boundary. In comparison with the ceramic production area in Xianyang (at least 1,700,000 m^2), the scale of the concentrated production area inside Chang'an appears to have been disproportionally small.

In addition to the size difference, the assemblage of products manufactured shows another deviation from the tradition that was widely seen in the Warring States period. Most of these workshops in the northwestern corner of Chang'an produced goods that only served royal members or high-status elites—including terra-cotta funerary figurines, ceramic building material for temples, and iron chariot fittings (Bai 2011; Xu L. 2021) (Figure 2.1). Coins were minted inside Chang'an, but the production was entirely controlled by the state after the monopoly policies, making it essentially a state industry. Kilns for ceramics identified inside were often regularly aligned in a row (Zhongguo Shehui Hancheng 1994; Zhongguo Shehui Hanchenggongzuo 1994), indicating that production was coordinated (e.g., workers produced in units simultaneously). However, kilns or facilities that were associated with the manufacturing of daily use ceramic vessels (e.g., *fu* cauldron and *guan* jar) were very few inside this production section. Most of identified kilns produced tiles and terra-cotta for high-status elite tombs. Kilns for firing architectural ceramics—i.e., tiles and bricks—have occasionally been found inside the capital city, but most, again, seem to have been destined for imperial construction projects. The assemblage of ceramic products even appears to be distinctive from the scenario inside Xianyang, in which large quantities of daily use ceramic vessels were still manufactured in addition to architectural ceramics.

Within the craft production area, at least one ironworks has been discovered, but the features and remains identified indicate that it operated on a small scale. Only two cupola furnaces have been found adjacent to the three kilns, probably used for firing ceramic molds. Meanwhile, casting molds identified through the excavation suggest that products were primarily related to chariot-fittings (i.e., axis sleeves and bites). Stack-casting[62] was employed to increase production capacity, similar to the technique evidenced by other ironworks. No manufacturing waste associated with agricultural implements or daily use tools, however, has yet been found inside the city, suggesting that the ironworks might have served primarily for elites or high-rank officials[63] dwelling in the capital.

While the role of the craft industry inside the capital was relatively limited, the government set up large-scale workshops and assigned officials to manage coin minting after the implementation of the monopoly[64] within the capital hinterland, particularly inside the royal park area known as the Shanglin yuan. Including various palaces, gardens, pavilions, and sections for raising royal hunting livestock,[65] the entire Shanglin yuan stretches over 300 *li*, and covers a large area in present-day Xianyang, Huxian, Zhouzhi, and Liantian, and the outskirts of Chang'an, an area almost encompassing the entirety of modern-day Chang'an city and adjacent districts (Figure 2.2). Within the section of Jianzhang palace, archaeological fieldworks have identified some of the palace foundations and associated water drainage systems (Zhongguo Shehui & Xi'anshi Yanjiuyuan 2018). During Wudi's reign, the Han state centralized minting authority into the hands of the three subordinates of Shuiheng duwei,[66] who took charge of the imperial minting of coins within the area of the royal Shanglin yuan (Xu L. 2020, 2021) (Figure 2.6). The location of the bronze mint within the privileged land belonged to the Emperor and the royal family might reiterate the idea that all natural resources were claimed by the emperor and that the minting authority was centralized within the hand of the emperor from various local kingdoms from Wudi's reign onward.

Through pedestrian and magnetic surveys, the bronze mint at present-day Zhaolun village in Huxian was attested to be the location of one of the three subordinates overseeing coin minting, known as Shanglin Zhongguan (Xi'an Zhongxin 2004). With an area of 2,560,000 m^2 (or 2.5 km^2), the bronze foundry was the largest craft production workshop that has been discovered in ancient China so far. According to textual records, more than 100,000 convicts, most of them punished for minting privately, were sent to work at this workshop during Wang Mang's reign,[67] which might be one reason that the bronze foundry was at such an unprecedented scale. Remarkable amounts of molds for casting bronze coins and manufacturing waste (e.g., slag and copper ingots) have been found. While Shanglin Zhongguan was also considered to oversee the production of luxury goods for the royal family, current evidence suggests that the site only served as an official minting center, and the manufacturing of other luxury products, e.g., bronze vessels and mirrors, appeared to have occurred elsewhere.

Outside the Chang'an capital and mausoleum towns, several ruling towns have been identified by national survey projects in past decades in the vast hinterland inside the Guanzhong basin (Guojia 1998), but almost none of them have yet been substantially investigated. According to the previous study of the settlement pattern of walled towns in the *sanfu* region (Chen B. 2007, 2016), most of them were of an area smaller than 500,000 m^2. Below I will briefly introduce discoveries in three locations, namely Yaoshang, Yueyang, and Nangucheng, as representative samples[68] illustrating the organization of craft production in ruling towns inside the Guanzhong basin (Figure 2.6).

Given the large population of the *sanfu* area, we might have expected that the high demand would have been addressed through local production. Nonetheless, kilns and other production features associated have only sporadically been reported in residential sites or county towns outside the capital. The only example relatively well understood at this stage is the one at Yaoshang, near the ruling town of Meixian in present-day Mei County (Shaanxi Yanjiuyuan 2011) (Figure 2.6). With an area of more than 70,000 m²,[69] the ceramic workshop must have been a medium-scale production center. The excavation area covered 2,000 m², and most features so far identified have been garbage pits. Other features include eight wells, four moats, six urn burials, and two adult burials. Artifacts including daily use vessels and architectural tiles, ceramic-making tools (e.g., paddles), and molds for making ceramic figures and tiles, have been discovered from excavation. Among the manufacturing waste, molds for casting iron plowshares, bronze belt-hooks, and, probably, chariot-fittings, were reported. However, the amount of iron and bronze manufacturing waste is limited in comparison with the debris associated with ceramic production. Workers in the ceramic workshop probably engaged merely in the occasional production of metal goods, on a part-time basis. The survey also identified rammed earth walls to the north and southwest of the excavation area, indicating that the workshop might have been situated at the center of Meixian during the Han period.

In contrast to the restricted finds of ceramic materials, more traces of iron manufacturing have been discovered, but again not on a significant scale. In Yueyang, the second largest county town in the Guanzhong basin covering about 4.5 km², iron slag was found at three loci roughly datable to the Qin and Han period. But each locus is small in scale. For instance, locus V was about 200 m × 150 m, based on the distribution of slag and red-burnt soil. At least ten molds for casting plowshares were found at the site. Other molds for casting chariot-fittings were identified. Ceramic production tools such as peddles and unfinished products have also been found (Liu & Li 1985; Shaanxisheng Wenwu 1966), indicating that some forms of multi-crafting existed. Significantly, Yueyang once served as the capital for both the Qin and Han states for a short period of time,[70] and numbers of large-scale palaces have been confirmed through archaeological investigation (Liu et al. 2020a, 2020b). The text on the Zhangjiashan bamboo slips also mentions that Yueyang[71] was a higher ranking county (literally a "1000-*shi* (bushel)-rank magistrate-counties", *qiandan zhi xian*), whose governor Xianling received a relatively large salary (1,000 *shi*). But nothing in the surviving remains suggests that iron manufacturing in this significant center was conducted on a very large scale.

The discovery of remains associated with iron manufacturing has also been reported from a number of smaller sites. A preliminary investigation was made in the 1950s of an iron foundry discovered at Nangucheng. Situated in present-day Fengxiang, the site might have been associated with the ruling town of Yong in the Han period. As explained earlier, Yong remained a "sacred area" in which large-scale imperial sacrificial rites were performed (Shaanxi Yanjiuyuan et al., 2020). During this investigation (Qin 1980; Shaanxi Fengxiang 1962), both ceramic and stone molds for casting agricultural tools, including plowshares and hoe-heads, were identified in the southeastern corner of the walled town[72] in an area of less than 30,000 m^2 (Figure 2.6). No large-scale waste deposits have been reported, comparable to those found in the surveys of large ironworks in Henan and Shandong. It has been claimed that the foundry at Nangucheng may have been connected to one of the Tieguan established by Wudi (Bai 2005), but the site's date has yet to be confirmed. In sum, no evidence of large-scale manufacturing has so far been identified, and the ironworks appeared to specialize in only limited types of products.

Having explained the general organization of craft production through the three cases, I will turn to Taicheng ironworks in present-day Yangling city, Shaanxi province, around 70 km to the west of present-day Xi'an (Figure 2.6). As I will demonstrate later, the general nature of this ironworks probably resembled that of the Nangucheng foundry and other small-scale ironworks. Since the findings of an archaeology excavation conducted in 2011 have been fully published, I am able to conduct a comprehensive discussion about the organization and daily operation of such small-scale ironworks. As the area of the Taicheng ironworks was less than 10,000 m^2 (Figure 2.7), it clearly operated on a scale smaller than other known ironworks beyond the capital. Ceramic typology and coin finds date the site securely to the Early and Middle Western Han periods, probably before the establishment of the iron monopoly (~202–140 BCE) (Shaanxi Yanjiuyuan 2018a:75–77). The excavation area of 500 m^2 was selected and concentrated on the part of ironworks with dense remains, based on the survey and augering results. Midden and trash pits discovered, thus, were probably the most representative features of workers' production activities that could be found from the ironworks. To the north of the ironworks at the same site, a large-scale cemetery in contemporary use has been identified. A total of 294 tombs have been excavated (Figure 2.7), providing interesting information about the community associated with the Taicheng ironworks. No residential quarters have yet been identified (Shaanxi Yanjiuyuan 2018a:7).

Within the ironworks, a total of 39 features were excavated in 2011 within the 600 m^2 excavation site. All these features should be associated with dumping or garbage pits; no features clearly associated with iron melting or refining have been found. Besides manufacturing waste, some remarkable tile fragments have been unearthed, but no house foundations have been found. The production of casting molds must have required facilities, such as a storage pit for preparing clay. So far, nothing has been found which is unmistakably associated with ceramic production.

Based on the assemblage and amount of remains and the shape, some features, such as the garbage pit H3, were used specifically for dumping manufacturing waste. Three main types of remains were discovered: manufacturing waste, faunal remains, and ceramic vessels. The manufacturing waste included slag, tuyeres, furnace linings, and casting molds, but no iron

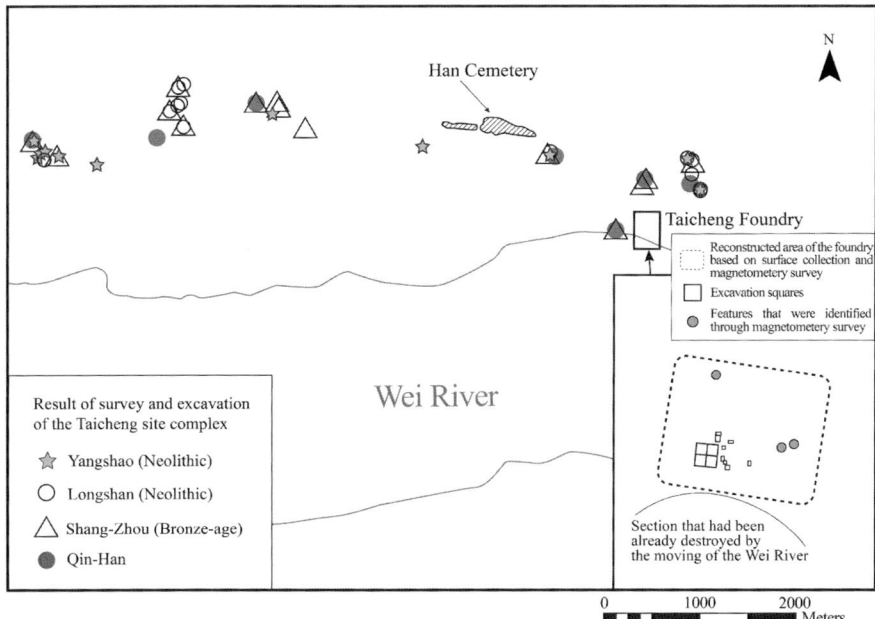

Figure 2.7 Location of the Han cemetery, ironworks, and settlements of various periods identified through a survey in the Taicheng site complex (after Shaanxi Yanjiuyuan 2018a:Fig 3; also note that the survey results did not show large-scale residential sites in contemporary with the ironworks).

ore or furnace features have yet been discovered at the site. According to the evidence of the molds, the final products mainly included farming tools like hoe-heads and plowshares. Interestingly, the shape of the molds and the product assemblages were very similar to the materials found at other ironworks mentioned before, suggesting that the function of Taicheng might have been similar to other ironworks in the capital region. I will further explain elsewhere the techniques and types of raw materials presented by manufacturing waste to contextualize the connection between Taicheng and other production centers.

Besides the four cases mentioned above, sporadic remains associated with craft production have also been found in the basin (Figure 2.6). It is difficult to fix the date of these remains. But by pulling together data related to craft industries, one can still catch a glimpse of their general organization inside the Guanzhong basin. Intriguingly, evidence of craft industries discovered within the greater Chang'an area was mostly irrelevant to daily use products for commoners. The coinage mint in Shanglin yuan and the ironworks and ceramic foundries in the northwest corner of Chang'an were all managed by the state and manufactured either prestigious goods or resources that were subject to tight state control. The archaeological discoveries therefore reinforce the argument at the beginning of this chapter that the capital, as well as its satellite cities, focused heavily on the function of exchange, trade, and consumption, instead of being a production center for daily goods. While there was a certain amount of minting and prestige-goods production, the craft production of daily use goods might have played little part in the overall economy of the capital, different from the scenario of the capital cities of the Jin states during the preceding Warring States period.

In the *sanfu* region, iron production in the local centers of Nangucheng, Taicheng, Yueyang (and probably also Yaoshang) also does not seem to have been organized on a massive scale. The production of ceramics may have been somewhat different from the scenario of the iron industry. The Yaoshang workshop is so far the largest ceramic workshop that has been identified in the entire region outside the capital. Since ceramic production centers have not been widely found, products from this center might have been supplied to residents in other counties or even to residents of Chang'an. It is also important to note that the Yaoshang workshop was only as large as 70,000 m^2, which is still smaller than the production zone inside the Xianyang capital before the Han period (at least 600,000 m^2). This pattern of the craft industry in the Guanzhong basin shows that local manufacturing was particularly sparse, contrary to what we might have expected in an imperial capital region. Viewing from this line of evidence, ironworks did not emerge rapidly in the capital region during the Han period. Even ceramic workshops in the capital Chang'an and in the *sanfu* region were relatively small. This suggests that the strategy of craft industry management changed significantly in the Han period. For daily use products, the Han state appeared to decentralize production centers that were often clustered within walled capitals during the Warring States period or dispersed them to other hinterland locations beyond the capital region.

To understand how iron or other craft industries generated connections between different parts of the Han society, we must look more carefully at the data and extrapolate their management and operation on the ground. Especially for iron, we need to consider the interaction between local production centers and other workshops beyond the capital. Since a regional or interregional transportation system unquestionably existed in the Han period, further study is needed to explore the role of iron in connecting various parts of society together and sustaining the demand for production activities in the capital. I will follow this line elsewhere and explore the techniques and assemblage of products demonstrated by ironworks within and beyond the Guanzhong basin. As I will demonstrate later, the cross-regional comparison of other ironworks and metal production centers between the Guanzhong and Guandong regions could further clarify general changes in the production system caused by the formation of a new imperial network and transformation of social relations.

Notes

1 Based on the identification of *xian* in Zhou et al. (2016). This number also include *xian* associated with the controversial Taichang commandery.
2 Even after the turmoil during the Wang Mang reign, Chang'an continued to be one of the political and economic centers during the Eastern Han period; see Ma (2000).
3 See Li F. (2006:18) for a useful discussion of definition of social setting, which is generally referred to "landscape" in archaeological literature.
4 For the discussion of Luoyang as the pivot point of the ideological universe from the Western Zhou onward, see Feng (2015).
5 *Shiji* 99.2716; modified from the translation in Watson (1993[1961]:237). For an in-depth discussion of the geo-topography of Guanzhong, see Shi (1991).
6 *Shiji* 129.3261. For the discussion of the concept of Guanzhong, see Hsing (2009); Xin (2008).
7 Besides controlling the traffic, the Han state also relocated kingdoms out from the Hedong region, as a way to strengthen its control over the eastern territories after Wudi moved the Hangu gate to further east; see Ma M. (2012).
8 Zhou Yafu, the commander of the Han force, said that "now as I am based on Xingyang, the rebels to the east should not be worried about" (*Shiji* 106.2831). Due to the geographical disadvantages of those kingdoms and wrong strategies, the rebels could not even conquer Suiyang (the capital of the Liang state), about 200 km to the southeast of Xingyang.
9 *Shiji* 129.3261.
10 The *daitian* system, generally referred to "ridge-and-furrow alternation", involved the use of alternate trenches (*quan*) for farming every year so that space would be optimized to permit the best growth within a given unit. The well-regulated alignment would also provide better ventilation and more sunlight for the growth of crops. For a detailed explanation, see Hsu (1980:112–114); Liu X. (2017).
11 Different from most other studies, Chen Yexin argues that the average temperature during the Han periods was lower than that during the Spring-and-Autumn period, and that the temperature during the Western Han period was cooler than that of the Eastern Han period (see Chen 2002).
12 *Shiji* 129.3272.
13 For a detailed discussion about the political significance of the national traffic network, see Nylan (2012); Sanft (2014).
14 During the reign of Wudi, the annual amount of staple goods transported to Guanzhong from its eastern territories, which were used to feed the population of Guanzhong and provision the frontier garrisons in the Hexi Corridor, amounted to six million *shi*, see *Hanshu* 24a.1142. At a later period, during the reign of Zhaodi (Emperor Zhao), the amount was slightly lower but still amounted to around 4 million *shi*, see *Shiji* 30.1441.
15 See Zhang (2016) for a comprehensive introduction of the drainage systems inside Chang'an.
16 For the discussion of the purpose of walled capitals in ancient China, see Xu (2017).
17 East–west long axis have also been identified in some mausoleum towns on the northern bank of the Wei River valley, such as Yangling. For the general layout and structure of the Yangling mausoleum, see Xianyangshi Wenwu (2010); Also see Zhu and Zhao (2018) for the orientation of long axis represented by all mausoleums during the Western Han period.
18 According to the site report of the tombs in Longshouyuan, residential remains were identified during the salvage excavation of the cemeteries. Unfortunately,

the remains have not been systematically reported. Also, the discovery of toilet at Miaojiazhai (Shaanxi Yanjiusuo 2007) in southern suburbs may indicate the existence of residential areas nearby.

19 For an in-depth discussion about the attendant tombs in mausoleums of the Han period and related ritual system, see Cao (2012).

20 For the archaeological investigation of each of these mausoleums, see Shaanxi Yanjiuyuan and Xianyangshi Wenwu (2012, 2013, 2014); Shaanxi Yanjiuyuan et al. (2011, 2021); Xianyangshi Wenwu (2007); Xianyanshi Wenwu and Shaanxi Yanjiuyuan (2019); Zhongguo Shehui (1996b); for the most intensive summary of previous archaeological works, see Xianyangshi Wenwu (2010).

21 This system was eventually abandoned in the final years of the Western Han, when the strategy of relocating the wealthy families from Guandong to mausoleums eventually created more social discontent and criticism than stability (*Hanshu* 27a.1341). As a result, no mausoleum towns were associated with the last four mausoleums: Yiling, Weiling, Kangling, and Yanling. Also, their mausoleum parks are relatively small.

22 In fact, some important officials in the central court lived in those mausoleum towns. For instance, Dong Zhongshu relocated his family to Maoling town after his retirement, and his family also dwelled in Maoling until the end of the Western Han.

23 *Hanshu* 28a.1547.

24 *Hanshu* 29.1678–1679, 1681, 1684–1685.

25 *Yantielun Jiaozhu* 5.68, "Jingeng".

26 Wang Y. (2004:187) hold a different idea and suggested that the crop yielding in Guanzhong might have been sufficient and stable, given that records about starvation occurred primarily in Guandong, not the capital region.

27 *Shiji* 29.1409–1410.

28 *Sanfu Huangtu Jiaozhu*, "cang", 6.347.

29 Lead isotopic studies have demonstrated that the ore sources (either lead or copper) used for bronze manufacturing primarily came from the Qinling Mountains during the Qin period, see Jia (2011).

30 It remains unclear how many coins had been minted by the Han state after it centralized the minting authority, given the lack of records in received texts. Also, textiles were used in the Western Han period as currencies (Lao 1971), which could supplement a good portion of coins as currency in circulation. Nonetheless, if we assume the *suanfu* (head tax) was about 120 *qian* during the Middle and Late Western Han period, and the population that needed to pay full *suanfu* was about 54 percent of the overall population, according to the Zoumaluo bamboo slips dating to the later Three Kingdoms period, each year the Han government needed to collect 32.4 million × 120 *qian* = 3.89 billion *qian*, which even does not include the so-called *kouqian*, or the head taxes from the population between 7 and 14 years old. For the discussion of *suanfu*, see Zang:265–309; for the demographic structure of population based on the excavated texts, see Yuan (2018:160–177).

31 *Hanshu* 24b.1280.

32 *Shiji* 129.3261; modified from the translation in Swann (1950:438).

33 *Shiji* 130.3286.

34 It is disputed as if the seal should be dated to the Warring States period or the Early Western Han period, see Tang (2019).

35 In fact, none of those "iron magnates" were originally from the Qin state. This supports my argument in Chapter 1 for regional variation in the Qin state.

36 *Qinjiandu Heji*, Shuihudi "Miscellaneous Excerpts from Qin Status", Chen W. (ed.) (2014:179); Hulsewé (1985:112, C14).

37 *Liye Qinjiandu Jiaoshi* (*di er juan*), Chen W. (ed.) (2018:186).
38 For the origin and transformation of the duties of Dasinong in the Han period, see Chen W. (2018); Wang (2008).
39 While Duguan theoretically was subordinate to Dasinong in the central court, local administrative units (i.e., *jun* and *xian* government) also involved in the management, such as coordinating the supply of labor force and materials to those offices; See Tong (2014) for the study of the Duguan system.
40 *Qinjiandu Heji*, Shuihudi "Statutes on Stables and Parks", Chen W. (ed.) (2014:55); transl. Hulsewé (1985:28, A9).
41 *Qinjiandu Heji*, Shuihudi "Statutes on Currencies", Chen W. (ed.) (2014:100); transl. Hulsewé (1985:54, A47).
42 Ibid.
43 *Ernian lüling*, "Statutes on Forts and Passes", Zhangjiashan (2001:493); transl. Barbieri-Low and Yates (2015:1125).
44 *Ernian lüling*, "Statutes on Finance", Zhangjiashan (2001:192); transl. Barbieri-Low and Yates (2015:929).
45 One characteristic of the financial system of the Western Han period is that the revenue for the royal family was independent from that for maintaining the operation of the state administrative system. For the original idea of such observation, see Kato (1993[1918]). Lin Yide's recent research provides an extensive work about the incomes of the Shaofu institute, which took charge of the revenue for the royal house; See Lin (2008).
46 *Yantielun Jiaozhu* 10.132 "Cifu".
47 As Wagner already pointed out, the original proposal for specific policies was submitted by Dongguo Xianyang and Kong Jin before the full implementation year (117 BCE), probably around 119 BCE (see Wagner's analysis in 2008:171 and references therein). Also, Jin Wen argues that the original idea to centralize iron and salt production into the state's Han was proposed by Zhang Tang. Dongguo Xianyang and Kong's proposal was more about the specific and practical plans to implement the idea (see Jin 2011:112–114).
48 *Yantielun Jiaozhu* 1.1 "Benyi".
49 *Yantielun Jiaozhu* 4.57 "Cuobi".
50 *Shiji* 129.3277. But in *Hanshu* 91.3690, Mr. Zhuo only had 800 slaves (*tong*). For relevant discussion, see Wagner (1993:258–259).
51 *Shiji* 129.3278; *Hanshu* 91.3691.
52 For the locations of these iron offices, see the introduction in Chapter 3.
53 One illustrative example will be the change of the management system of Shujun Xigong, which was basically centralized by the Gongguan system after Wudi's reign; See Bai (2014).
54 *Yantielun Jiaozhu* 6.84 "Fugu"; 7.101 "Feiyang".
55 *Yantielun Jiaozhu* 5.68 "Jingeng"; transl. Gale (1967:33).
56 While the monopoly policies of iron and salt might have been temporarily suspended by Gong Yu during Yuandi's (Emperor Yuan, ruling reign 48–33 BCE), these policies were quickly re-instated in 41 BCE; See *Hanshu* 24b.1176.
57 *Hou Hanshu* 4.167.
58 The Zoumalou bamboo slips from present-day Changsha dating to the Three-Kingdom period recorded a large group of *shizuo* (state-attached artisans). Some of them were specialists producing iron implements. In other words, the type of state-controlled factory specialized in iron agricultural implements might not have been abandoned during the Eastern Han period, even though the monopoly of iron was no longer strictly implemented; See Yu (2006).
59 Some scholars suggest that, before the implementation of the iron monopoly, the iron industry was controlled partly by the Han government, partly by local

Kings, and partly by private merchants. I agree with Kageyama (1984:274–278) that the iron offices in the Qin and Early Western Han period were already existed, and probably were responsible for the production of iron or steel weapons instead of agricultural implements.

60 Some studies even suggest that the iron industry in the Guanzhong basin comprised an essential role in the entire regional economic system (e.g., Choi 1998).

61 Some scholars (e.g., Zhangsun et al. 2017) argue that a production center for mirrors might have located nearby Chang'an, even though no empirical evidence has yet been discovered in the entire Guanzhong basin.

62 Stack-casting refers to a process whereby molds were stacked in a pile so that products could be manufactured in large numbers simultaneously; See Henan Bianxiezu (1978); Hua (1983).

63 In the Han period, chariots were normally used only by officials and other elites (Zhuang 2016). Chariot fittings are unlikely to have been affordable by ordinary people.

64 *Hanshu* 24b.1169.

65 e.g., see *Shiji* 58.2084.

66 Outside Chang'an, Chengcheng is the only coin mint that has been identified and studied. This site is a small-scale foundry site located at present-day Potou village in Chengcheng, about 70 km east of Xi'an. Its major function is a coinage minting foundry. A well-preserved kiln was also excavated during the excavation (Shaanxisheng and Chengcheng 1982). Molds include ceramic, bronze and stone molds. It is likely that the site was responsible for mold production. The site might belong to the town of Cheng or Congquan county, indicating that some minting during the Western Han period was practiced outside the Shanglin yuan.

67 *Hanshu* 99c.4167.

68 While there are some other craft production sites reported in the literature, such as the ironworks in present-day Hancheng (Shaanxi Huacang 1983), the detailed information of these cases has not yet been published. Therefore, I can focus on three representative examples here in order to illustrate the potential organization of these production sites.

69 This is merely a rough estimate, and the core area of the ceramic workshop might have been smaller.

70 Yueyang was the Qin capital before the Qin state relocated to Xianyang. It was also briefly the capital of the Han state before Liu Bang eventually settled the capital at Chang'an, as I explained earlier.

71 *Ernian lüling*, "Statutes on Salaries", Zhangjiashan (2001:193); transl. Barbieri-Low and Yates (2015:965).

72 I also conducted a small-scale survey in 2011 and identified plowshare molds from the ironworks, confirming the records published almost half a century ago.

3 Iron making in the center of the Han state[1]

From the 7th century BCE onward, cast iron technology was gradually established in the Central Plains as well as different peripheral states. The need for high temperature for cast iron production determined that the manufacturing of iron implements needed to be conducted on a relatively large scale. The production of iron also required a reliable exchange network to efficiently transport ore sources, fuel, and final products in bulk. Each stage thus involved a large number of laborers and connected different parts of the empire with each other. I will first turn to the techniques employed in iron smelting, refining, and particularly, converting iron to steel in this chapter, in order to contextualize the connection involved in the production and consumption process. The basic explanation of techniques employed in each production stage, often referred to as the "operational chain" in previous studies, will lay the essential foundation for interactions related to the iron industry that would occur at various scales, which I will further elaborate in Part II.

The explanation of various techniques in iron making is essential for understanding the potential manufacturing origins of iron implements, which are often the primary concern in the discussion of the distribution system. To cast light on the procurement of iron objects, the origins of raw materials and manufacturing places of final products must first be known archaeologically. Unfortunately, these two issues have not yet been comprehensively studied in the literature on cast iron artifacts in ancient China. So far, very few iron objects in the capital area of the Han state have been subjected to metallurgical analyses (Beijing 1996; Du & Han 2005; Liu C. 1999; Liu et al. 2019; Shi et al. 2019; Zhang 2017; Zhao et al. 2020). No conclusive evidence is available from the literature and published data of iron mines to confirm ore sources or the exact manufacturing locations of the iron objects from Guanzhong. More critically, previous metallurgical studies of iron objects excavated from the region have only demonstrated that the most-commonly found techniques were cast iron and a type of steel named steel decarburized from a solid-state of cast iron. Since very few slag inclusions surviving from ore, which usually include essential information for provenance analyses, are still present in most objects due to the high-temperature smelting

DOI: 10.4324/9781003259220-5

process of cast iron, it is almost impossible to geochemically determine the provenience of cast iron. Nevertheless, metallurgical analyses of iron can still provide the essential technological profile to characterize, as indirect evidence at least, whether the techniques used in products were similar between different production and consumption locations. In particular, if a comparative study could be conducted by integrating various evidential components, such as the manufacturing waste, potential raw materials discarded at the manufacturing site, and final products from the same community, such a comparison of manufacturing techniques might still shed light on the operation of the manufacturing and potential provenance of raw materials, semi-products, and final goods across the region. The review of iron making techniques, therefore, provides the basic framework for addressing the issues of distribution.

This chapter will start by reviewing the various production stages of iron making in ancient China. Since the current understanding of the various techniques derives from the studies during the past few decades of ironworks in the broader Central Plains (i.e., present-day Henan, Shanxi, Hebei, Shandong, and Jiangsu) beyond the Guanzhong basin, the second part of this chapter will take a closer look at these ironworks to further explain the requisite background of the Han iron production system. By piecing together various lines of fragmentary information about those ironworks, a more comprehensive image emerges, showing that iron manufacturing was seemingly concentrated in a number of clusters in the middle and lower Yellow River valley. In addition, a pattern of labor division is present within each of these clusters and between some of these clusters. While the grouping presented in the chapter is subjective to a greater or lesser degree, the purpose of the division is to underscore the potential collaboration, or some forms of labor division, between the ironworks within the same cluster. The macroscopic overview of those ironworks in the broader Central Plains also lays the foundation for understanding the techniques employed by the Taicheng ironworks within the Guanzhong basin. Through synthesizing evidence of various types of waste debris from the Taicheng case, I then consider the basic production system of the iron industry inside the capital region at the end of this chapter.

Since Chapter 2 already underlined that the production within the capital region was on a scale smaller than outside the capital region, the interregional comparison of the production systems in this chapter illustrates the greater detail of differences between ironworks inside the capital region and those located in Guandong. The explanation of the manufacturing techniques manifested by the case of Taicheng also throws light on the relations of ironworks inside and beyond the capital region, with regard to the supply of raw material and semi-products. Given the importance of iron manufacturing for agricultural production and social stability, the comparison of ironworks between Guanzhong and Guandong also compels us to further consider the organization of those small-scale centers represented by

Taicheng and their roles in integrating different social domains within the Guanzhong basin.

1 Iron making techniques and the operational chain in the Han period

There are two major traditions of iron making in the ancient world, as I briefly explained in Chapter 1 (for terminologies, see Table 3.1). Almost everywhere, the dawn of iron technology started with bloomery iron, where iron was smelted within a small furnace in solid-state. The final products were often called "sponge iron" as a mixture of slag and metallic iron. Forging and refining were thus required following the smelting process in order to remove impurities and to carburize the low-carbon iron (i.e., wrought iron) to steel during the forging process. In contrast to the system of bloomery iron, the manufacturing of cast iron needs higher temperatures and more fuel. Meanwhile, for making cast iron objects, workers might need to collaborate with other specialists (e.g., potters) to manufacture molds that can withstand the high temperature and stress generated but maintain the high performance of thermal conductivity during casting (Lam et al. 2017b. After casting, various processes of heat treatment, such as annealing, cold or hot working, and quenching, would be needed for certain types of finished products to enhance their physical properties.

Table 3.1 Definition of basic technical terminologies

Terminologies	Definition
Cast iron	Iron that was melted and cast, usually with about 4 percent of carbon (Wagner 1993:336)
Wrought iron	Iron with carbon content in the range 0.1–0.3 percent (Wagner 2008:89)
Bloomery iron	Iron was smelted by reduction of the ore to solid iron at a low temperature in what is called a bloomery (i.e., a small-scale hearth or a shaft furnace) (Wagner 1993:274)
Solid-state decarburization of cast iron	The annealing of a cast iron object in an oxidizing atmosphere in order to produce wrought iron or steel (i.e., iron with carbon content in the range 0. 5–1 percent) for smithing (Wagner 1993:291)
Malleable cast iron	An object was cast in its intended final form and annealed at a high temperature for a period of days to decarburize or graphitize the carbon in the structure (Wagner 1993:291)
Fined iron	The operation of converting cast into wrought iron or medium-carbon steel, probably through stirring, in a hearth or open fire, facilitated by a blast of air with charcoal as the fuel (Wagner 1993:290–291)

To better illuminate the role of iron production in the economic system, it is necessary to explain each main stage in iron manufacturing, namely mining, smelting and casting, and annealing. For the production of iron, the first step was ore mining and ore processing. In the clusters of iron manufacturing sites in present-day Henan that I will further discuss below, several locations—some of which included remnants of mining shafts—have been claimed as mining sites during the Han period. Unfortunately, none of those mining sites could be attested by recent archaeological surveys (e.g., Qin et al. 2016). Therefore, our current understanding of mining techniques, as well as the organization of mining workers, during the Han period remains limited. One critical reason is that most, if not all, middle or large-scale iron mines that were exploited in the Han period were often mined continuously in the late historical period or even right up to the modern period. Even though some were mentioned in early survey reports, the archaeological traces related to mining could easily have been obliterated by more recent mining activities.

The lack of archaeological evidence thus made us turn to historical records about ore miners. Textual records from later historical periods often inform that miners of iron and other minerals were often poor peasants or individuals who had fled from their registered town after losing their lands. Since miners were "refugees of justice" in mountain areas where the state would be difficult to keep a close eye on, mining regions were often viewed as the site of potential rebellion during the late historical period (e.g., He 2012). According to *Hanshu*, the Han state employed *tu*, or convict labor, together with *zu* (conscript labor) on a very large scale to mine copper or iron ores under the supervision of officials.[2] While the types of labor involved in iron production will be explained in greater detail in the next chapter, the limited records about miners in texts, regardless of which types of laborers they belonged to, were mostly related to the problems caused by their concentration in mining regions. In particular, there were at least two big rebellions close to the end of Western Han (15 BCE); both are relevant to mine workers.[3] The first was led by Su Ling, a fleeing convict laborer originally under the iron office of the Shanyang commandery (present-day southwestern Shandong). After killing and injuring a Zhangli (Senior Subaltern) to release other imprisoned convict laborers, Su Ling plundered an arsenal and gathered a force of several hundred bandits. *Hanshu* particularly comments on the scale of revolt, as "this band of rebels roved across more than 40 commanderies and kingdoms and persisted for several years".[4] Similarly, the second revolt was initiated by a group of conscript laborers under the iron office of Yingchuan commandery (present-day central Henan) and eventually spread to nine commanderies. For sure, the Han state must impose a strict management system to control those laborers congregated for mining, especially preventing them from escaping the mining or casting sites. But since convict miners usually were overly exploited, the outbreak of rebellion might have become unpreventable once the strict management was weakened by natural disasters or the corruption of the local government; both issues became widely seen during the end of the Western Han period.

After mining, the smelting of cast iron also required a large labor force. Since the blast furnaces for making cast iron are usually very large to enable them to generate the necessary high temperatures, the production of cast iron had to rely on a substantial supply of fuel, which was charcoal during the Han period, and a massive labor force to operate the bellow. For cast iron production at the pre-modern level, the most costly part often lies in fuel, instead of ore, because iron ore was relatively abundant in the natural world,[5] and a scarcity of ore was rare even without the technique of deep mining (Wagner 1993:408). The location of some ironworks in the deep mountain regions, such as the Tieshenggou ironworks in present-day Gongyi, were clearly chosen for the sake of procuring fuel and, probably, transferring those resources to other production centers. In the Han period, some ironworks were adjacent to urban centers in the plain areas, such as the case of Guxingzhen in present-day Zhengzhou. While the transportation of ore and fuel to those smelting ironworks would be costly, such locations were often operated on a scale even larger than those in the mountain areas, in which massive scale blast furnaces have been identified. In the case of Wangchenggang in present-day Lushan, for instance, one of the largest blast furnaces of the Han period has been found. The bottom part of the preserved blast furnace, which was oval in shape, measures 4 m north-south and 2.8 m east-west (Henan& Lushan 2002). Underlying the selection of the location was probably the purpose of monitoring the large number of laborers employed in iron smelting since it would be easier for governors to oversee laborers concentrated in an area adjacent to a ruling town than in deep mountains.

Ethno-historical documents about the cast iron industry during the Minguo period (early 20th century) in present-day Hunan (Wang Xiaoqing et al. 1934) can help illuminate the scale and organization of labor in smelting and casting behind fragmentary archaeological records. Based on historical records, a blast furnace measuring 7 m tall and 4.5 m at the bottom on each side, which was more-or-less equivalent to the case identified at Wangchenggang, would require at least six workers to operate at the same time merely for air blasting, charge loading, and slag removal during the modern period. Once smelting activities began, the blast furnace had to be operated day and night for several months. A sudden shut down of a blast furnace would lead to the solidification of iron liquid, making the entire furnace unusable. Therefore, four shifts, each of which hired six workers, were needed in order to continuously operate the smelting of one blast furnace. In the modern case, each operation of a blast furnace would last about nine months without any halt. In other words, the scale of labor involved in cast iron production is contingent on not only the size of the furnace but also the duration of the production period. Additional workers were also needed to repair and maintain the furnace during the time when smelting stopped. Skillfully operated, each modern blast furnace in Hunan could produce 136 *jin* (one *jin* is equivalent to 600 g during the Minguo period) of iron ingots by consuming 3,000 *jin* of iron sand and 10,000 *jin* of charcoal.[6] In the Han period, however, cast iron smelting used crushed ore instead of iron sand. Even for operating a blast furnace of the same size, much more ore and fuel would be required for each smelt. Given the scale of the labor force required, the smelting of cast iron would thus impose critical challenges for the organization of labor force, and created, inevitably, uncertainties for the centralized state to manage a large number of workers assembled at the same site for a long period of time, especially in locations not entirely under its control.

After smelting, the liquid iron was poured into molds to cast products of various types, or ingots (i.e., semi-products) for other ironworks that did not conduct iron smelting. The type of furnace employed in iron remelting was called a cupola furnace, which was found to be much smaller. Based on the reconstruction of the example from the ironworks at Dongpingling in Shandong (Shandong et al. 2019), the diameter of cupola furnaces was usually around 1–1.5 m. Therefore, fewer workers and less raw materials were needed to operate the furnace each time. To finish the casting, each ironworks also needed to produce casting molds on its own or to procure them from other production centers. While iron casting molds gradually gained in popularity,[7] ceramic casting molds remained the major type of mold throughout the Han period. Studies of casting molds show that the size of sand particles, which were the major component of ceramic casting molds, and the ratio between sand and clay were found to differ, depending on the types of casting molds used (Li & Chen 1995; Lam et al. 2017b). The variations indicate that mold-makers had a good understanding of the physical properties of raw materials and would adjust the proportions and types of sand and clay required according to their needs, such as using larger grains for making molds of larger size in order to enhance their strength.

Besides operating the blast furnace (e.g., operating the bellows to blast air into the furnace), a considerable number of laborers were also needed for the transportation of ore and fuel to the ironworks, in addition to the further processing of raw materials (e.g., crushing iron ores). Since cast iron smelting or remelting had to last for a long period of time once started, a considerable amount of daily necessities was needed to maintain the continuation of large-scale production. This is probably part of the reason that some of the known smelting ironworks are located in the plains regions, adjacent to the intersection of traffic routes, such as the case of Guxingzhen. While the transportation of fuel would be costly, the proximity to large-scale urban centers might give an advantage over the location in deep mountains for logistic supply and security control. Since blast furnaces like the one in Guxingzhen would also produce a large quantity of products in a single operation, the manufacturing of this ironworks required a developed transportation system to prevent waste and accumulation of unsold products. Therefore, a location adjacent to an urban center might be more favorable than that in deep mountains. As I explained in Chapter 1, ironworks during the Warring States period were often found inside crowded capital centers. The control over the transportation of raw materials, the ready access to a labor force, and the management of a concentrated labor force appeared to be the dominant factors underlying the rise of the cast iron technology as well as the location selection of production sites during the Warring States and Han periods.

Cast iron had undoubtedly been the most-dominant iron smelting technique since the Warring States period, but it should be noted that bloomery iron co-existed with cast iron for a long time. Bloomery iron was a more realistic technological choice in locations where fuel and labor were constrained (Larreina et al. 2018) and has occasionally been identified in the fringe of the Central Plains during the Warring States and Han periods. For instance, in the Zhaitouhe cemetery in present-day Huangling, northern Shaanxi, an iron ring, which may be a bracelet, has been identified as bloomery iron, along with a number of cast iron objects (Guo et al. 2014). Most of the occupants were probably members of the *rong* barbarian group subjugated by the Qin state, based on the characteristics of their burial goods (Shaanxi Yanjiuyuan et al. 2018). In the Yan state in northern Hebei, bloomery iron was reported for making iron armor and swords (Beijing Gangtie 1975). Bloomery iron has also been occasionally identified in analytical reports of sites of the Han period, such as the analysis of iron tools from the mausoleum of the Chu kingdom in present-day Xuzhou (Beikeda & Xuzhou 1997) and Han tombs in the capital region (e.g., Lam et al. 2018; Liu et al. 2019). It may be too early to confirm the origins, but bloomery iron should not be entirely excluded from the technological skill set of iron making during the Han time.

While cast iron is well known for its large-scale production, iron with such a high content of carbon would suffer from a lack of ductility and would be too brittle for making weapons or even farming tools. Annealing or decarburization was therefore required to convert cast iron to steel, which is superior in terms of both malleability and ductility. Without the techniques that can reduce the carbon content in the iron objects, cast iron would essentially be useless to ironworkers, and for this reason, it was not adopted in other regions until very late (Wagner 2008:167–170). Before the establishment of the Han dynasty, several types of annealing processes had been widely adopted during the Warring States period (Ke et al. 1993). The first type is called malleable iron.[8] By employing this method, batches of final products, such as axes or spades made of cast iron, would be annealed inside the kiln at a high temperature for a period of days to decarburize the casting iron (Wagner 1993:338, 351). Consequently, the proportion of carbon in the cast iron would be greatly reduced, and the final products are called grey cast iron[9] or mottled cast iron.[10] Evidence of malleable iron has been identified from a number of sites predating the Warring States period in the Central Plains (Li 1975) and the Han River valley to the south (Chen

J. 2014), suggesting the wide adoption of the annealing technique before the Han period.

Annealing an entire object homogeneously inside a kiln that was as cast would be difficult, not to mention the annealing of a batch of objects.[11] Perhaps the need to make malleable iron with the same degree of decarburization and to produce materials of higher quality gave birth to another annealing method, namely solid-state decarburization of cast iron, around the end of the Spring-and-Autumn period (Ke et al. 1993). During the Warring States period, this method has been identified in the three Jin states, such as the Zhonghang ironworks, and the Jiudian cemetery in the Chu state (Hubei 1995). By definition, the technique of solid-state decarburization refers to the treatment of annealing cast iron raw material in an oxidizing atmosphere within a refractory kiln in order to produce wrought iron or steel for smithing (Wagner 1993:291). This process generally is similar to the making of malleable cast iron. The major difference is that the latter— malleable cast iron—was usually cast in its intended final form, whereas the solid-state decarburization would produce semi-products for further forging. The ceramic molds for casting iron bars have often been claimed as important evidence for manufacturing such raw materials.

The challenge of homogenously decarburizing as-cast products still remains in the case of solid-state decarburization. To conduct heat treatment on small iron bars or ingots might enhance the success rate of decarburization, but this compromise might have imposed a constraint on the size of iron lump for making an implement as large as a sword. Ancient blacksmiths might have employed the so-called "welding technique" to weld multiple pieces of iron or steel together into a bigger piece for making an entire object.[12] Yet, this process would require a high level of forging skill and a good control of timing to weld pieces together. Otherwise, large welding gaps with an oxidized layer would exist within the new welded piece of iron, which would eventually impact the quality of the final products (Han 1987). In this vein, the invention of fined iron in early China is supposed to address, at least partially, the problems of solid-state decarburization. Generally known as *chaogang* in Chinese literature, this technique refers to the operation of converting cast iron into wrought iron or medium-carbon steel iron in a hearth or open fire, facilitated by a blast of air with charcoal as the fuel (Percy 1864:579). This finery process is also known as the "indirect process" of steel making, in contrast to the "direct process" that reduced iron from ores directly by using a bloomery furnace. The production of high-quality objects, such as swords, often used fined iron as the raw material through the so-called multiple-folding technique, which means repeated heating, folding, and hammering steps were employed to improve the qualities such as strength and ductility (Wagner 1993:283–284). In some cases, the fabrication technique of quench-hardening was also employed to enhance the quality of the final products.

Given the importance of fined iron in the stimulation of early iron development, there has been much scholarly debate over when and where this technique was first invented. Surprisingly, a recent discovery suggests that the Qin state may have seen the early adoption of fined iron technique (Liu et al. 2019). According to the metallurgical analysis of iron implements from a Qin cemetery in Xinfeng in Shaanxi, two iron swords, one chisel, and one iron spoon were demonstrated to have been made from fined iron. Meanwhile, other iron tools were made of steel-state decarburized cast iron and other forms of malleable cast iron after the alloying treatment, which basically represents the assemblage of techniques that would have been employed by other territorial states predating the Han era (Han & Chen 2013; Han & Duan 2009). In a previous study of ironware from a stone workshop inside the Qin Shihuang mausoleum, which specialized in the manufacturing of stone armor, several iron implements were reported to show characteristics of fined iron (Liu et al. 2010), suggesting that the use of fined iron products inside the Qin state was by no means exceptional.

The earliest discovery from the Qin state instead of its contemporaries with more advanced iron industry appears to present a challenge to my previous argument that the iron industry in the Qin state was comparatively less developed. While a good number of iron products from the Qi and Chu states during the Warring States period have been subject to metallurgical analysis, no objects of fined iron have been reported (e.g., Chen J. 2007). Nor have any fined iron objects been identified in the assemblage of analyzed iron samples from the three Jin states, which includes a collection of more than 60 pieces of iron. One possible explanation for the advance of fined iron as a new technique in the Qin state may lie in the influx of new artisans and their technical knowledge from other states, which would have narrowed the differences in the technical foundation between the Qin state and its rivals. As being explained in Chapter 1, the gradual unification by the Qin state probably allowed the regime to mobilize resources within its territories, including resources, population, and even technology. The Xinfeng cemetery where early fined iron objects were found, for instance, was about 6 km to the northeast of the Qin Shihuang mausoleum (Shaanxi Yanjiuyuan 2016). Diagnostic ceramics show that at least 50 percent of tombs in this cemetery, which includes more than 500 tombs, fall within the narrow time range of the second phase of the Late Warring States (roughly speaking, post-dating the 250 BCE) and Qin unification period (221–206 BCE). The chronology indicates that a dramatic population increase was evidenced in this case. A good portion of the occupants might have been re-settled migrants (or their descendants) removed by Qin Shihuang from other regions,[13] probably beyond the capital region, to the ruling town near his mausoleum in order to support various construction projects. Whether or not these fined iron objects were locally manufactured or introduced by migrants, there is good reason to believe that the large-scale mobilization of population following the wars which led to its unification might have introduced technological advances into the iron industry. The appearance of new techniques, thus, should not

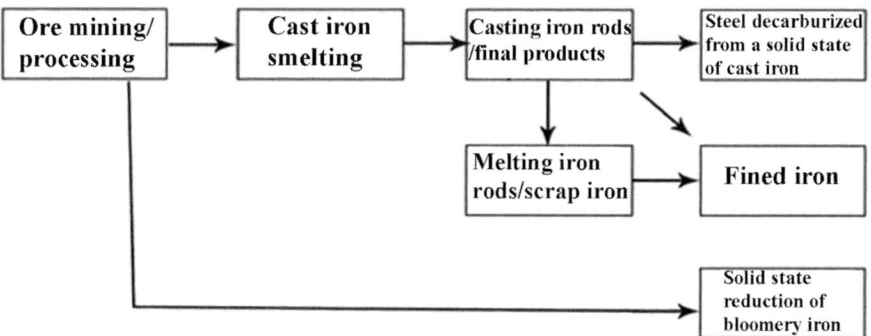

Figure 3.1 Operational chain of iron manufacture and techniques in ancient China.

easily lead us to overlooking the less developed characteristic of the iron industry before the short-lived Qin empire.

By synthesizing the previous discussion in the survey about iron technology and more updated discoveries and analytical results, a complete operational chain of iron making in ancient Chinese ironworks might include the steps illustrated in Figure 3.1 (for terminologies see Table 3.1). As highlighted and identified in previous studies (Wagner 1993:288–289), there were at least three ways through which wrought iron (iron with carbon content in the range 0.1–0.3 percent) and steel (iron with carbon content usually in the range 0.5–1 percent) were manufactured during the Qin unification and Western Han period: direct reduction by using the bloomery process, fining of cast iron (or fined iron below), and solid-state decarburization of cast iron (Chen & Han 2000, 2007; Wagner 1993:288). To a certain extent, this scheme is generic, but it should provide the basic framework for understanding the iron metallurgy technique of ironworks in the Han period. To further contextualize the technical scheme and illustrate how the constraints and advantages of cast iron technology shaped the organization of the iron industry in the Han period, I turn to the archaeological discoveries of ironworks beyond Guanzhong. Through an examination of the various clusters of iron production centers in the broader Central Plains region, I try to illustrate the operation of the iron industry under the ruling of the Han state and supplement the archaeological evidence to the discussion in Chapter 2.

2 Industrial clusters in the broader Central Plains region

When iron mining and production came under the empire's direct control after the implementation of the iron and salt monopoly in 117 BCE (Wagner 2008:192–210, 246), various approaches were adopted to reshape the iron industry. Besides the "nationalization" of pre-existed ironworks, some new ironworks were established under the direct control of Tieguang at the commandery level, which also resulted in the widespread distribution of iron works throughout the territories within the Han state.

The information about ironworks in surviving texts provides important background for archaeological discoveries. However, it is often difficult to match archaeological data to textual records. By marshaling the locations of iron offices recorded under each commandery in the Treatise of Geography in *Hanshu* (Chapter 28) and Treatises of Commanderies and States in *Hou Hanshu* (Chapters 109–113), previous scholars (e.g., Li 2000; Yang 1978; Wagner 2001:32) have already noted that present-day Shandong province had the highest number of iron offices (a total of 12 iron offices), followed by Henan (seven iron offices) and Jiangsu (six iron offices) (Figure 3.2). Also, five iron offices were located within present-day Shaanxi province. By contrast, the archaeological records show a different pattern. Figure 3.3 maps all known locations with remains associated with iron production, including iron smelting, casting, and mining sites found in the broader Central Plains region, which basically consisted of more than 90 percent of all ironworks in the Han period that have been thus reported (Bai 2005:Appendix 1). It is clear from a glance at the map that the production sites in Henan significantly outnumbered those found in Shandong province. Also, most of the currently known locations of iron manufacturing are concentrated in Henan province. More importantly, the largest ironworks and production

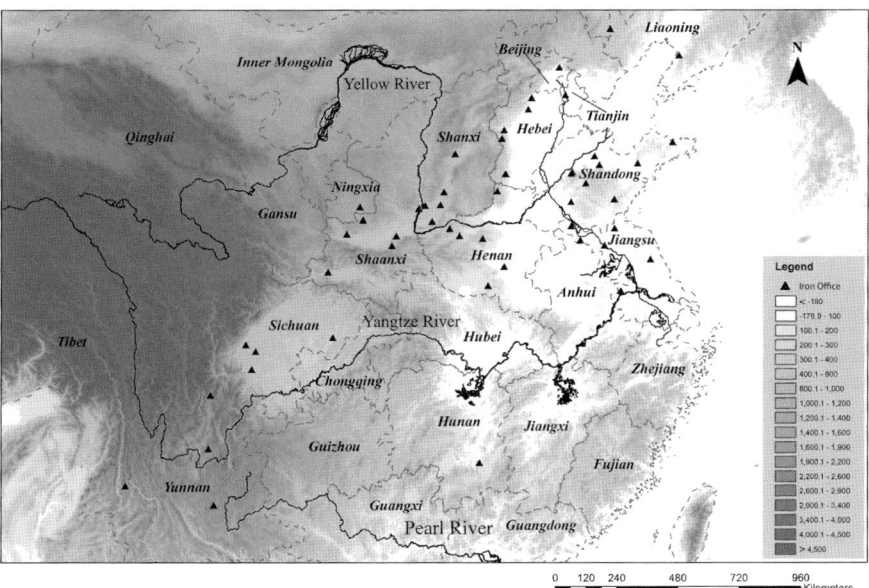

Figure 3.2 Locations of iron offices mentioned in *Hanshu* and *Hou Hanshu*.
Source: Wagner (2008:Table 1).

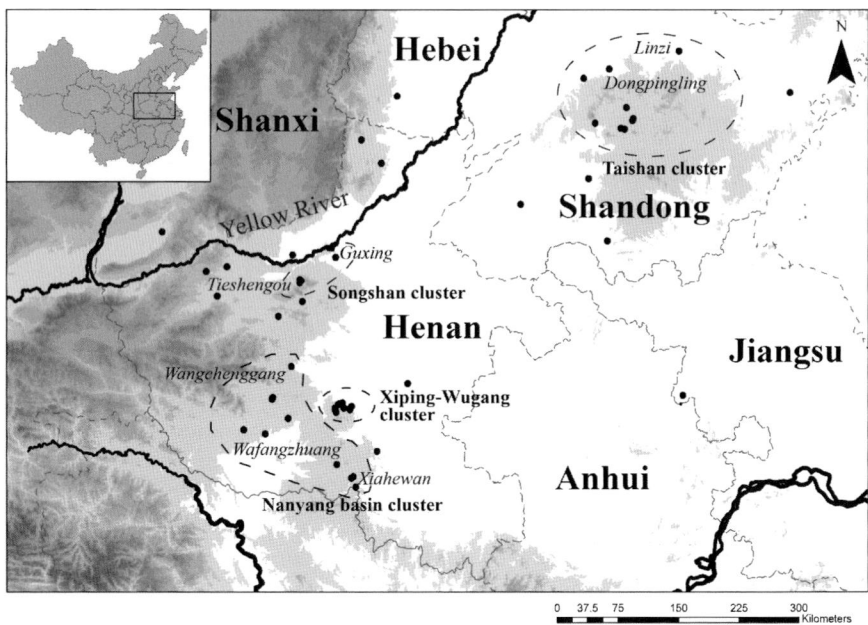

Figure 3.3 Locations of ironworks that were archaeologically found in the broader
Central Plains region.
Source: Bai (2005: Appendix 1).

sites that employed the largest blast furnaces during the Han period were
also located in present-day Henan, one at Guxingzhen and the other at
Wangchenggang.

Several factors may account for this discrepancy. For instance, the records about the location of iron offices only indicate whether an iron official
existed inside a commandery. However, each iron office in the Han period,
particularly those in present-day Henan province, often controlled multiple
ironworks at the same time. Meanwhile, some ironworks associated with
Xiaotieguan—officials only took charge of small-scale remelting and casting centers—are difficult to identify via fieldwork, resulting in their underrepresentation in some regions. While archaeological data cannot present a
complete picture, the pattern of known locations is in favor of the argument
that present-day Henan province was probably the most important region
of iron manufacture in the empire and produced iron products on a scale
probably unmatched by other regions.

Based on the proximity of these locations, the inscription records on
molds or tools that show their affiliation with different iron offices, and the
techniques employed in production, I tentatively divide these production
sites into at least four clusters (Figure 3.3). Readers need to bear in mind
that the clustering division does not necessarily mean that all production

sites were under the control of the iron office in the same commandery. Nor do I mean that each cluster was independently operated from other clusters. In the cluster in Shandong centered around the Taishan Mountain (the Taishan cluster), for instance, I included ironworks that were affiliated with three iron offices into the same group because of their potential relations reflected by inscriptions and production stages conducted by the ironworks.

The most widely known of the several clusters in Henan is the cluster in the northern hills of the Songshan Mountain (the Songshan cluster) (Figure 3.3). This cluster includes Guxingzhen (Zhang 2009; Zhongguo Yejin 1978), Tieshenggou (Henan Wenhuaju 1962; Zhao et al. 1985), and other production sites associated with Henan commandery in present-day Zhengzhou-Gongyi regions. From the large-scale excavations conducted during the 1960–1970s, casting molds and products with inscriptions of *heyi* and *hesan* have been found respectively. Arguably, the character *he* was the abbreviation for the Henan commandery, and the two ironworks would have been under the management of the same iron office of the Henan commandery, using the numeric marker (e.g., *yi*, the Chinese character of "1", and *san*, the Chinese character of "3") to differentiate products from different ironworks (Li 2000).

The geographic locations of these two ironworks also indicate that their function might be rather different, as I suggested earlier. The Guxingzhen ironworks is located in the floodplain adjacent to a Han walled town in present-day Zhengzhou, covering a massive area of more than 120,000 m^2. Besides blast furnaces, its features also included wells, kilns, houses, and facilities for crushing iron ore. In contrast, Tieshengou only covered about 20,000 m^2 and is located in the mountain area to the north of the Songshan Mountain, where it was more convenient to procure fuel and ore sources than in the plain areas. As previously mentioned, mine pits have been reported near the Tieshenggou ironworks (Henan Wenhuaju 1962) and claimed to be associated with the production site. Based on the analysis of features and manufacturing remains, Tieshenggou included facilities related to smelting, casting, and annealing, suggesting that the site was responsible for all steps in the iron production process. Interestingly, one of the largest iron smelting furnaces dating to the Han period, and possibly one of the largest furnaces in the pre-industrial world as a whole, has been found at the Guxingzhen. The furnace is oval-shaped with a long axis of 4 m. According to reconstruction, the volume inside the chamber of the furnace would have been at least 50 m^3. As two side-by-side furnaces were found,[14] at least two production units would have operated at the same time under the supervision of iron offices, producing probably at least one ton of cast iron each day (Figure 3.4)[15] Within the excavation area of Tieshenggou, eight smelting furnaces, one smithing furnace, one furnace for decarburization, and one fining furnace have been identified. But the blast furnace at Tieshenggou was relatively small, and no large blast furnaces have yet been reported at the Tieshenggou ironworks.

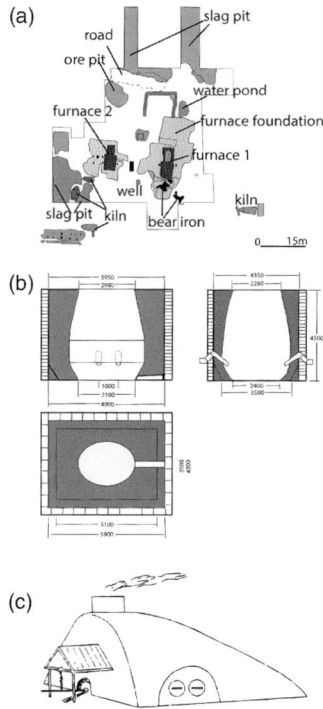

Figure 3.4 The layout of the Guxingzhen ironworks and reconstruction of one of the blast furnaces (a: Layout of Guxingzhen ironworks, after Zheng-zhou 1978:Fig 2; b: the reconstructed profile of the blast furnace no. 1 employed in Guxing, redrawn from Wagner 2001:Fig 11; c: the recon-structed working scene, redrawn from Wagner 2001:Fig 12).

Besides its location, the products from Tieshenggou were also different from the assemblage of Guxingzhen. Most of the casting molds from the lat-ter site were used for casting iron plowshare-heads and cast-iron bars, prob-ably as semi-products. Judging from the scale of cast iron manufactured and the types of iron products found at the site, other types of iron implements, such as spades and axes, might have been produced by the ironworks. In contrast, only a few casting molds have been identified from Tieshenggou. As the furnace's smaller size suggests, the scale of cast iron manufactur-ing, especially finished products, at Tieshenggou was probably smaller than at Guxingzhen. Tieshenggou ironworks probably served primarily as the transportation, or preliminary processing, center for ore or semi-products to other ironworks under the management of the same iron office, whereas Guxing specialized in smelting and casting a wider range of final products. If so, a labor division between these ironworks might have been employed in order to maximize the geographical advantage of each site.

To the south of the Songshan cluster was the Nanyang basin cluster, which includes a number of ironworks inside the Nanyang basin and in the mountain areas surrounding the basin. All these ironworks centered on a large production center at Wafangzhuang in Wan city (present-day Nanyang) (Henan Wenwu 1991a; Li & Chen 1995) (Figure 3.3), which was one of the *duhui* metropolitan cities in the Han period well known for its commercial development.[16] Covering more than 120,000 m^2, the ironworks dated from the Middle Western Han to the Eastern Han period, and was probably established against the backdrop of the iron monopoly. The ironworks was also located next to a minting factory and ceramic workshop (Henan Wenwu 1994; Li & Chen 1995). All these workshops could share fuel and certain types of raw material, which provided the conditions for the transformation of Wan into a large-scale manufacturing and commercial center (Wang Z. 2019). Features found at the site include iron cupola furnaces, iron smithing hearths, mold-firing kilns, and (probably) refining iron furnaces. Plentiful casting molds for casting plowshares and other types of production tools (e.g., hammers and sickles, and chariot-fittings), together with a considerable number of iron tools and weapons, representing the assemblage of iron implements found almost elsewhere during the Han period. It is also noteworthy that some casting molds from the site belonged to "mother-molds" of plowshares. This type of mold could be used for casting reusable cast-iron permanent molds, an important approach to achieve mass production during the Han period.[17] Since no ore remains have yet been reported from Wafangzhuang, the ironworks is thought to have primarily conducted melting, casting, and refining, and relied on semi-products or scrap iron supplied by other smelting centers in the same cluster.

Another large-scale iron production center has been identified to the east of Nanyang, at present-day Xiahewan in Biyang (Figure 3.3). Covering more than 120,000 m^2, the ironworks was about the same size as the Wafangzhuang ironworks (Henan 2009). Since Biyang was part of the Nanyang commandery during the Han period, this ironworks would have come under the same iron office which managed Wafangzhuang. The survey report identified considerable ore remains from the site, indicating that Xiahewan was a large-scale smelting center similar to Guxingzhen. Further to the southeast of the Nanyang basin, in the deep mountains of the Tongbai Mountain, at least four mining and/or smelting sites have been identified (Figure 3.3). Even though more fieldwork is needed to shed further light on these small-scale locations, it has been plausibly argued that these sites might have been upstream factories which were set up to satisfy the strong demand for ore and semi-products (ingots) from ironworks further inside the basin, such as Xiahewan and Wafangzhuang (Li & Chen 1995).

A number of mining and iron production sites have also been found on the northern rim of the Nanyang basin in present-day Nanzhao county (Figure 3.3). Further to the north, another large-scale ironworks has been found located in the northeastern hills of the Funiu Mountains, in present-day Wangchenggang, Lushan county, in which one of the largest furnaces of the Han period has been identified (Henan & Lushan 2002; Henan et al. 2021). Since the site is estimated to cover about 360,000 m^2, Wangchenggang has been claimed as the largest ironworks of the Han period yet discovered. While the ironworks was geographically beyond the Nanyang basin, these production locations to the north of Wafangzhuang would have been managed by the iron office in the Nanyang commandery, as Lushan and Nanzhao were both within the territory of the Nanyang commandery in the Han period. Besides large-scale blast furnaces, the discovery of iron ore from Wangchenggang confirms that iron smelting was practiced on the site. The discoveries of ceramic molds for casting agricultural tools and facilities for manufacturing fined iron indicate that the Wangchenggang ironworks also engaged in the production of final products, similar to the situation at Guxingzhen. Arguably, Wangchenggang might have supplied semi-raw materials to the remelting and casting centers inside the Nanyang basin, illustrating again some forms of labor division. Supported by production sites in the mountain areas and nearby large-scale centers in the foothills such as Wangchenggang, the Han state was then able to fully maximize the labor force congregated within the *duhui* metropolitan center and to transform Wan into a production hub for iron implements.

The third major cluster was found in the present-day Xiping-Wugang area to the east of the Nanyang basin. Since the cluster is adjacent to the Nanyang basin cluster, it remains unclear whether production sites within this group would supply raw materials to other centers in the nearby cluster like Wafangzhuang. Previous surveys and scientific analyses of remains have identified at least ten locations related to mining, smelting, and even refining, within the cluster (Qin et al. 2016). Since no cast molds were found in previous surveys, this cluster probably only conducted iron smelting to produce semi-raw materials. In addition, evidence of refining has been found from at least one location within this cluster, indicating that the cluster might have produced some tools via the forging of fined iron. Surviving texts in *Zhanguoce* mentioned that an iron production center of weapons belonging to one of the three Jin states, the Han state, was located in the Xiping-Wugang area.[18] During the Han dynasty, the empire might have reused the pre-existing mining and iron production systems and integrated them into the imperial network. By contrast, most of the ironworks within the Nanyang basin were built from scratch during the Han period.

Further to the east in Shandong province, the spatial relations of the ironworks are less straightforward than those of their counterparts in Henan. Most of the ironworks so far discovered are in sites surrounding the Taishan Mountain, as illustrated in Figure 3.3, and form a relatively concentrated cluster. Two of these ironworks have been systematically excavated and reported, and they were different in terms of their scale and the types of products produced.

The first example comes from the site located inside the Dongpingling walled town in present-day Zhangqiu, the capital town of the Jinan commandery. The ironwork covered more than 20,000 m², and its operational life stretched from the Middle Western Han to the Eastern Han period (Shandong et al. 2019, 2020). A total of 11 cupola furnaces, together with facilities for refining and a considerable number of garbage pits have so far been found. The major types of products from the ironworks, according to ceramic casting molds, were hoe-heads. Plentiful iron tools and weapons have been discovered at the site. Most importantly, at least two caches of iron ingots were identified, one of which contained more than 3,600 ingots weighing about 550 kg (Shandong et al. 2019). Since no iron ore has yet been found through excavation, the location is likely to have been a remelting center specializing in the casting of agricultural, and potentially other iron implements through forging on a relatively large scale. Like Henan, the Jinan commandery might have controlled multiple ironworks. An ironworks found in present-day Jinan city has been suggested as the other workshop under the control of the iron office of the Jinan commandery (Han et al. 2012; Zhongguo Shehui & Jinan 2018). According to the preliminary excavation report, this ironworks also specialized in casting spades, hoeheads, and various types of vessels, but no clear evidence of iron-smelting has been found. In other words, the two ironworks associated with the Jinan commandery specialized in melting, casting, and probably forging, by using scrap iron or ingots imported from other ironworks.

The Dongpingling case also provides rare evidence documenting a complex supply system of various production materials that was not captured by other textual records. One casting mold inscribed "*taiyi*" (the initial title of the first ironworks associated with the iron office of the Taishan commandery) has been found at Dongpingling (Shandong et al. 2019). Assuming the interpretation of the term "*taiyi*" is correct, at least one of the suppliers for casting molds might have come from the iron office of the Taishan commandery in present-day Tai'an, to the south of the Taishan Mountain. Even in today's iron industry, Tai'an and the adjacent Laiwu area are well known for the abundance of iron ore deposits (Li 2009; Liu 1989). Numbers of mining and iron production sites—some of them on a relatively large scale—have been reported within the basin in the southern foothills of the Taishan Mountain, known as the Tailai basin (Figure 3.3). The production centers inside the Taishan commandery probably supplied semi-products to the ironworks to the north of the Taishan Mountain, through the same transportation system which supplied bulky casting molds. If so, the operation of the two ironworks in the Jinan commandery relied on a network that required the collaboration of iron offices associated with different commanderies.

To the east of Dongpingling lies another essential production center in Linzi city, which was a metropolitan city between the Warring States and the Han periods.[19] The organization of the iron industry also presents patterns that have not been observed in other centers. At least six site complexes

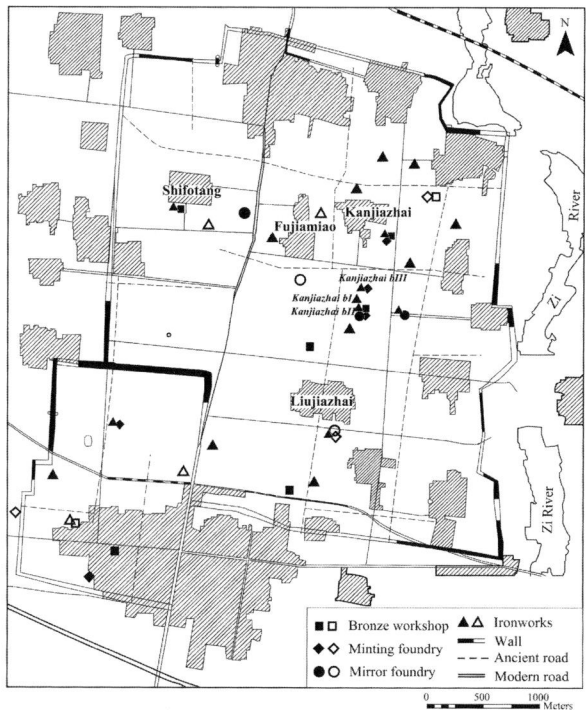

Figure 3.5 Layout of Linzi walled city and location of various craft workshops (redrawn from Zhongguo Shehui et al. 2020:Fig 5-1).

associated with iron production, two of which were larger than 400,000 m², have been found inside the urban center constructed during the Spring-and-Autumn period (Figure 3.5). The recent excavations at the village of Kanjiazhai have shown that this site complex consists of at least three locations, and produced cast iron and bronze mirrors. This discovery allows us for the first time to understand the internal organization of multi-crafting inside Linzi (Yang et al. 2013; Zhongguo Shehui et al. 2020; Yang 2021).

Fieldwork at Kanjiazhai makes it clear that some forms of labor division must have existed within the workshop area. Of the three locations at Kanjiazhai, Locus bI was associated with an ironworks dating between the Middle Western Han and Eastern Han periods. Forging hearths and kilns, probably for decarburizing cast-iron products, were aligned in a row, indicating that multiple units of workers were in action at the same time. Locus bIII conducted iron smelting/melting and casting alongside bronze minting. Its production activities date from the Early Western Han period, slightly predating the features at Locus bI. By contrast, Locus bII was a large bronze foundry specializing in bronze mirror production, and it is the only mirror production center so far archaeologically confirmed. Diagnostic casting molds attest that the bronze mirror foundry dates at the latest from the Early to the Middle Western Han periods. Collectively, these discoveries suggest that Kanjiazhai was a multi-crafting site complex, and that its operations were conducted on a massive scale.

While no remains of blast furnaces have yet been found, the studies of iron manufacturing waste identified at Kanjiazhai and other locations inside Linzi indicate that those ironworks conducted not only ore smelting and casting but also refining processes (Du et al. 2011, 2012; Liu et al. 2020). In other words, the production activities in Linzi basically include all the procedures outlined in Figure 3.1, a pattern different from the production system represented by the ironworks at Dongpingling or even at Wafangzhuang. Previous studies suggest that there were at least two large iron mines located in the southern foothills of the Taishan Mountain to the south of Linzi (Du et al. 2011, 2012). It seems that the multiple locations inside Linzi city, together with iron mines to the south of Linzi, constituted an independent production system. However, as our knowledge of the production and distribution system of Linzi mines is relatively limited, I have for the sake of convenience assigned Linzi to the Taishan cluster.

As I explained earlier, the map of four major clusters should be viewed as a conceptual tool for understanding the patterns of ironworks during the Han period. Due to the lack of contextual information and other ironworks nearby, I can only group together a limited number of sites. Several ironworks that were shown on the map, such as the ironworks in Tengguo Gucheng (Tengzhou, Shandong) (Shandong Jiningshi 1991), would not be introduced here. Also, there were doubtless more than four clusters of ironworks in the Han period. For instance, several ironworks have been found in the western part of Henan, which was the Hongnong commandery in the Han period. Located at the eastern entrance of the Guanzhong basin, these ironworks probably also supplied goods to either the capital region or the important political center of Luoyang. In addition, an ironworks has been discovered at Yuwangcheng in present-day Xia County, southwestern Shanxi (Shanxi 1994). Its remains include casting molds for chariot-fittings, vessels, and agricultural implements. *Hanshu* mentioned that the Hedong commandery, in which the Yuwangcheng ironworks is situated, was rich in its salt and iron resources.[20] More ironworks might have existed and clustered around the site. Similarly, iron manufacturing remains have been found from the urban center of Handan in present-day Hebei, another metropolitan center in the Han period (Duan 2009).[21] Since large urban centers could facilitate the mobilization of labor and the delivery of final products via the transport network—factors which might account for the prosperity of the ironworks of Linzi and Wafangzhuang—it is reasonable to suppose that an iron production center similar to the scale of the two cases mentioned above existed within the Handan urban center.

The clustering pattern mentioned above merely sketches out the general structure of the iron industry to the east of the Guanzhong basin. Their size,

ganization, and products might have differed considerably. But each clus-
r included at least one major center casting objects on a large scale, and
agricultural tools were usually the major types of goods manufactured by
these ironworks. The widespread discovery of molds from these ironworks
for casting agricultural implements is clearly related to the popularity of
ox-drawn equipment and the emphasis on agricultural production in the
Han period (Wagner 2008:224–228). Since fined iron was quite widely employed in production during the Western Han period, types of manufactured products from these sites probably included tools made by hammering
or forging, which would not have left such clear traces for archaeologists.
Nonetheless, other types of iron implements, such as iron weights, spades,
sickles, hammers, chariot fittings, and cast-iron molds have only been found
in a few ironworks (e.g., Wafangzhuang). At least judging by the types of
casting molds and final products found at the site, not all of them would
have produced a wide range of implements. By looking at the assemblage of
products from known cases, there seems to be a division between different
ironworks in terms of the products that they produced, which was contingent on the geographic location, access to resources, and, probably, the degree of supervision by the bureaucratic system.

To have brought the iron industry to its full development, the Han state
must have developed an extensive system to administer the ironworks and
coordinate production activities in various regions. Each iron office also
had to oversee multiple ironworks that engaged in different parts or stages
of production, as in the Guxingzhen and Tieshenggou ironworks. In order
to make casting production more efficient, these ironworks must have coordinated volumes of raw material provided as well as the timing of transportation. The same principle is also illustrated by other examples. At the
Dongpingling ironworks, the raw materials—iron ingots—must have come
from other production centers, either in the Taishan or Qi commanderies.
Archaeological evidence, therefore, indicates that these ironworks were
part of a coordinated network based upon a basic form of labor division,
sometimes even across different commanderies. Moreover, most of these
ironworks in different clusters specialized in the manufacturing of certain
types of agricultural tools. In contrast, only a few centers manufactured a
wide range of farming tools, vessels, and chariot fittings. This pattern indicates that subordinates of the same iron office, or even offices from different
commanderies, coordinated not only the transportation of raw materials
but also the finished products. Since some big ironworks evidently manufactured far larger amounts and types of products than others, and also relied
on supplies from other centers, a complex system spanning across several
regions was needed to transport finished products, raw materials, and even
production tools. Such a system certainly characterized the iron industry
during the Han period.

Because of the substantial development of the market system in the
Han period, the interregional transportation of iron implements stretched

beyond the Central Plains. As demonstrated by typological and scientific studies, iron implements were transported for long distances during the Han era. For instance, in Lingnan, on the southern border of the Han state, the types of iron implements found in Han tombs include swords, knives, lamps, caldrons, and several types of tools. Significantly, the typology of these iron products resembles that of the objects found in the capital region. Metallurgical analyses of iron products have also indicated that cast iron was the major type of raw material (Lam et al. 2020; Zhang M. et al. 2020). However, no cast iron foundries dating back to the Han period have been found anywhere in Lingnan. In fact, remarkably few iron workshops have been discovered in southern and southeastern China; only three ironworks have been so far identified, based on either archaeological or textual materials,[22] implying that iron implements found in the peripheries must mostly have been imported from outside, probably from the large-scale clusters in the broader Central Plains. The logistical problems of supplying finished products to other regions might have been one reason why ironworks in these clusters tended to be organized on a relatively large scale.

Given the unique technical characteristics of cast iron, the pattern of clustering production, and the evidence of long-distance distribution, cast iron products were not only implements which spelled "life and death for farmers", but they were also the medium through which the state could knit communities in various regions into a wider political and economic network. In order to understand how the flow of iron would intersect with the wide spectrum of the population and generate connectivity across large regions, a fine-grained analysis of manufacturing and transportation at the regional scale is necessary. Yet, no such comprehensive analysis has been attempted. For this reason, the case study of the capital region below provides critical information supplementing the macroscopic structure of the iron industry sketched out above. In the section below, I look at the manufacturing techniques of the Taicheng ironworks and iron implements from a cemetery near the Taicheng, to provide the framework for addressing these issues.

3 Iron-making in the Han capital region

In this section, I shift to focus on the capital region from the eastern part of the Han territories. Even though the capital region in and around Chang'an was undoubtedly the political and economic core of the Western Han, its iron industry has long been underexplored because only a handful of artifacts (Beijing Keji 1996; Du & Han 2005; Liu C. 1999; Zhang 2017), mostly from cemeteries, had been analyzed up until the discovery of Taicheng. As mentioned earlier, several ironworks have been discovered inside the capital Chang'an and other urban centers (e.g., Zhongguo Shehui 1995, 1997), but no systematic analysis has yet been conducted on manufacturing remains. Meanwhile, although celebrated for its agricultural production and advanced farming techniques, Guanzhong is not known for being a resource-rich area of iron. In this regard, the iron workshop named Taicheng, which is located within the area of Taixian during the Han period, and iron objects used as burial goods from a cemetery in the same community (Figure 2.7) shed particularly useful light on the iron industry in the region.

While remains from the ironworks provide information about the production system, the surviving material at best yields only a partial picture about the type of iron goods used by ordinary people in their daily lives. Burial goods from the cemetery associated with the Taixian therefore fill an important gap in our knowledge. To the northwest of the ironworks, the cemetery is one of the largest cemeteries outside Chang'an yet reported in Guanzhong. A total of 294 middle/low-rank burials have so far been excavated, of which more than two-thirds date to the Early Western Han period, contemporary with the ironworks (Shaanxi Yanjiuyuan & Yanglingqu 2018). Similar to the assemblage of iron objects from other cemeteries in the region, a total of 77 iron items have so far been found, of which almost 50 percent were iron vessels (including 23 caldrons and 16 plate-shaped lamps). The discovery of the Taicheng ironworks and the nearby cemetery provides a valuable opportunity for synthesizing the analytical results of manufacturing waste from the production site and the techniques of iron manufacturing from residential sites. A synthesis of these two lines of evidence enables us to reconstruct with a high degree of confidence the production and supply system in the Taixian settlement during the Han period.

The cast molds from the ironworks provide the most direct evidence of the type of products manufactured. A systematic study of molds published in the site report of the ironworks demonstrates that there were only three types of molds, for casting hoe-head implements, plowshares, and mattock chisels (Figure 3.6). More than 90 percent of molds discovered from the ironworks were of the first two types. There is no evidence to suggest that any iron vessels, chariot fittings, or other types of products (e.g., iron rods for smithing) were cast at the site. Nor have other types of agricultural tools such as sickles and hammers been discovered at the site, even though they have been commonly found in several other ironworks, including Wafangzhuang. The molds excavated from the site amount to at least 170 sets of hoe-head casting molds and 160 sets of plowshare casting molds (Shaanxi Yanjiuyuan 2018a:45). Only a limited number of product types were made at Taicheng, similar to the situation in other melting/casting centers, such as Dongpingling in Shandong province. It is also noteworthy that the types found at Taicheng represent the types of products manufactured by other ironworks in the capital region. Plowshare molds and chisels have also been reported from previously known ironworks such as the one at Nangucheng in Yongcheng.

While fieldwork has not so far turned up any kilns, the ironworks probably produced at least some of the molds for its own production. Over-fired waste products and molds without casting gates (i.e., the channels through which liquid cast iron was poured into the assembled molds) have been

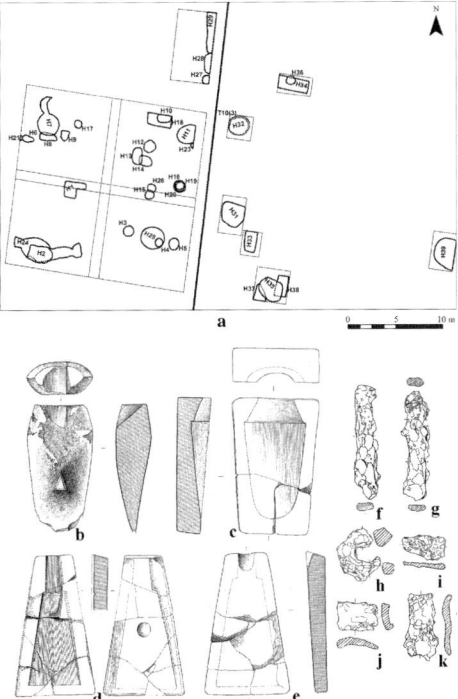

Figure 3.6 Plan of various excavated features at Taicheng and manufacturing remains found in the ironworks (a: after Shaanxi Yanjiuyuan 2018a:Fig
5; b: plowshare core, redrawn from Shaanxi Yanjiuyuan 2018a:Fig
15-2; c: plowshare mold, redrawn from Shaanxi Yanjiuyuan 2018a:
Fig 79-2; d: hoe-head mold, redrawn from Shaanxi Yanjiuyuan 2018a:Fig
42-2; e: hoe-head mold, redrawn from Shaanxi Yanjiuyuan 2018a:Fig 76-
4; f–k: iron pieces, redrawn from Shaanxi Yanjiuyuan 2018a:Fig 33).

found in several garbage pits (e.g., Shaanxi Yanjiuyuan 2018a:256, 301). If
the Taicheng foundry did not include facilities for mold production, this
type of waste would have been dumped adjacent to the production site,
rather than being transported to the casting site. Its presence confirms that
casting molds were manufactured on the site. Besides firing kilns, facilities
for clay or sand sorting and stations for preparing casting molds probably
also existed in this ironworks.

In addition to casting molds, furnace fragments, tuyeres, iron fragments,
and hammer scale (i.e., the oxidized surface layer of an iron object that falls
off during the hammering or forging procedure), other types of debris from
the ironworks were comprised mainly of slag remains. The microstructure and chemical composition of the large corpus of slag provide the most
critical line of evidence in relation to the techniques employed at the site.
According to a recent metallurgical study (Lam et al. 2018), most of the

slag remains subjected to analysis were waste products from the melting process. Two pieces of samples were likely related to finery, given the micro-structure identified. In other words, the Taicheng ironworks might also have engaged in small-scale fined iron production alongside cast-iron manufacturing. Since no ore fragments or slag clearly related to the smelting process have yet been identified, this also raises two important questions that need to be addressed by further research. Given the difficulty of transporting heavy, bulky iron ingots, did the ironworks use collected scrap iron as its only source of raw material? Also, is it possible to determine whether most objects used locally were manufactured by the nearby ironworks? The two questions can only be addressed through a more systematic analysis of the iron fragments from the site, including vessel fragments, broken pieces of iron tools (e.g., ring-pommel knives and axes), and irregular-shaped fragments whose original types were unknown.

Scientific analysis of iron samples shows that these fragments were made by various techniques, and thus might have come from multiple sources (Lam et al. 2018). It is worthwhile to explain the details of the results here to facilitate the discussion of the supply system of the ironworks. The majority of samples analyzed, which comprised 57 samples out of 107 pieces of analyzed metal (Figure 3.6:f-k), are either white cast iron, grey cast iron, or mottled cast iron. In other words, almost all iron samples analyzed were made using the cast iron technique. These cast iron samples could be either raw materials for melting/smelting or, if their shapes are irregular, manufacturing waste, such as bear iron. Also, four samples out of the total 107 analyzed were identified as fined iron, and another is potentially a bloomery iron.[23] The four samples identified as fined iron, or which used fined iron as their raw material, were probably fragments of some sort of tools, instead of semi manufacturing waste of cast iron manufacturing. In addition, among the seven samples identified as solid-state decarburization of cast iron are two special rectangular, thick bar-shaped objects that are very likely semi-products (Figure 3.6:f, g). Molds for casting this type of iron bar have been found at other large-scale iron foundries (Henan 2006; Li & Chen 1995), but not at Taicheng. The study of iron fragments, therefore, indicates that a wide range of raw materials were collected for use in production, including scrap iron and semi-products (or raw materials) procured from other production centers.

Since studies of iron found in ironworks only provide information on the types of iron techniques that were employed in manufacturing agricultural tools, the study of iron objects from the cemetery offers valuable insights into the kinds of iron implements that were used by contemporary residents. Studies have been made of the analysis of another set of samples, consisting of eight ring-pommeled knives, four large knives, four swords, four small knives, one nail, one tube (attached to a halberd), one axe, one *cha* spade, and one *ji* halberd. Results show that 11 pieces of them were steel/wrought iron made by solid-state decarburization of cast iron, in addition to one malleable cast iron and five objects of fined iron. It seems that solid-state decarburization of cast iron was the primary material used for manufacturing iron tools and weapons found in tombs. Although bar-shaped steel objects found in garbage pits, such as the one bar-shaped objects mentioned above, could also have been used for making iron implements that were found in the cemetery, no casting molds for making knives or rods were discovered during the excavations of Taicheng, unlike in other sites. In addition, of the four sword samples analyzed, the three with preserved metallic bodies have been identified as fined iron. The study of iron swords from Han tombs near Chang'an also shows that the objects were made of fined iron (Zhang 2017; Zhao et al. 2020). While evidence of fined iron manufacturing was found at Taicheng, the scarcity of such remains among the copious amounts of slag identified at the site suggests that the production of fined iron might not have occurred on a large scale and very regularly.

In reviewing the evidence from metallurgical analysis, melting and probably refining were the main techniques employed in iron production. By synthesizing the evidence from the production site that has been discussed before, the basic procedures of the ironworks would have included at least the following steps (Figure 3.7): mold making (e.g., clay preparation and mold firing), raw materials preparation (e.g., fuel, flux, and scrap iron sorting, crushing, and transporting), melting and casting, refining and smithing, and garbage cleaning (e.g., repairing furnace lining and dumping manufacturing waste). Whether charcoal burning took place at this location still cannot be addressed by the evidence we have collected so far. But Taicheng was the type of ironworks that was probably responsible for the entire production process from mold making to casting or even hammering or refining pig iron.

Although Taicheng was able to manufacture some types of iron tools, the comparison of the products from the ironworks and the assemblage of iron implements from the cemetery suggests that some objects included in

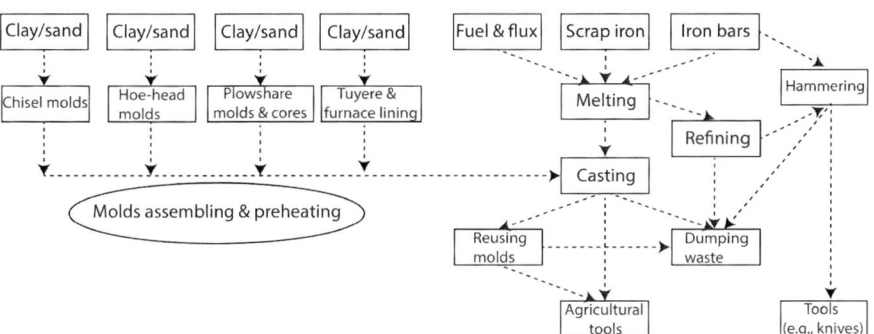

Figure 3.7 Process flow diagram showing the reconstructed production system at Taicheng.

tombs might not have been made by the Taicheng ironworks. As mentioned above, no vessel casting molds have yet been identified from the ironworks. Iron cauldrons and lamp stands must have been procured via exchange, even though it might have been more economical to produce them near a ruling center. More importantly, metallurgical analyses have demonstrated that ring-pommeled iron knives, the major type of implements found in the burial sites, were made of solid-state decarburization of cast iron (Lam et al. 2018). Given the complete absence of molds for casting iron rods at the ironworks, such knives might not have been manufactured entirely from casting to forging at Taicheng, even assuming that the ironworks would have produced this type of object through smithing scrap iron or forging imported semi-products (e.g., iron rods). The lack of evidence for large-scale manufacturing of semi-products, such as casting molds for iron rods or fined iron, indicates that the raw materials needed to sustain iron production were brought in from outside. The manufacturing of final iron products to support daily life might have relied upon other ironworks, especially those beyond the capital region, such as the one at Wafangzhuang, via external exchange.

The Taicheng ironworks, and probably other known ironworks similar to the Taicheng ironworks in terms of scale and assemblage in the region, appeared to have been a small production center making limited types of agricultural tools, primarily for farmers in Taixian or adjacent settlements. Even where the procurement and supply of iron raw materials were concerned, the operation of the ironworks also might not have been addressed solely by the recycling of scrap iron, given the relatively small amount of fragmented iron tools found to date. It appears that the ironworks must have relied on an exchange system to a great extent. More importantly, no other large-scale ironworks in the region comparable to ironworks like Wafangzhuang in the broader Central Plains have yet been discovered inside the capital region. The management of the Taicheng iron industry must have involved, at least partially, interregional exchange and transportation to secure the supply of raw materials or finished products from other clusters of ironworks outside the capital region for the local community.

Returning to the question that I raised in Chapter 2. The small scale of production might have potentially imposed a big challenge for the increasing demand of iron in the capital region as the Han state consolidated its rule. By looking at the ironworks in the broader capital region, I argue that the Han state, and probably the Qin state after its unification as well, employed a strategy of labor division in the management of the manufacturing system. Besides bringing ironmasters or artisans into the capital to increase local production, the Qin might have linked the iron production system and local societies to the broader system in regions alongside the Yellow River valley that were already developed before the Qin's unification. Following the Qin legacies, the Han state might have employed the same approach and further established large-scale ironworks beyond Guanzhong in regions where the iron industry was well established, especially after the implementation of the iron monopoly. The developed bureaucratic system of the Han state was known for its efficiency in managing and transporting information from the bottom village-level administrative unit, known as *li* ward, up the chain of management to the central court. In this light, such a system would have provided an important infrastructure that helped to link the various clusters of iron production centers into an exceedingly large-scale iron provision system through the coordination of the transportation of goods, raw materials, and labor force.

The study of the remains from the Taicheng ironworks has confirmed that small ironworks in the headquarters region relied upon the recycling of scrap iron as raw materials. But underlying local small-scale manufacturing the role of interregional exchange was also essential in the operation of the ironworks. Since the small ironworks could only address the demands for agricultural tools and, potentially, small numbers of other tools, certain iron products that were important in daily life in Taixian still required imports from other workshops, including those outside the capital region. Besides operating an internal system aimed at recycling material from nearby settlements, these ironworks and the nearby community must have relied on an external system for the procurement of raw material and supplies of finished products. In addition to local recycling, importation from a more extensive iron provision system beyond the capital region likely played a no less important role in the iron-related economic system. This mechanism of interregional exchange might also explain why so little manufacturing evidence has survived, given the huge demand for iron products in the capital region.

In addition, the strategy of regional division mentioned before would have reinforced the dominant role of the capital region, besides further integrating its economic system into the eastern territories through the transportation and supply of iron goods. The strategy would markedly transform the territories to the east of Guanzhong into necessity providers, supplying iron agricultural tools and other strategic materials like bronze and iron weapons, for those consumption centers inside the capital region. The labor division would also transfer the most labor-intensive parts during the entire process of iron-goods making, which would have become a factor contributing to social instability, to regions relatively distant from the capital. It is important to point out that the strategy of division is fundamentally different from the regional division of labor in the sense of modern economies; the latter assumes that a region or country will specialize in the production of a particular kind of good for which it has a comparative advantage[24] in order to maximize profits through trade. The regional division system in the Han period, however, was structured by the state mandate. Its aim was to exploit local resources in order to supply local demands and other ironworks beyond the area, particularly the capital, so that the production of metal products could eventually strengthen the economic and military power of the central court in the capital core.

Recognizing the characteristic of small-scale production of ironworks in the capital region, the following issue has to address how iron production was organized and interacted with the apparently nucleated, factory-like production centers outside the region. Given its small size, would such an ironworks have been an independent household production center, or in fact a small-scale centralized factory linked with other production centers outside the region? Since the small-scale ironworks had to rely on an external supply system, would its operation have fallen under some forms of state management? Also, what sort of men were the iron workers? Most importantly, what role did the small ironworks play in the integrated market system and the establishment of imperial connectivity inside the capital region? In the following two chapters in Part II, I present an in-depth analysis of remains to probe the organization of the ironworks in the capital region. I try to explain whether small-scale ironworks differed from their larger counterparts with regard to their organization. To further characterize the interaction surrounding the making and distribution of iron products, I also explore the relations between iron workers and their local communities through the supply of daily food. These two aspects can help to clarify the changes in social relations caused by the establishment of small-scale ironworks in the capital region, and the ways through which the iron industry in the capital was integrated into the grand production and distribution system portrayed above.

Notes

1 The analytical results of iron objects from the Taicheng ironworks discussed in this chapter is revised and elaborated from some material in a previous publication (Lam et al. 2018).
2 See *Hanshu* 72.3075. This passage mentions that the Han state employed *zu, tu*, and officials in various Tieguan to mine copper and iron. In addition, the passage indicates that more than 10,000 state laborers were exploited in the production related to copper and iron.
3 *Hanshu* 26.1311; *Hanshu* 10.314.
4 *Hanshu* 26.1311. Similar record about Su Ling's rebellion can also see *Hanshu* 10.323.
5 The abundance by mass of iron ranks the second among all metal in the earth crust and major rock's type, see https://en.wikipedia.org/wiki/Abundance_of_elements_in_Earth%27s_crust.
6 The smelting of cast iron also required flux (usually limestone) to facilitate the formation of slag. Unfortunately, the Minguo report did not include the amount of flux in the records.
7 For a general discussion about metal molds during the Warring States and Han periods, see Li (1994[1981]); Wagner (2008:154–159).
8 Malleable iron refers to wrought iron or medium-carbon steel that was made by cast iron through the annealing process; See explanation in Wagner (1993:290–291).
9 Grey cast iron means the type of cast iron with carbon in the form of microscopic graphite flakes; See Wagner (1993:344). This type of iron would be made by a prolonged consolidation process of cast iron liquid, or the heat treatment process of cast iron.

10 Mottled iron means the type of cast iron showing a mixture of grey and white-cast microstructures; See Wagner (1993:476).

11 Wagner suggested that, assuming the annealing temperature was 1,000 degrees, it will take 1.2 days to anneal a hoe-head, and at 910 degrees will give 4.3 days. But if the temperature dropped to 750 degrees, it would take 12 days. This is difficult enough in a modern electric furnace for holding constant for long periods. A variation of at least 50 degrees, probably much more, must be expected in a primitive annealing furnace; See Wagner (1993:359).

12 Welding usually refers to forge welding, which means two pieces of iron to be welded together are heated in the forge hearth to a very high temperature, typically in the range 1300–1400 °C; See Wagner (1993:274).

13 The anthropometric measurement of occupants' skulls suggests that results are statistically similar to samples from Zhou cemeteries in Shanxi (Chen & Deng 2017) instead of other comparative groups in Shaanxi. By taking the face value of the results, one may argue that the occupants might have had closer genetic relationship with communities outside the Qin territory, and that some members might have been migrants relocated in Guanzhong probably caused by the eastward expansion of the Qin state. Of course, this suggestion has to be supplemented by more evidence from ancient DNA analysis in the future.

14 For more information about the organization, see Chapter 4.

15 Based on the reconstructed size of one of the blast furnace and comparison with modern blast furnaces, Wagner suggested that the yield rate was probably several hundred tons per year, and that the area of forest needed to supply the necessary charcoal would have been several km^2 (Wagner 1993:265).

16 *Shiji* 129.3269.

17 For more in-depth discussion about "mother-molds", see Wagner (2008:156–159).

18 *Zhanguoce Zhanzheng* 26.5.1480, "Su Qin's persuasion wins Han for the Alliance"; transl. Crump (1996:460).

19 During the Han period, Linzi first belonged to the Qi Kingdom, then the Jichuan Kingdom, and eventually the Qi commandery after the rebellion of the Wu-Chu Kingdoms. It remains uncertain how the political disturbance and changes of the administrative system would impact on the organization and management of ironworks.

20 *Hanshu* 28b.1648. The exploitation of salt resources in this region might have been started as early as the Xia-Shang periods, or the 2nd millennium BCE; See Chen et al. (2010).

21 Since no large-scale excavations focusing on residential and workshop areas have been conducted, the date of those iron manufacturing remains still remains unclear.

22 For the excavation of those ironworks in the Han southern frontiers and related discussion, see Hunansheng et al. (2019); Lam et al. (2020).

23 Both fined iron and bloomery iron objects would include large numbers of densely-packed and deformed impurities, but their microstructure characteristics are different. For the details of identification, see Lam et al. (2018).

24 For two counties producing both A and B goods, if country 1 used the same unit of labor to produce more A goods but less B goods than what county 2 did, then country 1 can produce type 1 goods at relatively lower opportunity costs, i.e., having comparative advantage. As a result, country 1 will then intend to produce more type A goods for exportation while importing more from country 2.

Part II

4 Organization and labor division of ironworks[1]

The analysis of manufacturing remains in the preceding chapter indicates that the Taicheng and other small-scale ironworks in the capital region must have maintained a strong connection with an external production system to import raw materials and semi products. The concentration on limited types of products also indicates that residents even near the ironworks had to rely upon other production centers to procure a wide range of daily use goods. This raises several questions. Did the new imperial network also lead to any transformation in the way ironworks were organized in the region? Given the relatively small scale of the production area and its focus on limited types of goods, would the organization of labor in those ironworks be different from other large-scale counterparts? This and the following chapters in Part II take a closer look at archaeological remains from a microscopic perspective in an attempt to find out answers. By investigating the internal organization and the supply of daily necessities, these chapters further illuminate the operation of ironworks in the capital and their social relations with broader parts of the empire.

With regard to the Han economic system, previous studies (Kageyama 1984:271–284; Wagner 2008:156–159, 186–188) have suggested that, before the implementation of the monopoly on iron production in 117 BCE, most production took three basic forms. Besides the large-scale factory-like units controlled by the state that were introduced earlier (e.g., Guxingzhen and Wafangzhuang), those ironworks owned by ironmasters might have been operated akin to the system of iron plantations that were in operation in America during the 17th and 18th century conducted by self-sufficient communities under the head of iron masters in isolated areas, usually adjacent to forests where a reliable supply of charcoal could be found (Gordon 1996:33–44). Small-scale household units owned by private merchants or ironmasters also existed in the Han period, especially in small county-level towns. Potentially, these three types of organizations might have had various ways of interaction with the Han state. For instance, large scale factories were often managed by the state and had to rely on state support to produce goods for meeting a mandated quota. The operation of small-scale household production, in contrast, would have been driven primarily by the

DOI: 10.4324/9781003259220-7

commercial development and social demands in adjacent towns or cities. Since Taicheng was located in an area distant from iron ore deposits, and its primary operational period preceded the introduction of the iron monopoly, one may assume that the small-scale ironworks like Taicheng would be classified as household production units run by family members who made their living through selling iron goods, thus presenting an organization different from that of large-scale state factories. As explained in the Introduction, the connectivity of an imperial network was determined by various dimensions, including the way through which workers were organized and collaborated to finish various production steps. The investigation of the organization of both small production units and large-scale factories can thus provide a critical aspect of information for studying the iron industry and its contribution to the connectivity during the Han period.

The identification of the way workers were organized through the distribution of remains within sites, however, has been recognized as very controversial,[2] especially if only part of the workshop is excavated. For a quick illustration, we can use the case of Taicheng as an example. While it was known that the scale of the Taicheng ironworks was small, it remains unclear whether the workshop was in fact a household-production site operated as a family business or a small-scale factory that required more complicated coordination of workers, similar to other large-scale ironworks in the Warring States period. Archaeological records can only reveal a partial image of ancient societies instead of a full picture. Some frameworks derived from anthropological insight and examples from ethnographic fieldwork, therefore, will be helpful here, serving as a blueprint to piece together fragmentary records. In order to evaluate and interpret the forms of organization that various ironworks represented, terminologies that have been employed in previous literature need to be clarified. Furthermore, such an explanation also lays down the foundation for the investigation of "embeddedness" (i.e., the intensity of craft specialization and the connection with other members in the neighborhood or broader area) in the next chapter, a topic which is relevant to the interaction with the local economic system through which workers procured food to support their production.

1 Understanding the social organization of workers in "silent" records

Archaeology has a long interest in understanding how things were made in the past. Various models in archaeology have thus been proposed to conceptualize the forms that craft specialization would take, by focusing on attributes such as the scale of production units, the intensity of production, and the participation of elites or authorities (e.g., Clark & Parry 1990; Peacock 1982; Santley et al. 1989; van der Leeuw 1977; Sinopoli 1988). Of these conceptual frameworks, Costin's (1991) four-parameter framework probably has the broadest applicability to the classification of types of production in archeological study. In this framework, context, intensity, scale, and concentration are the four related dimensions that can articulate degrees of specialization and classify production sites into eight types (Table 4.1). Such a conceptual framework has also been demonstrated to be a useful heuristic tool for clarifying organization and management in several case studies in Bronze Age China, such as the production of salt and jade earrings (e.g., Flad 2011; Sun 2008), and it is therefore worthwhile here to first explain how these types of organization could be interpreted from archaeological evidence.

In Costin's framework (Table 4.1), the four parameters can be summarized as the time engaged in production, the distribution of producers, the requisite labor force and production area, and the relationships between producers and those who control the products. "Context" refers to the physical environment and "the social, political, and economic, and ideological milieus that structure relations among producers and between producers and consumers" (Costin 2007:150). "Attached" and "independent" specialization were usually used to distinguish two types of production system "context", corresponding respectively with those under the aegis of political institutes or elites and those without obvious governmental or elite involvement (ibid:152). "Intensity" is a scalar parameter with full-time and part-time at the two ends of the continuum, depending on the proportion of time devoted to a specific type of productive activity within a worker's overall time spent on production (Flad 2011:17), either in one day or another period of time. Although "scale" is literally contingent on size, in Costin's framework (1991) this parameter is also determined by types of social relations involved in the production, such as kin-based or using hired laborers (Flad 2011:23). The last parameter, "concentration", refers to the distribution pattern of specialists, and is contingent on the extent to which workers manufacturing the same type of products were centralized within a relatively small area. For instance, large-scale ironworks in urban centers could be viewed as a typical representation of centralized production. Using the four parameters, the eight forms of organization Costin identifies can serve as a conceptualizing tool for characterizing the ways workers were employed and the connection between the producer community and the overall management system.

Through incorporating these parameters—context, intensity, scale, and concentration—we can better conceptualize the term small-scale household production and clarify its differences from other types. It can be seen that this type of independent household production, which represents one potential type of ironworks organization mentioned above, is probably equivalent to an individual or community workshop that employed kin-based part-time labor, either within a nucleated or dispersed layout (Costin 1991:8), whereas state-run iron factories more closely resembled large-scale attached specialization by employing full-time, non-kin-based craftsmen, which would have been a nucleated convict or nucleated/retainer workshop.

Table 4.1 Definitions of the four parameters (upper) and eight types of specialization in Costin's framework (lower) (based on Costin 1991:11, 13, 15, 16; 2007:152)

Context: affiliation of producers and the sociopolitical components of the demand for their wares. Attached specialization makes and distributes goods under some ruling elites or states. Independent specialization makes and exchanges goods without overt elite or state involvement	*Concentration*: the distribution pattern of specialists across the landscape. Nucleated and dispersed are at the two extremes of this parameter	*Scale*: standing for the size of the workforce and principles of labor recruitment. Small, individual kin-based units and wage-labor forces that were employed based on skill are the two extremes	*Intensity*: referring to the amount of time producers spent in craft production. Part-time and full-time are the two extremes of this parameter

Types of "context"	*Types of specialization*	*Types of concentration*	*Types of scale*	*Types of intensity*
Attached specialization	Dispersed corvée	Dispersed	Kin-based?	Part-time
	Individual retainer	Dispersed	Kin-based?	Full-time
	Nuclear corvée	Nucleated	Labor	Part-time
	Retainer workshop	Nucleated	Labor	Full-time
Independent specialization	Individual Dispersed workshop	Dispersed Dispersed	Kin-based Labor	Part time? Full-time
	Community Nucleated workshop	Nucleated Nucleated	Kin-based Labor	Part time? Full-time

Even though these parameters derived from theoretical frameworks for identifying independent household production appear to be comprehensive and self-evident, applying such a framework in a specific context is easier said than done. In the case of Taicheng and similar small-scale ironworks, for instance, it is difficult to determine whether the identified production site was part of a nucleated community workshop or a small household center, based on the assemblage of remains identified. Also, without the help of other direct evidence representing the identities of workers, such as their burials and associated burial goods, the evidence related to manufacturing waste or even final products would be of limited use in determining whether workers were part-time or full-time, or kin-based or non-kin-based laborers.

The employment of these concepts as a means of differentiating independent household production units from other types of organization through the analysis of evidence for final products, manufacturing remains, and associated features in an archaeological setting of the Han period is also hindered by other challenges. First, small-scale iron production sites in settlements in the capital region have yet to yield clear evidence or background information (e.g., inscription records) showing ways of affiliation with the state. Nonetheless, evidence for distinguishing attached and independent specialization is essential for the identification of independent household production units. In an archaeological context, evidence in this regard includes artifacts or features that bear political symbols, such as seals or high-status architecture, indicators showing whether the raw materials were accessed by a limited number of people, and signs showing who controlled the process of distribution process (Costin 2005:1072; Flad 2011:27). Moreover, no other residential sites have been excavated within the Taicheng ironworks or other workshop complexes. Given the constraints of the archaeological evidence at hand and the absence of other textual records, it is difficult to identify the extent to which a specific ironworks might have been affiliated with the state and to determine the exact type of organization represented.

The clarification of the other two parameters, namely scale and intensity, through excavated features or remains related to manufacturing is no less complicated in the context of the Han empire. In theory, as a nucleated or retainer workshop would employ mostly full-time non-kin-based workers, evidence for long-term dwelling and daily residential remains should rarely be found near the production area of this type in the way one might expect near a modern industrial site (Santley & Kneebone 1993). As Chapter 2 introduced, the excavation and survey of ironworks in the capital region to date appear to confirm that no household structures were located within the surviving part (Shaanxi Yanjiuyuan 2018a:10). However, it is worthwhile considering whether this apparent absence of evidence might be contingent upon preservation since those sites were often partially destroyed in later historical periods. Meanwhile, examples such as the Taicheng ironworks have yielded considerable iron manufacturing waste and remain associated with food consumption. The concentrations of manufacturing waste, the absence of clear evidence related to residential houses, as well as the assemblage of other finds are collectively ambiguous when attempting to determine if small-scale (perhaps including large-scale) ironworks operated as an independent household production center, or a nucleated retainer, or even a nuclear corvée workshop.

In this regard, ethnographic and ethnoarchaeological studies of household craft production in prehispanic and modern Mesoamerica (e.g., Arnold

2014; Feinman 1999; Hirth 2009) can help elucidate the nature of independent household production units. Based on these comparative examples, management as a means of balancing various risks is always a fundamental feature of kin-based, independent production units in household settings documented by ethnographical records of pottery production. For potters working in household settings to be fully independent and entirely responsible for their own survival, and the ultimate distribution of the ceramics they produced, they need to employ various strategies to balance risks and reduce the impact of market fluctuation. Diversified economic strategies, such as farming or providing another service to the community, were thus adopted to supplement income lost due to changes in the pottery market. In contrast, potters in state-subsidized ceramic workshops can specialize solely in manufacturing. In comparison with full-time nucleated workshops, independent household production units, or individual/community specialization, as described in Costin's (1991) framework, cannot rely fully on a relationship within a specialized supply network that only interacted with limited groups of customers and produced goods continuously throughout the year. Archaeologically, a self-supporting system for daily necessities, the production of multiple types of craft products, and intermittent production should be viewed as more reliable evidence than the size indicating independent household-level production (Feinman 1999; Hirth 2009).

The ethnographic records published recently about a family-run cast iron foundry in Huize in present-day Yunnan, China (Yang & Li 2011; Yang et al. 2010) provide another set of useful information to further characterize household production in the context of iron production. Located inside a household in the town of Huize, this case is a small-scale ironworks specialized in casting two types of plowshares (Figure 4.1), which is similar to small-scale ironworks in the Han period. The ironworks was run by the owner together with six to seven hired workers.[3] All laborers worked inside a small station adjacent to the residential household of the owner. Within its six months of operation during the year, this small ironworks cast about 1,200 plowshares each month using sandstone casting molds with one furnace. During the non-production season, the owner had to rely on farming or repairing iron implements to make a living.

Given the small scale of production of the ironworks described in the previous paragraph, labor division between different production stages existed only in a primitive way. The making of casting molds using sand-stone—the most complicated procedure in the entire production process—was finished by the owner. Since such skill was only shared within the owner's family, other laborers were hired primarily for labor-intensive tasks, including filling fuel and ore, removing iron slag, and pouring iron liquid into molds. All these duties were shared among all workers without a clear division of labor. As a result, each worker usually had to perform multiple roles during remelting and casting. The modern ethnographical work shows that the way thereby those workers were collaborated was in a simple manner, unlike the

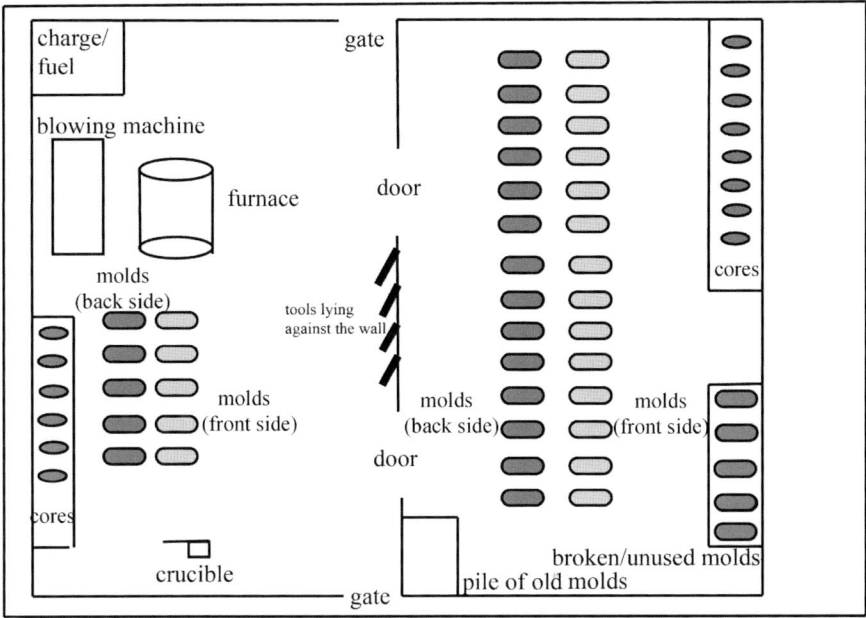

Figure 4.1 Plan showing the organization of the modern ironworks in Huize (after Yang et al. 2010:Fig 32).

situation in a factory in which each step is taken charge of by only one group of workers. Because of its small scale and rudimentary form of collaboration, the ironworks could only produce iron plows on a moderate scale for customers in the same county or towns nearby.

Readers must note that significant differences might have existed between the Han empire and modern China, not to mention pre-hispanic and modern Mesoamerica, in terms of their geographical conditions and social backgrounds. However, using analogies in ethnoarchaeological reasoning can still provide a conceptual tool for understanding the organization of various types of ironworking sites. Drawing together these strands from comparative examples, an independent household production unit can potentially be distinguished from workshops of the nucleated retainer or nucleated corvée/convict type, depending on whether kin-based labor was primarily employed in part-time specialization seasonally or year-round. Also, the site should at least not present evidence, such as an office building or seals, indicating that the elites or political institutions had the authority to directly control or oversee some or all components of the manufacturing process (Costin 2007:153). More importantly, household production might be expected to involve multiple types of economic activity including food production, and have associated evidence for residence on-site, in which workers may need to participate in most, if not all, procedures. If all of the characteristics of household production described in ethnographic work were shared by Han-era small-scale production, then the relationship between the production community and the overall economic system in which the production and distribution took place would present characteristics different from those of large-scale ironworks, or a different form of connectivity. While some of these domains might not be easily identified via archaeological evidence, comparing those small-scale ironworks with other cases with less ambiguous contexts, such as the Zhonghang and Guxingzhen metal production centers mentioned before, might offer additional help clarifying various parameters.

Of course, conducting a typological study of workshops using the four-parameters framework is only one way to speculate on types of labor organization. Other aspects, such as the way through which workers collaborated inside the workshop, are also essential in understanding the organization of archaeological and historical cases. In this vein, the framework proposed by the historian of science Ursula Franklin (1999) provides another useful classification for conceptualizing various types of collaboration. She proposed two concepts, namely holistic and prescribed specialization, to characterize two types of collaboration. The former refers to the system in which the same worker (or a small group of workers) was responsible for most or if not all production tasks. Instead of being made on an assembly line, products handcrafted by such a small group of workers would benefit from better quality control and more unique qualities.[4] In contrast, prescribed specialization indicates that "the making or doing of something is broken down into clearly identifiable steps" (Franklin 1999:12). In addition, each step will be carried out by a separate worker, or a group of workers, and the same set of tasks was conducted repeatedly. In a non-kin-based, factory-like workshop setting, the entire workshop is often subdivided into different sections. Each step of production will then be finished by independent groups of workers. The skills employed in production will demonstrate a relatively high degree of standardization, in order to maximize productivity. In archaeological records, the segregation of remains associated with different production steps might indicate operations of this type of organization.

Products that are mass-produced and require a sequence of separately executable steps prescribed with sufficient precision, such as bronze ritual vessels[5] in ancient China, often needed the collaboration of workers in a factory-like setting (Li 2007). Yet it is important to note that the assembly-line labor division might not be the only way of organizing labor for large-scale production. In the study of bronze arrowheads and crossbows from the Qin Shihuang's mausoleum, Martinón-Torres et al. (2014) differentiate the large-scale manufacture of standardized objects into two types of production models: single flow line production and cellular production; both cases would generally be called prescribed specialization in Franklin's framework.

Parallel to the widely known "Ford's model" pioneered by Henry Ford and the Ford Motor Company, the single flow line production means that the entire procedure was broken down into different parts and each production unit only performed each procedure, in which the production moves along an assembly line in a constant flow. While the efficiency would be greatly enhanced since workers needed to focus on limited procedures, any failure in collaboration would result in substantial waste, such as over-producing stocks of final products or components that could not be sold out or consumed in time. The second model, also known as cellular production, similarly involves the flow line in which the products move from one station to another on the assembly line to improve efficiency. However, workers in this case are first divided into small cells or units, and each cell takes charge of several stations. The division of workers into small units allowed some of these workers to produce only when demands were in place in order to reduce the risks of overstocking. Most importantly, workers at different stages in each unit would collaborate together, such as checking errors before passing down the products to the next stage, to reduce the waste from mass production of a single component and increase the flexibility to respond to consumers' needs, an approach that was developed by Toyota Motor Corporation in their car manufacturing and thus referred to as the "Toyota model".

By combining chemical analysis of bronze and statistical analysis of metric measurements of bronze crossbows and bundles of arrowheads buried with terra-cotta soldiers, Martinón-Torres et al. (2014) found that some variations often existed in different parts of bronze weapons. For instance, the same type of crossbow accessories found in different batches, such as triggers and string-hooks, are often varied in terms of their size and shape. Consequently, a particular trigger variant has to be assembled with one particular type of string-hook.[6] Based on the divergence represented, Martinón-Torres et al. proposed that bronze casters might have been divided into small units, and each unit produced batches of crossbows and other weapons, such as arrowheads, at the same time with their own technical preferences. In other words, accessories of triggers or other weapons were not manufactured by a flow-line in a highly standardized manner and then assembled together. One reason underlying this design probably lies in the quality control of strategic goods like bronze weapons that were hugely demanded by the Qin state in the unification wars. Cellular production, as explained earlier, would be more preferable in terms of the control of quality and waste reduction to an entirely streamlined model due to the multiple quality control checks in the production process. In addition, this model allows more flexibility for workers in each unit to adjust or make changes during the production process. For this reason, the cellular mode was probably more favorable in the manufacture of strategic materials such as bronze crossbows and arrowheads that were desperately required in the Qin state.

In most of the archaeological production sites, features that were found were often garbage remains, leaving a mixed pattern of debris and remains associated with various types. Through synthesizing the location of major manufacturing features and the operational chain of the site, I suggest that an archaeological reconstruction could still provide a glimpse of the basic organization evidenced by material records. The coordination of units or workers at different steps, if identified, would be useful for addressing how the workplace was structured. Other issues to examine include the spatial relationship between production and other daily activities that occurred at the site. As I explained before, there are no comparable metal production sites in the capital region predating the Han period published. Looking at other production sites in other territorial states before the Han period, however, contributes to understanding Taicheng or similar cases and addresses, at least partially, the core issue here of whether there was any transformation of labor organization in the iron industry that coincided with the emergence of the Han empire.

2 Making for the masses: the emergence of concentrated workshops predating the Han period

As noted by many previous studies, the technology of the iron industry was rooted in the pre-existing bronze industry.[7] Following Franklin's idea, I consider that technology is involved with not only techniques but also the organization and planning of labor. Since the evidence of a number of metal foundries has been published, the organization manifested by ironworks in the Warring States period offers more background for understanding the emergence of ironworks during the Han period. Two examples are thus particularly important for illustrating the social context and relations between workers in metal production centers before the Han period, and they both belonged to the Jin states. In Chapter 1, I addressed how the technology in the Qin state inherited a great duel from these contemporaries. The organization of metal workshops in these two states therefore provides insight for understanding the ironworks during the Qin and even the later Han periods.

The first example discussed here comes from the Niucun bronze foundry, which is situated in a site complex named Houma in present-day Houma city, Shanxi (Shanxi 1993; Shanxi Houma 1995). Houma is thought to have been the capital of the Jin state from the Middle of the Spring-and-Autumn period onward (Shanxi Houma 1996). The major components of the Houma capital consist of three adjacent walled towns, and the Niucun bronze foundry[8] was to the south of two of the walled towns, known as Taishen and Niucun. Its proximity to the capital clearly implies the association with elite management or state control of the foundry. Covering an area of 960,000 m^2, the entire bronze foundry consists of multiple locations (Figure 4.2). Among them, loci II and XXII are where extensive, systematic excavations were conducted during the 1960s, covering more than 4,000 m^2. Based on

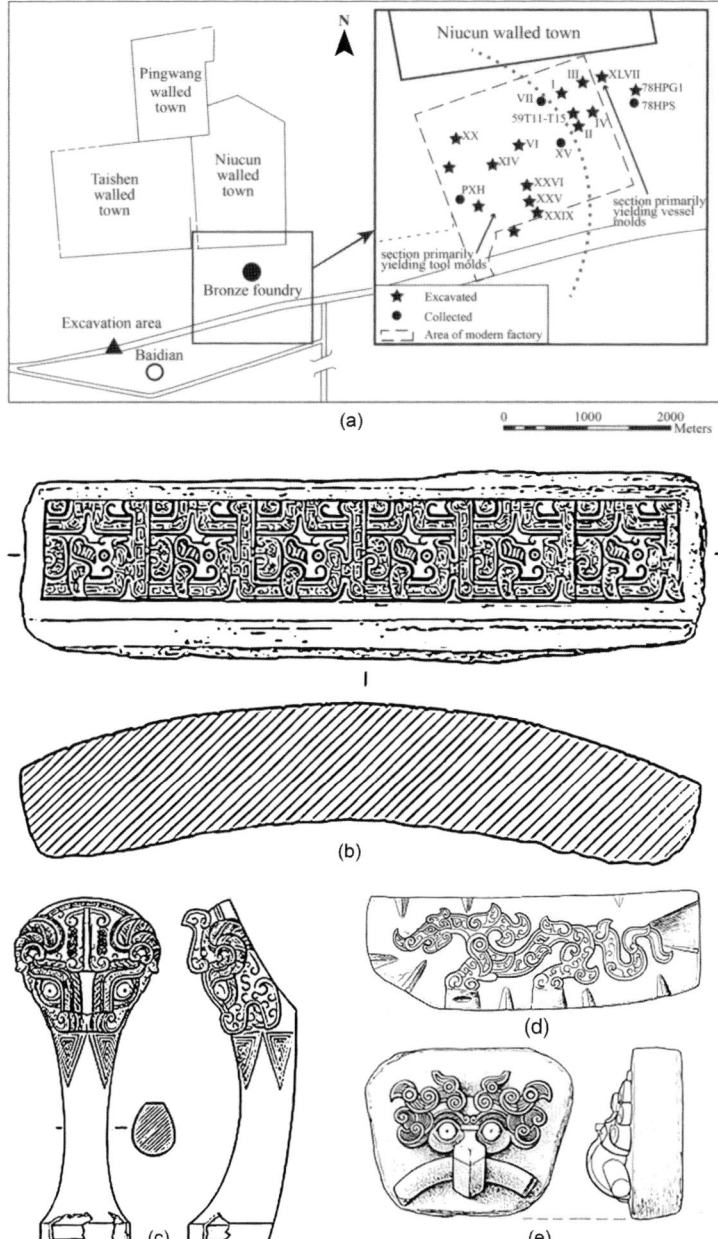

Figure 4.2 Location of the Niucun bronze foundry and molds/models for bronze manufacturing (a: location of various loci at the Niucun site complex, after Shanxi 1993:Fig 3; Shanxi 2012:Fig 2. The triangle represents another bronze foundry contemporary with the one at Niucun; b: example of a "pattern block" from locus II, redrawn from Shanxi 1993: c–e: examples of molds and models for casting various appendages; c: redrawn from Shanxi 1996:Fig 54; d: redrawn from Shanxi 1996:Fig 220; e: redrawn from Shanxi 1993:Fig 139).

typology, the site report suggests that the foundry dates from the Middle Spring-and-Autumn to the Early Warring States period—a critical time-frame of technological development witnessing the emergence of cast iron technology, but no evidence shows any iron melting or smelting activities taking place there within this time frame, even though the powerful Jin state was one of the iron-production centers during the pre-Han period (Han & Duan 2009).

Previous scholarship (e.g., Bagley 1993, 1995, 1996; Wan 1975)[9] has pointed out that the Niucun foundry in Houma adopted various techniques to increase manufacturing efficiency and speed up production. One of the techniques was the so-called "pattern block", which is a decorated model with positive carving for creating a strip of clay carrying negative imprints (Figure 4.2:b). Mold workers could then insert those imprinted strips in-side the place for a decorative band on a casting mold. During the Shang and Western Zhou periods, craftsmen needed to carve, incise, or stamp on each piece of section molds to create the decoration band before assembling them into a complete set for casting an entire vessel. Through the pattern block technique, decoration on bronzes could then be duplicated from only limited pieces of the decorative model so that the efficiency could be greatly boosted. In addition, the manufacture of bronze vessels was streamlined by another new technique, namely the "multiples casting" approach, through which different appendages, such as ear-handles and legs, were made sep-arately and then inserted into the molds for casting the main part of vessel body (Figure 4.2:c–e). All appendages would be locked in place when the assembled section mold was cast. Apparently, these two methods were in the interest of greatly reducing the time on manufacturing vessels and the probability of failures during one of these complicated procedures. The new technologies would also significantly raise the speed and efficiency of bronze production compared to the previous period insomuch that bronze vessels could be massively produced to meet social changes during the Spring-and-Autumn period (Bagley 1995; von Falkenhausen 2006:156–161; Yu & Gao 1985).[10] Since the amount of tool products produced by Niucun is extremely large, they might have been utilized mostly by non-elite individuals, even though the organization and management of production were probably still under the control of elites.

Along with the appearance of new molding techniques, the assemblages of ceramic molds from different loci also display several distinctive patterns, hinting at another approach to enhance efficiency through labor division. According to the site report (Shanxi 1993:3–5), the assemblages of molds from loci II and XXII, which are distanced from each other by about 1,000 m, were very distinctive (Figure 4.2). The percentage of molds for making woodworking or agricultural tools at locale XXII well outnumbered molds associated with ritual vessels. More than 10,000 mold fragments have been recovered from the locus, and over 90% of them are chisel/axe molds. Other types of casting molds, such as *kongshoubu* (coin) and small amounts of belt-hook molds have been found, but they only account for around 2% of the entire assemblage of casting molds. The chisel mold fragments found through the excavation might represent at least 6,000 individual pieces of bivalve molds (Zhang 1997). The assemblage of molds from locus II, however, is different from XXII and dominated by models or molds for casting sets of ritual vessels and musical instruments that were commonly found in contemporary high-status tombs. Also, only a limited amount of furnace fragments and slag have been identified in this locale, in contrast with the situation in locus XXII, where considerable furnaces and tuyere fragments were identified together with casting molds. It is likely that the excavated area in locus II was the section for the mold-making procedures or storage before casting.

Manufacturing waste has also been discovered in other loci adjacent to II and XXII, attesting to the idea of labor division. Near locus XXII, a pit that contained a significant number of chariot fitting and belt hook molds was found. Around 200 m to the south of this locus, more than 10,000 complete pieces of shovel-like *kongshoubu* (coin) cores were found at locus LIV (Shanxi 1993:3). In contrast with the scenario represented by locus XXII, the casting molds identified from other areas adjacent to locus II belong to ritual vessels. Based on this dichotomy, the site report proposed quite correctly that the northeastern corner of the foundry was a section that specialized in the production of ritual vessels, and the other part belonged to the locations for tools manufacturing (Figure 4.2:a). It is obvious that the bronze industry evidenced by the Jin state during the Spring- and-Autumn period was subdivided internally into at least two parts, which separately focused on the manufacturing of prestige goods and daily-use products. Because of its scale of production, foundries for bronze tools or coins might have adopted strategies and management systems attempting to enhance efficiency, which would also lay the foundation for the emergence of large-scale ironworks in later periods.

Since the speeding up of production efficiency was clearly an idea central to the bronze production at Niucun, and the new manufacturing technique of casting an entire vessel by joining several pre-cast appendants together embodied a basic form of assembly-line production, it opens to speculation whether the organization of casters and mold-makers in each location were also organized in a streamlined way to further enhance the production speed similar to the "prescribed" type of labor division, in which the entire complicated procedures were separated and carried out by different groups of workers who concentrated on certain production procedures. One potential way to speculate on this issue is to look at the details of the organization represented by the distribution of debris and production facilities at each production location. In the case of the Niucun site complex, debris of molds and furnace fragments were dumped with other residential waste (e.g., animal bones and serving vessels) in trash pits of relatively uniform size, which does not entirely match with the conventional definition of a workshop.[11]

Yet, there is little doubt that the context was considered to be a concentrated production area, since a significant amount of manufacturing waste has been found there together with other direct evidence of manufacture, such as kilns.

In Figure 4.3:a, I map the distribution of various features and two major types of casting molds in locus XXII, based on the records in the site report. The intra-site distribution map shows a rather mosaic pattern. The foundry includes three major types of features, i.e., subterranean houses and semi-subterranean houses, wells, and garbage pits. Debris associated with casting procedures (e.g., slag and furnace fragments) were identified in these features throughout the location. The distribution of debris did not show a clear-cut segregation pattern in which bronze remelting activities were concentrated at a particular location. Through close scrutiny of the distribution map of various features, it also appears that houses and wells were distributed almost everywhere within the entire locus (Figure 4.3:a). Those house features would have been used as storage facilities or indoor working spaces for making casting molds and other preparations for casting. The community of workers at Niucun would consume water on a large scale, thus requiring multiple wells to increase the supply, but wells would also be important facilities for production. By carefully reading the map, wells and houses were distributed throughout the entire excavation area, instead of concentrating within a limited area. According to the proximity of wells and houses, these houses and wells seem to be separated into several groups or clusters. Since the production and daily activities of casters had to center on these features, it is plausible that casters working in the locus were also divided into several small clusters or groups to manufacture bronze tools at the same time.

The same pattern was also found in the distribution of casting molds in locus XXII. The two main types of casting molds—chisel/axe and *kongshoubu* coin molds (Figure 4.3:b & c)—were only studied here, because the numbers of other types of molds were too limited for my observation. Based on the distribution map (Figure 4.3), these two types of molds were both observed from various parts of the foundry. While the quantity of *kongshoubu* molds is comparatively smaller than that of chisel/axe molds, the latter type of molds appears in at least two clusters that I divided in Figure 4.3. Furthermore, the distribution pattern of chisel/axe and *kongshoubu* molds suggests that the production of different types of artifacts was unlikely to be carried out by separated groups of workers. This pattern of producing several types of products along with remains associated with various procedures also appeared in other loci. In locus II where ritual vessels, musical instruments, weapons, and belt-hook molds or models were recovered, most features include models or pattern blocks for making various ritual vessels, musical instruments, tools, and even chariot fittings,[12] indicating that mold makers often made multiple types of products by employing the latest pattern block technique. While a preference for mass production increasingly determined

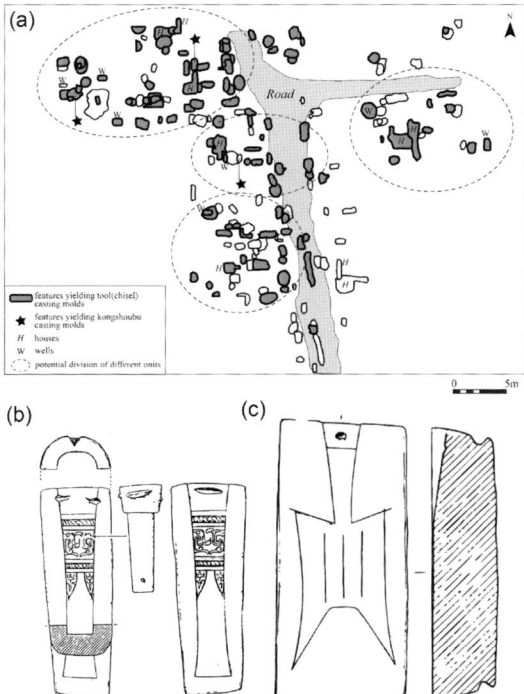

Figure 4.3 Distribution of various types of remains and features in locus XXII and the two main types of casting molds from the locus (a: layout of locus XXII, Late Spring-and-Autumn period, after Shanxi 1993:Fig 19; b & c: molds for casting chisel/axe and *kongshoubu*, b: redrawn from Shanxi 1993:Fig 39-7, c: redrawn from Shanxi 1993:Fig 46-1).

the new techniques employed in bronze making, workers at locus II might have produced molds for a wide range of products for the casting section in other loci, instead of focusing on a particular type of vessels to maximize the quantities of goods produced.

Based on the types of remains within the entire Niucun foundry, each locus seems to represent the division of labor by focusing on certain types of products. Such production zones might have been the most impactful organizational change to enhance production efficiency in response to the new social demands of ritual vessels and production tools (Bagley 1995, 1996). Nonetheless, it seems unlikely that each location would have been further subdivided into sections that only took charge of certain steps of the entire production process. Nor was the location divided entirely based on product types. The distribution pattern in these loci was so ambiguous that it is almost impossible to discern the existence of any sub-divided groups based on the types of debris. To explain the organization underlying such patterns, readers must bear in mind that various factors might have contributed to such ambiguity, including the depositional process, waste management, and clearance of contemporary waste; all these factors should be taken into account in the discussion of organization. In all possibilities, however, one critical factor may lie in the way labor was divided at the location. If casters and mold-makers in such a large-scale foundry were organized in a cellular model, in which workers in different groups would take charge of multiple tasks, including different procedures and even different types of products, the distribution of discarded remains would correspondingly represent a rather mosaic pattern without a clear-cut division of debris associated with different production stages such as the case of locus XXII illustrated.

The second case to look at in this section, the Zhonghang ironworks (Henan 2006), is located in the capital walled town of the Zheng and Han states in present-day Xinzheng City, Henan (Figure 4.4). The capital first belonged to the Zheng state during the Spring-and-Autumn period and was later, in 375 BCE, conquered and occupied by the Han state, one of the three successor states after the partition of the Jin state by three rival families. The layout of its walls is trapezoidal in form and consists of two sectors

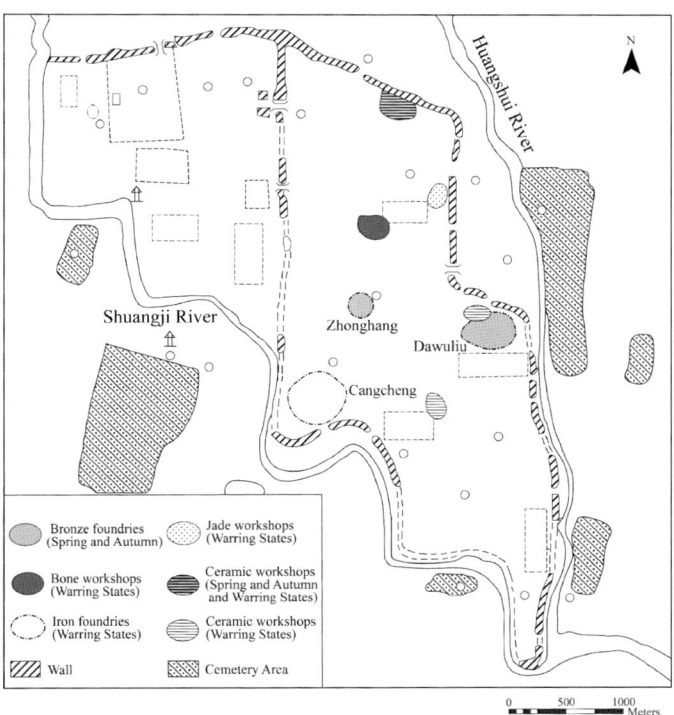

Figure 4.4 Plan of the Zheng-Han Gucheng (Xinzheng) and location of the Zhonghang ironworks (redrawn from Ma 1999:Fig 2; Wang 2010:Appendix 2).

divided by a wall in between. Situated inside the larger compartment, the Zhonghang cast iron foundry, roughly dating between 375 and 230 BCE, was established directly above a bronze foundry and a sacrificial venue dating to the Spring-and-Autumn period associated with the Zheng state. About 19 bronze caches and 80 sacrificial horse pits have been discovered underneath the Warring States stratum of the ironworks, which had been intensively excavated within an area totaling about 8,000 m^2 (Figure 4.5). While no intact furnace features have been identified, the discovery of furnace fragments suggests that the melting procedure would have taken place nearby the excavation area. At Zhonghang, like Niucun, furnace fragments and molds have been found in the same contexts. Iron and bronze furnace remains, which were identified through macroscopic observation, were also discarded *en masse* in at least 15 features scattering quite evenly throughout the excavation area. Since no evidence proves that the waste was deposited in provisional dumps beforehand, it seems reasonable to assume that various types of manufacturing waste were discarded adjacent to the locations where the manufacturing activities originally took place. In addition, the center part of the ironworks was an "empty" area free of garbage pits or features associated with production activities. At least 80 tombs contemporary to other manufacturing waste were found, including both adults and juveniles. The occupants of those burials might have been workers or family members[13] dwelling near the site (Figure 4.5:a).

Judging by the manufacturing evidence from Zhonghang, the scale of production appears to be enormous. The ironworks primarily manufactured *jue* axes and *chu* hoe-heads, two basic types of agricultural tools, and at least 1,000 sets of molds were found, also similar to locus II. Given the large numbers of casting molds identified at Zhonghang, the ironworks was clearly engaged in the manufacture of agricultural or production tools, as it was in Niucun locus XXII. The casting molds from the Zhonghang site included a wide range of goods, including iron bars (a kind of semi-products), bronze ornaments, and bronze coins; both types of manufacturing required the same fuel supplies and used similar techniques for making casting molds. Similar to Niucun, a number of metal workshops, either belonging to separate production centers or different locations of the same foundry, were found inside the urban center (Henan 2006). Previous fieldwork already uncovered at least three contemporary metal production workshops situated inside the walled town (Ma 1999). Of the other two workshops, one is located in Cangcheng (Liu 1962), while the other one is located in Dawuliu (Henan 1993, 1994; Ma 1999) to the east of Zhonghang (Figure 4.4). Primarily agricultural tools and coin casting molds were found but only very few remains for manufacturing weaponry (or, for that matter, waste products or semi-products of weaponry), an assemblage similar to that found at Zhonghang. Since those foundries were roughly contemporary, the evidence reveals a trend similar to Niucun, that multiple workshops were set up in order to boost the scale of production. From a brief look at the layout,

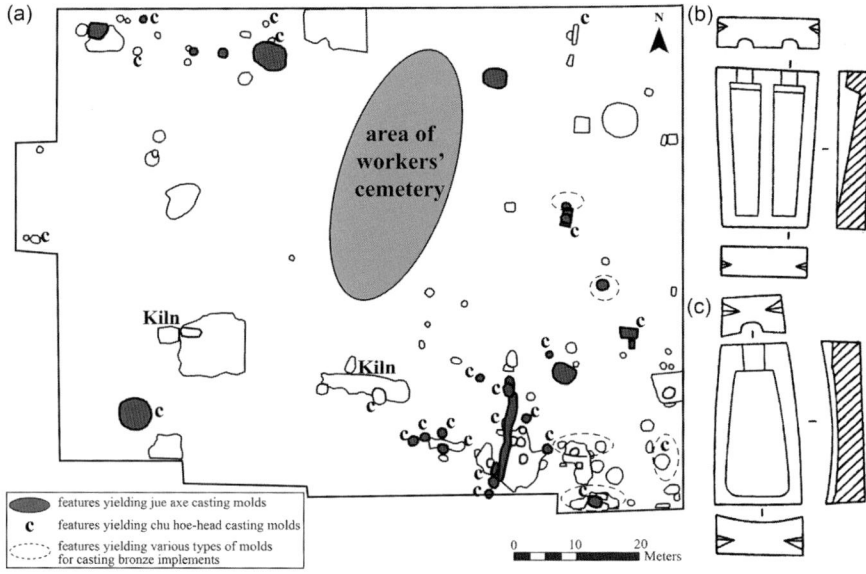

Figure 4.5 Distribution of various types of remains and features at Zhonghang ironworks and the two main types of casting molds for making iron implements from the ironworks (a: layout of the Zhonghang ironworks, after Henan 2006:Fig 491; b & c: molds for casting *jue* axe and *chu* hoe-heads, b: redrawn from Henan 2006:Fig 503-1, c: redrawn from Henan 2006:Fig 505-12).

the Niucun and Zhonghang foundries discussed here also seem to represent similar types of production organization because they both (1) operated on a relatively large scale; (2) were located in an area that was relatively segregated from other parts of the city; and (3) were engaged primarily in the production of agricultural tools. These three parameters show that the two foundries can be categorized as either nucleated workshops, nucleated corvée, or retainer workshops, based on the available non-quantitative information. But how were the iron and bronze industries organized at the same production site? Were various types of products actually segregated, similar to the subdivision of tools and ritual vessels at Niucun, or did they involve cooperation among the same group of workers? A deeper investigation into the production activities and discard patterns of different types of manufacturing waste is thus necessary. Based on a comparative study of intra-site variations in the distribution of the debris belonging to the metal industries at the same site, the following section will try to extrapolate how the production activities were arranged and how the workers in charge of the production of different products interacted.

The spatial distributions of the assemblages of debris from each feature are shown in Figure 4.5:a, which illustrates the distribution of three types of remains: casting molds of iron axes, casting molds of iron hoe-heads, and casting molds of various bronze objects (Figure 4.5:b & c). The distribution map of the discarded remains in the iron foundry presents several noteworthy patterns. The two types of casting molds for iron tools were found in most features together with other debris throughout the site, whereas bronze casting molds were found primarily in the southeastern part of the foundry (Figure 4.5:a). Nonetheless, bronze casting molds were found in nine features, four of which also yielded iron casting molds (Figure 4.5:a). The coexistence of remains suggests that bronze and iron objects might have been produced by workers in independent sections. No divisions between these two industries were presented in the case of Zhonghang. These patterns all point to the fact that the manufacturing waste of the two industries always coexisted in the same contexts or areas in the same foundry, and therefore the operations of the two casting processes took place very close to each other, possibly even at the same place by the same group of workers. In addition, no clear division between different types of products could be observed, nor did the procedures of iron manufacturing. There is little doubt that a labor force employed on such a scale would require management to make the production efficient. Yet, the distribution of remains and the layout of features yielded limited evidence to show whether the workshop area was divided into different parts based on different manufacturing stages or types of products.

The organization of the Zhonghang ironworks also indicates other commonalities with the locus XXII in Niucun. The ironworks appeared to produce certain types of products, instead of producing the whole repertory of daily-use iron goods. A certain degree of labor division between different production locations inside the capital town must have existed, probably to enhance the production efficiency. But within the area of each production center, the intra-site distribution of features suggests that the production processes were not structured based on a fully streamlined design. Nor could we observe a division pattern that was based upon the types of products or different stages. Various types of remains, for instance, molds for iron agricultural tools and bronze coins, were often found in the same contexts throughout the same location or production center.

Due to ambiguity in the intra-site distribution pattern of archaeological remains, it is not easy to draw a decisive conclusion about the internal organization of these two cases. But if the cellular unit was employed in the manufacturing of bronze weapons due to the consideration of quality control, we should again give some thought to the possibility that this principle might have been widely employed in organizing laborers in the production of other types of metal goods. Being a large-scale production center supplying masses of goods to residents within and beyond the capital city, the cellular mode of production might have provided the needed flexibility to adjust to different demands in terms of the types, quantity, or modification of manufacturing methods. The operation of multiple units for casting and other procedures at the same time would generate such a mosaic pattern of debris associated with different stages and features throughout the excavation area. Since the Warring States witnessed a substantial transformation that strengthened centralization, military reforms replacing chariot-military with infantry, and land-bestowing policies together with new taxation systems, the contemporary bureaucracy could have also provided the technological foundation to support the supervision and command of collaborating manufacturing units to meet the demands of mass production, which, in turn, laid down the foundation for the adoption of the cellular mode production in the production of iron and bronze implements.

3 The organization and nature of labor at ironworks in Guanzhong: a microscopic viewpoint

Besides the parameters indicated above, another important aspect with regard to the organization of production is the compositions of various types of labor force. During the pre-Han period, metal artisans and other craftsmen were mostly attached to the royal house or high-status lineage (Barbieri-Low 2007:41). Since these craft-specialized communities worked for noble families for generations, their status was thus probably hereditary. Only during the Warring States period did independent artisans gradually appear, along with the employment of state-controlled conscript and convict laborers in most craft domains (Lu 2018; Satō 1962; Sahara 2002[1994]). A good portion of craftsmen who produced goods at Niucun and Zhonghang were probably state-patronized craftsmen, but there is little known about the lives of workers mentioned in surviving texts predating the Han period (Lin 2014). Compared to the lack of information during the pre-Han period, surviving textual evidence from the Han period provides some valuable information for understanding the status of labor forces. The clarification in the greater volume of information available for the Han period helps not only to investigate the organization of ironworks but also lay the foundation for the exploration of the difference, if any, between ironworks in Guanzhong and other regions (e.g., Guxingzhen, Wafangzhuang and Linzi-Kanjiazhai locus bI) that were known to be state-run workshops. Therefore, it is worthwhile to explain the major types of labor in greater detail here.

By synthesizing textual evidence, previous studies have already suggested that labor force in various types of production included four general types: *yong, gong, zu, tu,*[14] which should cover the broad categories of craftsmen employed in most ironworks that we have already come across. Among the four categories, *yong* relates to waged laborers. During the Han period, those who were forced to leave their hometowns due to natural disasters or poverty often worked as hired laborers for entrepreneurs. The Han state would also hire waged laborers for state projects when the labor force of *zu* and *tu*, or conscript and convict labor, was not enough (Ma T. 2012). While hired laborers were likely used in iron production, especially in small private workshops predating the implementation of monopoly policies, I will focus on the last three types of laborers, as textual evidence, such as the passage disucssedin Chapter 3 (*Hanshu* 72.3075), clearly suggests that they constituted the majority of the workforce employed in making not only iron but also other craft goods.

In the Han period, *gong* was a community enjoying special status among the four categories. *Gong* literally means artisans and refers to skillful workers who had specialized techniques or knowledge essential to production. While some artisans might have been independent, and hired by the state workshop during a short period of time, most craftsmen with specialized knowledge were often under the control of *Gongguan*,[15] an administrative institute that manages craft production as attached labor. Luxury goods such as lacquerware and gilded bronze vessels were often made by *gong* workers' skillful hands. In the case of iron production, *gong* might be put in charge of procedures that require long-trained skills and knowledge, such as the preparation of the raw materials for mold making and smithing iron tools using the multiple-folding technique that was introduced in Chapter 3. For hard labor tasks, such as stoking the furnace during the smelting process, *gong* might also serve as a consultant supervising other low-skilled laborers.

In contrast to *gong*, *zu* and *tu* mean workers involved in hard-labor but low-skill parts in craft production and construction projects (Chen 1980:124, 193, 196; Yu 2006), and their exploitation by the state was conducted on a much more prevalent scale.[16] *Zu* literally stands for conscript labor. Each able-bodied man in the Han period had to serve as a conscript for a wide array of purposes, ranging from constructing canals and palaces, farming, to low-skilled jobs in state-sponsored workshops. Although each conscript's assignment would last about one month, the total number of conscript assignments in any given year would vary widely (Zang 2012:144–152). For independent artisans with specialized skills, they would be called on to serve as conscript artisans in official workshops instead of being used as low-skilled workers like *tu*, who would carry out hard labor duties such as loading fuel and ore to the blast furnace during cast iron production.

Tu in transmitted and excavated texts equates to convict laborers who committed crimes and were sentenced to hard labor (Wu 2012). For most common crimes, such as robbery, assault, forging documents, willful destruction of property, and so on, a penalty of hard labor for a four- to six-year term would be imposed (Barbieri-Low & Yates 2015:217, 226). These criminals comprised the largest group of unskilled labor in state-run workshops and construction projects. For male conscript labor, they were also given the dirtiest and most dangerous jobs, such as mining (ibid:231–232). For both convict and conscript laborers, their food ration was provided by the state. Each adult male would receive a ration of 2/3 *dou* (1.33 liters) of millet per day, and heavy labor would receive a larger ration of 5/6 *dou* (~1.66 liters) of millet. No provision of meat or vegetables was indicated in texts, but workers would be issued a set of clothes for the winter (ibid:236). Since the state only provided the minimum amount of food for them to survive, malnutrition would be very common.[17] In addition, it is not rare that those convict labor carrying out the most demanding labor were ill-treated by supervising officials. Even in the Yantie debate that I explained in the Introduction, the defender of the state monopoly policies, Yushi dafu (Sang Hongyang), acknowledged that "there may be subordinate officers who are not disinterested and do not give effect to the regulations, with the result that the people [conscripted laborers and convict labor who made and mold iron implements] are distributed and distressed".[18] Because of the unbearably harsh and brutal treatment, Su Ling, the convict laborer who was introduced in the previous chapter, and other state laborers had no choice but to join rebellions in order to escape the ironworks and the heavy yoke to which they were subjected. It is also important to note that, while conscript laborers were also employed in mining and other hard labor related to metal production, they worked only about one month in a year for the state. Officials overseeing craft production might not have overexploited them as badly as convict labor in order not to sabotage the formers' original farming production. The condition of conscript labor thus might not have been as miserable as convict laborers.

In the Han period, slaves (*nu*), or laborers serving non-redeemable work,[19] were also employed in craft production. These laborers were originally the wives and children of criminals with a warranty of hard labor or death penalty. While a good portion of them might have worked until they were dead, their social status was different from *tu*,[20] and were not the most harshly dealt with category of forced laborers. *Nu* slaves were used primarily as servants in household or smaller-scale state-run industries like textile production. During the Han period, some experienced male slaves with high skills were often employed in the manufacturing of luxury products such as lacquerware and bronze vessels. Slaves who mastered skills and knowledge in iron production might also have been sent to work for iron offices as technical consultants (ibid:254). In addition, iron plantations owned by masters or merchants and private minting foundries might have employed slaves[21] before the implementation of the iron monopoly, instead of more costly waged labor. Nonetheless, the scale of slaves employed in iron production was disproportional to the massive scale of convict and conscript laborers evidenced by textual records. Since a myriad of infractions in the Han legal code would stipulate penalties of hard labor, the pool of convict laborers would be easily refilled even with what was likely a high mortality rate caused by the harsh working environment. Also, the large numbers of convict and conscript laborers employed in state-run craft industries such as iron render the labor system of the Han empire remarkably different from that in its contemporary counterpart, Rome, in which slave labor was the main source of workers employed in various types of production and construction (Scheidel 2011, 2012; Yates 2002).

Since state-run ironworks often employed convict and conscript labor on a large scale, the production operation would have needed a management system to oversee those laborers who were not only reluctant to work but also prone to rebel against officials. While the management system left very few traces in surviving texts, the layout of various facilities might provide some clues for understanding how workers were organized at the production workshops. A brief glance at the layout of the ironworks discussed previously will demonstrate that facilities were often organized in an orderly manner. Some features for the critical steps, such as furnaces or the kilns for firing ceramic molds, were aligned in a row or in a systematic way. At Guxingzhen ironworks in the Songshan cluster introduced in the previous chapter, for instance, two side-by-side large-scale blast furnaces were found to be surrounded by various associated facilities, including ore crushing pits, mold-firing kilns, and houses for workers to process raw materials (Figure 3.4). The aligning pattern of features was also identified in other ironworks, such as Dongpingling and Linzi (Kanjiazhai locus bI) in the Taishan cluster. In the former case, at least two cupola furnaces aligned in a row were identified, indicating that they might have been operated at the same time by multiple units (Figure 4.6:a). Centered on these key facilities for iron melting were pits that contain considerable amounts of raw material (e.g., iron ingots), pits for clay-mining, and kilns for firing casting molds; all of them consisted of the critical steps in iron manufacture. In the latter case, six kilns have been found to be arranged in a row (Figure 4.6:b). Judging from the structure and layout, those kilns would be used simultaneously for the decarburization process of iron pieces and casting molds, near the area for melting and refining.

Underlying such spatial organization of furnaces and kilns, laborers would have been divided into different units to conduct the same stage of procedure at the same time, forming the collaboration that I view as "horizontal", which is different from the collaboration of sequential stages, or "vertical", in an assembly line. Given the large-scale of production represented by these examples, the multiple production units could not only enhance production efficiency but also provide a necessary tool for supervising those unfree laborers grouped in a confined space to work. Such well-organized alignment can also be often seen in the layout of royal ceramic workshops inside the capital Chang'an introduced in Chapter 2. Excavations have found that kilns for firing tiles or bricks for palaces or terra-cotta figurines were often aligned in a row. Inscriptions, often consisting of an abbreviation of an office title and a number, attest that the workshops were managed by the state and that state laborers were divided into different units coded by a numeric system to produce ceramics at the same time (Lam 2019). In contrast, ceramic workshops that produced daily use goods, which were less likely to be directly controlled by the state, did not show such an organized layout of kilns.[22] In this sense, the systematic and organized alignment might have been a "governing tool" through which the bureaucratic system could coordinate hard laborers and monitor the quality of products. Arguably, the cellular model of organization that was potentially manifested by previous

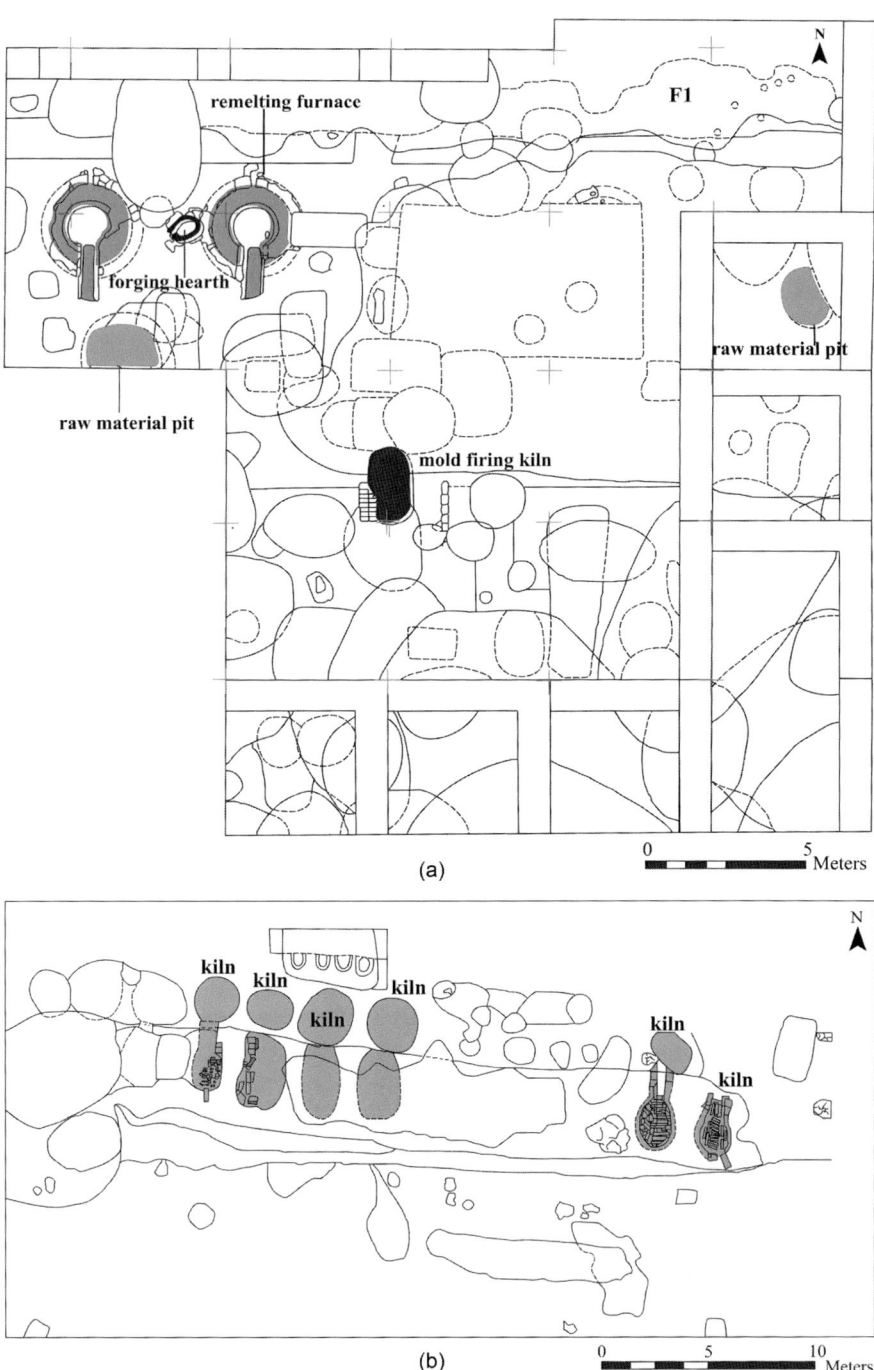

Figure 4.6 Plans of large-scale ironworks in the Taishan cluster during the Han period (a: Dongpingling, after Shandong et al. 2019:Fig 3; b: Linzi, Kanjiazhai locus bI; after Zhongguo Shehui et al. 2020:Fig 3-8).

large-scale metal workshops at Niucun or Zhonghang also belongs to the type of "horizontal collaboration" discussed here. Perhaps due to the development of the bureaucratic system and the tremendous increase in the convict laborers employed in various kinds of production during the Han period, the organization of space became more standardized, thus leaving more recognizable patterns in archaeological records.

Moving from Guandong to Guanzhong, the Taicheng ironworks appeared to stand in striking contrast with all cases mentioned above in several ways. The excavation and survey of the entire Taicheng complex did not attest to any household structure or kiln within the surviving part of the ironworks (Shaanxi Yanjiuyuan 2018a:10). Due to the absence of features directly related to production, I have to turn to the assemblage of remains in each garbage pit and their intra-site distribution to extrapolate the internal organization of the ironworks.

Given the discovery of various types of waste debris, the excavated area at Taicheng should be close to the casting and smithing locations. The analytical results explained in Chapter 3 suggest that all steps related to iron production took place within the area of ironworks, although the procedure for mold making might have been relatively further away from the excavated area. By separating out the remains found from each feature, a quick glance can also show the uneven distribution of remains across the ironworks. Although slag and molds were quite commonly found, there are only five features (H35, H15, H25, H5, and H4) (Figure 3.6) that yielded significantly low amounts of manufacturing remains. This special part of the foundry might have been related to workers' daily activities, such as resting or food consumption and therefore yielded very few examples of manufacturing waste (Figure 4.7). In contrast, the northern part of the excavated area was used for raw material sorting, iron casting, refining, forging, repairing furnace walls, and even mold making, although the specific location of these activities cannot be deduced at this stage based on remains from garbage pits. Related to this issue, the scarcity of serving vessels at the site, such as bowls, cups, and plates, was also notable (Shaanxi Yanjiuyuan 2018a:60–69). Such types of ceramics would be viewed as evidence of long-dwelling at the site and were often found at large-scale ironworks. Together with the absence of any cemetery within the ironworks, the organization of Taicheng might be very close to that of a centralized, full-time workshop in which workers came to work but did not dwell at the site after their shifts.

The joining signs left on both plowshare and hoe-head molds yield another important line of evidence that further speaks to the organization of workers at Taicheng. On the upper edge of hoe-head molds, two types of signs made by stamping or tube-lining were found, namely one-stroke and three-stroke markers (Figure 4.8). Such markers may facilitate the alignment of the two pieces of molds to assemble into a set for casting, but their variation does not seem to suggest any major functional difference.[23] It seems likely that these two types of signs were made due to the presence

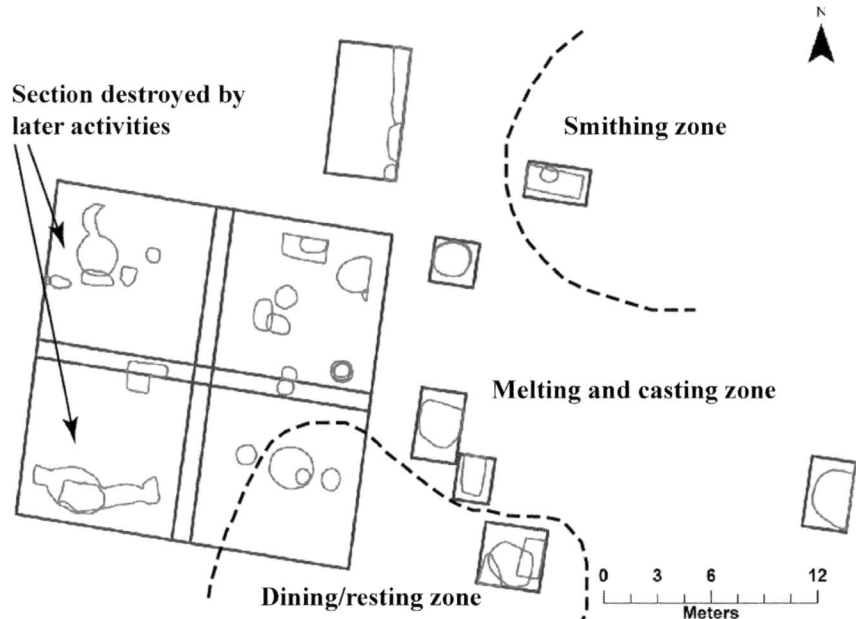

Figure 4.7 Plan showing the internal organization of the Taicheng ironworks (after Shaanxi Yanjiuyuan 2018a:Fig 5).

Table 4.2 Counts of assembling markers on hoe-head molds

	| | |	|	*Total pieces(individual)*
H3	17	1	110
H31	5	7	38

of at least two groups of workers working at the same time.[24] The intra-site distribution of molds with these two signs also shows a noteworthy pattern. In Table 4.2, I focus on two features in which a large number of molds were found since the small number of molds in some features might not be statistically significant. Molds with the first type of signs (one-stroke markers) were predominant in H3 (17:1) (Table 4.2), whereas products with the second type of signs (three-stroke markers) were found alongside products with the first type of signs from the other features, H31.

Supporting evidence also comes from the joining signs on plowshare molds and cores. Markers that were probably made by stamping on the upper edge of certain numbers of plowshare molds were identified, and they show a wide range of variation (Table 4.3). Similar to markers on hoe-head molds, these joining signs were intended to facilitate the assembly of two

Table 4.3 Counts of assembling markers on plowshare molds

	Assembling markers							
	Upper edge							
Types	⊥	–	‖	│	│_│			
Frequency	1	1	10	9	2			
	Bottom edge							
Types	│	—	‖	‖│	T	///	‖\│	7│
Frequency	5	3	2	1	1	1	1	1

(a)   (b)

Figure 4.8 Photographs of joining markers and spacers on casting molds (a: two types of joining markers on the top edge of hoe-head molds; b: two types of spacers on plowshare cores, photographed by the author).

pieces of molds and a core in between before the casting procedure. Similarly, on the surface of both sides of a plowshare core was found a protruding feature called a "spacer", which was the protruding part on both sides of a core to create the cavity between the core and the casting surface of the two molds after they were reassembled together to hold molten cast iron liquid (Figure 4.8). A total of five types of spacers were found on both large and small plowshare cores, indicating that the preparation of plowshare cores might have been divided into multiple groups. The intra-site distribution of different types of cores also presents a noteworthy pattern. The diamond (N = 8) and triangular- and rectangular-shaped markers (N = 13) were predominately found in H3. Meanwhile, cores with triangular-shaped spacers (N = 8) were found in the same context. But in H31 and other features (e.g., H33, H34, and H36), more often than not only the triangular-shaped spacer was identified (Table 4.4). Again, since the variation of spacers did

Table 4.4 Counts of different types of spacers on plowshare cores

		▲	▲ over ▢	■	◆	Total pieces (individual)
Large	H3	10	14	2	9	43
	H31		2			20
Small	H3	3			2	9
	H31	6				18

not appear to be functional, the pattern suggests that cores might have been similarly made by workers who were divided into multiple groups.

Collaboration of multiple units may also have existed during the casting procedure. Let's envision a streamlined scenario. If casters procured molds from all mold production units regardless of who made the products, the assemblage of molds and cores with various joining markers and signs would have generated a more mosaic pattern. When casting molds were damaged, casters would have discarded broken pieces bearing various signs into garbage pits nearby the casting area, thus creating a rather random combination of signs and marks on molds. Given the discrepancy of joining signs found in different garbage pits, however, it is likely that potential collaboration also existed between mold-making workers and casters. One possibility is that casting workers might have been divided into various groups, and, for some reason, each group procured casting molds from only certain groups of mold-making artisans (for illustration, see Figure 4.9). Working together as a unit, the collaboration between mold-makers and casters would potentially facilitate the control of the quality and quantity of products produced, such as checking with molds before casting and reporting to mold-makers issues that were found. As explained before, the cellular model might be more flexible in adjusting to the demands and controlling the quality of the final products in comparison with the streamlined production models. Meanwhile, such a division of labor would have served as a tool of supervision, especially in the case of state-controlled workshops. The concentration of molds with certain types of signs and markers in several garbage pits also opens to speculation whether the group of workers who produced certain types of plowshare or hoe-head molds engaged in casting using their own tools. Given that no production facilities have yet been identified, current data from the site do not allow us to overstretch such interpretation of the distribution of remains. Nonetheless, the variation of joining signs and markers on casting molds at Taicheng reveals the existence of labor division and coordination of units, a cellular principle that was attested by other large-scale ironworks. Even though the size of

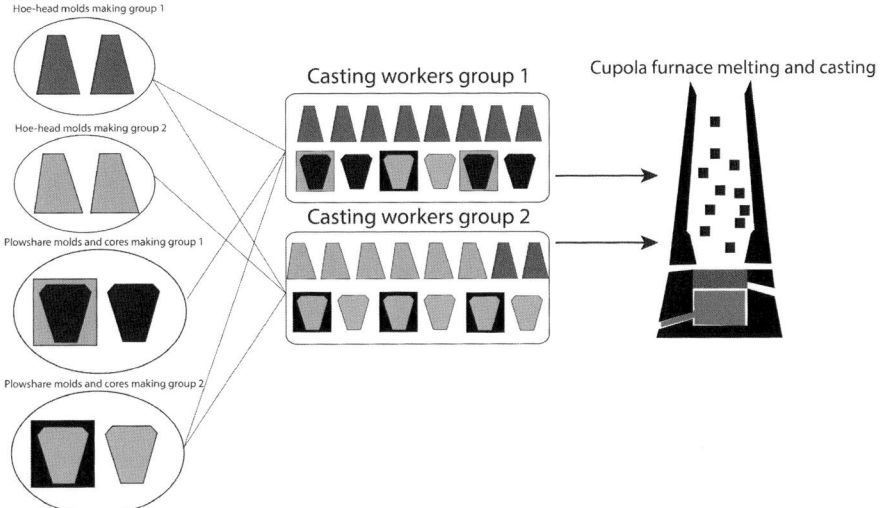

Figure 4.9 Hypothetical scheme showing the connection between workers taking charge of different stages of production at Taicheng (this scheme shows that the production of the same type of molds might have been conducted by different groups of workers. Molds of the same type but with different colors represent those products with different joining markers. Meanwhile, molds were not randomly passed down to casting workers. Each group or team of casting workers seemed to have had a connection with a specific group of mold workers. The assemblages of casting molds used by different groups of casting workers might, therefore, be different).

the production area would be viewed as being of a household level, the collaboration of different units represented by the evidence of casting molds suggests that the Taicheng ironworks was operated in a way that aimed to increase the efficiency of mass production, which is different from the modern case in Yunnan as explained earlier.

Even using only the small selection of casting molds discussed above, evidence from Taicheng throws light on the labor division and worker collaboration at ironworks during the Han period. Given the intra-site distribution of casting molds and other manufacturing waste, the organizing principle of small-scale ironworks in the capital of the Han empire was probably similar to other nucleated intensive production centers organized by the state instead of a family household workshop. As noted by several studies of craft production in regions outside ancient China, the development of an expansive empire and associated interregional connected network may not necessarily lead to an explicit transformation of craft specialization, either in terms of the technique, organization, or size of workshops,[25] even though such changes were often assumed to appear alongside the rise of an imperial entity. Building on the network connecting to production centers in various regions, the ironworks were able to procure raw materials beyond Han's capital region. But since maintaining constant supply was difficult given the limitation in transportation at that time, the cellular production model might have provided the flexibility to better cope with the fluctuation of supplies from other ironworks while ensuring that the ironworks provided sufficient tools for agriculture at the node of the iron transportation network. A centralized coordination over those units would thus be a key mechanism that fully made the local production become part of the national production system, no matter whether most workers were convict laborers controlled by the state or hired waged laborers. Reiterating the major theme of the book, connectivity did not only result from the trade and exchange of goods, but it was also generated at the more microscopic level, such as the coordination of cellular production mode through daily routines at minor settlements like Taicheng. In this light, the huge social demand for iron implements in the Han period might have been addressed by the network of small-scale centers, each of which was collaborated by a cellular production model.

Through this chapter, it is evident that the organization of laborers in iron production, or perhaps in the production of other metal goods, was an important governance tool for the Han state. Due to the lack of other textual information, however, it is hard to further extrapolate the state's involvement and specific type of organization. Certain issues in the framework explained in the beginning, such as intensity, cannot be addressed via the scrutiny of the layout. Also, the identification of horizontal collaboration has not yet fully ruled out the possibility that the Taicheng ironworks was managed as an independent household production center. Without the help of textual evidence, we must admit that the nature of the labor force cannot be fully illustrated via the study of manufacturing waste and final products. In the next chapter, I further explore the daily life of workers. In particular, I will examine the coordination between the workers and local communities in the supply of food that was evidenced by faunal and related remains, in order to situate iron production in a broader range of social relations.

Notes

1 The discussion of the theoretical framework about craft specialization is revised and expanded from the summary originally in Lam et al. (2019).
2 In archaeology, this type of distribution is also known as "intra-site" distribution, and has been discussed in the organization of craft production, see Carr (1984); Greenfield and Miller (2004); Hietala (1984); Simek (1989).
3 Nowadays only six workers are enough to carry out the production, since electricity has been widely adopted in the labor-intensive procedure such as bellow operation. But before the arrival of the electrification era, more workers were needed for the operation of an ironworks on a scale even as small as Huize.
4 Holistic technology does not mean that "people do not work together, but the way in which they work together leaves the individual worker in control of a particular process of creating or doing something" (Franklin 1999:11). In this sense, Huize ironworks mentioned above also belonged to this category.

5 It is known that bronze vessels in ancient China usually were manufactured by a process called piece-mold technique, which involves complicated procedures. To start with, mold makers would first use clay to build a model that looks like the final product. Then mold makers would place soft clay around the model to construct the mold, which would be cut into segments and removed from the core. During the mold-making process, ornaments would be executed on each piece of mold segments using various methods, such as stamping and adding raised ridges, so that high-relief motifs could be created on the surface of the final bronze product. To finish the casting, section molds would be assembled around a separate core. Spaces or chaplets would be placed between the core and molds to create the space for holding the melted bronze liquid, which then became the final product after the casting process. For the specific process of building section molds and the creation of ornament on the inner surface of casting molds, see Nickel (2006:9–10, 15–16). It is important to note that Robert Bagley disagrees with the idea of using tubing to create decoration on casting molds. Instead, decorative motifs should be made on the mold first (see Bagley 2009). Scholars working on casting molds from Anyang, however, suggest that both scenarios exist according to their close examination of molds from Xiaomintun (see Li et al. 2007). In other words, both ideas of decoration making-techniques probably hold true.

6 For an in-depth introduction about the analytical results and variations of bronze weapons from the Terra-cotta Warriors Pits, also see Li X. (2020b).

7 The number of bronzes manufactured in the Shang-Zhou periods indicated the scale of production was already tremendous in the pre-industrial world. The production and use of bronze agricultural tools during the Bronze Age, however, was very limited relative to bronze vessels and weapons. Furthermore, the excavations of bronze foundries dating to the Late Shang dynasty, like Xiaomintun (Yinxu 2007; Zhongguo Shehui Anyang 2006; Zhongguo Shehui 2020), northern Miaopu (Zhongguo Shehui 1987), and Xiaotun palace area (Shih 1955; Zhongguo Shehui 2004) in Anyang, as well as to the Western Zhou era—like Lijia (Zhouyuan 2007) and Kongtougou (Shaanxi Yanjiuyuan & Beida 2019) in Zhouyuan—have discovered limited amounts of molds for tools. Only during the Spring-and-Autumn period has the large-scale production of metal agricultural and woodworking tools been identified in archaeological cases, such as Niucun. Therefore, only this example is discussed for the purpose of illuminating the organization of bronze production.

8 According to previous archaeological works, there were at least two bronze foundries affiliated with the Jin Houma capital. Besides Niucun discussed here, the other one is located about 1.5 km to the south of the Taishen walled-town (Shanxi 2012). Nonetheless, this foundry has not been investigated as systematically as the Niucun foundry.

9 For a synthetic summary of those bronze production sites and manufacturing techniques, see Shanxi Houma (1996).

10 For a more updated discussion about the bronze manufacturing techniques of Jin-state bronzes, see Nan et al. (2019).

11 The definition of a workshop or manufacturing site thus appears not to be perfectly applicable in this case. According to Santley and Kneebone's definition, a workshop is a segregated area where a high density of debris is found without any domestic waste. In a residential setting, the wastes from "household domestic activities are normally placed in the same dumps, and there is little variation in midden content from one household to the next" (Santley & Kneebone 1993:39). In the Niucun case, residential waste was dumped in the midden within the workshop area and mixed with manufacturing waste.

12 For instance, the products made by the models and molds in one of the houses in locus II, F13, included *ding* vessels, *hu* vessels, belt-hooks, mirrors, and

chariot-fittings. In addition, a number of molds were used for casting appendages such as rings and figurines.

13 Inside the Niuchun bronze production site, a similar pattern was found at locus XXII which included a considerable number of tombs contemporary to the production activity buried inside the foundry area.

14 Based on the conditions of labor as a continuum of coercion, and gauged upon criteria of degree of control over work, restriction of movement, and restriction of life choice, Barbieri-Low divided labor (artisans) into seven types: self-employed artisan, wage labor artisan, independent artisan, apprenticed artisan, conscripted artisan, convicted-criminal artisan, and slave artisan (Barbieri-Low 2007:212–213). But for the discussion here, the four categories should be comprehensive enough for understanding the types of workers involved in iron production.

15 For an explanation of the Gongguan system during the Han period, see Gao (2019).

16 According to *Hanshu* 72.3075, more than 100,0000 people (*zu* and *tu*) were exploited for minting coins and mining copper and iron annually during Yuandi's reign (48–33 BCE). Therefore, Gong Yu, who were appointed the Yushi dafu (imperial counsellor) by Yuandi, criticized the state-labor system that "since an average farmer can feed seven people with his labor, more than 700,000 people somewhere were therefore starving".

17 Hulsewé provided an interesting information about the food rations for prisoners during the Second World War, which was, to a certain extent, comparable to convict laborers during the Han period in his translation of Shuihudi documents. As he stated,

> during the Second World War the prisoners of war of the Japanese in Singapore received 500 grams of raw rice daily as their main rations, with 50 grams extra for heavy work. This was supplemented by a modest quantity of vegetable fat and some self-grown vegetables, including red peppers. Occasionally they received a small piece of dried fish, but meat hardly ever.
>
> (Hulsewé 1985:33)

As I will explain later in Chapter 5, 1 ml of dehusked millet grain is equivalent to about 0.6355 g. The ration of 2/3 *dou* is equivalent to about 845 g of millet grain. However, since no other food was provided to state laborers, the food ration for a convict or conscript laborer in the Han period does not appear to be much better than a prisoner of war in modern times.

18 *Yantielun jiaozhu* 6.84, "Fugu"; modified from the translation in Gale (1967:34).

19 For the detailed differentiation between slaves and other types of laborers during early Imperial China, see the discussion in Yates (2002:314).

20 The issue of "slavery" in the labor system for state-sponsored industries and projects has attracted a lot of attention in previous scholarship. For instance, Wilbur (1943a, b) long ago synthesized evidence mentioned in texts, and concluded that, in the Han period even after the salt and iron industries became government monopolies, the government basically employed a large amount of corvée and convict laborers in the industries as well as large-scale projects such as the construction of mausoleums.

21 As Barbieri-Low (2007:252) suggests, "at least during the third to early second centuries BCE, private industrialists used slaves for those tasks in which the government would normally use convicts or a mixture of convicts and conscripts, activities such as iron mining and smelting".

22 One example can see the ceramic workshop in Linyi, Shanxi (Shanxi et al. 2012), which is one of the few cases of ceramic workshops that have been relatively well published.

23 Undoubtedly, these signs and markers were used to facilitate the mold assembling and to make sure the two pieces of molds align together. But according to modern ethnographic work (Yang & Li 2011; Yang et al. 2010), workers that are experienced in the process usually do not need to use these markers. In other words, the presence of markers and signs suggests that the scale of production was conducted on a relatively large scale.

24 Readers should note that at this stage it is difficult to tell as if different markers or signs were made by workers at the exact same time, even though these features date to the same archaeological phase.

25 In the study of craft industry in southern India during the Vijayanagara period (1336–1646 CE), for instance, Sinopoli (2003:313) provided an illuminating example in this regard. She suggested that the traditional model viewing the development of craft production as a process through which initial small-scale household industries was superseded by large and more complex organization units, alongside the political complexity process characterized by differentiated divisions of labor and expanded political economies, did not happen in South Asia. Evidence for a high degree of centralized administrative involvement in or control of craft production was absent (ibid:302); instead, small workshops structured at the household level remained. In this case, production was increased not by intensification through dramatic technological changes or organizational transformations, but by the increase of the total number of producers (ibid:157).

5 Food and economic embeddedness of iron production communities[1]

Craft production involves not only the processing of raw materials and the distribution of final products. Its efficient operation also requires constant supplies of daily necessities, especially food, to workers, if the production is conducted on a large scale. Besides consumers, other residents who support the operation of ironworks and transportation of raw material as well as iron products will be involved in the web of social relations created by the entire production sequence. The channel of food procurement and consumption can thus convey some important information about the organization of laborers and other aspects of their social lives.

In the previous chapter, I cast light on the similarities between Taicheng and the two metal production centers—Niucun and Zhonghang—in terms of the organization of labor. I also argued that, based on the intra-site distribution of remains and markers made by casters, there may have been collaboration across multiple cellular units in each case. Nonetheless, some issues underscored by the frameworks introduced in Chapter 4 have yet to be fully addressed. For instance, the measurement of the degree of intensity, or the so-called full-time versus part-time specialization, remains under-addressed in the case of small ironworks in the capital region. What other lines of evidence could shed light on the decision of producers and owners to diversify economic strategies and balance various risks? While I suggest that Taicheng is unlikely to represent a small independent household, whether the food supply system of cases like Taicheng would be different from other large-scale counterparts, given their size differences? In this chapter, I propose that the record reflecting the consumption of meat, i.e., animal bone remains, should be considered in the study of craft production, as this aspect will illuminate social relations between workers and the community in which they were situated, that otherwise cannot be generated from manufacturing debris alone.

In order to explain the approach to studying food consumption during craft production, I introduce the concept "economic embeddedness" in this chapter. This is a useful framework for synthesizing various lines of evidence potentially related to risk balancing and diversified economic strategies introduced in the preceding chapter but could not be easily addressed

DOI: 10.4324/9781003259220-8

by the distribution of debris. To employ this theoretical framework in the archaeological case study, I particularly look at faunal records associated with iron production sites. Together with other records about food represented by plant remains and textual evidence, we can gain insights into the connection between producers, adjacent communities, and customers (or patrons) in craft production, or in general the social relations between workers and their neighborhood.

It must be admitted that foodways in archaeological records include not only faunal but also botanic remains and evidence representing how food was prepared and served. The focus on faunal remains can best provide the basic information just about the type of meat consumed, the procurement of meat (self-raised or procured from market), and probably the manner in which domesticated animals were raised for the food supply. These aspects can be viewed as only one portion of contemporary foodways. This chapter will look specifically at records of animal remains, however, since animal bone assemblages have been more often published in the archaeological literature of craft production centers during the Qin and Han periods when compared with archaeobotanical remains. Animal bone remains, therefore, are more available for the comparative analysis of ironworks organization with which we are concerned here. In addition, the system of meat procurement and animal raising reflected by animal bone remains can also provide indicators, probably as important as botanical remains, for understanding the social relations as well the duration of times workers engaged in the production activities.

1 Food supply system and economic embeddedness

The last chapter shed light on various issues raised by the application of frameworks as a conceptual tool in the study of archaeological cases. As explained at the end of Chapter 4, there might not be explicit changes in either the manufacturing techniques or degree of workshop concentration presented alongside the emergence of a new imperial system (e.g., see Sinopoli 2003:32, 302). Drawing on Sinopoli's work on textile production during the Vijayanagara period (1336–1646 CE) in southern India, one approach to addressing these questions is to focus on the movement of products and raw materials between various economic spheres, as an alternative means of evaluating the relationships between craft production and state economies (ibid:36). Tracing the movement of final products in archaeological records will involve additional sets of questions, which I address specifically in Chapter 6. But in line with Sinopoli's idea, the movement of necessities for workers' subsistence should be incorporated, so as to understand the way through which production was integrated within broader social, economic, and political contexts. By studying the supply system for food, our understanding of the degree of interaction taking place within communities between specialists, patrons, and customers can be much enhanced.

154 *Food and economic embeddedness*

For illustrating the implication of food supply in the discussion of organization, I employ the concept of "economic embeddedness" to synthesize records, primarily related to faunal remains. I consider this concept as the representation of the degree of economic connection between producers, customers and adjacent communities that was established through the exchange of all types of manufactured products and the procurement of daily necessities to maintain the manufacturing in a craft production center. In addition, the embeddedness manifested by craftsmen would be shaped by various factors, including the market exchange of meat and other daily necessities, the capacity of the production center to be self-sustaining, and its relations with other members of the local community. It must be noted that the framework "economic embeddedness" is conceptualized in a way different from the widely known term "embeddedness" used in economic historian Polanyi's work (2001[1944]), which refers to the type of economic activities in pre-capitalist societies that were contingent upon social relations rather than rational calculation. As Feinman and Garraty (2010) compelling argued, Polanyi's definition underestimated an important fact that embedded "social relations" often played an important role even in modern economies. As a scalar variable, economic embeddedness here does not build upon the assumption of any non-rational calculation.

To facilitate the illustration, I try to provide a short, hypothetical example to explain the types of connections that constitute economic embeddedness. Let's imagine a large-scale ironworks named X in an urban center, similar to the site of Wafangzhuang introduced in Chapter 3. It would be very different from a family-run production center, Y, in smaller neighboring settlements at the same time, which was far smaller, employed far fewer non-relations craftsmen producing limited types of products, and only spent part of the year farming or working as hired laborers to supplement its income for the family year-round. In contrast, the workers in the X workshop were probably a mix of *gong* artisans and a large number of *tu* and *zu* (conscript and convict laborers) who collaborated and performed different tasks at different stages in the production process, or even in cellular units. As a state industry, each worker in the factory-like workshop X also received a food and clothing allowance commensurate with their status.

Now given the fact that workshops X and Y have both long been lost to the ages, it is difficult to know with certainty how they operated based only on features and manufacturing waste in these two sites, especially without any textual background. Nevertheless, there are several ways we might be able to trace some of the organizations in the archaeological record, such as the state-directed provisioning and the source of food supplies that were captured by archaeological evidence. Besides the status and diets of workers, the relationship between the state, groups of workers, and the communities that they are situated, or various kinds of embeddedness represented, can also be referred to by the provisioning system of daily necessities, especially food, represented in archaeological records.

The reason why animal remains, or more generally meat consumption, is relevant to the discussion here is that the types of meat consumed and the mechanism for procuring meat would reflect, at least partially, the nature of craftsmen and their organization. For instance, it is believed that full-time specialized craftsmen have to obtain meat from other members or through an exchange system, as most of their time would have been dedicated to production activities. According to the archaeological study of the urban food supply during the Bronze Age in Mesopotamia by Zeder (1988), indicators of such specialized meat provision can be accessed in the study collection through the management and distribution in the range of species, body-part representation, and age profiles for slaughtering.[2] Bone remains can therefore provide useful indicators with which to evaluate the intensity of craft specialization and the connection of food supply with other community members or neighboring areas, which can then be generalized as various degrees of economic embeddedness.

Using the concept of economic embeddedness, the dichotomy of part-time versus full-time specialization in Costin's framework can also be better articulated. In contrast to full-time nucleated or retainer workshops, household production units could not fully rely on an embedded relationship within a specialized supply network. Meanwhile, specialists in such settings only interact with limited groups of customers throughout the year. As a result, independent household production units usually have to diversify their economic strategy using various sources of income and food in order to support themselves (Hirth 2009). Conversely, a full-time and non-kin-based workshop (nucleated convict workshop or nucleated/retainer workshop), whether it was independent or state-controlled employing retainers, might not need to diversify its economic strategies because of more reliable supplies. In addition, as full-time laborers, the workforce is more reliant on their neighboring communities for support than part-time workers within independent household production units, who should have more time to spend on farming or husbandry as a means of procuring food resources to sustain themselves (Flad 2011:19). The major distinctive domains that characterized household production lie in the self-sufficiency in daily necessities (e.g., Feinman 1999; Hirth 2009; also see discussion in Chapter 4) to balance the risk in production.

Regardless of whether they were of independent or attached specialization type, full-time production units based on waged labor, retainers, or convict labor would have been deeply embedded in a specialized exchange network and relied on their patrons or other local specialists to procure raw materials and food. Workers in such situations would apparently be less self-sufficient and less flexible, thereby creating a unique type of economic embeddedness that was presumably distinct from the form of household organization discussed above. Of course, each type of organization sometimes employs more than one type of labor. For instance, a kin-based household production unit could employ some waged labor for low-skilled work and rely on the food market to a certain extent. Similarly, a state-run iron factory might have employed mostly convict laborers with a few *gong* artisans. Nonetheless, the cost of food, especially meat, was relatively expensive in the Han period. A strong degree of reliance on an external meat market for an independent production unit presumably could not be feasible. Consequently, the various degrees of reliance on an external food supply system and the self-sustaining food production system together could make the dominant species in the assemblage of animal bones and plant remains different between major types of production centers in archaeological cases.

For heuristic purposes, I consider that the types of organization relating to the study of the iron production centers might be synthesized as being embedded in the local economic system in at least two main ways (Table 5.1). The first of these can be labeled "simplistic economic embeddedness", which is the type occurring within local communities and is characterized by a self-sustaining mechanism that diversifies the supply. This case is more or less equivalent to "individual" or "community" specialization in Costin's framework, in which a self-sustaining food system and the crafting of multiple products were the major strategies for survival. As a result, no indicators should appear showing a deep reliance on a specialized food supply system, such as the concentration of consumption on animals that could be raised near households (e.g., pigs and chicken). For the second type, termed here "deep economic embeddedness", full-time workers in a retainer workshop or nucleated workshop (Table 5.1) produce limited types of goods and might be heavily reliant upon relationships with limited ranges of customers or suppliers. Because of their full-time manner of specialized production, the communities within nucleated retainer workshops were reliant upon a specialized food supply network and were associated with mechanisms that could efficiently draw customers to a location to access their products (Flad 2011:20) as well as distribute food to the workshop.

With the explanation laid out above, one possible way to identify deep economic embeddedness would be through its presentation in an urban food chain of meat supply. The food supply system for ironworks in the walled capital during the Warring States period probably belongs to this type. In such a scenario, many tasks are outsourced, and many hands are involved in meat butchering and distribution in such a setting (Landon 1997:160). The way in which meat was supplied might be characteristically different from cases in minor centers or rural areas that were less dependent on the urban food chain. Meanwhile, a low frequency of wild foods[3] such as game animals and wild plants is expected in the assemblage because food products would not have been raised or hunted by urban residents. Non-local and exotic food items would also be more likely brought into the city through a market system (e.g., Bowen 1992, 1994, 1998).

Besides the types of animals, body parts assemblage would reflect the change towards deeper embeddedness. Reitz's study (1986) of faunal remains from 16 sites in Georgia and South Carolina during the colonial and

Table 5.1 Types of economic embeddedness and corresponding types of workshop organization

Types of organization	Evidence of multiple types of craft production	Subsistence patterns	Archaeological evidence of faunal remains	Types of economic embeddedness
Individual/ community workshop, or independent household production (independent household-level production involved non-kin based members involved in a part-time manner)	Might engage in multiple types of craft production or have seasonal alternation; multiple types of craft production might involve goods that do not share similar types of resources such as farming or textile	Primarily based on a self-sustaining mechanism	Associated with husbandry	Simplistic
Nuclear corvée/ convict[a] (attached production involved non-kin based part-time labor)	Evidence for multiple types of craft production is very rare or indicates the sharing of fuel or raw materials	Evidence related to self-sustaining mechanism is very rare	Very few faunal remains would be found because of the low social status	Medium
Retainer workshop/ nucleated workshop (full-time non-kin based specialization that is with or without state involvement)	Evidence for multiple types of craft production is very rare or indicates the sharing of fuel or raw materials	Evidence related to self-sustaining mechanism is very rare	The taxa, assemblage of body parts, and age profile of faunal remains are likely to indicate that meat consumption heavily relies on an external source	Deep

a In Costin's framework, the attached production involved non-kin-based part-time labor refers to "Nuclear corvée". But in the Han context, corvée and convict labor were often used at the same time, especially for large-scale projects with low-technical requirements. Even though convict labor usually served for the state much longer than the duration of corvée, labor of these types were generally low-status and received very limited subsidies from the state. Therefore, we add convict labor to this category.

post-colonial period, which include both rural and urban contexts, demonstrated that faunal assemblages in rural areas always show more diverse patterns than their counterparts in urban centers. In a market economy, meat is professionally butchered and sold by retailers. As the commercial slaughtering of large mammals is prohibited within the dwelling areas of urban centers and occurs in specialized slaughterhouses that were far removed, more often than not slaughtering waste and non-meat anatomical elements are rarely found or are of low frequency (Henry 1987a, 1987b; Schulz & Gust 1983). As a result, the body part assemblage in urban contexts often concentrates on certain meat elements.

Another signature of the change in food reliance can be detected in the so-called kill-off patterns. Calculated by the proxy on bones indicating the age of animals when they were killed, such as the epiphyseal lines on long bones and tooth eruption, the kill-off pattern can illuminate how decisions were made to select animals of different ages to slaughter. Based on a study of Colonial New England, for instance, Bowen (1998) proposed that the increasing market for beef and emerging market for wool would eventually lead to commercial and specialized husbandry. As a result, the kill-off pattern of cattle in archaeological contexts should show that the majority of cattle were killed during their prime, whereas sheep and goats were slaughtered during old age given their value for continued wool production, along with the growth of a more specialized and intensified animal husbandry. For these reasons, taxonomic assemblage, body parts representation, and kill-off patterns in urban contexts are likely to demonstrate a pattern distinct from those in rural contexts that relied less on a specialized food chain (Landon 1996).

It must be acknowledged that types of economic embeddedness would not have corresponded precisely to specific types of specialization. For instance, workers in some types of organizations, for example a nuclear conscript/convict workshop, might also have some allowance of food from the government, such as the case of the conscript/convict labor system in the Han period evidenced by texts. Since these types of workers usually provided goods or services directly to the government, rather than to a specific group of customers in adjacent communities, and only a small ration of food would be provided, I consider that the degree of economic embeddedness of this kind of workshops probably fell somewhere between that of independent households and nucleated/retainer workshops (Table 5.1). In addition, some types of organization discussed in relation to previous conceptual frameworks, such as "individual retainers", "dispersed corvée", and "dispersed workshop", might not be differentiated when applying the concept of economic embeddedness. Instead, their identification must be contingent upon evidence explicitly suggesting official management, spatial relations with other local residents, and materials that can indicate the identity and rank of workers. Nonetheless, faunal records from independent household production centers, especially those located distant from major ruling centers, might reflect a pattern different from that in urban centers. Using the degree of embeddedness represented by food to evaluate the data, it is possible to outline the connection of ironworking communities with the broader communities.

In using the consumption patterns primarily reflected by animal bones to evaluate the reliance on an external food supply system, I assume that workers in a full-time specialized workshop working throughout the year had to rely on the supply from the state or intensive support from neighboring communities, probably through the meat market (Flad 2011:19). Thus, the bone assemblage in a retainer or nucleated workshop is expected to be different from an independent household ironworks, in that the latter would try to retain its flexibility and employ self-sustaining economic strategies such as raising livestock in the environs of the workplace. Meanwhile, information on plant remains will also be included in some cases if such data are available. As noted by previous archaeobotanical studies, the presence of carbonized grain from features is often attributable to the occurrence of cooking and crop processing activities nearby.[4] Using the procurement, exchange, and preparation of food as an analytical unit, the goal of this chapter is to evaluate the extent to which ironworking communities were attached to or had relationships with other communities in order to procure food and other daily necessities.

In addition to the reliance on a specialized food supply system, other factors may also have played a role in shaping the records evidenced in an archaeological context. For instance, the selection of meat products was also subject to social factors such as the functional differences of sites, cultural preferences for food, market availability, garbage disposal, and the like (Henry 1987b; Huelsbeck 1991; McKee 1987; Rothschild 1989; Rothschild & Balkwill 1993; Schiffer 1987). More critically, scholars have claimed that meat cuts from different body parts sometimes would reflect rank differentiation and thus be consumed by members of different statuses, in addition to the discrepancies between the dietary system in urban centers versus rural areas (Schulz & Gust 1983).[5] In order to articulate various factors involved in the food provision system, it is thus necessary to adopt a comparative approach. The comparison of datasets including animal bones and plant remains between Taicheng, the representative case in Guanzhong, and other cases (e.g., the Zhonghang ironworks in Zheng-Han Gucheng and Kanjiazhai workshop complexes in Linzi) in the broader Central Plains can provide important context in the interpretation of economic embeddedness.

The Han period's rich textual records and other related discussions of food in the literature (e.g., Hayashi 1975; Sterckx 2011) can also provide background information about the food supply system and social relations therein during the Warring States to the Han periods. Previous textual studies of Han period cuisine suggested that chickens usually were the major source of meat for commoners during that period (Yu 1977) because of the relatively high price of most types of meat in relation to the low wages of laborers. According to excavated written sources from the Hexi Corridor, in northwest China, livestock such as pigs and sheep/goats ranged in price from 200 to 1000 *qian*, and their meat was usually sold for about 2.5–7 *qian* per *jin* (equivalent to 244g) (Ding & Wei 2016:166–168) (Table 5.2). In places where animal husbandry was less well developed than in the Hexi Corridor, the price of meat would have been even higher. It is noteworthy that meat prices were already relatively high compared to the generally low incomes of ordinary people during the Han era, which was clearly stated in *Hanshu*:

> Now [at that time] if a man supporting a family of five persons [including himself] cultivated on hundred (*mu*) acres of [arable] land, each year from each arch he would harvest one and a half *shi* [of grain], making [a total of] one hundred and fifty *shi* of unhusked grain *su*. Out of this would be taken one tenth for taxes-in-kind......For food per person for one moon [he would require] one and a half *shi*, and for five persons for an entire year ninety *shi*......Deducting expenses which cost three hundred [coins]......For clothing usually each person required three hundred coins and five persons through the whole year would use one thousand five hundred, [so there would be] a deficit of four hundred and fifty [coins]. [Moreover] expenses in times of afflictions, illnesses both slight and grave, deaths, burials, as well as [military] taxes *fu* and other government levies were not included [here].[6]

Since this excerpt is claimed to record the incomes during the Warring States period (about 400 BCE), caution must be exercised when projecting the description to the Han period. In particular, the average yield rate for one *mu* would have been higher than 1.5 *shi*, thanks to the use of more effective farming techniques.[7] Nonetheless, since the tax burden was greater during the Han period, it is unlikely that the revenues of a family of five people would have been greatly increased. For this reason, only during the time without natural disasters and external warfare would ordinary people be well supplied, as one of the quoted paragraphs in *Hanshu* Chapter 24a at the beginning of this chapter noted. For hired waged labor, their incomes would have been only about 8–12 *qian* per day during the Qin and Early Western Han period (Ding & Wei 2016:279–282), which was low relative to what a meal containing meat would cost.[8] In Junyan, the Han northwestern frontiers, one *jin* of meat usually ranged from 2.5 to 9 *qian*. Given that meat (especially beef, pork, and mutton) was relatively expensive in the Han period (see Table 5.2), ordinary people (waged labor, farmers, and probably small merchants) might have found it impossible to regularly afford (Yu 1977), beyond consuming the occasional household chicken or pig to supplement their diets. Therefore, "those who guarded gates in villages and lanes ate fine grain and meat" were conceived as one of the signs of prosperity and sufficiency when the "nation lived without general disturbance" during the reign of Wendi, Jingdi, and the beginning years of the Wudi.[9]

Table 5.2 Price of livestock mentioned in textual records (unit: *qian*)

Types of livestock	Price for each animal, source: Song (1994)[a]	Price for each animal, source: Liu T. (1999)
Horse	5,454	
Cattle	1,200/1,818/3,750	2,500/3,000
Sheep/goat	150/177/500	250
Pig	300/900	
Dog	100/121	
Chicken	23/70	36
Rabbit	29	
Fish		3.33

a In the excavated documents, usually several prices were listed for each type of livestock, probably related to the fluctuation in the market.

Archaeologically, it is thus expected that investigation would identify certain food patterns in contexts associated with independent household production in the Han period. An independent household unit would rely primarily upon a self-sufficient food provisioning system rather than procuring meat from the market (Table 5.1). Presumably, excavated faunal assemblages might consist primarily of chicken bones with a smaller component from domesticated livestock such as pigs, which could be raised in a courtyard. In contrast, the consumption of meat in a nuclear corvée or convict workshop should be low as a result of their low status and the minimal amount of staple food provided, even though the workforce was economically embedded in and reliant upon local communities for its food. Animal bones should therefore be rare within any midden deposits present, and probably would not include those of valuable livestock, such as cattle. In contrast, retainer workshops, in which the majority of workers were *gong* state-supported artisans, and nucleated workshops employing mostly waged labor, should both show the strongest degree of economic embeddedness among the category of workshops under consideration here. In the latter case, most workers relied upon a specialized food provisioning system, and faunal remains beyond poultry are more likely to be found. Yet, evidence of food preparation would be scarce in the latter case. In the following section, I will use case studies of the Warring States and Han periods respectively to illustrate how this framework can facilitate the discussion about small-scale iron production in the capital region.

2 Deep economic embeddedness in Warring States' metropolitan areas

To better understand the social relations manifested by the pattern of food consumption in those Han ironworks, I will first look at the faunal remains from Zhonghang. This collection of faunal remains provides a means of understanding the food system associated with a concentrated factory-like workshop in a walled capital. Ideally, using datasets in the Guanzhong basin might have been more relevant, making datasets comparable. But Zhonghang is the only available case related to craft production with a thorough faunal-remain database for comparison in the pre-Han periods (even including the Han period) that has been hitherto fully published.[10] Within the intensively excavated area, all zooarchaeological results were systematically published both in the full site report (Luo et al. 2006) and in an online database.[11] In addition, the context of the Zhonghang ironworks is unmistakably associated with a centralized nuclear workshop. Since the Zhonghang site is adjacent to palaces and high-status architectures within the capital, its location and proximity to buildings that are indicative of governmental control suggest that they were most likely attached to the state and related to a specialized supply system (c.f., Fargher 2009). While the site is located beyond the Qin-Han capital core, its natural setting in general is similar to the Guanzhong basin. Any discrepancies between Zhonghang and the Taicheng case that will be examined below are likely related to the food strategies or supply system associated with urbanization and changes in the management of ironworks, instead of their geographical environment. This example was thus appropriate for comparatively assessing the degree of specialization and social connections of the other ironworks in the Han period.

Before taking a closer look at the assemblage of faunal remains at Zhonghang, a brief introduction about the types of animals consumed during the earlier Western Zhou period in the region will help further contextualize the results and interpret the implications for social organization. One important case in this regard comes from a stone earring workshop at Qijia in Zhouyuan, one of the headquarters of the Western Zhou dynasty with a dense population, located in present-day Shaanxi (Ma 2010). According to the analytical report, the assemblage in the stone workshop was dominated by cattle, which consists of 37 percent of the assemblage of NISP[12] of all identified taxa. Other majority taxa include sheep/goats (22 percent) and pigs (20 percent). Together with cattle,[13] these three types of domesticated animals represent about 80 percent of taxa identified in the assemblage. Deer, rabbits, and chicken were comparatively few. It is likely that the assemblage of faunal remains represents the types of domesticated animals that were primarily consumed in urban centers during the Zhou period or even earlier during the Late Shang period (Hu 2012; Li et al. 2010; Li et al. 2011).

Looking at the dataset in Zhonghang, a great deal of similarities can be observed. The assemblage of faunal remains in this ironwork is relatively similar to the broader tradition represented by the earring workshop during the Western Zhou period. In terms of the faunal assemblage, the NISP values of all identified species at Zhonghang consist primarily of cattle, pigs, sheep/goats, dogs, and horses (Table 5.3). In the assemblage, the percentage

Table 5.3 Taxonomic representation at the Zhonghang and Taicheng ironworks

		Zhonghang		Taicheng	
		Count	%	Count	%
Bos taurus	Cattle	562	28.4	97	18.8
Sus scrofa	Pig	398	20.1	49	9.5
Ovis aries/Capra hicus	Sheep/goat	78	4	37	7.2
Canis sp.	Dog	75	3.8	73	14.2
Equus caballus	Horse	117	5.9	19	3.7
Odocoileus virginianus	Deer	90	4.6	3	0.6
Rodentia	Rodent[a]			14	2.7
Unidentified fish				3	0.6
Gallus gallus	Chicken			3	0.6
Anas sp.	Duck			1	0.2
Unidentified birds		7	0.4	7	1.4
Large mammal		324	16.3	59	11.5
Mammal		323	16.4	150	29.1
Total		1,974	99.9	515	100

Data source: Luo et al. (2006); Shaanxi Yanjiuyuan (2018a: Table 13).
a   Rodent that was found in the assemblage may be intrusive.

of cattle (28.4 percent) is significantly higher than all other species, followed by pigs (20.1 percent); both taxa represented the major types of meat consumed. In addition, deer and horse bones at Zhonghang account for 5.9 percent and 4.6 percent of the total NISP respectively, and these values are higher than those of sheep/goats (4 percent) and dogs (3.8 percent). At Zhonghang, the small portion of sheep and goat bones in the assemblage appears to be the main discrepancy between the Warring States ironworks and Western Zhou stone earring production center. For some reason, sheep and goat husbandry might have experienced a decline during the Warring States period. In the Zhonghang assemblage, there are only two specimens identified as bird bones. The meat contribution of poultry in this case might not have been very high, but the low frequency might also be related to the archaeological recovery and collection methods employed during excavation.

While sheep and goat husbandry does not seem to have played a key role in the meat provision system for ironworkers in the Zheng state in comparison to the case during the Western Zhou era, the similarity of the overall range of husbandry within the assemblage between the two cases suggests that a meat supply network associated with the urban system was often characterized by a reliance on cattle and pig consumption. Supporting evidence can be seen in other datasets contemporary to Zhonghang. According to the report of faunal remains from ironworks and bronze foundries in the Kanjiazhai site complex in Linzi, the three major types of animals consumed calculated by NISP during the Warring States period include pigs (169), cattle (115), and dogs (108), which account for the 35 percent, 28 percent, and 22 percent of the total NISP respectively, together with small amount of horses, sheep and goat, and deer bones. Except for the prevalent consumption of dog meat in the Qi state, the meat subsistence patterns between Zhonghang and Linzi are rather similar. While Linzi is relatively far from Zhonghang and the Guanzhong basin, a heavy reliance on beef seems to be the common characteristic of a specialized meat provision system, especially in urban centers during the pre-Han period. In addition, the prominent role of cattle was probably associated with a developed transportation system that was able to procure cattle from farms outside the urban centers.

The body part assemblage at Zhonghang can help to further characterize the meat procurement system reflecting a deep embeddedness. In order to better depict the acquisition pattern of different cuts of meat at Zhonghang, I use "recovery rates"[14] to represent the proportion of different skeletal elements of the three major species: cattle, pig, and dog. In Figure 5.1 (for illustration of the body parts with the first two highest recovery rates, see Figure 5.2), the cattle bone assemblage appears to be dominated by cranial elements, followed by humeri, scapulae, and tibiae; the latter group represents relatively meaty parts. Lower limb bones such as metapodials were not well represented at Zhonghang. Similarly, distal limb bones such as the calcaneus, talus, and phalanges, bones of the axial skeleton such as axis and atlas, and humeri and femurs are scarcely not represented relatively in the Zhonghang assemblage, suggesting not every part of the cattle corpse was evenly presented in the remains discovered.

In the body parts assemblage of pigs (Figure 5.3; for illustration of the body parts with the first two highest recovery rates, see Figure 5.4), it is also of interest to note that, like cattle, the skull and mandible are similarly the most dominant elements. Although some meaty elements, such as humeri and femurs, were represented in the Zhonghang assemblage with a recovery rate of about 20 percent, appendicular bones, especially those related to more meaty party like limb bones, are significantly underrepresented. The lower limb bones, such as metapodials and phalanges are also significantly

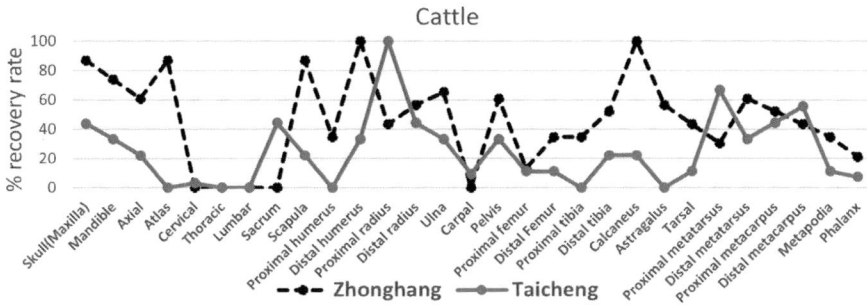

Figure 5.1 Recovery rates of cattle elements from Zhonghang and Taicheng.

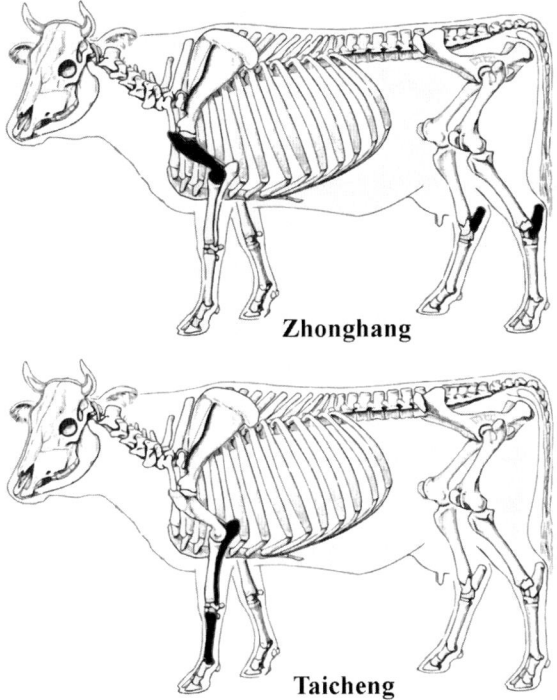

Figure 5.2 Illustrations that show the elements with the two highest recovery rates among the cattle skeletons in the Zhonghang and Taicheng assemblages (redrawn from König & Liebich 2020:Fig 1.28).

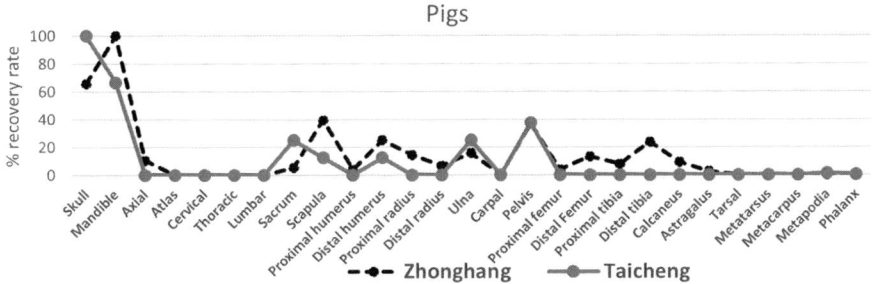

Figure 5.3 Recovery rates of pig elements from Zhonghang and Taicheng.

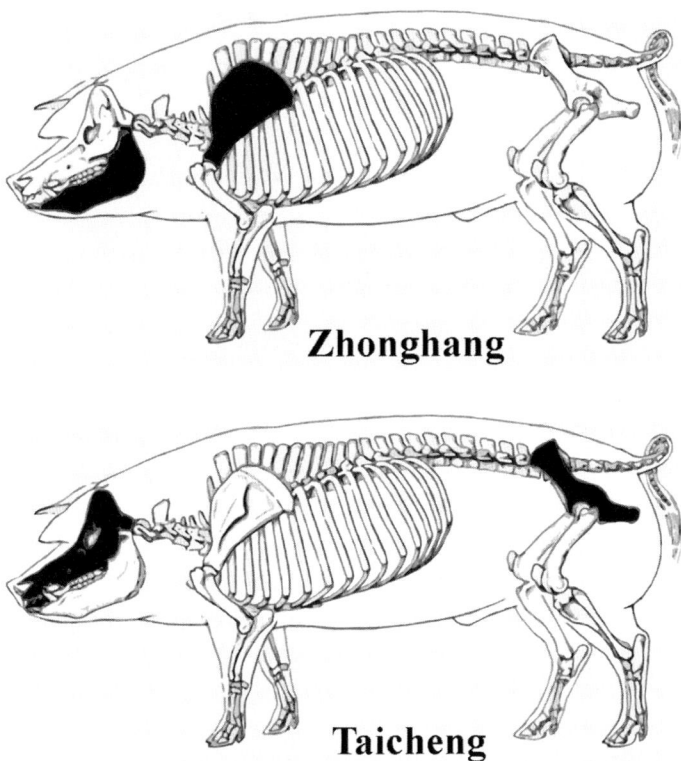

Figure 5.4 Illustrations that show the elements with the two highest recovery rates among the pig skeletons in the Zhonghang and Taicheng assemblages (redrawn from König & Liebich 2020:Fig 1.27).

underrepresented. In other words, this case demonstrates a prominent discrepancy between cranial and post-cranial elements, which indicates that only a portion of the slaughtered animals arrived at the site.

The estimation of slaughtering ages of animals can further reveal associated livestock exploitation strategies and meat production systems.[15] In Figure 5.5, I present the "survivorship score",[16] or "the proportion of specimens that survived beyond the age at which an element fused" (Zeder et al. 2015) based upon epiphyseal fusion data for different elements and the degree of tooth wear as a usual practice (e.g., Grant 1982; Silver 1969), for cattle and pigs at Zhonghang (Figure 5.5:a, c). Even though the Zhonghang site yielded insufficient dog bones to calculate the kill-off profile of that species, the age profiles of cattle and pigs allowed the further extrapolation of the utilization pattern. The Zhonghang cattle bone data show that a remarkably high proportion of cattle were killed at a relatively old age. According to the epiphyseal fusion data from limb bones, the survivorship rate of age class E (42–48 months) is close to 80 percent. As the majority of animals represented by the assemblage survived beyond the age of 42–48 months (four years old) when killed (Figure 5.5:a),

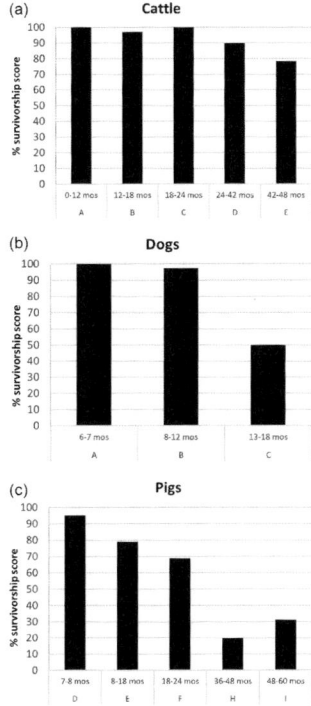

Figure 5.5 Kill-off patterns of cattle (a), dogs (b), and pigs (c) based on epiphyseal fusion at Zhonghang (mos = months) (age stages and grouping of cattle bones fusing are following Brunson et al. 2016; Silver 1969; age stages and fusing of dog bones are following Silver 1969). The estimated pig age of each stage is based on Grant (1982) and Zeder et al. (2015).

cattle husbandry was evidently not aimed at specialized meat production. The majority of cattle consumed at Zhonghang was probably raised as draft or traction animals and killed when old or they died of natural causes and were sold on the market.

The age profile shows that pigs were raised by another strategy. According to the degree of tooth wear and eruption (Figure 5.6:a), the prime slaughtering age of pigs at Zhonghang was between 18 and 24 months, and there is no evidence to suggest that any of the pigs slaughtered had reached three years old. But a comparison of the tooth wear and epiphyseal fusion data generates a somewhat confusing image of the slaughtering ages of pigs at Zhonghang. The survivorship scores of age classes H and I are 20 percent and 31 percent respectively, while the minor increase can be attributable to the small sample number in class H (Figure 5.5:c). Although there seems to be a big drop from class F to classes H and I (Figure 5.5:c), the survivorship scores of class I suggest that about 30 percent of pigs survived beyond

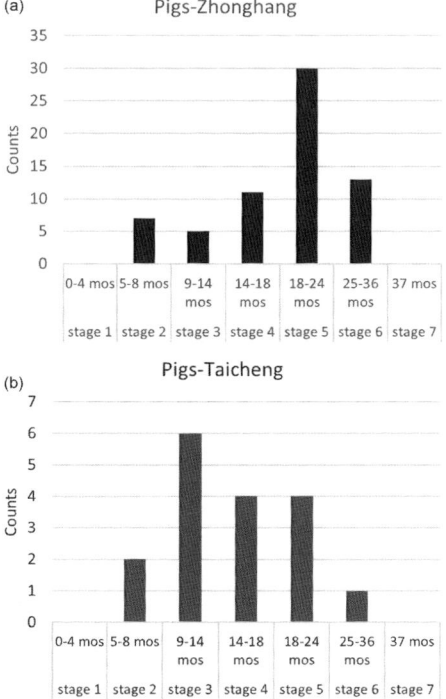

Figure 5.6 Eruption and wear stage of teeth in pig tooth-rows and loose teeth (mandible) at Zhonghang (a) and Taicheng (b). Mos = months. The estimated age of each stage is based on Grant (1982) and adjusted based on the Bronze Age pig assemblages at Yinxu by Li (2011).

48 months when slaughtered. This discrepancy might be partially caused by destructive taphonomic processes, leading to the underrepresentation of juvenile pigs. Another possibility is that the age estimation formula based on the degree of tooth wear does not correspond well with the actual data. Perhaps given the differences in food or living environment, the wear rate of pig teeth during the Warring States of China was slightly lower than that predicted by the standards we adopted here (Li 2011; Ma 2008), which could lead to an underestimation of slaughtering ages of archaeological specimens. To maximize meat production, the best slaughtering age for pigs not raised by modern industrial husbandry would fall within the range of 1.5 and 2 years old (Li 2011). While the majority of pigs consumed by workers at Zhonghang were killed probably for maximizing meat production, the existence of animals slaughtered relatively late in life indicates that a self-sustaining system might also have partially contributed to the subsistence of laborers at Zhonghang, in which a pig would have been killed only when needed.

Given the social setting of Zhonghang, it is not surprising to see that the types of meat procured by workers are similar to the assemblage of a specialized meat supply system in an urban center. The procurement system characterized by the body parts assemblage and killing profile further attests that workers must have relied heavily on other specialists through the meat market, in order to procure the meat to support themselves, or manifest deep economic embeddedness. The pattern of animal remains found at Zhonghang also represented the status of certain craftsmen in the ironworks. The relatively plentiful supply of meat suggests that some state food subsidies would have been delivered to craftsmen with special skills at the state-run ironworks, such as those with the knowledge needed to direct the construction of furnaces, prepare charges using the correct ratios of ores, fuel, and flux, and operate furnaces for successful smelting, as well as the manufacture of clay casting molds. The amelioration of the living standard of those workers could eventually enhance and contribute to the stability of production activities that were essential to the state economy. For workers carrying out labor-intensive tasks, such as fuel and ore loading and bellow operating, they might have also belonged to the convict or conscript labor pools, or in general low-status labor,[17] and thus received very few, if any, meat portions. It remains unclear the extent to which the faunal remains from the ironworks represent those low-status workers. Nonetheless, the food remains found at Zhonghang might have at least reflected the dietary system of those high-status artisans, in addition to their deep embedded social relations represented by the meat cut and kill-off slaughtering patterns.

3 Food supply and the embeddedness of iron production in the capital region

Since the Zhonghang ironworks was situated inside a large urban center, its social setting was markedly different from that of Taicheng and other ironworks inside the capital region, which were typically much smaller, and located in lower-ranked administrative towns. In addition, a good portion of workers in Zhonghang might have dwelled near the site and were recruited as long-term labor, as indicated by the discovery of the cemetery inside the ironworks. In contrast, cemeteries were not identified through archaeological fieldwork within the area of the production site at Taicheng. In spite of the difference in scale and structure, these two broadly contemporary ironworks both concentrated on manufacturing similar types of products using iron casting technology, and thus provide comparable datasets that can enhance our understanding of the daily lives of iron manufacturing communities through meat consumption records.

The bulk of faunal remains from Taicheng came from 16 features, primarily from the southern section; some of them might have been related to the disposal of manufacturing waste. Due to the much smaller scale of excavation, and probably also the smaller scale of the operation, the number of identified animal remains was 515 (Table 5.3), far fewer than the number recovered from Zhonghang. In the taxa assemblage, cattle and dogs (their bones account for about 25 percent and 24 percent of the total NISP, respectively) were clearly the two most important species in the diet of the workforce, based on the statistical results of NISP, a result seemingly inconsistent with the Han textual records mentioned earlier that suggested that commoner households might have relied on poultry for their meat intake.

Certain nuanced differences between the taxonomic assemblages from the Taicheng and Zhonghang sites can also be easily identified. One discrepancy lies in the fact that pigs seem to have played a more significant role in the workers' diet at Zhonghang, whereas workers at Taicheng relied more heavily on dog meat. In the case of Taicheng, pigs made up only a small part of a worker's diet, while sheep and goat account for just 4 percent of the NISP, suggesting that the reliance on sheep and goat husbandry further declined over time. In spite of these variations, these two studies show that cattle were the dominant taxon at both sites, while pigs and dogs were also important at Zhonghang and Taicheng respectively. The increase in dog meat in dietary consumption was probably indicative of broader consumption patterns during the Han period, instead of an idiosyncratic feature of the Taicheng example. For instance, the zooarchaeological study of the remains from the Kanjiazhai workshop complex in Linzi (Han period), Shandong, similarly shows that the three major taxa in the NISP assemblage are pigs (142), cattle (131), and dogs (106), which account for 30.9 percent, 28.5 percent, and 23.1 percent of the total NISP, respectively (Li Z. 2020). The consumption of dog meat appears to be a new contemporary cuisine fashion across the state reflected in the archaeological record, which was also supported by commonly seen records about dog butchers selling dog meat in markets in contemporary texts.[18]

Other species identified from Taicheng include horse, chicken, deer, and fish. Fish and deer bones account for less than four percent of identifiable specimens, and resources obtained through hunting or fishing appear to have played only a limited role in subsistence. Even though small bone remains (e.g., those of birds and fish) were identified through flotation, their number is very low (Table 5.3). As is typical of many zooarchaeological studies, the majority of small bone fragments, whether hand collected or from flotation, were unidentifiable to either species or body-part elements. Overall, about 90 percent of identifiable faunal remains[19] associated with the ironworks belong to the major species of domestic mammals mentioned above, similar to meat consumption tradition in urban centers since the Western Zhou period.

As alluded to earlier, the reliance on beef (and to a less extent, pork) appears to be a common characteristic of a system of specialized meat provision. The Taicheng animal assemblage reflects the same pattern. It is noteworthy that cattle and horses in the Han period were still considered the most valuable species of livestock during the Han period. However, the appearance of horse and cattle remains in the bone assemblage in Taicheng does not indicate that these husbandries were slaughtered specifically for meat supply. As the "Statutes on Stables and Parks" in Shuihudi Bamboo slips mention,

> ......when those who use government horses and oxen lose horses (or oxen)...the county where they have died; the county investigates and... sells the meat. It immediately collects the sinews, hides and horns, as well as fully collecting its value in cash.......[20]

In other words, when a horse or cow belonging to the government died, the local official had to follow the governmental rule to immediately sell every part of the carcass (e.g., meat, hide, and horn) and collect the cash from its sale, in order to make good out of a bad situation. It is possible, therefore, that horse and cattle bones found in the site, rather than reflecting the animals' having been reared primarily for meat, might originally have been government-owned livestock sold to the meat market when they were old or had died.

In order to further understand the supply system underlying the procurement of meat at the Taicheng site, I present the discovery rates of different skeletal elements represented by the two major species: cattle and pigs. Although the sample size is small, the assemblages of body parts seem to reveal several interesting patterns. For cattle (Figure 5.1; for illustration of the body parts with the first two highest recovery rates, see Figure 5.2), the proximal radii, proximal metacarpals, and distal metatarsals all appear to be well represented in the body parts assemblage as their recovery rates are higher than 50 percent. Skulls and mandibles are also represented elements in the assemblage, but the examples of these cranial parts discovered from the site are very fragmentary and of relatively low discovery rate. The atlas and axis, which typically survive destructive forces well,[21] are also poorly represented in the Taicheng assemblage (Figure 5.1). In general, the recovery rates of axial elements and cranial bones are relatively low, and this is unlikely to have resulted solely from poor preservation.[22] In addition, the bones of forelimb and hindlimb extremities (e.g., phalanges, carpals, and tarsals) had very low recovery rates, while other less meaty lower parts of limb bones (e.g., metatarsus and metacarpus) are generally better represented. Another remarkable pattern in the assemblage is that, while some limb bones are well represented, robust elements like distal humerus and tibia that can survive destructive forces well (Binford 1981:281–337) were not well represented in the body parts assemblage. Market preferences and transportation factors may both have contributed significantly to the assemblage composition representing the workshop dietary, and workers appeared to procure only part of the butchered body from the market.

At Taicheng, dog bones have the second largest NISP value in the assemblage (Table 5.3). Would those dogs be raised at the site by workers, instead of coming as butchered meat from the marketplace? Like cattle, some portions of the elements were underrepresented. The most common elements in the assemblage of dog bones are the skull (calculated based on maxillae) and mandibles (Figure 5.7; for illustration of the body parts with the first two highest recovery rates, see Figure 5.8). The high recovery rates of these elements are not surprising because they are robust and diagnostic. Beyond the cranial elements, femurs are also well represented with a recovery rate

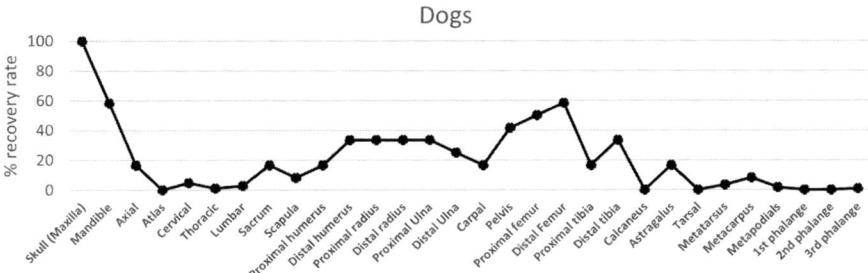

Figure 5.7 Recovery rates of dog elements from Taicheng.

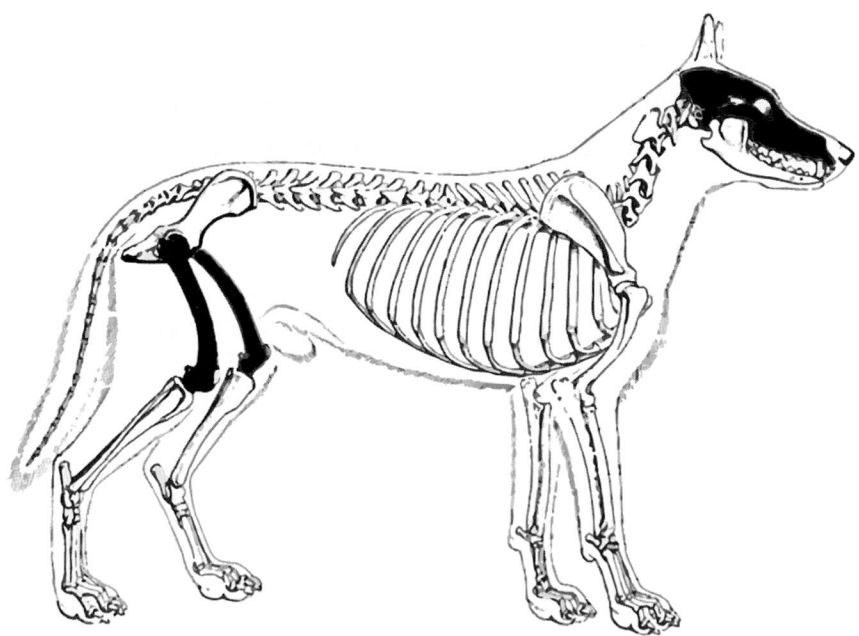

Figure 5.8 Illustrations that show the elements with the two highest recovery rates among the dog skeletons in Taicheng (redrawn from König & Liebich 2020:Fig 1.26).

of over 50 percent. The figures for the forelimbs are slightly lower, and the recovery rate for distal humeri and proximal radii is only 33 percent for both. The small bones of the forelimb and hindlimb extremities and post-cranial axial bones are also particularly lacking in the assemblage, indicating that dog carcasses might have been delivered to the site as butchered cuts of meat. According to the assemblage, it is unlikely those dogs consumed might have been raised by workers themselves and then butchered as a whole within the workshop area.

In the pig bone assemblage, significant differences also exist in the proportions of elements present, similar to the patterns of cattle and dogs (Figure 5.3; for illustration, see Figure 5.4). Pig post-cranial bones are remarkably underrepresented in comparison with cranial elements. Limb and axial bones were similarly scarce in the pig assemblage. Among all limb bones, the proximal ulna has the highest recovery rate, but still only represents 25 percent of the assemblage. This pattern is quite different from that of cattle and dog bones. For these two taxa, the recovery rates of limb bones are much higher in the body parts assemblage. The dominance of skulls in the Taicheng assemblage is even more pronounced than in the Zhonghang case. The overwhelmingly head-dominant pattern in pig assemblages may mean that other portions of carcasses were rarely brought to or consumed at the site.

The patterning in body parts assemblage suggests that the consumption preferences for different species varied to a certain extent. For cattle, and pigs as well, one dominant feature of the recovery pattern was the presence of skulls and the less meaty parts of limbs versus rich meat-rich parts of animals. This patterning indicates that workers at Taicheng might have only rarely consumed meaty portions like loin associated with the axial skeleton. Such meat-bearing elements might have been intensively processed before deposition or traded elsewhere, never entering this archaeological assemblage. Also, the underrepresentation of the small bones of the distal forelimb and hindlimb in the assemblage, which were often discarded nearby specialized butcher sites, indicates that processed carcasses brought to the site were likely to have been in the form of small-sized cuts of meat, one indicator suggesting the existence of an urban meat supply network. While meat was an important part of workers' diet, their options were rather limited.

Judging from the age profile, the majority of beef consumed by workers at Taicheng in general were from old or worn-out animals, whose meat was tough and considered undesirable (Bowen 1998). This pattern is also similar to what was evidenced in Zhonghang. According to the epiphyseal fusion of long bones[23] and calculated survivorship score, most cattle consumed at Taicheng were relatively old animals, such that 60 percent of animals in the assemblage had survived beyond the age class E (estimated epiphyseal fusion at between 42 and 48 months) when killed (Figure 5.9:a). Also, at least eight cases of pathology were found on cattle bones in the Taicheng assemblage (Shaanxi Yanjiuyuan 2018a:69). These cases were all related to arthropathy,

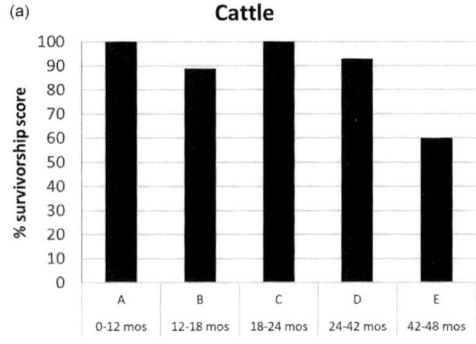

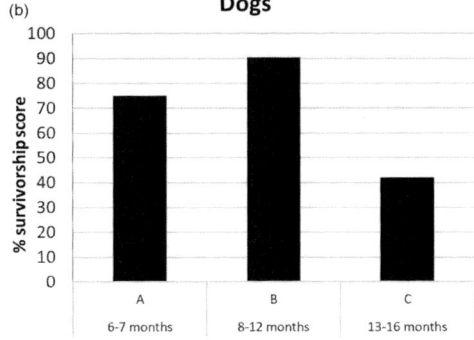

Figure 5.9 Kill-off patterns of cattle (a) and dogs (b) based on epiphyseal fusion at
    Taicheng (mos = months) (age stages and grouping of cattle bones fusing
    are following Brunson et al. 2016; Silver 1969; age stages and fusing of
    dog bones are following Silver 1969).

probably resulting from long-term traction work such as plowing and pulling.
Based on the killing ages and the pathology, these animals might have been
raised primarily for traction (plowing) or as draft animals, rather than for
specialized meat production. One source of such aged cattle was probably
this type of government-owned livestock mentioned in excavated texts, which
at the end of their lives were disposed of through the market system.

When compared with cattle, the slaughtering ages of pigs and dogs present a distinctively different pattern at Taicheng. The slaughtering ages of
pigs were estimated based on the degree of tooth wear and eruption because
too few limb bones survived. The counts of pig teeth by mandible reflecting different stages of tooth eruption and degree of wear are also listed in
Figure 5.6:b, showing that about 70 percent of pigs fall within the slaughtering age range of 12 and 24 months old based on tooth eruption data. In
particular, the pig data peaks at stage III, corresponding to 9–14 months
old. No data indicate that any pig was killed older than three years of age.
A similar pattern can be seen in the killing-age of dogs. In Figure 5.9:b, the

counterintuitive increased survival rate[24] of dogs from a younger (age class A) group (75 percent) to an older group (age class B) group (~90 percent) is most likely a result caused by stochastic variation due to low sample numbers. However, the survivorship score of age class C, which is much lower than either class A or B at about 40 percent, suggests that most dogs consumed were juveniles or young adults (see also Figure 5.5:b for a similar trend at Zhonghang). It seems very likely that these pigs and dogs were raised primarily for the production of meat. Overall, the slaughtering ages indicate that these livestock might have come from two different production systems: cattle perhaps originally being raised as traction or draft animals, whereas pigs and dogs were probably raised to maximize meat production and were primarily killed before becoming adults.

In general, the kill-off profiles of pigs and cattle reflected by the assemblages of the two ironworks of the Warring States and Han periods suggest that these two sites relied to a certain extent on a specialized meat supply system. Based on the kill-off profiles, the systems that provided pigs for Zhonghang and Taicheng both butchered the livestock before they reached adulthood. Those in charge of meat supplies at these two sites appear to have procured only certain parts of carcasses. Meanwhile, the workforce at both sites consumed beef from old cattle that could have first been used for other purposes, such as wagon pulling, before they eventually became the workers' supper. The only difference between the two examples lies in the fact that more pigs at Zhonghang might have survived to a greater age when killed. Therefore, the age-at-death patterns and the body parts assemblage at both sites indicate that the majority of livestock consumed, including cattle, pigs, and perhaps even dogs, were probably processed or butchered by other specialists. These patterns further imply that the livestock consumed were unlikely to have been raised in the backyard of domestic dwellings by the ironworkers themselves. However, at this stage, it is not possible to determine whether the workers procured their meat through the market, directly from other specialists, or via other routes such as the state supply network.

Faunal remains only provide partial information about subsistence practices. It is important to incorporate botanical remains in order to better understand the foodways if such data are available. At the Taicheng site, the study of palaeobotanical remains shows that very few millets and wheat grain have been found, even from features that were not particularly associated with the discarding of manufacturing remains (Shaanxi Yanjiuyuan 2018a:489), indicating that the processing of crops or the preparation of food might not have taken place within or near the excavation area. A similar pattern has been identified in the recent report from the Wangchenggang ironworks in the Nanyang cluster (Figure 3.3). Only a few crops remain—14 seeds, comprised of seven millet grain and seven wheat grain—have been identified in soil samples systematically collected from the excavation covering about 1,000 m^2 (Liu et al. 2021), again suggesting that food cooking or preparation might not have occurred within the excavation area.

A sharp contrast, however, was presented in the botanical records from the Kanjiazhai site complex in Linzi city. Considerable amounts of crop remains have been discovered in features at locus bII and bIII dating to the Warring States and early Han period, some of which also contained large volumes of manufacturing debris and were located adjacent to work areas. Also, large quantities of crop seeds have been identified at features at locus bI that were in operation between the Middle and Late Western Han periods. A total of 1,979 seeds, including millets, wheat, and rice, have been found (Chen et al. 2020; Zhao 2020). While the impact of other factors such as preservation and biases in excavation should be subjected to further study, the sharp discrepancy represented by these ironworks dating to the Han period might indicate some differences in the subsistence practices at these ironworks. Owing to the lack of botanical remains, indicating that cooking or food preparation was unlikely to occur nearby, it seems plausible that most workers at the Taicheng and Wangchenggang might have consumed food prepared by other specialists. In contrast, the presence of a large number of carbonized crop remains in Linzi suggests that food preparation might have taken place adjacent to the workshop area. If so, the operation of Taicheng must rely on other specialists to not only provide but also prepare the food, which in turn supports my viewpoint that Taicheng was a full-time ironworks representing a deep economic embeddedness.

In this chapter, I have argued that the study of ironworks' foodways could serve as an important line of evidence for discussions concerning contemporary social relations and their connectivity to other external communities. Building on the argument in Chapter 4, one of the key ideas that I aimed to further investigate is whether small-scale ironworks such as Taicheng were more likely to be independent household production units or a small-scale nucleated factory with a high degree of specialization in production. Chapter 4 explained that the intensity of manufacturing proposed in Costin's framework is one critical parameter for addressing the issue. One productive approach is to look at the supply of meat as if workers would have provided their own supplies of meat—most likely from poultry and pigs—that could be raised in the yards behind workers' dwellings. From a comparative study, it was somewhat surprising to find that the ironworks from the Warring States to Han periods had a similar range of domesticated animal taxa, including in both cases significant components of cattle, pig, dog, horse, and sheep/goat bones, albeit in different proportions, given the differences in the size and context of these two sites. Furthermore, beef and pork were brought to the ironworks in smaller cuts, and the consumption pattern seems to favor specific animal cuts. Kill-off patterns illustrate that livestock in both cases were raised to a specific age range for killing to optimize the utilization of animals, either in terms of meat production or for other purposes like traction and pulling. Interestingly, poultry were relatively rare in the assemblage of faunal remains at both Zhonghang, Taicheng, and other ironworks. The taxonomic assemblage at Taicheng also shows that workers relied heavily on domestic animals for their meat, while wild resources were barely exploited. At least, the limited exploitation of poultry and pigs at Taicheng appears to contradict the conventional wisdom that sees such sites as self-sufficient household production units.

The comparison of elements and age profiles further indicates that both ironworks relied heavily upon an external supply system, which was an important line of evidence that otherwise would not be derived through looking at manufacturing waste. The animal bone assemblages show that butchery activities were almost absent on these sites. The range of elements present also suggests that meat was procured through external specialists. The age profiles illustrate that the majority of livestock were raised to a specific age range for killing in order to optimize the utilization of the animals, either primarily for meat production, or following a life of traction or draft work. All these lines of evidence stoutly support that meat resources in the ironworks would have come from a specialized animal husbandry and well-managed meat production system, probably through the market system.

The deep reliance on an external supply system for meat and other food at Taicheng, together with the evidence of organization outlined in Chapter 4, appears to further challenge the over-simplistic assumption built upon texts that equates "small-scale" ironworks with a household-level of production center, thus indicating that the iron industry in the capital region had a more complicated structure. The broader social setting within which full-time specialized ironworking communities like Taicheng were able to operate, including the procurement of raw materials, the manufacturing of small range of final products for meeting the intensive demand, the efficient distribution of final products that could satisfy the needs of customers, and the receipt of regular supplies of meat and other foodstuffs in return, must be embedded with a developed exchange and supply network. The clarification of the degree of economic embeddedness enjoyed by ironworks thus helps to elucidate the connections and interactions of workers with their social settings. It is perhaps not a surprising result that the Zhonghang faunal remains match the pattern expected of an urban food supply chain. But it is significant and interesting to find that the patterning of faunal records from Taicheng—which at best was a medium-ranked county center—are similar to Zhonghang in terms of the dominance of beef, body-part representation, and kill-off patterns for major taxa. When all these lines of evidence are viewed together, a strong degree of economic embeddedness and integration within a specialized food supply system is therefore indicated.

Building upon the deep economic embeddedness represented, we can further enhance the understanding of the management of Taicheng. If it is valid to view Zhonghang as a potentially state-controlled ironworks situated in an urban center and highly specialized in production—i.e., a workshop that relied mostly upon the state for its provisioning or the market to obtain meat produced by others—then, according to the evidence related to food, Taicheng should be similarly categorized as a workshop employing full-time specialized labor either in an independent nucleated or attached retainer workshop manner. Although family-run household workshops could also rely on the market-oriented food chain to a certain extent, the high degree of reliance on a specialized food provisioning system at Taicheng, added to the lack of other evidence for craftworking or self-sufficient food production, suggests that Taicheng, and other similar ironworks in the capital region predating the monopoly, were unlikely to be operated by part-time specialists in household production units.

Another critical result underscored by the comparison of faunal remains is that some changes, though perhaps relatively subtle, could be identified from the Late Warring States to the Han period in terms of the food supply system inside metal-production centers. For instance, the remains of deer, which were often assumed to be hunted wild animals, became extremely rare in the ironworks in the capital region. In addition, the consumption of animal parts was even more selective in the case of Taicheng. The lack of botanical remains further suggests that food preparation did not occur at the site. Presumably, the degree of economic embeddedness represented by the case of Taicheng might have been more intensified than the case in the Warring States period. In Chapter 4, I suggest that a horizontal collaboration was evidenced by the Taicheng case. The food supply system seems to further suggest that the collaboration was embedded within a centralized food supply network. Whereas the operation of the iron industry at the county level in the capital region was at a smaller scale, its degree of specialization might have been more intensive than some of its preceding production systems.

Within the constraints of the current evidence, it is difficult to determine the extent to which the state played a managerial role in Taicheng's operation. Since the faunal remains from Zhonghang might be accounted for by the state subsidy given its attached nature, and the fact that meat was expensive in the Han period, the similarity between Taicheng and Zhonghang may imply, to a great extent, that the Taicheng ironworks might also have involved some degree of state support, whether via the direct control or wage subsidies. One cannot even rule out the possibility that some workers with high skill there might have been retainers or attached artisans who were partially supported by the state. Since the deep embeddedness in the Zhonghang case is also the result of state supply, the similar pattern reflected by Taicheng's operation might have involved some degree of centralized administrative control of the mobilization of resources, but such an idea must be further attested.

Traces of the daily lives of ironworkers are rarely preserved in archaeological records. Regardless of whether the Taicheng ironworks was independently run or state-owned, its full-time manner of intensified production of limited types of goods and its deep reliance on a specialized food supply system together provide new information concerning the rise of the iron industry during the Han period. The pattern of faunal remains reminds us that a larger food supply network was the prerequisite even to the establishment of small operations such as Taicheng. If such a network was operated by a meat market, would the market system also play a role in other aspects of the iron industry in the region, such as contributing to the widespread distribution of final products—iron implements—within the capital region? In the next chapter, I examine evidence that is closely related to distribution and the potential market system of final products within the capital region, as a means for understanding the gradually well-integrated world during the Han period.

Notes

1 The framework of "economic embeddedness" and zooarchaeological data in Taicheng in chapter has been modified and expanded based on my previous publication (Lam et al. 2019). Also, zooarchaeological and palaeobotanical data from numbers of more updated publications have been incorporated into the discussion.
2 For instance, see cases in Gidney (2000); Redding (2010).
3 This by no means indicates that wild species would be completely absent in urban archaeological records. Based on the example of Charlestown, indigenous wild animals that were able to adapt to the growth of the city and animals that were attracted to the urban center were found in the assemblage (Reitz & Zierden 2014; Zierden & Reitz 2009). Thus, it will oversimplify to view all non-domesticated animals in an urban setting as the result of hunting wild game.
4 In most cases, crop grain was preserved in archaeological contexts because it was burnt and carbonized before entering into the depositional environment. Also, such burning behavior was often associated with cooking. For the explanation, see Zhao (2010:54).
5 It must be noted that many other studies have called for caution on the simple assumption that occupants of a site with low social or economic status necessarily consume fewer meaty portions, and consequently, more fragments associated with low-valued parts elements are a reliable indicator of lower status (Crader 1989; Henn 1985; Lyman 1987; Schmitt & Zeier 1993).
6 *Hanshu* 24a.1125; modified from the translation in Swann (1950:141–142).
7 According to the bulk density mentioned in Yuelu Qinjian, Wu Zhaoyang and Jin Wen suggested that 1 *ml* is equivalent to 0.6355 g of millet or 0.75 g dehusked millet grain in the Qin-Han periods. Also, the *mu* mentioned in *Hanshu* here is the so-called small *mu* unit (length ~ 100 *bu*), not the big *mu* unit (length ~ 240 *bu*) that was employed by the Qin state after the Shang Yang's reform and the Han period (Wu & Jin 2013). If we convert the *mu* here to the big *mu* unit, the yield rate of 1 *mu* would then be 36 *dou* (or 3.6 *shi*) (ibid; but see the rectification in Jin (2021:407), since Jin Wen acknowledged in his later publication that they overestimated the yield rate during the Warring States period in Wu & Jin 2013). The recently published excavated texts *Duxiang qinian kentian zubu* from Zoumalou (Ma 2013) mentioned that average yield rate was 3.98 *shi* per *mu* during early Wudi's reign in present-day Changsha region. Chen Xingyu proposed that the average yield rate in the Central Plains or agriculturally developed regions was about 4 *shi* per *mu*, based on the records in contemporary texts such as *Huananzhi* (Chen X. 2020). Also, it is important to note that the yield rate should be contingent on local environment, and presented regional variations to a certain extent in the Han period. The excavated texts *Tangyi yuanshou ernian yaojubu* from Tushantun, Shandong, which include the yield rate in present-day Nanjing

area in 1 BCE, was only between 2.58 and 2.1 *shi* per *mu* (see Qingdaoshi & Huangdaoqu 2019).

8 *Zhangjiashan Suanshushu* mentioned that 1 *dou* of *mi* (rice) is about 1.5 *qian*. In northwestern China, bamboo slips from Juyan indicated that the normal price of 1 *dou* of *mi* ranged from 3 *qian* to 34 *qian*. Each adult male would need at least 2/3 *dou* (1.33 liters) of millet or other crop grain per day to survive. Therefore, the price of meat, even just for a small amount, appears to be expensive compared to the price of crop grain.

9 *Hanshu* 24a.1135; modified from the translation in Swann (1950:175–177).

10 Unfortunately, the ancient diet during the Late Bronze Age (Western Zhou) and Early Imperial period in the Guanzhong basin, are still poorly understood through zooarchaeological analyses. Especially during the Western Han period, up until now we only have preliminary reports on remains from a small section of the capital (Hu et al. 2006) in this region. This dataset is by no means large enough for a quantitative comparison.

11 The database can be downloaded from http://www.archaeology.net.cn/html/cn/ xueshuziliao/kaogushujuku/dongwukaoguziliaoku/2013/1025/31728.html.

12 NISP is a common way to calculate animal bones of different species found in archaeological sites, which stands for "number of identified specimens for skeletal part" (Lyman 1984).

13 During the Shang and Zhou periods, cattle played probably the most dominant role in sacrificial rituals (Yuan & Flad 2005). Especially in the Zhou ritual system, the consumption of cattle was prescribed in the wide range of ritual activities (e.g., wedding, diplomatic, and funeral) of elites above the *shi* level. The high frequency of cattle remains in the assemblage of faunal remains might not necessarily indicate the relatively high-status of workers. Instead, the high frequency might be attributable to the sufficient supply of cattle to major urban centers during the late Bronze age, making beef more accessible to residents even though they were craft specialists.

14 The "recovery rate" stands for the ratio between the numbers of each element of each species found at the site versus the expected total numbers of such body parts based on the minimum number identifiable in the assemblage, where 100% would mean that the total number of an element is close to the maximum possible given the MNI (minimum number of individuals) calculations for that taxon in the assemblage. In zooarchaeology, this is a means to discern whether certain parts of a body were dominant in the assemblage, and imbalance between different parts of the skeleton is usually an indicator of a specialized meat supply system.

15 As the bones of young animals generally do not survive as well as those of adults of the same species (Landon 1997), age profiles can also help evaluate the skewing effects of post-depositional destructive forces on faunal assemblages. Possible taphonomic effects must therefore be considered together in order to build stronger arguments regarding the animal husbandry.

16 For the formula to calculate the survivorship score and specific method, see Zeder et al. (2015).

17 Lu (2018) suggests that some craft industries, such as iron mining, during the Warring States period already employed state-controlled free labor.

18 One of the founding generals, Fan Kuai, was a dog butcher before joining Liu Bang's revolution, see *Shiji* 95.2651. In the annotation of *Shiji Zhengyi*, Zhang Shoujie also explained that eating dog meat in the Han period was as common as eating lamb.

19 Bone fragments unidentifiable to species were classified according to size categories, but mammal bones of this type from the site only represented a very small proportion of the total assemblage.

20 *Qinjiandu heji*, Shuihudi, "Statutes on Stables and Parks", Chen W. (ed.) (2014:55); modified from the translation in Hulsewé (1985:28–29, A9).

21 Studies of the differential survival of body parts show that mandibles, maxillae, axis and atlas are usually surviving elements (Binford 1980, 1981; Lyman 1984) in most archaeological contexts due to their robustness.

22 It is noteworthy that cattle vertebrae and ribs are not surprisingly underrepresented in the Taicheng case. One potential reason is that fragments of these elements are difficult to identify down to species level.

23 While the tooth-wear is also useful for studying the kill-off pattern, the teeth data available for cattle in the Taicheng case are insufficient to draw any reliable conclusions.

24 In reality, the survival rate of an older group had to be lower than its younger group. For instance, if 30 percent of individuals in a juvenile group were slaughtered, the survival rate of an older age group (i.e., the percentage of individuals that could survive through that age range) should be lower than 30 percent.

6 Market integration and the distribution system for iron goods[1]

Moving from the microscopic perspective of ironworks in county-level centers and the Han capital Chang'an, I will recenter the discussion in this chapter on a more macroscopic issue related to connectivity, focusing on the distribution of final products on a regional scale. Alongside the development of bureaucratic and minting systems, market exchange gradually came to occupy an essential role from the Warring States onward. Iron implements were widely used as everyday commodities[2] during the Han period and transported to places distant from where they were made (Li 1994[1993], 2000). Meanwhile, Guanzhong was clearly linked to the middle and lower Yellow River valley, where clusters of large-scale manufacturing centers were dominant. How would the distribution and transportation system of iron implements inside the capital core transform and adapt over time? How did the regional distribution and supply system work on the ground after the goods were transported to the region? Specifically, did the distribution of iron daily use items, which likely entered circulation via the market network, become more accessible to the regional population of all ranks? Wang Mang (ruling from 9 to 23 CE), the usurper of the Western Han dynasty, sent down a decree in 17 CE to reiterate the importance of market exchange and state control in "equalizing" the prices of goods in order to justify his economic policies for his Xin dynasty. As the decree commands:

> Now salt has the priority of foods and delicious viands. Wine is the sen-
> ior of the "hundred" medicines, the delight of felicitous gatherings. Iron
> [may be called] a fundamental in framing. Celebrated mountains and
> great marshes are the storehouses for rich and abundant resources. [The
> seven markets which equalize prices] *wujun* and [the system of credits
> and loans] *shetai* are [means by] which the "hundred clans" (the peo-
> ple) procure equalization [of prices and to which] they look in order to
> supply their wants......The six (that is, salt, liquor, iron, other products
> from natural resources of mountains and of marshes, and coinage) are
> such that families registered as common people cannot [be allowed to]
> manufactured in their own homes (or without license in shops). [For
> them] they must necessarily look to markets.[3]

DOI: 10.4324/9781003259220-9

Given the importance of the market in the circulation and supplies by specialists, whether there would have been sufficient supply for not only the capital but also minor centers in the region owing to the development of the transportation network? More importantly, how did the distribution patterns in the Han period differ from those in place under the Qin state along with the development of the Han imperial system that further connected various regions into a unified political entity?

In addition to the emergence of large-scale manufacturing centers, the transportation network at various scales would have played a critical role in the supply network of commodity exchange (Carrier 1995:61), contributing to the archaeological phenomenon of the widespread distribution of iron implements in the Han period. We know from textual evidence introduced in Chapter 3 that local governments oversaw the transportation of metal commodities from their regions. Anyone leaving a county would have their cargo inspected and registered before being allowed to pass through the exit gate. At the same time, Han bureaucrats were also responsible for administrating marketplaces in every town (Gao 2008; Kamiya 1994; Sahara 2002[1985]). The mechanism through which iron implements were distributed among centers of various ranks in the capital region will be surveyed here as a means of understanding the connectivity within the capital associated with the rise of imperial power.

As explained at the outset of this book, commodities are goods that were produced on a large scale and involved a specific relationship between producers and those who sponsor or manage the production. Commodities are typically transported or exchanged through systems that go beyond the direct link between producer and consumer, and are more often transacted via the so-called marketplace exchange (i.e., centers or institutions in which market transactions take place) that could link discrete and distant people and places together within an economic area. Given a market's connections with disparate parts of an empire, its study can also provide key insights into the development and practice of imperial processes (e.g., Smith 2004). In archaeological literature, however, the definition and identification of the terminology "marketplace exchange" have been hotly debated in various archaeological studies.[4] It is necessary to first engage with theoretical discourses to clarify this terminology. This chapter also aims to identify the kinds of archaeological evidence that would be relevant to investigating marketplace exchange, such as the distribution pattern of iron implements, that could illustrate the movement of goods and answer questions about systems of exchange.

In this chapter, integration refers to degrees of connections that have been stimulated by the movement of goods between hands, which is different from the overall theme of the book—connectivity—in the sense that the latter concerns the connection more broadly shaped by the political system and economic exchange, such as the phenomenon of the widespread distribution of Han style materials and the underlying idea shared by various communities. Integration focuses more specifically on the distribution mechanism of similar types of commodities and tries to explain how it was shaped by various factors such as marketplace exchange and state redistribution. Since residential areas of commoners remain significantly under-represented in the dataset, the examination of the presence of iron implements in various types of archaeological contexts would provide the most direct evidence of integration related to the iron production system. Due to the rich published material on burials in the body of archaeological scholarship, the comparison of distribution patterns of iron, together with those for other types of objects as supporting evidence (e.g., bronze objects), from tombs of commoners of moderate social status, can provide some insights into the degree of integration, albeit insights that would have been misleading to a certain extent given the offering made in funerary rituals might not have been indicative of their use in everyday life.

Parallel to the concept of connectivity, integration could be conceptualized at various scales. Instead of inter-regional exchange, I look at the regional level within the capital region, as a proxy for understanding the transformation of connectivity in the case of the Han empire manifested by the iron industry. To facilitate the description of varied patterns, I first conceptualize the issue of regional integration and propose a tripartite framework to explain three forms of integration that one may identify in archaeological records: dendritic, administrative-integrated, and fully integrated. Building on this proposed framework and indicators of each type, this chapter then uses statistical analysis to investigate the distribution patterns of everyday iron and bronze items from commoners' tombs within the capital region of the Qin and Western Han empires. The archaeological evidence was examined in order to understand whether changes occurred in the way ordinary people in various centers procured metal goods. Through the investigation of market integration juxtaposed with the manufacturing system explained before, this chapter suggests that iron was not only a necessity to maintain social stability but also a medium through which the force enhancing the connectivity among the imperial subjects was generated. The study of integration also sheds new light on dynamic mechanisms of administrative control over the movement of material culture and, more critically, how the Han empire played its role in the formation of the early market system.

1 Conceptualizing regional integration and market exchange in ancient China

Much has been written about market exchange practices during the Qin-Han periods, indicating some forms of integration should exist and clarifying its essential role in the imperial finance system (von Glahn 2016:95–97; Zhang 2006). This is one reason that the implementation of monopoly policies to control the manufacturing and selling of two types of important daily materials—iron and salt—greatly expanded the income sources to meet the costs caused by a series of military campaigns on northern and northwestern frontiers (Nishijima 1986). Economic texts compiled during the Warring States-Han periods, including the *Guanzi* and the *Yantielun*,[5] extensively discussed issues relating to the market economy such as regional variation in the availability of different resources and economic principles based on quantitative calculations (Chin 2015:32–34). In archaeological records, evidence of coinage systems,[6] long-distance trade products such as lacquerware and bronzes (Barbieri-Low 2007:118, 125, 137; Hong 2006:218–221; Liu Y. 2018; Wu 2007), and scenes of physical marketplaces were depicted in artistic representations of the times (Liu 1973) have been discussed with regard to the market exchange system represented by the evidence of trade and interregional exchange (see discussions in Bang 2009; Gao 2008:-108–112; Hsu 2006[1965]:143–146; Huang 2003; Scheidel 2009, 2015; von Glahn 2016:151–154; Zhang 2006:222–225). Transaction records about the long-distance distribution of crops and textiles have also been widely found in excavated texts. Apparently, market exchange was prosperous in the Han period and essential to the state's economic system.

Unfortunately, ancient texts and these lines of archaeological evidence often only provide brief macroscalar but variegated narratives about the mechanisms and role of market exchange. How daily commodities were transported between settlements of various scales and what role the distribution of such goods via various levels of the market system played in organizing the economic foundations have yet to be clarified through empirical study. Unlike later historical periods, in which rich textual materials allow the investigation of marketplace distribution (i.e., how different markets were distributed across a region) and even how regional cultural traditions were shaped by market behaviors (Han 2017; Skinner 1964, 1965a, 1965b), textual records at similar resolution are lacking for the Qin-Han periods. We must turn to other "indirect" evidence in archaeological contexts to understand the mechanism of market exchange.

For a long time in the literature, the role of market exchange in a contemporary sense, namely a system that was adjusted primarily by the force of supply and demand, has been widely debated in ancient economies, especially in societies without currency (Polanyi 1957:255–257, 2001[1944]:45, 49, 69; Finley 1999[1973]:84).[7] A growing body of archaeological scholarship has come to recognize that markets existed far more widely in ancient economies than has previously been portrayed (Hirth & Pillsbury 2013; Manning & Morris 2005). Meanwhile, recent studies have also noted that ancient markets usually operated without some of the fundamental features that have only appeared in modern, industrial settings, including the well integration of market systems into settlements of varying scale, large-scale divisions of labor, extensive trading networks, and a fast spread of information over long distances (Morley 2014). Pre-industrial market exchange was often hindered by various technological constraints relating to goods transportation and the communication of information.

In this vein, a productive archaeological investigation of market exchange, particularly in the context of the Han empire, needs to address how exchange and transportation in the past operated as a process for generating different degrees of economic integration in any given socio-political unit. It seems more accurate to consider past market behaviors as constituting a type of transaction that was often embedded within or operated in parallel with the political involvement in practices such as redistribution.[8] Consequently, the archaeological evidence related to marketplace exchange would come in many forms. In order to describe the role of the market in ancient settings in a more meaningful manner, I suggest that market exchange should be conceptualized as a "multi-layer" process, as proposed by historians Alan Bowman and Andrew Wilson (2009:24–27) in their discussion of the Ancient Roman economy. Given the technological limitations of transportation in past societies, it is necessary to differentiate the integration generated by market transactions into three spatial scales: local (or sub-regional), regional, and interregional (across the regions of an entire empire), and to interrogate each of them separately, instead of viewing the ancient market system as a whole. Since the distribution of daily goods in the past was likely to be a combined effect of various exchange mechanisms—not solely market exchange—from each of these levels or scales, studying the degree of integration using material culture should clarify how ancient markets served to integrate cities with county and village towns and thereby provide a practical approach for articulating the economic structure of connectivity.

Having explored some fundamental issues relating to ancient market exchange, this chapter attempts to spotlight Han China's regional economic structure, the major concern in this book. The regional market is perhaps the most critical among the three levels of integration identified above, inasmuch as it facilitated long-distance exchange and provided necessities to local communities at lower-level centers. In previous discussions of ancient markets in China, however, the regional aspect appears to be the least clear when compared with interregional and sub-regional levels of exchange. For instance, the widespread discoveries of Han-style bronze mirrors and lacquerwares[9] have already been recognized as evidence of the interregional exchange system that operated across different parts of the Han empire (Barbieri-Low 2007:118, 125, 137).[10] Meanwhile, the evidence of an intraregional market system—the periodic marketplaces—was even considered to be commonly found in the capital center[11] as well as sub-regional governmental centers during the Han period or even earlier, according to textual records (Gao 2008:110; Zhang 2006:237–250). By contrast, intermediate-scale (i.e., regional) integration, which is concerned here with the mechanisms by which major centers or market systems were integrated within a specific region and the extent to which the state was involved in the transportation process, has not been comprehensively investigated for the Han period. Part of the problem is that no framework capable of piercing the various lines of non-text archaeological evidence together to understand the system yet exists. To mitigate this difficulty, I propose three models: dendritic, administrative integrated, and fully integrated, for conceptualizing different forms of regional scale market exchange that occurred in the Qin and Han periods.

Among previous attempts to explore the exchange of daily commodities using various archaeological indicators,[12] Hirth's (1998) "household distribution approach" based on cases from Mesoamerican archaeology provides a broadly applicable framework for understanding market exchange beyond a particular case study region. Since the market system was ambiguous before the post-classical Mesoamerica in inscriptions or ethnohistorical records, Hirth proposed this approach to examine the frequencies of exchanged goods and homogeneity of assemblages from households of different ranks. Hirth (1998:455) explains that the force of market exchange allows customers of different ranks to gain access to the same assemblage of goods because products flow primarily through independent economic channels rather than hierarchical political networks. As a result, market exchange tends to generate a distinctive distribution pattern of goods in archaeological contexts, that a homogeneous assemblage of goods would have been found among all households in a small area regardless of their differentiation by economic status.

Previous studies employing the "household distributional approach" in Mesoamerican archaeology have demonstrated its value for understanding market exchange at a relatively small spatial scale, such as when archaeologists are concentrating on features within a site or site cluster (Garraty 2009; Hirth 1998; Hirth & Pillsbury 2013). However, when addressing the question of market exchange at a regional level covering relatively large areas, such as the Guanzhong basin, I argue that another well-established approach should be combined with this one, namely Renfrew's (1975, 1977) "fall-off distribution" approach. Renfrew suggests that the spatial fall-off patterns in abundance of goods with distance from source may demonstrate the existence of various forms of exchange (especially market exchange) across a large regional landscape. These two approaches can be used in concert by replacing households with settlements of different ranks (e.g., capital city and minor centers). Once production or major transportation centers have been identified, if the assemblages of certain types of objects in centers of different ranks are relatively similar or their relative frequencies give no clear indication of declines of occurrence with distance from sources, also known as "monotonic depletion" (Renfrew 1977:72–73), from the production center to peripheries, then the pattern might indicate a developed market system is operating to influence the distribution of goods. Accordingly, the study of spatial fall-off patterns in conjunction with the distributional approach appears to be a crucial methodological step towards addressing regional integration via the proxy of commodities

As mentioned before, the form and degree of market exchange are never static. Anthropologist Carol Smith (1976a, 1976b) proposed before that all market systems can be generally differentiated into two basic types: "normal" and "abnormal;" these two types manifest very distinctively in terms of intervention by administrative forces, transportation efficiency, and means by which goods were transported (Smith 1976a:28, 33–39). The normal market system refers to the scenario in which settlements and market centers are organized according to the so-called "market principle in a central-place system," within which lower-ranking centers or markets usually exist in conjunction with two or more higher ranking centers in order to facilitate distribution and reduce costs (Christaller 1966:72; Smith 1976a:20–21, 1976b:8). By contrast, an abnormal market system, also called a "dendritic system", transports goods through limited or even single paths that connect higher with lower-ranking centers (Kelley 1976; Smith 1976a:34–36). In the latter case, marketplaces remote from major centers are under-developed and constructed primarily for the sake of administrative control rather than economic considerations. Goods produced at high-level or administrative centers could only be transported downstream to lower-level locales through a less-developed exchange network.

As I underscored earlier, it must be recognized that significant differences in terms of economic and political settings existed between the Han empire and the case studies from which the above models were derived; this needs to be taken into account when considering the past realities of Han society. Nonetheless, the investigation of fall-off distribution patterns of goods and their correlation with hierarchies provides one fundamental way for assessing archaeological evidence for regional integration and state control over the market exchange. Despite various constraints, these three frameworks—household distribution, fall-off distribution, and normal/abnormal market—can be synthesized for investigating the mechanisms underlying the distribution of goods, which received little mention in Han period texts.

By combining the distributional approach with discussions about market forms, I propose at least three types of integration: dendritic, administrative-integrated, and fully integrated would be manifested by the distribution pattern in which the market existed (Table 6.1; Figure 6.1). The three hypothetical market models can serve as a basic conceptual tool for a general description of miscellaneous patterns reflected in archaeological records. Table 6.1 compares their features, while Figure 6.1 provides schematic diagrams for each of the three models and related changes in social relations. As regional cores, Xianyang and Chang'an were likely to play a key role in the redistribution, and probably production, of iron objects and other commodities found in the region. This chapter employs these models to evaluate the degree of integration of regional and lower-level centers at different distances from the capital and thus varying degrees of peripherality, in order to assess the extent to which marketplace exchange was present in these locations.

Based on these models, I envision that the assemblage of goods and frequency of tombs yielding goods in different places will vary primarily

Table 6.1 Types of market exchange and indicators for three exchange models

	Dendritic model	Administrative-integrated model	Fully-integrated model
Exchange in the capital	Capital dominates production and transaction	Capital dominates production and transaction	Capital may not dominate production and transaction; goods are more evenly distributed outside the capital
Exchange in centers outside the capital	Goods produced in the capital are consumed locally; goods manufactured in the capital cannot be distributed to peripheral major or minor centers	Exchange between the capital and major centers, especially those closer to the capital, is increasingly active and frequent; the distribution pattern is not entirely monotonic depletion	Goods manufactured in the capital are easily distributed to major and minor centers
Expectation for assemblages in archaeological record	Assemblages in the capital sharply distinguished from lower-rank centers; most commodities found in the capital; frequencies of types found in the capital are very low in lower-rank centers	Assemblages in the capital and nearby major centers are more homogeneous; frequencies in major centers are less likely to show monotonic depletion; sharp difference in the frequencies of artifacts between capital and lower-ranking, peripheral centers	Assemblages in the capital, major, and minor centers are more homogenous; frequencies of the same type of commodities in capital or major centers are not always higher than those in lower-rank or peripheral centers

depending upon the intensity of market connection and interaction with administrative control (Table 6.1). While immigration was undoubtedly present in the Guanzhong basin, residents there in general followed similar cultural practices and funeral rituals, as demonstrated by most typological studies of burials and funeral ceramics in the region (e.g., Han & Zhang 2011; Xiao J. 2007). It is unlikely that certain types of metal objects predominantly

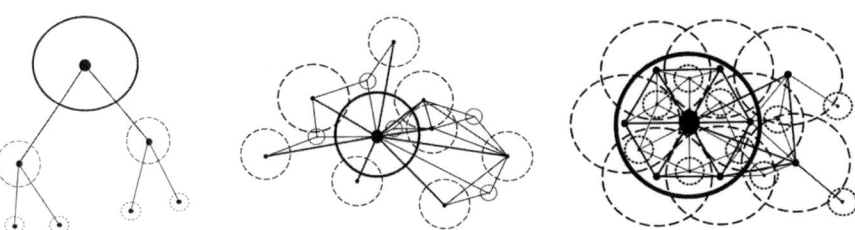

Figure 6.1 Schematics for three market-exchange models: dendritic (left); administrative-integrated (center); fully-integrated (right). Key: circle drawn with a solid black line represents the market area covered by the capital (largest solid black dot at the center of the circle); circles drawn with dashed lines represent market areas covered by administrative centers (black dots) other than the capital; medium size dots represent major (first-rank) centers; small dots represent minor or second-rank centers; straight lines between solid black dots represent market connections between centers (redrawn from Minc 2006:Fig 1; Smith 1976a:Fig 4) .

appeared only in a small area because of a unique local tradition. Although social status could to a certain extent impact access to goods and thus the composition of assemblages and the farming tools more likely to be associated with these peripheral areas are rarely found in burial contexts, it may still be possible to draw valid conclusions from the variability identified in commoners' tombs with a large sample size from different settlements in the capital region. I consider that variations in the frequencies of tombs yielding goods between different locations represent at least three ideal types, which can be juxtaposed against a continuum, with developed marketplaces only concentrated in major centers on the one hand, and relatively free distribution among centers of various ranks due to the widespread distribution of marketplaces on the other.

The first type is called a "dendritic" model. It exists in a region where a major administrative center dominates the overall production or distribution of most everyday commodities. In this case, although markets might be well developed at the main center, such as the capital in the region, regional marketplace exchange via a network between the capital and other lower-ranked centers is relatively underdeveloped. This hinders the transportation of goods from the main center or capital to other consumption sites. Because the movement of goods is central to the institutional apparatus of power at the capital in some cases, the capital in the region might dominate the manufacture of all craft products or the procurement of final products from outside. But the transportation of goods from production centers located in the capital to the majority of consumers across the region is relatively inefficient. The lack of a well-integrated market system outside of the capital severely impacts the transportation of goods, leading to assemblages of goods in the capital that are dramatically different from those in all lower-ranked centers. Consequently, frequencies of objects may be significantly higher in the capital because that is where resources are concentrated. In addition, the collection of certain types of goods found in the capital may be very rare in lower-ranking centers. When all these factors are combined, the volumes of commodities in other lower-rank centers stand in sharp contrast to the pattern revealed in the capital.

The second type I call an "administrative-integrated market" model. In this case, perhaps due to a greater density of marketplaces in a region or an improved level of connectivity between marketplaces, the market system is relatively well-developed in other major or first-rank centers at some distance away from the capital. As a consequence, the differences in frequencies of objects and assemblage compositions with distance from the core are less pronounced. Either the regional network is more evenly developed or administrative forces serve to accelerate the supply of goods only between capitals and relatively minor or second-rank centers. The difference between capitals and other major centers in terms of their access to goods might be less pronounced than in the dendritic model, while the discrepancy between the capital and lower-rank centers still persists. This exchange system inevitably contributes to the formation of more homogeneous goods assemblages in first-rank centers outside the capital.[13] Nonetheless, consumers in the capital, regardless of their social status, might have greater access to items within a given assemblage of goods offered by a particular manufacturing or redistribution center. As a result, the frequencies of goods in major centers would still be relatively higher than in minor centers.

The third scenario is a "fully-integrated market" system, in which minor centers are much better connected with one another and with the capital than is suggested by the other two models. This, in fact, reflects the form of integration caused by market exchange that has usually been conceptualized and discussed in previous archaeological studies, where the better connections between centers significantly counterbalance the limitations of transportation costs and technology (Garraty 2009; Hirth 1998). Also, the exchange of goods primarily follows the economic or transportation principle, whereby goods are allocated to customers who demand the items regardless of their social status (Smith 1976a:19–20). Because of such a well-developed market network, residents throughout the region can generally access the same assemblage of products, whether they live in the capital or in distant, minor centers. The result would be a relatively homogeneous assemblage of goods in the archaeological record. Eventually, the assemblage of commodities in the same kind of archaeological units (e.g., households, cemeteries) within centers of different levels would include similar types of objects. Within a large region, the frequencies of certain types of objects might still vary between different centers due to transportation costs or communication barriers, but neither capitals nor major centers would reveal a higher percentage or frequency of types of goods.

By proposing the models discussed above to evaluate structural variability in market systems, the survey of iron final goods in the capital region in the following sections is designed to investigate the accessibility of goods, or consumption patterns, in settlements of different levels and at varying distances from the regional core center or capital, as a way to evaluate how social relations would be involved, strengthened or altered through the transaction and consumption process.

As Feinman and other scholars have noted, the issue of equifinality relating to post-depositional issues must be of concern in the archaeological study of markets (Feinman & Garraty 2010; Feinman & Nicholas 2012; Smith 1999, 2010). Equifinality refers to forces that result in the representation of similar artifact assemblages in different archaeological features after the long depositional process, even though the original conditions of those features would be very different.[14] Since many of the iron objects recovered from tombs are badly preserved and heavily corroded, and the original forms of many objects are often unrecognizable to the extent that site reports just label them in general as "iron ware", the assemblage data for iron objects published might have been somewhat skewed by natural post-depositional processes. In contrast, bronze objects are often much better preserved than iron in the same environmental contexts.[15] Although certain bronze objects such as bronze weapons and chariot fittings were to a certain extent related to rank,[16] other items in the assemblage such as coins, mirrors, belt-hooks,[17] coffin decorations, digging tools, and knives, were already being manufactured on a massive scale and have been found in tombs representing various social ranks, indicating they would have been available to ordinary people by the Warring States period. For this reason, I suggest that bronze and iron objects should be examined together in order to better understand the distribution patterns of each object type, even though the focus is on iron. If a market system indeed existed and contributed to the distribution of iron goods or other everyday goods, then the types of bronzes that were less closely related to status, for example, mirrors, will perhaps better reveal an underlying market distribution pattern.

The application of the three models to examine the distribution of objects across settlements of different ranks requires us to understand the provenances of sources, either in terms of raw materials or final products. As I discuss in Chapters 2 and 3, iron production during the Qin period may well have been concentrated in the capital. Meanwhile, evidence of iron production in the Han period is generally very small in comparison with contemporary ironworks in the eastern part of the empire. Only limited types of agricultural tools, and occasionally chariot-fittings, were manufactured at such small ironworks. No primary centers as large as Wafangzhuang introduced before were found. Presumably, these local production centers in the capital region were set up to supplement goods that were in the most demand and to reduce the cost of transportation through recycling scrap iron to make iron agricultural tools for local residents. The majority of the iron daily goods largely consumed in the capital region could at least in some cases have been imported from large-scale production centers outside the capital region. Since the canal system might have been one major channel of transportation from the east, the Chang'an capital would be a redistribution center rather than a major manufacturing center, at least to residents to the west of Chang'an.

The production system of bronze ware in the region, in contrast, appears to be relatively not well understood. As was seen with iron ores, modern geological surveys have shown that no large copper mines were located within the Wei River valley (Zhongguo Kuangcang 1996). Archaeometallurgical studies have indicated that the Qin state might have exploited copper resources in the Qinling Mountains in the eastern part of Gansu (Jia 2011). Bronze manufacturing remains dating to the Warring States period have been found in Xianyang (Shaanxi Yanjiusuo 2004b) and Yongcheng (Tian 2013), indicating that some bronze objects were likely to have been locally manufactured in more than one center. Bronze manufacturing sites dating to the Western Han period have also been found surrounding the capital, including in the northwestern corner of Chang'an (Zhongguo Shehui 1995) and in Shanglin yuan (Xi'an Zhongxin 2004). The surveys and excavations of these sites indicate that they were used primarily for minting coins, while no remains associated with the production of bronze daily goods such as mirrors and weapons have been found. Whether the supply of copper and other alloying minerals came from the Qinling Mountains also remains controversial.

More lines of evidence related to bronze manufacturing have been found outside the capital region. For instance, the best archaeological evidence for the production of bronze mirrors, which are the most common type of bronze artifacts found in burial assemblages, was discovered in Linzi in present-day Shandong (Bai & Yasuji 2007; Zhongguo Shehui et al. 2020). In addition, studies of textual records of bronze weapons (crossbows) and vessels show that these items were primarily manufactured in the Henan commandery in present-day Henan province (Liu & Zhang 2006) and the Shu commandery in present-day Sichuan province (Bai 2014; Wu 2007). Collectively, textual and archaeological remains appear to show that the production system of the bronze industry was somewhat similar to the one producing iron. The majority of bronze and iron items found in tombs in the capital region, in fact, would have been probably shipped into the capital region using an imperial transportation network, such as the Cao canal, that connected the capital to other parts of the empire and to other lower-level settlements within the region (Zhang 2016). With such historical background, the capital region of the Han period thus seems to be an interesting example for the application of the three models to reveal the regional exchange and the structuring principles of the market system within the context of Qin and Han empires.

Having presented the background information above, the chapter addresses the following issue: whether the production and transportation systems of metal objects within the capital region might have undergone a significant shift between the Warring States period and Qin-Han periods? Before the collapse of the Qin empire, the majority of iron and bronze objects discovered in the Wei River valley were likely to have been manufactured locally. At least no evidence relevant to the inter-regional distribution of metal goods has been reported. The Qin capital center might have played a more dominant role in manufacturing than its successor, Chang'an. In contrast, most types of bronze and iron daily items discovered in the Western Han period were probably imported from workshops outside the Wei River valley, which has been explained in Chapter 3. Because of the transportation infrastructure linking the capital region to other production centers, Chang'an might therefore have served as both a manufacturing and redistribution center for various final products or raw materials. The capital region of the Qin-Han states thus provides an important opportunity for applying the framework described above to examine the mechanism for distributing metal goods and to examine whether it changed in parallel with a major transformation in the political and production system.

2 Dendritic distribution of metal in the Warring States period

In the Qin state, the development of the cast iron industry became more evident in archaeological records after moving its capital to Xianyang in the Late Warring States period. Some cast iron manufacturing remains dating to the Qin period have been identified in the capital area at Xianyang (Shaanxi Yanjiusuo 2004b) and probably in the area of the mausoleums, but their scale remains unclear. While iron might have been imported during the unification warfare, it seems reasonable to assume that the capital area (Xianyang) was one potential manufacturing center for iron items found in the region during the Late Warring States and Qin unification periods. Iron workshops might have existed in some other centers, such as the Qin Shihuang mausoleum to support the massive manufacturing of goods for his after-death world, although no large-scale manufacture compared to Guandong has yet been discovered.

In order to interpret changes in the distribution patterns in the capital region, I collected published Qin burial data[18] from Guanzhong (Table 6.2; Figure 6.2) for a combined sample total of more than 1,700 tombs. High-status tombs such as those with sets of bronze ritual vessels were removed from the dataset to limit the effect of social status on the data. Qin period burials were mostly shaft-pit tombs or catacomb tombs of similar size. It is important to note that the traditional social hierarchy that had developed in the Bronze Age was no longer reflected in the burial practices of the Qin state following the Lord Shang reforms (von Falkenhausen 2004; Shelach & Pines 2006; Teng 2002, 2013). Most of the Qin tombs post-dating the Middle Warring States period are relatively similar in terms of their size and structure. Tombs with exceptional scales were rarely reported.[19] These

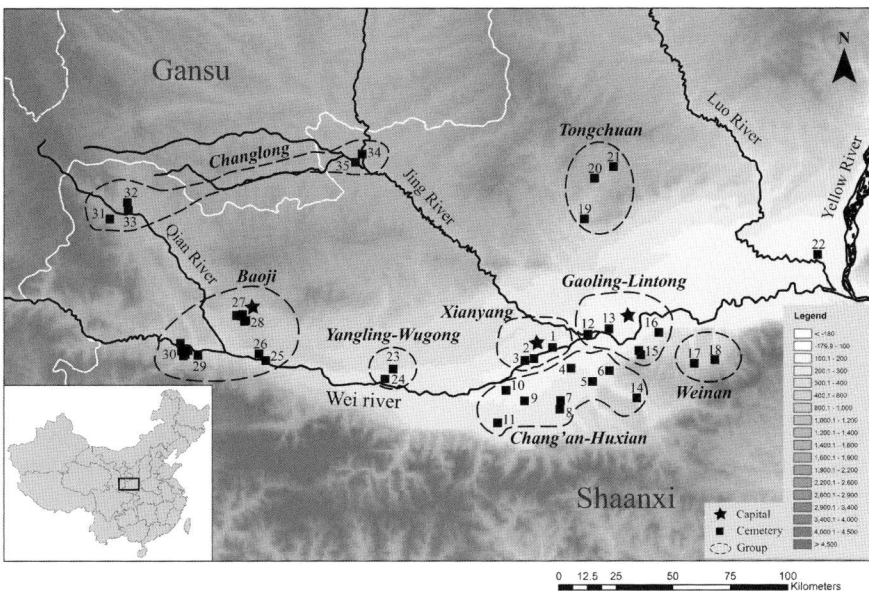

Figure 6.2 Distribution of Warring States cemeteries of the Qin State in the Guan-zhong basin, including parts of cemeteries dating to the Spring-and-Autumn and Qin unification periods.

Sources: (1) Shaanxi Yanjiusuo (2004b); (2) Xianyangshi Wenwu (2005); Shaanxi Yanjiuyuan (2018c); (3) Xianyangshi Wenwu 1998; (4) Shaanxi Yanjiusuo (2006c); Shaanxi Yanjiuyuan (2018b); Shaanxi Yanjiuyuan (2008a); (5) Jin (1957); (6) Zhang Zhongyi (1959); (7) Wang (1994); (8) Xi'anshi (2004b); (9) Zhongguo Kexueyuan (1962); (10) Shaanxisheng Wenguanhui (1975); (11) Cao (1989); (12) Shaanxi Yanjiusuo (2003b); (13) Shaanxi Yanjiusuo (2004a); (14) Zhong-guo Shehui Shaanxi (1988); (15) Qinyong (1980); Shihuangling (1983); Shaanxi Yanjiuyuan (2016); (16) Shaanxi Yanjiusuo (1998b); (17) Shaanxi Yanjiuyuan and Weinanshi (2011); (18) Shaanxi Yanjiusuo and Qinshihuang (2006); (19) Ma (1959); (20) Shaanxi Yanjiusuo (1986); (21) Shaanxi Yanjiusuo and Beijing (1987); (22) Shaanxisheng and Dalixian (1978); (23) Gao and Zhao (1996); Shaanxi Yanjiusuo (2006d); Xianyangshi Wenguanhui (1992); Xianyang-shi Wenwu (1996); (24) Zhongguo Shehui Wugong (1996); (25) Shaanxisheng Wenwu (1965); (26) Baojishi and Baojixian (1980); (27) Shaanxisheng Gongzuozhan (1991); Shaanxi Yanji-uyuan et al. (2013); Yongcheng (1985); (28) Shaanxisheng Yongcheng (1980, 1986); Shang and Zhao (1986); Yongcheng (1980, 1986); (29) Su (1984); (30) Baojishi (1991); Baojishi and Baojishi (1979); Tian and Lei (1993); Zhao and Liu (1963); (31) Baojishi and Longxian (2001); (32) Gao and Wang (1988); (33) Shaanxi Yanjiusuo (1998a); (34) Shaanxi Yanjiusuo (1984); (35) Zhong-guo Shehui (2007).

small- and medium-sized tombs might therefore represent people from a wide spectrum of society, although most low-status bond-servants or slaves are still unlikely to be represented here as they usually did not have typical tombs that are recognizable in the archaeological record. It can reason-ably be argued that the frequency and distribution of goods found in the graves selected for this study reflect their availability to ordinary people of middle-ranking social status, rather than their availability to all members of society.

Table 6.2 Tombs found at eight burial groups dating to the
Warring States-Qin periods

Area	Number of tombs
Baoji	106
Chang'an-Huxian (Chang-Hu)	584
Changlong	148
Gaoling-Lintong (Gao-Lin)	572
Tongchuan	7
Weinan	52
Xianyang	461
Yangling-Wugong (Yang-Wu)	16
Total	1798

To illustrate the fall-off pattern, I divided the Qin period burial dataset into several spatial clusters or "groups" based on the location of tombs and the proximity of cemeteries to the capital (Figure 6.2). These divisions were created in an attempt to provide relatively comparable groups for purposes of statistical analysis. Since they are not entirely congruent with the administrative *xian* county divisions promulgated by the Qin empire,[20] they are therefore somewhat subjective. Also, given the nature of the data, the size of each group is not identical, and the numbers of modern cities or counties covered by each group vary greatly. For the same reasons, the area divisions for the Han period that are introduced below are somewhat different from that of the Qin dynasty in terms of the geographical coverage of each area and the number of clusters.

This section aims to use the framework proposed above to evaluate if the patterning of objects buried or discarded in tombs in different groups was contingent upon another crucial factor: the hierarchy of settlements. I also need to reclassify the collected data to employ the framework of fall-off distribution, following the criteria below. This study ranks each group as either the capital city (main or core center), first-rank (major centers slightly inferior to the capital but superior to other centers), or second-rank (minor centers inferior to the capital and first-rank centers) based on the hierarchy of major settlements included in each of these groups (Table 6.3). Historical texts combined with archaeological data provide valuable evidence for determining the rank of settlements. For the Warring States period, I classified Chang'an-Huxian (Chang-Hu) and Baoji as first-rank settlements. Since several major palace complexes were located in the Chang'an area, and it may have been part of the Xianyang capital at the time, the political importance of Chang-Hu should be relatively higher than other groups. Also, since Yong, a key site in Baoji, was a ritual center where the inauguration ceremony for the First Emperor was said to have taken place,[21] the group of Baoji should be important in terms of its political role. It is noteworthy that the Gao-Lin (Gaoling-Lintong) group, while it is adjacent to the capital,

Table 6.3 Ranking of various burial
groups at various centers during
the Warring States-Qin periods

Center	Rank
Xianyang	Capital
Baoji	First-rank
Chang-Hu	First-rank
Changlong	Second-rank
Gao-Ling	Second-rank
Tongchuan	Second-rank
Weinan	Second-rank
Yang-Wu	Second-rank

included primarily resettled migrants from the eastern territory, and most individuals might not enjoy the status as prestigious as those in Xianyang. Thus I categorize it as a first-rank center.

Certain treatments of data were also adopted to better illustrate inherited subtle patterns. Due to the potential impact of the individual economic status of those buried in the statistical study below, I only calculate the frequency of occurrence of certain types of iron and bronze items. Although the exact quantity of each type of iron and bronze objects in each tomb is presumably contingent upon the level of integration of market exchange in the settlement, it also might be influenced by the social status of the occupant of the tomb. Wealthy occupants were more likely than other people to have metal objects buried with them. In addition, a considerable number of Qin and Han tombs were looted over time, even though ironware usually are not the targets of plundering. Therefore, I only take into consideration the presence or absence of iron and bronze objects, rather than their quantities, and instead use the frequency of burials containing certain types of bronze or iron objects as a major proxy for illustrating the market system and availability of daily commodities to the general population in the capital region.

As I noted in Chapter 1, the major types of iron objects found in Qin tombs included knives, belt-hooks, and vessels (Bai 2005; Lam et al. 2017a). Iron digging or farming tools such as spades have occasionally been found, but they seem to have been discarded in tomb backfill instead of placed in coffins as burial goods. With few exceptions, iron weapons such as swords, spears, and arrowheads have not been frequently found in the studied assemblages. Other iron objects included lampstands, but they were primarily found in tombs dating to the Late Warring States period or later. In comparison with the Han period, iron cauldrons, vessels in general, and long swords are rarely found in Qin tombs; their numbers are not high enough to be included in the assemblage list for this study of distribution patterns (Bai 2005; Teng 1993, 1995).

The collection of bronze objects from Qin tombs selected for the study of distribution patterns includes everyday goods (e.g., belt-hooks, mirrors, and cauldrons), tools, coffin decorations, chariot-fittings, and weapons (including halberds, swords, spearheads, and arrowheads). Since the last two broad groups are relatively rare in the assemblage, I suspect that these items might have been associated with individuals of special social rank and therefore controlled by the government to a certain extent. To make the bronze assemblage data comparable to those for the iron assemblages, I present data on bronze belt-hooks, knives, mirrors, bells, bracelets, chariot-fittings, vessels, weapons, and coffin decorations, but exclude data for heirloom objects (e.g., coins) or that appear very infrequently in tombs.[22]

Since my aim is to understand the frequency of metal objects in various tomb clusters, I also grouped similar types of objects into generic categories such as iron or bronze knives and bronze or iron belt-hooks. Objects such as iron scissors that appeared only occasionally were collected into broader generic groups such as "iron tools". For the purpose of comparison, the following section also only considers the major types that appear in most clusters, including belt-hooks, knives, and swords. If a generic group appeared in just two or three clusters with a low frequency, then I intend not to include those items in the presentation of results here because of their low distribution range. After the process of reclassifying objects into more generic groups, the frequencies of occurrence of each type are then compared in order to reconstruct distribution patterns. Building upon the reclassification, I further aggregate all iron or bronze items into the general categories of "iron objects" or "bronze objects" in order to more clearly illustrate the distribution patterns produced when the percentage of metal objects is plotted against a site's proximity to the capital.

The bar graph in Figure 6.3 clearly shows a discrepancy in the distribution of iron artifacts between various groups of settlements. The types of iron artifacts are particularly few in number and very rare in most lower-rank centers such as Changlong, making the assemblages in Qin tombs at the capital (Xianyang) distinguished from other centers across the entire capital district. While the Qin state originated in the Longdong region, namely eastern Gansu and northwestern Shaanxi, the area of Changlong then became a buffer zone between the Qin state and various barbarian groups

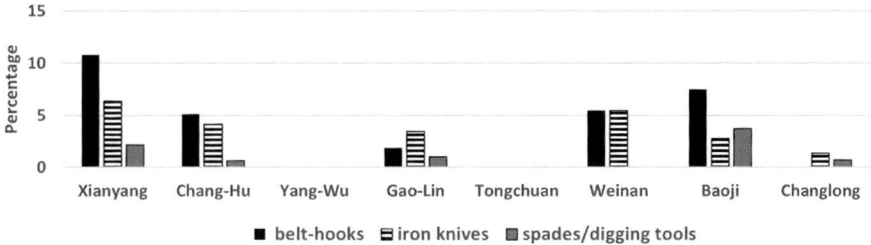

Figure 6.3 Percentage of tombs containing iron items at eight burial groups in Guanzhong from the Warring States through Qin periods.

in the Hexi region,[23] especially when the capital was eventually resettled in Xianyang further to the east. Other phenomena should also be noted in the frequency data. First, in Xianyang, the capital of the Qin state after 350 BCE, about 6 percent of tombs included iron knives and about 11 percent of tombs yielded at least one iron belt-hook (Figure 6.3). Second, inter-site comparisons show that the percentages of iron belt-hooks and knives in Xianyang and Chang-Hu (including Chang'an) are relatively higher than those in Yangling-Wugong (Yang-Wu), Changlong, Gao-Lin, Weinan, and Baoji. Due to its proximity to Xianyang, Chang'an had already assumed an important role during the Late Warring States period and served as part of the capital area. Several Qin cemeteries, whose occupants were claimed to be residents in Xianyang, were found in the later Chang'an area.[24] Its residents might have had little difficulty obtaining commodities that were being manufactured in the Xianyang area.

In general, what these figures suggest is that, while iron was not rare in the Qin state, iron objects were not ubiquitous in the Qin state beyond the capital area throughout the Warring States-Qin period. Even in first-rank centers such as Baoji, the types and frequencies of iron objects are relatively low. This discrepancy is even more noticeable between the capital and peripheral or second-rank centers. In addition to the scale of the iron industry that was discussed in previous chapters, the poorly developed market economy in the Qin state at this time would also have limited the circulation of iron implements. After aggregating all iron items together into the broad category "iron objects," the succinct version of the distribution pattern also indicates an intriguing pattern, that the percentage of tombs containing iron objects relates to the proximity to the capital (Figure 6.4:a). Judging from the current statistical results, it is reasonable to say that for the small to medium-sized tombs examined, the ones in the capital area were more likely to yield iron knives and belt-hooks than those that were remote from it (Figure 6.4:a). Also, tombs in the capital appear to include iron objects more frequently than those in both the first-rank and second-rank settlements (Table 6.4, $p < 0.001$). While it is impossible to exclude other factors, such as funeral rituals, involved in deciding which objects would be included in tombs, the sharp discrepancy suggests that iron implements were unlikely to be well distributed within the Qin capital region during the Late Warring States or even before the Qin's unification in 221 BCE.

The percentage of tombs containing major types of bronzes (Figure 6.5) reveals a pattern somewhat similar to that manifested by the distribution pattern of iron objects. As mentioned above, the most common type of bronze object found in Warring States burials is the belt-hook. In the Xianyang area, the percentage of tombs containing this kind of bronze object is as high as 42 percent. Bronze belt-hooks have been found in other areas included in this study, however, the percentage of bronze belt-hooks in Xianyang is much higher than in other areas. For example, only about 10 percent of tombs in Changlong and Weinan contained bronze belt-hooks, a pattern

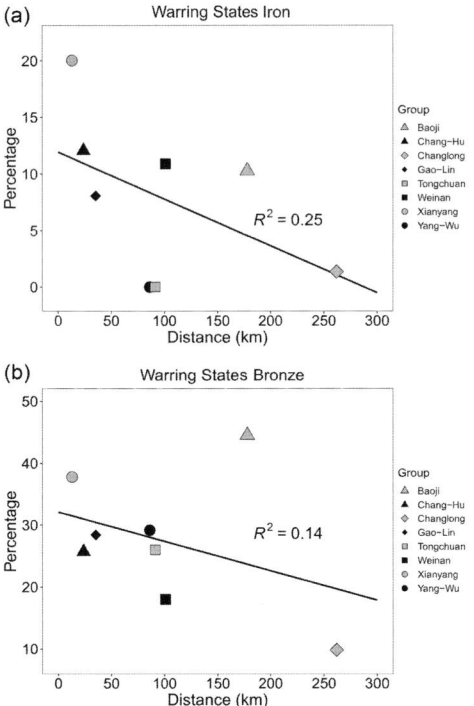

Figure 6.4 Graph showing a correlation between distance to Xianyang city and percentage of tombs containing two types of metal goods at eight burial groups from the Middle Warring States through Qin unification periods (ca. 350–206 BCE) (a: iron objects; b: bronze objects; X-axis: distance from an area to Xianyang city calculated by the average distance between the cemeteries in the area to the capital; Y-axis: percentage of tombs containing any one of four types of iron objects in the area).

similar to the inter-site distribution of the iron belt-hooks discussed above. In one of his widely-known metaphors, philosopher Zhuangzi criticized the hypocrisy of rulers who usurped the throne but promoted the sages' virtues (also known as Confucian morals) at the same time, and said "He who steals a belt-hook pays with his life; he who steals a state gets to be a feudal lord."[25] Clearly, belt-hooks should be viewed as a type of common commodity in the Warring States period, and their frequency in some areas in the capital region might be closely relevant to scarcity, probably due to the limited capacity of the distribution network for centers in the extremity.

Given the rather long history of the bronze industry, it is worthwhile to take the factor of multiple manufacturing centers and the potential alteration in the distributions into consideration. While the frequency of bronze belt-hooks in the Changlong area is not ubiquitous compared to the pattern in Xianyang, small numbers of bronze knives together with bells, mirrors,

Table 6.4 Comparison of percentages of iron and bronze objects found in Warring
States-Qin tombs from capital, first-rank, and second-rank settlements

	Capital	*First-rank settlements*	*Second-rank settlements*	*Comparison*
	(N = 461)	*(N = 690)*	*(N = 795)*	p^a
% Iron objects in tombs	20.0	11.7	6.8	p < 0.001
	20.0	11.7		p < 0.001
	20.0		6.8	p < 0.001
		11.7	6.8	p < 0.01
% Bronze objects in tombs	37.8	28.6	24.1	p < 0.001
	37.8	28.6		p < 0.001
	37.8		24.1	p < 0.001
		28.6	24.1	p = 0.05

a   For each category (iron and bronze), the p-value in the top row represents a comparison
between all three types of settlements: capital, first-rank, and second-rank; p-values in the
second, third, and fourth rows represent comparisons between two of the three types of
settlements.

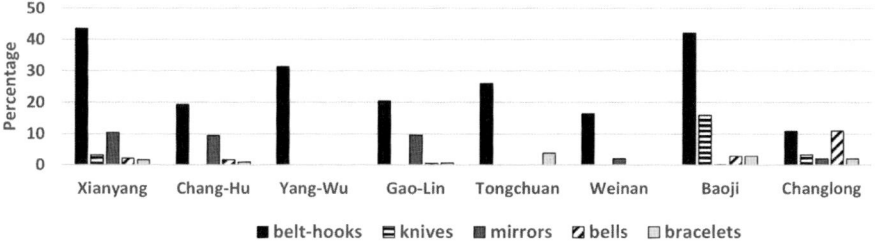

Figure 6.5 Percentage of tombs containing bronze items at eight burial groups in
Guanzhong during the Warring States through Qin periods.

and bracelets still have been identified there. However, bronze knives are
almost absent from Chang'an burials. Its percentage in Xianyang is relatively low, even lower than the percentage in Baoji. The inter-site comparison reveals a distribution pattern somewhat different from that of iron
knives (Figure 6.5). Compared with the iron industry, the bronze industry,
especially the section of tool manufacturing, had a much longer history
of development in the Qin state. After the Warring States period, bronze
knives also became relatively accessible to commoners as everyday products or burial goods. Probably skewed by the local production in Yong[26]
or other unknown locations, the percentage of other bronze items in assemblages does not present a clear correlation to distance from the capital (Figure 6.4:b). The less dramatic differentiation between the capital and

lower-ranked places also seems to be in alignment with the administrative model of distribution. A difference between the center and peripheral areas is still present, but it is not as distinctive for bronze as for iron objects.

With all these subtle discrepancies, the intergroup variations in bronze objects still display an interesting parallel with the patterning of iron objects. During the Warring States-Qin periods, the percentages of tombs in Xianyang containing at least one bronze object are generally higher than for other areas (Figure 6.4:b). Meanwhile, the Weinan and Changlong figures are relatively low, probably because of their distance from the capital and their proximity to the borderlands of the Qin state. The percentage in Baoji is second highest, which may be attributable to its unique political significance as a capital city that was used for more than 300 years. Even after the capital was moved to Xianyang, Baoji continued to serve as a ritual center. Other types of bronzes such as mirrors that are usually less common in assemblages are more often found in Xianyang than in other areas. In general, tombs in the capital area and first-rank settlements seem to yield bronze objects more frequently (Table 6.4, p < 0.001), regardless of whether the items indicate high social status or not. By evaluating the descriptive figures, the distribution and consumption clearly concentrated the capital area, a pattern emerges more or less aligned with the dendritic model, and we see the distribution networks surrounding the manufacturing and consumption of iron products as well as bronze objects concentrated on individuals or communities within the capital region but not extended very far away.

3 Appearance of an integrated market in the Han capital

For the Western Han tombs of middle to lower rank from the same region (Table 6.5; Figure 6.6), the reclassification of a dataset similar to the processing of Qin data had to be conducted for the purpose of comparison. The unearthed text, the *Zhilü* (Statutes on Salaries) from Zhangjiashan (Barbieri-Low & Yates 2015:964; Zhangjiashan 2001:193) that I quoted before provides

Table 6.5　Numbers of tombs found in nine burial groups dating to the Western Han period[27]

Area	Number of tombs
Baoji	35
Chang'an	1054
Fufeng	22
Gao-Lin	30
Longxian	39
Meixian	45
Weinan	19
Xianyang	27
Yangling	306
Total	1564

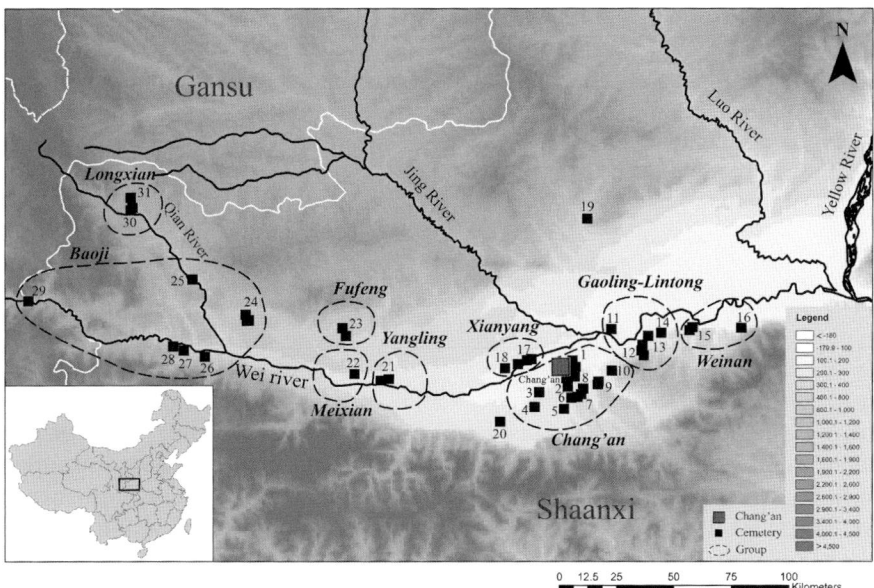

Figure 6.6 Map of Western Han cemeteries in the Guanzhong basin.

Sources: (1) Cheng et al. (1992a, 1992b); Han and Cheng (1991, 1992); Shaanxi Yanjiusuo (1987, 2003c, 2006b); Shaanxisheng Wenwu (1960); Sun and Chong (2001); Wang and Kong (1987); Xi'anshi (1997a, 1998a, 1998b, 1999); Xi'anshi and Zhengzhou (2004); Xi'anshi Yanjiuyuan (2018); Zhongguo Shehui Chang'an and Xi'anshi Yanjiuyuan (2014); Zhongguo Shehui Tangchengdui (1991); (2) Xi'anshi (1997b); (3) Xi'anshi and Zhengzhou (2004); (4) Xi'anshi (2009a); (5) Shaanxi Yanjiusuo (2001); (6) Xi'anshi and Zhengzhou (2004); (7) Xi'anshi and Zhengzhou (2004); (8) Xi'anshi (2004a); (9) Shaanxi Yanjiusuo (2003a); (10) Zhang Zhongyi (1959); (11) Shaanxi Yanjiusuo (2004a); (12) Shaanxisheng Peihe (1989); Wang (2004); (13) Unpublished data provided by Yang Qihuang; (14) Shaanxi Yanjiusuo (2004c); (15) Cui (1992); Cui and Wang (1998); (16) Xibei (1989); (17) Xianyang (1986); Xianyangshi Wenwu (1999, 2004, 2006); (18) Xianyangshi Wenwu (2000); (19) Ma (1959); (20) Zhuo (1980); (21) Gao and Zhao (1996); Shaanxi Yanjiuyuan and Yanglingqu (2018); Xianyangshi Wenwu (1996); (22) Shaanxi Yanjiusuo and Baojishi (1989); (23) Shaanxi Yanjiuyuan (2010); Zhouyuan (2001); (24) Shaanxisheng Yongcheng (1980, 1986); Shaanxi Yanjiuyuan et al. (2013); Shang and Zhao (1986); (25) Wang (1975); (26) Shaanxi Yanjiuyuan and Baojishi (2013); (27) Zhang (1987); (28) Shaanxi Yanjiuyuan and Baojishi (2012); (29) Shaanxi Yanjiusuo (2006a); (30) Baojishi (2002); Shaanxisheng Baozhong (1999); (31) Tian and Yang (1998).

essential hierarchical information about various county centers. In the document, county magistrates were classified into three ranks relative to the political importance of the counties they governed (Xiao A. 2007). I assume that the highest-ranked counties, known as the 1,000-*shi* (bushel)-rank magistrate counties, were more important, at least politically, than other counties in the Han empire (Table 6.6). Thus, the Gaoling-Lintong (Gao-Lin) cluster is classified as first rank because it includes two counties (Xinfeng and Yueyang) where magistrates held a salary grade of 1,000-shi; Baoji also belongs to the first rank because Yong county magistrates had the same

Table 6.6 Ranking of Burial Groups at Various Centers during the Western Han period

Center	Rank
Chang'an	Capital
Baoji	First rank
Gao-Lin	First-rank
Xianyang	First-rank
Fufeng	Second-rank
Longxian	Second-rank
Meixian	Second-rank
Weinan	Second-rank
Yangling	Second-rank

salary grade. Xianyang is considered first-rank because most mausoleum towns, which were set up by the Han government to relocate rich and influential families migrated from the east, are located there (Ge 1990; Barbierilow 2021). While conventional studies divide the entire chronology of the Western Han into three phases (Han & Zhang 2011), the volume of published data in some areas is much lower for some phases and the parts that have been published are highly selective and biased. Furthermore, these cemeteries were usually partially excavated, and only tombs that were relatively well-preserved or contained rich assemblages of goods are mentioned in the publication. Because some areas lack sufficient samples to permit analysis within a fine chronological framework, I discuss the percentages of Western Han tombs as a whole that came from the same area or same cemeteries.

In the Han period, the tomb structure was different from the preceding period and changed significantly from shaft-pit and catacomb to brick-chamber tombs with a short entry ramp (Han & Zhang 2011). Some of the Han burials took the form of a pair of joint brick-chamber tombs, but very few of them had a long entry ramp with a chamber larger than 10 × 4 m. For this reason, I exclude examples of relatively large size with long entry slop and storage chambers, which usually include artifacts associated with a prestige status, such as figurines,[28] jade suits (or components of jade suits),[29] and sets of bronze vessels, representing occupants who might have been officials of relatively high rank, possibly very high-rank officials or elite members. These examples usually included individual cemetery gardens and external storage pits associated, such as the example of the Fengqiyuan cemetery belonging to Zhang Anshi's family (Shaanxi Yanjiuyuan 2009), who was appointed as a member of the Shangshu (Secretariat) during Zhaodi's reign (87–74 BCE), and the discovery of M115 at Zhangjiapu that includes two storage chambers on one side of the entry slop in which sets of ceramic and bronze ritual *ding* tripods have been found (Xi'anshi 2009b).[30]

During the Western Han period, the assemblage of iron objects in the entire Wei River valley changed in certain ways alongside the appearance of new types, indicating a new distribution system emerged. First, the major types of iron artifacts became more diversified. For instance, iron swords, vessels, and lamps occurred more widely in burial good assemblages (Figure 6.7). Another remarkable change was that iron belt-hooks rapidly disappeared. Yet, the most remarkable change in the regional assemblage pattern was that iron objects appeared more frequently in second-rank centers, even though some were far from the capital in Chang'an. In Figure 6.7, I show the percentage of tombs in different groups that yielded major categories of iron objects. Certain types of iron objects such as digging tools are absent from tombs in some areas, but each tomb cluster includes at least four types. The percentages of tombs containing the four major types of iron artifacts also reveal a rather mosaic-like scenario. In some areas, the percentages of burials containing certain types of iron objects are relatively high. For instance, the percentage of iron cauldrons seems to be particularly high in Meixian. However, the prevalence of iron swords and knives in Yangling appears to be the lowest in comparison with other areas, indicating the proximity to an ironworks did not result in significantly higher percentages of iron objects from tombs in local assemblages. Collectively, the data show that tombs in the Chang'an area no longer had a higher probability of containing more iron objects, even though the local population had greater access to iron resources or were closer to the transportation center. Nor do the data support the idea that burials in settlements of higher rank or with evidence of production show a higher prevalence of iron objects in tombs, either in terms of type or frequency.

To better illuminate such mosaic-like patterns, I aggregated all iron items into the generic category "iron objects" and calculated the percentage of tombs in each area containing at least one type of iron objects (Figure 6.8:a). The result clearly reinforces the idea that there is no clear correlation between distance from the Western Han capital and the percentage of tombs containing iron objects. In particular, no clear-cut distributional patterns can be identified, especially in relation to the distance of different burial groups from the capital. Although the percentages are subject to variation due to the small numbers of published tombs in some burial groups, the pattern is nevertheless distinguished from that of the Qin assemblage, which

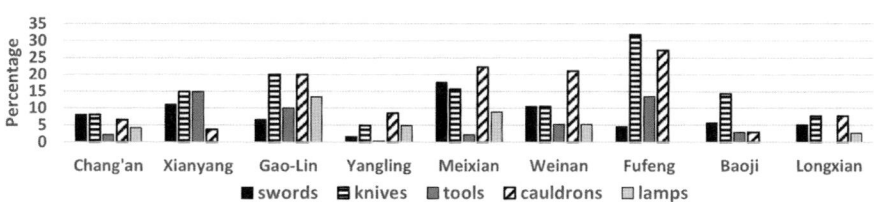

Figure 6.7 Percentage of tombs containing iron items at nine burial groups in Guanzhong during the Western Han period.

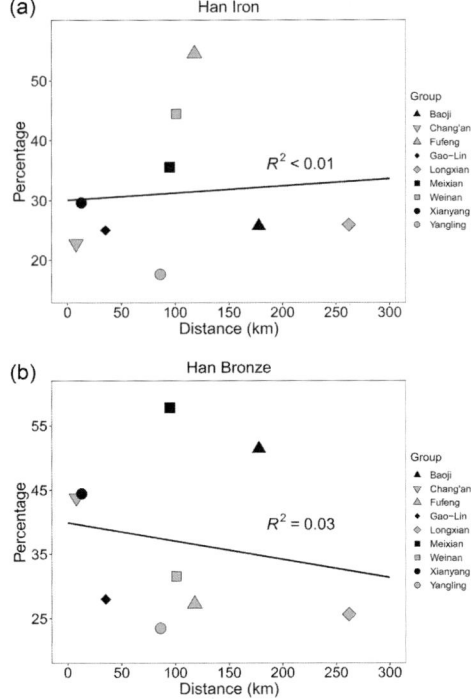

Figure 6.8 Graph showing a correlation between distance to Chang'an city and percentage of tombs containing two types of metal goods at nine burial groups during the Western Han period (a: iron objects; b: bronze objects).

was characterized by a low percentage of tombs yielding limited types of iron objects at lower-level centers vis-à-vis the high concentration of iron objects in the capital area.

In Chapter 3, I explained that the consumption of iron objects, whether final or semi-finished products, at local centers in the Wei River valley would have largely depended upon access to goods being supplied by external sources via an interregional transportation network, of which Chang'an was the key redistribution center. Even though the ironworks might have been organized by the design to boost production efficiency, they only focused on the manufacturing of rather limited types of products, and the scale of production might not have been large enough to provide sufficient access to all minor centers. The iron assemblages and distribution patterns during the Western Han period further indicate that an active regional market system would have contributed to the transportation and movement of goods within the entire capital region, probably from the Chang'an center. In addition, the distribution of types present in the Han iron assemblages appears to be more homogeneous than during the Warring States period,

Table 6.7 Comparison of percentages of iron and bronze objects found in Western Han tombs from capital, first-rank, and second-rank settlements

	Capital	First-rank settlements	Second-rank settlements	Comparison
	(N = 1054)	(N = 92)	(N = 431)	p^a
% Iron objects	22.77	26.63	23.73	p = 0.749
in tombs	22.77	26.63		p = 0.459
	22.77		23.73	p = 0.77
		26.63	23.73	p = 0.583
% Bronze	43.8	41.73	26.45	p < 0.001
objects in	43.8	41.73		p = 0.643
tombs	43.8		26.45	p < 0.001
		41.73	26.45	p = 0.004

a For each category (iron and bronze), the p-value in the top row represents a comparison between all three types of settlements: capital, first-rank, and second-rank; p-values in the second, third, and fourth rows represent comparisons between two of the three types of settlements.

and the frequency of vessels and tools contained in tombs seem to follow a market-dominated pattern, in that the frequencies of occurrence do not decrease in line with the increase of distance from the capital center in the same market zone. The percentage of iron objects in the capital was also not higher than that in first-rank (Table 6.7, p = 0.459) or second-rank Han settlements (Table 6.7, p = 0.77), even though residents near Chang'an would easily procure more objects, or objects that were made with higher-quality decorations.

Judging from the distribution pattern, economic integration appears to have improved by the Han period and it was no longer dominated by a "dendritic model" of market distribution. The well-integrated regional market system might also be attributable to the expansion of the state network from the core to the Hexi Corridor after Wudi's reign. Consequently, residents in previously distant areas in the Guanzhong basin such as Longxian became a traffic point on the imperial pathway, Huizhongdao,[31] which connects Guanzhong to the Hexi Corridor, and thus they gained more access to iron assemblages similar to those obtained by residents in Chang'an. Distance or political rank was no more a key factor in the distribution patterns of iron daily use goods in the capital region during the Western Han period.

In parallel with the iron assemblages, the strong influence of the distribution network centered on the capital gradually declined in the case of bronze assemblages during the Han period. A quick look at the bar chart in Figure 6.9 reveals again a sharp difference between the Han and Warring States-Qin periods. Han tombs yielded bronze objects more frequently and indicated rather homogeneous assemblages, while most tomb clusters from the Warring States-Qin periods do not have assemblages containing mirrors,

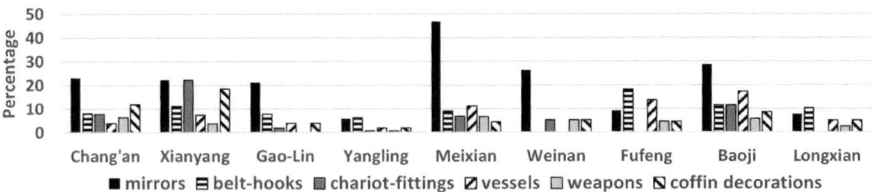

Figure 6.9 Percentage of tombs containing bronze items at nine burial groups in Guanzhong during the Western Han period.

bells, belt-hooks or bracelets. The availability of bronze daily use objects during the Han period seems to have been less dependent on proximity to production centers. The low-scale exchange between centers within these areas already existed before Qin unification, but the pattern illustrated by Figuure 6.8:b does not appear to explicitly indicate the existence of a large, regional market network. After the collapse of the Qin dynasty and reunification under the Western Han, however, the bronze industry began to develop similarly to the iron industry, enlarging the scale of production. Besides mirrors, bronze assemblages include more items such as chariot-fittings and some bronze vessels, and crossbows, and tombs in each area contain greater or lesser percentages of objects from most of these categories. While some of the products were potentially cast by foundries near Chang'an, evidence showing the local manufacture of mirrors, weapons, and tools is scarce in the region, indicating that they were imported from other state workshops in various commanderies beyond the Guanzhong basin, also known as Gongguan work office (Gao 2019), through redistribution centers. In general, the fall-off pattern did not center on the capital, and the phenomenon of capital city dominance over the production and distribution of bronze utensils, tools, and weapons simply disappeared.

Aligned with the distribution pattern of iron objects, the frequencies of bronze objects in most areas also do not correspond to the distance of each area from the capital, Chang'an, during the Han period (Figure 6.9). For instance, in Baoji and Meixian, the percentages of Western Han tombs including bronze mirrors are more or less similar to Chang'an. There is no clear evidence demonstrating a close correlation between distance and access to bronze items (Figure 6.8:b). Echoing the distribution pattern of iron objects, the percentage of bronze daily use items in the capital was not significantly higher than that in first-rank settlements (Table 6.7, $p = 0.643$), even though the percentage in second-rank settlements is lower than both the capital (Table 6.7, $p < 0.001$) and first-rank settlements (Table 6.7, $p = 0.004$). One potential reason is that copper in the Han period was, as it is today, much more expensive than iron. The price of copper and iron was not explicitly recorded in texts. But one important source comes from *Shiji* Chapter 129, which states:

[Whomever in] market-towns and commercial metropolises sold annually [any one of the] following categories to the specified quantity was also equal [in wealth with the head of a great hereditary] family *jia* of a thousand chariots......

13. Bronze utensils, to the weight of thousand *jun*

14. Plain wooden and iron vessels, (and/or) of *xie* and *qian* (gardenia and madder plants for dyes or medicinal purposes), to the weight of a thousand *jin*......[32]

In this passage, Sima Qian recorded that those merchants who sold one thousand *jin* (about 250 kg) of iron or 1,000 *jun* (about 62 kg) of copper or bronze would make the wealth equivalent to the annual incomes of an elite family with 1,000 chariots, which was about 200,000 *qian* according to the same passage. Assuming the income record is accurate, some scholars suggest that the price for copper (or bronze) per unit was at least four times that of iron (Ding & Wei 2016:305). A sharp discrepancy was even present in the sparse records of price. For instance, during the Middle-Late Western Han period, an iron *cha*-spade only cost 3 *qian* (ibid:111), which was a very low value compared to the price of meat and crop prices introduced before. Perhaps in the capital region, the price for the same type of agricultural tools was even lower. In contrast, the inscriptions on a bronze clothing iron dating to the Eastern Han period indicate that this product weighing three *jin* was worth 300 *qian* (ibid:105). A bronze mirror with delicate decoration would also cost about several hundred *qian*. In this light, some bronze objects, such as mirrors, were argued to be "light luxuries" (Guo 2018), and these might not be affordable to a good portion of ordinary people due to their relatively expensive prices, which might have contributed to their higher presence in some first-rank settlements.

In sum, the distribution patterns of bronze and iron objects in the Han period bear a degree of similarity. During the Han period, the distribution shows relatively homogeneous patterns in terms of types of bronze goods and the percentage of tombs containing them in each area in the capital core. No clear linear fall-off patterns can be identified in the graphs of the relationship between frequency and distance (Figure 6.8:a & b). If a developed regional market system was responsible for distributing iron products from production sites to different local centers, then the similar distribution patterns for bronze items identified in archaeological contexts indicate that these products were probably distributed by the same mechanism, although distribution to outliers such as Meixian might still have been affected by intervention from administrative centers due to their political or economic importance. The variation in the availability of some everyday bronze objects between different centers probably reflects the fact that some of these goods were more readily available or residents in some centers were able to afford them. Nevertheless, the dendritic model was by no means the major mechanism responsible for the distribution pattern observed for the Western Han period, reflecting a more integrated system.

In the opening of this chapter, I suggest that the regional scale mechanism of market exchange is essential to our understanding of the economic foundation and connectivity of the Han empire. It must also be noted that, although most commoners could access metal products, the production of iron was largely controlled by these states after the implementation of the salt-iron monopoly in the Western Han dynasty in 117 BCE. Besides the manufacturing process, the Qin-Han states managed sales of these objects, probably by maintaining prices and controlling the quality of objects sold in marketplaces at settlements of various ranks (Gao 2008). The Han state even imposed a restriction on the transportation of iron, particularly prohibiting iron from leaving Han-controlled territory (Barbieri-Low & Yates 2015:1117). The involvement of the state in manufacturing, transporting, and distributing products would unavoidably combine with the force of "marketplace exchange" determined purely by demand and supply. This is the reason for the proposal of classifying various types of theoretical connections (dendritic, administrative-integrated, and fully-integrated) that underlie market exchange. An empirical investigation of distribution patterns can therefore articulate the operation of regional market exchange and shed light on the theme of this book: the evolution of imperial integration and social relations transformed by the exchange system.

To clarify the social function of market integration in the distribution of commodities and the creation of connectivity, this chapter has examined the distribution patterns of iron and bronze items within the capital region. Combining integration studies with models of market exchange, the distribution patterns of iron and bronze objects, albeit overlooked in previous studies of tombs, can cast light on several mechanisms by which regional market exchange linked the local communities to the macro-scale interregional network and created a new type of social relations. Reiterating my previous argument that market exchange was rather less developed during the Qin period, the distribution patterns seen in the Warring States-Qin data indicate that the exchange of goods in the core region should actually be considered an example of "dendritic exchange," in which the exchange of metal commodities was primarily controlled by the capital at Xianyang. While the marketplace might have been relatively developed in Xianyang, an integrated link between the capital and other minor centers might not have thus existed. Meanwhile, burials in the capital and other areas demonstrate a substantial difference in terms of the percentages of tombs having metal objects. Burials in the capital area more frequently contain bronze and iron objects than those in other first- or second-rank centers. Perhaps due to the lack of a suitable network beyond the capital, surplus supplies of metal goods manufactured inside or near the capital could not be effectively distributed on a large scale to other settlements of lower rank. Although a small-scale administrative-integrated market system between the capital and first-rank centers might have existed for the transportation of bronze or iron objects outside the capital during this period, the entire network was focused only on the capital, and movements of goods to lower-rank settlements appear to have been hindered by the limitations of transport capacity. Despite the fact that market exchange was obviously present inside the capital, it is unlikely that a fully-integrated market exchange system existed across the Qin state and entirely transformed various communities in the region. This situation might have changed little before the Qin unification that connected the economic network to a broader region and brought in various new techniques and resources to the headquarters of the empire.

In contrast, a defining feature of the iron and bronze assemblages of the Han period is that the percentage of tombs containing metalwork is not dramatically different between the capital and lower-ranking centers. Probably reflecting to the new imperial system, this presents a more "fully-integrated" scenario compared to the Qin period. Iron knives, swords, and cauldrons appear to have been prevalent in burial contexts in various areas and centers, and the assemblages are relatively homogeneous. The percentage of tombs in the capital (Chang'an) containing at least one type of iron and bronze object is no longer significantly higher than for any of the other areas discussed in this study, and their distribution implies that a new system of market exchange was serving to integrate different local centers through the consumption of iron and bronze objects.

According to the distribution patterns of iron and bronze implements during the Warring States and Western Han periods, I argue that the existence of a well-developed, integrated market system centered on the capital should be foregrounded in any attempt to understand the economic influence of the capital region as one of the major factors structuring the widespread distribution of material cultures such as iron and bronze implements and the material representation of connectivity. As I alluded to earlier, after making Chang'an its capital, the Western Han empire transformed the Wei River valley into not just a political headquarters, but also a central locus for imperial consumption. The iron production remains identified in the Guanzhong basin suggest that it was relatively small-scale compared to its huge population. Meanwhile, there is no clear evidence to suggest that a majority of the everyday bronze goods found in tombs could have been manufactured locally. Following the strategy of the Qin state, one approach that the Han state employed to meet the massive demand for iron implements was probably through the imperial project linking various consumption centers in Guanzhong together as an integrated market network, and connecting it to the imperial project to the east of Guanzhong that consisted of multiple clusters of centralized manufacturing centers. But the large-scale interregional transportation network controlled by the state alone could not efficiently supply goods to various centers in the region. A well-integrated regional distribution network must also have existed and cooperated with the interregional system to distribute metal products, semi-finished products, and even raw materials from other regions to settlements of different sizes within the Wei River valley. In this light, the Han capital and its surrounding capital region were able to serve as a convergence point for the entire empire described in historical texts not only because of its interregional transportation infrastructure but also because it developed a regional system that connected the capital to settlements of different rank as well as production centers specialized in limited types of goods in Guanzhong, providing the important social setting in which the broader connectivity of the Han state addressed in the book would emerge.

Summarizing the major discoveries in this chapter, the distribution patterns reflect the evolution of the market economy and commodities exchange in the region of the political headquarters, which was changed to be closer to a fully-integrated system, even though some administrative centers still partially dominated the transportation and supply of bronze objects. Meanwhile, the distribution of commodities to ordinary people in settlements of various ranks had to rely upon an interregional market network that permitted transaction and the movement of goods in and out of the political core, creating the connectivity evidenced. Given the lack of more detailed textual records relating to the manufacture and distribution of goods, however, it is impossible at this stage to identify how the state was involved in and controlled regional "market exchange", especially during the Early Western Han period. At the very least, though, the sheer numbers of iron and bronze objects found in the centers indicate that market networks in the Han period appear to have been much better developed and more fully integrated than in the Qin period, and that these goods became more accessible to consumers during the Han period. These changes in the distribution patterns and increasing integration of the capital region would in turn better integrate various parts of the Han state via the circulation of goods, thus strengthening the authority of the Han state together with the bureaucratic system. The focus on regional market systems might provide some perspectives through which a larger body of questions, including what mechanism led to the widespread distribution of iron implements in the Han period, can be further explored.

Notes

1 The chapter has been substantially revised from my previous publication (Lam 2020). Also, more updated data of iron and bronze objects in Qin tombs that were published more recently have been incorporated into the original statistical analysis.
2 Other ancient texts in the Han period also often suggest that iron tools, particularly agricultural implements, were commodities circulated through market exchange (see *Yantielun jiaozhu* 36.429 "Shuikan").
3 *Hanshu* 24b.1183; modified from the translation in Swann (1950:347–349).
4 For the summary of the debate, see discussions in Feinman and Garraty (2010).
5 Relevant chapters in these received texts include *Guanzi jiaozhu* 5.88–90 "Chengma", 80–86.1397–1543 "Qingzhong"; *Yantielun jiaozhu* 1.1–28 "Benyi",

3.44–59 "Tongyou", 29.387–445 "Sanbuzu", 36.429–430 "Shuikan". Also see Cheng and Zhang (2019); Chin (2015:31–68); Schefold (2019); Sterckx (2020) for the discussion about the overall economic thoughts illustrated by those "economic texts" about agrarian economies, commercial trade, and state control over the economic system.

6 See Emura (2011) for an extensive study of the coinage system during the Spring-and-Autumn and Warring States period. Kakinuma (2011) offers an in-depth study of the coinage system as well as other exchange media (e.g., gold and textiles) during the Western Han period.

7 To be more specific, the classical viewpoint often holds that the contemporary sense of market exchange did not function as a major structuring principle in pre-capitalist society, since ancient exchange was often based on personal relationship instead of rational calculation. A number of studies in Sociology already pointed out the importance of social relationships involved in market economies (Lie 1997; Plattner 1989; Swedberg 1994), contradicting the argument that the market exchange in the modern capitalist society was impersonal and only adjusted by the rational calculation of price. For the dichotomy between ancient versus modern economies that was frequently disputed in archaeological literature about markets in other regions, see Feinman and Garraty (2010).

8 According to Earle (2011:238), redistribution involves the movement of surplus (e.g., crops and craft products) primarily by the power of the central institute. For examples of political involvement in determining the distribution of goods, one can see Roman period examples in Bang (2008); Hitchner (2005); Mattingly (2006); Millett (2001).

9 While the production of some of these items was under the state control via the Gongguan system, associated inscriptions on these items such as mirrors demonstrate that they were clearly circulated as marketable commodities; See Guo (2016, 2018).

10 It is noteworthy that, in addition to lacquerware and mirrors, some products that were not preserved well in archaeology, such as textiles, were often transported across a long distance. For instance, the recent excavated texts suggest that textiles were exported to Linxian from other places in Lingning commandery and Xiajun county in present-day Hubei (Tongxian), see Zhang (2019).

11 Ancient texts such as the *Sanfu huangtu* (*Sanfu huangtu jiaoshi* 2.93, "Chang'an jiushi") mention at least nine marketplaces operating in Chang'an, the capital of the Western Han empire. For the discussion of specific locations of these markets, see Qian (2020).

12 There are voluminous scholarship in archaeology dedicated to this topic, for instance see Blanton (1996); Braswell (2010); Brumfiel (1980); Dahlin et al. (2007, 2010); Hirth (1998); Nichols et al. (2002); Shaw (2012); Smith (1978). For a summary of the application of various indicators of market exchange in archaeology, see Garraty (2010).

13 Even though the parameters used to describe diversity can be generalized into the three of categories of richness, evenness, and heterogeneity, most previous research (e.g., Garraty 2009; Minc 2006) only focused on heterogeneity, and advocated the use of Brainerd–Robinson coefficients, devised for archaeological research, to describe this dimension. But here we will primarily compare the number of types identified and investigate if each cluster has all major types of iron or bronze artifacts. Because the occurrence and frequencies of iron and bronze objects in tombs are subject to various factors, as I already explained, and the percentage of assemblages calculated in this work only reflects an "overall" pattern represented in a cluster, the use of percentage to run BR coefficients could generate very biased results. Therefore, I preferred to focus on a

much simpler approach using "richness" to describe to what extent assemblages are similar.

14 Equifinality has originally been adopted in zooarchaeology to discuss the transformation of archaeological records by post-depositional factors. For definition, see Lyman (2004).

15 In comparison with iron, bronze objects are more likely to be targets of looters and less likely to remain after looting. Destructive looting might therefore have a greater impact on the assemblage and distribution patterns of bronze objects than iron objects.

16 The treatise of "Records on Clothing" (Part 1) in *Hou Hanshu* mentioned that the using of horse-chariot is not only a privilege of state officials. The using of different color of umbrella cover and chamber decorations also embodies hierarchical meaning (*Hou Hanshu* 118.3647). For a discussion about the embodiment of hierarchy of chariot-patrol scene in murals, see Zhuang (2016).

17 Belt-hook was a type of accessory that was used to fasten the belt, and belt-hook use was a custom widely adopted during the Warring States. For the basic introduction about its function, see Wang (1985). For a more updated discussion of the ancient belt hooks, see Wang (2012).

18 Since the burial data in publication are still accumulating, I only collected data that published before 2020 in order to facilitate this statistic study.

19 One exceptional example is the high-status tomb at Poliucun, Xianyang, which occupant was claimed to be one of the commandery-in-chiefs of the Shu commandery. The dataset discussed here excludes such kind of tombs with voluminous prestige goods, such as lacquerware, jade, and, in particular, bronze ritual vessels; see Shaanxi Yanjiuyuan (2020).

20 A systematic discussion about the county division within the Guanzhong basin during the Qin period can be found in Hou (2009).

21 *Shiji* 6.227.

22 Bronze coins also became popular during the Warring States period. Bronze coins of different dates are often discovered in the same tomb, suggesting they might have been passed down from previous generations as heirlooms or been in circulation for long periods. Since this issue cannot be resolved, coins were excluded from this study.

23 *Hanshu* 99b.4117.

24 For the discussion of the residents and dwelling locations within the Xianyang area, see Liu (1990); Xu (2000:169–170).

25 *Zhuangzi jishi* 10.320, "Qu Jie"; for translation of the verses, see Watson (2013:70).

26 As indicated in Chapter 2, there is a bronze foundry inside the Yong capital (Tian 2013), but its details such as the size and products remain unknown.

27 While Han cemeteries have been widely found in the region, a good portion of them, unfortunately, has not been fully published, even though they include significant numbers of tombs. Dataset of this kind cannot be incorporated into this table; See Shaanxi Yanjiuyuan (2017a)Xi'anshi Yanjiuyuan (2017, 2019b); Xianyangshi Wenwu (2017) as examples.

28 Chai's study (2017) provides an extensive study of the discoveries of figurines in burial contexts within Chang'an area.

29 In the Han period, offices only with exceptionally high-status, such as Huo Guang, were bestowed with jade suit, during their funeral ritual (*Hanshu* 68.2931), and relevant records were very rare in texts. However, jade pieces, which were probably components of a set of jade suit, were occasionally found in tombs, especially those of relatively large size; see M20 at Yangtouzhen in southern suburbs of Xi'an as an example (Xi'anshi Yanjiuyuan 2013).

30 Examples that probably belong to high-ranking officials or elite members also include Shaanxi Yanjiusuo (2003c); Shaanxi Yanjiuyuan (2017b); Xi'anshi (2003, 2004a, 2004c); Xi'anshi Yanjiuyuan (2012, 2019a).
31 *Hanshu* 6.195. For the analysis of the specific location of the Huizhongdao, see Bi (2010).
32 *Shiji* 129.3274; modified from the translation in Swann (1950:434–435).

Conclusion
Management of iron and the *shihuo* system

Of the eight [objects of] government in the "Great Plain", the Hong-fan [of the Book of History]. The first was called *shi*, "Food" [for the people]; and the second, *huo*, "Media of Exchange." The former may be said to be the excellent grains and [other] edibles produced by the agriculturalists. The latter may be defined as textiles, woven of vegetable fibers and of silk, of which wearing apparel can be made; as well as metals, knife [money], tortoise shells, cowries [et cetera], with which wealth may be divided, benefits distributed, and [what the people] have exchanged for [what they] have not. The two [objects of government] are fundamental for the maintenance of the people.

(*Hanshu* 24a.1117; modified from the translation in Swann 1950:109–110)

This book set out to address how the iron industry in the capital core and its relations with other production centers beyond the region contributed to Han's successful administration of such vast territories. I argue that the connectivity evidenced by the manufacture and distribution of iron implements, particularly daily-use goods, is crucial for addressing the issue put forward above. Given the broad territories covered by the Han state, an integrated system for the transportation of goods and information centering on the capital region was a precondition for the success of the management of the empire. The production of iron in various parts of the empire and the interregional distribution of iron contributed to the formation of a network that held the empire together and maintained the dominant role of the capital over other regions. Drawing on the anthropological insight that was explained in the Introduction about potential changes along with the trend toward mass production, I consider that connectivity in the case of the iron industry was shaped by various dimensions, including not only interregional transportation but also changes in the production organization and the emergence of a more integrated market system for final products in the capital region. The connectivity generated through iron production also linked the capital region and workshops beyond Guanzhong, consolidating the state control of the economic domains relevant to iron production.

DOI: 10.4324/9781003259220-10

Through combining various strands of evidence related to the iron industry in the capital region, chapters of this book center on the underlying factors that contributed to this connectivity, and elucidate changes in the social relations transecting various parts or stages of iron manufacture and distribution, from ore miners, casters, communities in the neighborhood, to customers, along with the development of the Qin and Han empires.

The rise of the iron industry was a remarkable phenomenon in ancient China. Within 200 years, tools that were made from the cast iron technique replaced most of the implements used in daily production that were made from other materials. Chapter 1 underscored the regional discrepancy in terms of the development of the iron industry and the widespread popularization process. While there is evidence for early experimentation in iron-working in the Qin state, iron technology in the region did not appear to have enjoyed any widespread adoption during the subsequent Warring States period. In comparison with the Jin states and Chu state, the discovery of cast iron implements appeared to be less pervasive in residential areas, burials, and craft production centers in the Qin state. Nor were any large-scale iron production centers confirmed in the walled capital city of the Qin state. Meanwhile, only sporadic evidence shows that iron making technique was employed in the manufacturing of weapons, which theoretically would have given a cutting-edge advantage to the Qin state in military campaigns. By viewing all lines of evidence together, the iron industry in the Qin state might not have been as strongly developed as its counterparts, and the underdeveloped pattern might have continued even until the epilogue of the unification warfare. Such discrepancy might also have disclosed the originally undeveloped market system in the Qin state compared to other territorial states, and foreshadowed the strategy employed by the Han state to transform the regions where a more developed iron industry was situated into the supply centers for other parts of the empire, especially the capital core.

Through illustrating the social setting of the capital core and the state management of the iron industry, Chapter 2 attempts to cast in higher relief the types of iron-related connectivity that took place inside the Han capital region. The construction of a large capital city and ringing satellite cities together with various canals, storage facilities, and road networks transformed the Guanzhong basin into a convergent point concentrating population and resources from various parts. Since textual records clearly state that the control of the iron industry was a bureaucratic responsibility for the central institutions and local governments, and that the Han state had to maintain the sufficient supply of iron goods to residents for agricultural production, it opens to speculation whether the production of iron implements in the capital core would have conducted on a large scale to meet the demand spurred by the population density and pressure for agricultural development. In the examination of various craft industries and their social setting, however, one intriguing pattern in the scale and assemblage of manufacturing remains is that most production centers of everyday

goods were relatively small in the capital region compared to those in eastern territories. What is even more surprising to see are the discrepancies between archaeological discoveries of relatively small-scale ironworks, such as Taicheng, and the large demand for iron products in the region, which hints at the importance of interregional exchange and the regional network that has been emphasized elsewhere in this book.

In Chapter 3, I argued that regional labor division was a key aspect in understanding the supply of iron to the capital and the connectivity established by the iron industry. Beyond the Guanzhong basin, ironworks discovered hitherto enhance our understanding of iron offices described in texts. Most iron-related archaeological discoveries are located in the broader Central Plains regions, centering on present-day Nanyang basin, Songshan region, and the northern and southern foothills of the Taishan Mountain in Shandong. A review of evidence suggests that ironworks in those clusters often specialized in different procedures of iron production. Such a design of labor division was probably planned to maximize the resources required for production, particularly fuel, labor, and ore, in the geographical setting in which ironworks were situated. Some of those ironworks, such as Wafangzhuang and Guxingzhen, also manufactured a wide range of goods on a large scale, apparently in support of settlements in other parts of the empire.

Represented by Taicheng, ironworks in the capital region were able to employ most of the iron or steel-making techniques that were utilized during the Han period. But these ironworks only specialized in the manufacturing of a small portion of products used in daily lives. The operation of the ironworks, I believe, also had to connect with the interregional network for resources that were not locally available or sufficiently supplied such as iron billets or other semi-finished materials. Through the comparison of iron manufacturing techniques between the ironworks and its adjacent cemetery, it is very likely that a good number of daily-use items, for instance vessels and spades, were obtained through a market network from production centers outside Taixian or even the capital region. Furthermore, the study of the production system and iron implements used by residents implies that ironworks in the capital region were probably subsidiary centers on the nexus of transportation routes to replenish parts of iron tools popular in daily lives. This understanding echoes the point made earlier that the local iron industry had to be embedded within an extensive network for raw materials and final products. The operation of the small-scale ironworks was thus an important part in generating the connectivity between cities in the capital region and other territorial areas.

In the Han period, Guanzhong and various regions were increasingly integrated by an interregional network through which the provision of iron became more sufficient for the demand in farming, craft production, and other daily activities. Besides the import of a large amount of goods into Guanzhong, the ironworks in the region were also investigated in great detail in order to illuminate how the interaction between the local iron

industry and other large-scale production centers in Guandong took place. *embedding locally*
In Chapters 4 and 5, I attempt to investigate the labor organization through
the intra-site distribution pattern of manufacturing remains and evidence
of food consumption by workers at large-scale ironworks in Warring States
and Han urban centers as well as the small-scale ironworks in Guanzhong.
The comparative study tries to address whether the difference in size might
have manifested different types of management over iron workshops, as well
as the interaction with communities in the adjacent county-level settlements
so that the connectivity that occurred inside the capital region—one main
theme of this book—can be better illuminated.

One argument in Chapter 4 is that the collaboration of multiple units and
the potential centralized supervision represented by ironworks were key
features characterizing iron production in the Warring States and Han pe- *Zhangguo fondom?*
riods. Iron and bronze foundries in the Warring States period, which were
often found to be organized as large-scale, nucleated factory-like production centers, already demonstrated a division of labor within the whole site
complex, in which different sections or locations specialized in various types
of metal goods. Inside each section of these pre-Han ironworks and bronze
foundries, multiple types of products, and remains associated with different
steps of production, such as melting, casting, as well as mold preparation
and repair, were often found in agglomeration throughout the entire production area. Instead of being separated from each other, the distribution of *no*
remains associated with various production steps did not present a streamlined pattern in which one unit of workers was only put in charge of one specific stage of production. Since casters of bronze weapons for the Qin empire
might have been organized as cellular units, it is very likely that workers of
bronze and iron daily-use goods in large-scale factories were organized in
similar types of units, in which groups of workers carried out the production of the same type (or multiple types) of goods at the same time.

Considering the small scale of the Taicheng ironworks and limited types
of products produced, one would expect that most workers might have
played multiple roles during the entire production process without a complicated and clear-cut division. A close scrutiny of the intra-site distribution of
the Taicheng example in Chapter 4, however, reveals a type of organization
that was different from such an expected scenario. Regardless of its small
size, the organization of the Taicheng ironworks represents the organizing
principle evidenced in the preceding Warring States period, in which workers overseeing the same production stages were divided into several units. A
careful reading of the intra-site distribution pattern of casting molds with
different markers also implies that workers at different stations or procedures might have in some ways collaborated with each other. With regard
to the basic organization attested by markers on casting molds, the iron- *??*
works in the capital region demonstrated the "horizontal collaboration"
that I coined in the chapter to categorize the collaboration of units overseeing similar stages. Even though any direct evidence showing the actual

communication between workers was not archaeologically preserved, the collaboration of multiple units was represented by the intra-site distribution of remains in the minor production sites. Some forms of centralized supervision and coordination would also be involved, no matter whether the ironworks were entirely controlled by the state or not. Clearly, one should not take for granted that small-scale cases like Taicheng might have been operated in a way similar to the contemporary ethnographical example of a household-level production center introduced in this chapter.

In order to further investigate the ways through which casters engaged in production and potential social connections between ironworks and their neighboring communities, I employ the concept of economic embeddedness in Chapter 5 to examine records relevant to food consumption in ironworks. I have highlighted that the heavy reliance on other specialists for meat supply, probably through the meat market, was attested by both large-scale and small-scale ironworks in the capital region during the Warring States and Han periods, indicating that all these cases were production centers employing externally provisioned, full-time specialists or artisans. Especially in the case of Taicheng, those workers at the site might have demonstrated an even stronger extent of embeddedness by relying on other specialists to procure meat or prepared food. Arguably, this seemingly small-scale workshop was unlikely to be an independent household production unit as one may presume according to its size. Also, a developed food market was the prerequisite for the operation of such full-time specialization in order to allow ironworkers (including both skilled artisans and laborers conducting hard labor) within minor centers like Taixian to procure enough food supply. Together with the understanding about the horizontal collaboration from the preceding chapter, the supply of food suggested that the operation of ironworks in minor centers, in one way or another, was probably managed by a centralized coordination.

As ironworks in the capital region must have connected to the overall economic system in the political core region, it opens to further speculation about the extent to which the market was integrated for the transportation of iron finished goods in settlements of various ranks. In particular, with the regional labor division and interregional exchange evidenced in previous chapters, how was the regional exchange transformed alongside the consolidation of the Han empire? The regional integration through the market exchange of ironware is examined in Chapter 6. To disentangle various issues involved in market exchange, I survey the distribution of metal objects in the capital region during the Warring States and Western Han periods, respectively, as a means of depicting various degrees of integration represented. The allocation pattern of iron and bronze objects from burials in the Guanzhong basin demonstrates that the transportation network for the distribution and procurement of iron commodities in the region might have witnessed a significant transformation. On the regional scale, iron and bronze daily objects in the Late Warring States period were included in tombs with a high frequency in the capital region compared to the low frequency in centers far beyond the capital, suggesting that the regional transportation system might have remained in its preliminary form during the Warring States period. On the contrary, the allocation pattern of iron and bronze daily objects that were included as burial goods presents an ambiguous pattern regardless of the distance of any given location to the Chang'an capital. Together with the establishment of ironworks in the region that were coordinated to produce certain types of objects, residents, regardless of where they dwelled, might get access to the same assemblage of iron objects, and thus mitigated the pattern of concentrated consumption in the capital in the Han period.

The intensification of integration in the capital region and a better-connected world represented by settlements, infrastructure, and craft industries as a response to the imperial transformation was often found in other ancient empires.[1] Through various aspects related to iron production from the Warring States to the Han era illustrated in this book, it is not hard to discern changes of connectivity evidenced in the capital region and beyond. Nonetheless, readers might not be surprised by this conclusion, since unearthed administrative records already attested to a well-integrated system for the transportation of information.[2] As I already clarified in the introduction, my intention of looking at the evidence of iron is not to merely reconfirm what is by now a common knowledge in Han archaeology and history. Instead, the perspective of connectivity is employed as a tool for understanding, in the case of the Han empire, how changes in the craft industry were mediated through the contemporary political needs and re-shaped social relations. Resonating with the recent focus in scholarship on the actual transformation on the ground in the imperial study that I also outlined in the Introduction, this study of the iron industry during the Han period tries to cast light on the role of the manufacture and distribution of iron products that contributed to the formation of the new connected world.

By looking at the production and distribution system in the capital, one interesting pattern is that no obvious changes in the organization were evidenced by the iron industry compared to various transformations caused by the intensification of commodity production in 17th-century Europe (Carrier 1995). The granular study of Taicheng ironworks shows that its organization was in fact similar to other large-scale iron production centers. In the capital region, changes in the iron industry presented primarily in the increase in the number of small ironworks. The strong continuity of the organization of iron production is probably attributable to the tradition of centralization in the management of the iron industry that emerged before the Han period. Meanwhile, those ironworks inside the capital region not only were well integrated to the local community but also linked Guan-zhong to centers beyond the region through the developed bureaucratic system during the Qin-Han periods, through which the transportation of raw materials, fuel, labor force, and final products would have occurred.

In order to supply enough goods to the capital, the operation of such a network also had to transform other territories that had advancements in iron technology before into the exploited zones of resources and supplies. The integration of lower-level administrative centers in the capital region as well as the interregional exchange network was a key aspect in understanding the issue of connectivity in the case of the Han empire, which might have significantly contributed to the dominance of the capital and the penetration of active imperial power into various administration units, especially after the official implementation of monopoly policies.

The network associated with iron production and distribution also benefited the connectivity between the core and more distant regions, such as frontiers in the north and northwest, thereby contributing to the connectivity that we saw in the quoted passage about the traffic scene in the Introduction. Iron as mundane goods was not widely recorded in unearthed textual records. Only sparse records about the transaction of iron agricultural tools have been found in the administrative records from frontiers.[3] Yet, the demand for iron daily-use tools on frontiers was by no means low. To support the extending garrison systems, the Han state instituted *tuntian* on frontiers and converted a good portion of guard soldiers to farmers,[4] but iron farming tools such as spades, hoe-heads, and plowshares were unlikely to be manufactured on a large scale in the Hexi Corridor as sporadic evidence has been identified so far. Given the concentration of ironworks in present-day Henan and Shandong provinces, and the lack of ironworks in other peripheral regions, it is plausible that the clusters of production centers might have produced and supplied goods to other regions of the Han state such as the northern and northwestern frontiers. But to transport to the Hexi region, bulk final products must be moved to the hub of the empire—Guanzhong basin—before continuing the transportation to further west. In other words, the connectivity evidenced in the capital region was not only the result from an imperial project to enhance the originally less developed industry; the connection between the capital center and the eastern territories through iron production also paved the way for the further consolidation and integration of other parts of the Han empire into a macro-scale imperial supplying network, in which the capital became an important transmission point.

Such a well-connected system also throws light on the unique nature of the Han iron industry. While a small-scale production unit like Taicheng would be flexible, especially via its cellular unit production, other large-scale iron factories were notorious for the huge costs that were recorded in the *Yantielun*. The transportation of fuel—charcoal—and other raw materials on land to the centralized foundries adjacent to ruling towns such as Guxingzhen and Wafangzhuang, would be very costly during the Han period. Any untimely delivery of information between those collaborated ironworks might have generated unnecessary waste, either in the form of over-produced products or redundant labor force. This is also the reason why the mass production in the integrated network was criticized as wasteful in the Han period. Even for ironworks as small as Taicheng, any miscommunication in the supply and delivery of fuel, semi-raw materials, and probably prepared food might have caused disruption in the production of goods that were desperately needed in the area. The risk of responding poorly to fluctuation might have been inevitably high compared to those independent household-production units like the case in modern-day Yunnan. Despite all these issues, it is noteworthy that the overall nature of centralization in iron production might not have much changed up until the end of the Eastern Han period, or even later. While monopoly was argued to be not fully implemented in the Eastern Han period, the sporadic records about iron offices suggest that the state-controlled production system, and the integrated network to make it functional, lasted at least in some regions. In other words, throughout the entire Han period the widespread distribution of iron implements and the network of the iron industry might have come at the cost of huge expenditure and waste. One may wonder why the Han state was in favor of the seemingly "uneconomical" mass production and connectivity that had to be maintained by huge cost. Even though the development of agriculture and iron techniques would fuel the demand and spurred the production scale, I suggest that other considerations,[5] including generating state finances and political needs of strengthening the control of iron production regions, should be taken into account in understanding the organization of the iron industry during the Han period.

In a recent study of economic history in late historical China, historian Liu Zhiwei (2019) suggested, based on his close knowledge of Ming and Qing economies, that the economic system in imperial China was operated in a way different from the contemporary sense of economics. Contemporary economists typically hold that humans are living in a natural situation in which means are scarce. Consequently, any economic action results in the frugal use of means to maximize limited resources. Most economists are familiar with this definition: "Economics is the science which studies human behavior as a relationship between ends and scarce means which have alternative use" (Robbins 1945[1932]:16). While it is naïve to think that the economic system remained unchanged from the Han through the Qing periods, Liu argued that the term *shihuo*, which was often used in official history to categorize economic activities, might have provided a better framework for understanding the mechanism of the imperial economies (Liu 2019). Literally, *shihuo* is a synonym for food (*shi*) and goods (*huo*), and *shihou* chapter in official history, such as the quoted passage at the beginning of this chapter, often describes the ways through which the state supplied subsistence in order to meet the needs of its ruled subjects. In ancient China, nature was often assumed to have provided for much more than human beings' needs. As Confucius comments on the root of poverty in society in the *Analects*:

I have heard that a nation or a family does not worry that it has little but that little is unevenly apportioned, does not worry that it is poor but that it is unstable. Because with equitable distribution there is no real poverty, with harmony, no real scarcity, with stability, no real peril.

(*Lunyu jishi* 33.1137; transl. Watson 2007:115)

Upholding Confucius' viewpoint, ancient historians and governmental officials, therefore, did not consider the root of the economic problem to lie in insufficient natural abundance for what people need for subsistence. Rather, the main goal of the state in activities that were broadly defined as "economies" was to maintain and coordinate the production of food—*shi*—and to sustain the goods—*hou*—to be circulated in order to meet the daily demands of ordinary people.[6] In this light, the economies in ancient China were conceived as a sphere in which a state, confronting abundant means, must employ strategies to manage and extract resources, at least partially, into the state's hand so that "wealth may be divided" and needs of political subjects would be met.

While this sounds similar to the modern economic concept, the economic idea in ancient China was grounded on an assumption that was remarkably different from the modern one. Since natural resources were not assumed to be scarce, it is not through the allocation of resources and the enhancement of production rate that more goods would be provided, and thus, demands would be met. Instead, the main goal of the state is to control, or even centralize, resources (land, population, and natural ores) so that sufficient goods would be exchanged and evenly distributed. It was the "evenness" of resource distribution that resulted in social stability, population increase, and eventually the accumulation of resources for royal or imperial consumption. The main task of "economic rationality" in ancient China was to divide and distribute wealth through the state entity so that people in various regions could have what they were lacking via exchange. This idea also resonates with the ideology discussed in Chapter 2 that all natural resources under heaven were claimed by the emperor as his own "properties". For this reason, the even distribution then became one of the main duties of emperors and their controlled bureaucracy. Current economic models, in contrast, focus on the allocation of limited resources and the increase of production efficiency in order to maximize the quantity of goods that would be produced and to overcome the limitation in natural resources, or to be "economical".

In this light, Liu further argues, contrary to our common understanding, that the market did not stem from the need for regional exchange in ancient China. By contrast, the market was generated as a tool of management in the *shihuo* system, through which tributes would be levied by the state. This idea is different from the modern one that presumes the market as a mechanism in which shifts in quantities of goods offered will naturally create modulation in supply and demand so that goods can be transported to where they are needed or more highly valued.[7] While markets in the *shihuo* system were also a means of distributing resources to other regions where resources are lacking, the circulation of goods was not dominated by regional specialization in a modern sense, in which regions specialized in the production of certain goods that they were good at, and used their surplus to exchange for other goods that they need (Chapter 3). It was the state's duty, rather than the market's "invisible hand", to maintain the circulation of goods to those who were in need and to prevent the overdevelopment of entrepreneurs and their overaccumulation of wealth. Subordinated to the imperial administration, the major role of the marketplace exchange in the *shihuo* system lies in mobilizing surplus, including crop and craft products, and turning various local goods into tributes,[8] since all goods were essentially tributes to the state. Reiterating to my point in Chapter 6, the market system was undoubtedly present in the economic system of the Han period, but the production and distribution of commodities such as metal goods appeared to be adjusted simultaneously by the domination of some administrative centers during the transportation process, instead of being solely determined by the force of the market exchange where resources are allocated by prices that are free to move in response to changes (Temin 2013:6). In some way such system can be categorized as a classic "redistributive economy", but this system was the one that employed the mechanism of the market as a primary means of redistribution. In such an economic system, wealth was created through the centralization of resources and the increase of exploitation of ordinary people for the state expanse, which was exactly embodied by the case of the iron monopoly represented in the Han period.

While an integrated network of the supply and circulation of iron was evidenced in archaeological cases, the *shihuo* system provides a framework that is promising to better describe the underlying mechanism driving the maximization and coordination of iron production. The integrated network of iron production in the Han period appears to have been structured under an economic rationale similar to what was prescribed by the *shihuo* system to ensure that goods would be collected and distributed evenly for the state. The connection of the production system between the core and eastern territories as well as the integrated pattern within the region apparently aimed at supplying goods to other regions, or in the *shihuo* sense to ensure the even distribution of those abundant natural resources among all political subjects through the exploitation of ore-rich regions. If the major purpose for the design of such a well-connected pattern was more than tracing for profits beyond the state treasury and responding to local needs, various perplexing "uneconomical" ways for mass production and supply could then have been better understood. As Wagner already has remarked concerning the Han's economy, "the [Han] government side sees society as a coherent unit, united by trade, whose functions can be optimized by appropriate interventions from the center" (Wagner 2001:29). The connectivity evidenced by the iron industry in the capital region and beyond would have guaranteed resources and tributes to be redistributed in "that coherent unit" for the social stability of the Han's various parts, especially those far-flung regions,

Conclusion

spite the fact that the "experiment" of an integrated network underneath
the rationale of the *shihuo* system came at a huge price.

The success of the Han state, which managed to control its vast territories
from Shandong to the Hexi Corridor from east to west and from the Hetou
region to central Vietnam from north to south, was often conceived as the
result of its bureaucratic system, in which the large corpus of officials and
relatively high literacy rate guaranteed the delivery of the imperial message,
the collection of census data and local information, and the extraction and
redistribution of resources, including labor, staple crops, husbandry, tax
revenues, and other tributes. But neither coercive force nor the bureaucratic
system alone guaranteed the stabilization and integration of various parts
of the empire. The supply of iron was primarily for domestic and practical
needs for mundane daily activities. Yet, the manufacture and distribution of
iron objects played an important role, albeit often overlooked, in creating
the connectivity critical to the Han empire. Situated within the center of
the state redistribution network, the production and exchange of iron in the
capital were essential in generating the connections that laid the foundation
for imperial management and the collection of state finance, which might
not have been illuminated by other lines of sources. Iron tools were practical
implements commonly used in daily production, but the production, utilization, and distribution of these implements had significant implications in
the Han imperial system by generating the connectivity that linked different
parts of the Han state into the imperial network. While this study only focuses on one part of the Han empire, with the growing interest in the investigation of ironworks in the future, the reconstruction of the iron industry
and connections between other regions that are not primarily covered here
may contribute to further disentangling the convoluted and long-lasting debates over factors contributing to the state integration and consolidation in
studies of the Han empire.

Notes

1 For instance, the construction of road infrastructure in the case of the Roman
   empire appeared to stimulate the intensification of connectivity of various parts
   across the Mediterranean sea (e.g., see Hitchner 2012).
2 One important and updated reference for the coverage of the Han administrative system is Lai's work (2013). Korolkov's recent work provides an excellent
   example of the Qin period in that concern, based on the in-depth study of Liye
   excavated texts; see Korolkov (2021).
3 For instance, see the price records of iron tools summarized in Ding and Wei
   (2016).
4 For an in-depth analysis of the management and organization of the *tuntian*
   system in the Han frontiers, see Liu (1988).
5 Donald Wagner suggested before that the "implicit" technological choice (i.e.,
   no one explicitly made the choice but the choice of using certain technique was
   made) lay in the Qin-Han bureaucratic system. Since cast iron production is
   most efficient at a high level of production, and with a large and reliable labor

force (Wagner 1993:409), large-scale cast iron manufacturing was more easily forthcoming in the totalitarian state of Qin. While I agree that the emergence of cast iron production had to build upon a system, such as the Qin-Han bureaucratic institute, that would facilitate the centralization and movement of fuel and labor force, the bureaucratic system alone might not fully explain why the Qin and Han states were willing to maintain such a supply and distribution system at a high cost.

6 Similar idea of a state-controlled circulation system instead of allowing a more autarkic market system evidenced in texts is also proposed in Loewe (1985) and Schefold (2019). Watanabe Shinichirō (1989) also argued before that one of the major characteristics of the Han economic system was able to coordinate accumulated resource in peripheries through the coordination and redistribution system managed by the central court. The term *shihuo* proposed by Liu Zhiwei, nonetheless, appears to be an illuminative concept that concisely captures the nuance of the Han economic system.

7 See the summary in Feinman and Garraty (2010).

8 Liu Zhiwei also refers to this type of economic system in ancient China as a "tributary economy". Coincidentally, Roman historian Peter Bang in a slightly earlier publication proposed to use a similar term, "tributary empire", to reconceptualize the market system in the Roman period (Bang 2008). As he argued, "markets do not determine the structure of the economy. Instead, they play a crucial role in mobilizing the agricultural surplus and turning it into a disposable resource" (Bang 2008:62). Through looking at trading records of grain, he suggests that there was sparse evidence indicating inter-regional connection through a market system or an increase of labor differentiation, contradicting some previous studies that posit the expansive Roman empire heralded the arrival of market economies surrounding the Mediterranean Sea. In order to understand the significance of market within its temporary context, research focus should be recalibrated to the role of market in redistributing luxury goods and facilitating the mobilization of peasant surplus as tributes to the Roman state. In the case of the Han empire, however, the production and distribution did illustrate a seemingly more "integrated" world. The difference may hint at a more dominant role played by the Han state and its bureaucratic system in various economic domains in comparison with its Roman counterpart.

Glossary

Anling	安陵
Ba River	灞河
Bacheng gate	霸城门
Bai Canal	白渠
Baidian	白店
Baling	霸陵
Baoji	宝鸡
Baoshan	包山
Bei Palace (*gong*)	北宫
Beidi	北第
Bianjiazhuang	边家庄
Biyang	泌阳
Bloomery iron	块炼铁
Bojiawang	薄家湾
cang	仓
Cangcheng	仓城
Cao Canal	漕渠
Cast iron	生铁/白口铁
cha (spade)	锸
Changde	常德
Chan River	浐河
"Chang'an jiushi" (*Sanfu huangtu*)	《三辅黄图·长安九市》
Chang'an	长安
Changle Palace (*gong*)	长乐宫
Changling	长陵
Changsha	长沙
Changzi	长治
chaogang	炒钢
Chaoyi	朝邑
Chengcheng	澄城
Chengdu	成都
Chengguo Canal	成国渠
"Chengma" (*Guanzi*)	《管子·乘马》

Chengqiao	程桥
Chengxiang	丞相
Chidao road system	驰道
chu (hoe-head)	锄
Chu state (Kingdom of Western Han)	楚国
Chu state (Warring States Period)	楚国
Dahonglu	大鸿胪
Dasinong	大司农
Dabuzishan	大堡子山
daitian	代田
Dajiayuan	大家园
Dali	大荔
Danjiangkou	丹江口
Dasan pass *(guan)*	大散关
Dawuliu	大吴楼
ding (tripod)	鼎
Dong Zhongshu	董仲舒
Dongdi	东第
Dongfeng Reservoir	东风水库
Dongguo Xianyang	东郭咸阳
Dongpingling	东平陵
Dongshi	东市
dou (unit of capacity)	斗
Doufucun	豆腐村
duhui	都会
Duguan	都官
Duke Xian of Qin	秦献公
Duke Xiao of Qin	秦孝公
Duling	杜陵
Dunei ling	都内令
Dunhuang	敦煌
Duxiang qinian kentian zubu	《都乡七年垦田租簿》
Eastern Han	东汉
Eastern Zhou	东周
Ejin Banner	额济纳旗
Empress Lü	吕后
Erligang	二里冈
Ernian lüling	《二年律令》
Fan Kuai	樊哙
"Feiyang" (*Yantielun*)	《盐铁论·非鞅》
Feng River	沣河
Fenghuangquan	凤凰泉
Fengxiang	凤翔
Fenjin	汾晋
Fenshuiling	分水岭

fu (cauldron)	釜
Fufeng	扶风
"Fugu" (*Yantielun*)	《盐铁论·复古》
Fujiamiao	傅家庙
Funiu Mountains	伏牛山脉
Ganquan Palace (*gong*)	甘泉宫
Gansu	甘肃
Gaoling	高陵
Gaomocun	高陌村
Gaozhuang	高庄
ge (dagger-axe)	戈
Gobi desert	戈壁沙漠
gong	工
Gongcheng	宫城
Gongguan	工官
Gongyi	巩义
Gong Yu	貢禹
Great Unity	大一统
Grey cast iron	灰口铁
guan (jar)	罐
Guandong	关东
Guanghan	广汉
Guangguan	广关
Guanzhong	关中
Guanzhong-central policies	关中本位政策
Gui Palace (*gong*)	桂宫
Guo Zong	郭纵
Guxingzhen	古荥镇
Guyuan	固原
Han (Warring States period)	韩国
Han (a tribe of Qiang)	罕
Hangu pathway	函谷道
Hangu	函谷
Hangzhong	汉中
Hebei	河北
Hedong Commandery	河东郡
Henan Commandery	河南郡
Henan	河南
hesan	河三
Hetao region	河套地区
Hexi Corridor	河西走廊
heyi	河一
Hongnong Commandery	弘农郡
Hou Jiangjun	后将军
Houma	侯马

Hua Mountains	华山山脉
Huananzi	《淮南子》
Hubei	湖北
Hui River	浍水
Huize	会泽
Huizhongdao	回中道
"Hungfan" (*Shangshu*)	《尚书.洪范》
huo	货
Huo Guang	霍光
Huxian	户县
hu (vessel)	壶
Inner Mongolia	内蒙古
ji (halberd)	戟
jia	家
Jiangling	江陵
Jiangsu	江苏
Jianzhang Palace (*gong*)	建章宫
jin (unit of weight)	斤
Jincheng Commandery	金城郡
Jin state	晋国
Jinan	济南
Jinancheng	纪南城
Jing River	泾河
jing (well)	井
Jingdi (Emperor Jing of Han)	景帝
"Jingeng" (*Yantielun*)	《盐铁论·禁耕》
Jingjiazhuang	景家庄
Jingshicang	京师仓
Jingyang	泾阳
Jingzhao	京兆
Jingzhou	荆州
Jitian ling	籍田令
Jiudian	九店
Jiuqing	九卿
Jiuyuan	九原
jue (axe)	镢
jun (unit of weight)	钧
Jundushan	军都山
Junshu ling	均输令
Jun-xian system	郡县制
Juyan	居延
Kangling	康陵
Kanjiazhai	阚家寨
"Kenling" (*Shangjunshu*)	《商君书·垦令》
Kong Jin	孔仅

kongshoubu	空首布
Kongtougou	孔头沟
kouqian	口钱
kuangmai	穬麦
Kunming Canal	昆明渠
Kunming	昆明
Laiwu	莱芜
Lao Kan	劳榦
Langjingcun	郎井村
Langzhong ling	郎中令
Lantian	蓝田
li (administrative unit)	里
li (unit of distance)	里
Liangdaicun	梁带村
lianhu jing	连弧镜
Lijia	李家
Lingling Commandery	零陵郡
Lingnan	岭南
Linqiong	临邛
Lintong	临潼
Linxiang	临湘
Linzi	临淄
Liu Bang	刘邦
Liu Jing (Lou Jing)	刘敬（娄敬）
Liu Zhiwei	刘志伟
Liufu Canal	六辅渠
Liujiawa	刘家洼
Liujiazhai	刘家寨
Liulinxi	柳林溪
Liye	里耶
liyi	里邑
Longdong	陇东
Longshou Canal	龙首渠
Lord Shang	商鞅
Lou River (Tributary of Wei River)	洛河
lüli	闾里
Luoyang	洛阳
Lushan	鲁山
Majiazhuang	马家庄
Malleable iron	可锻铸铁
Maojiatan	毛家滩
Maoling	茂陵
Mei county	郿县
Meixian (in Han time)	眉县
mi (millet)	糜

mi (rice)	米
Mingguang Palace (*gong*)	明光宫
Minguo	民国
Mogou	磨沟
Mottled iron	麻口铁
Mr. Zhuo	卓氏
Nangucheng	南古城
Nanyang Commandery	南阳郡
Nanzhao county	南召县
Niejiagou	聂家沟
Ningxia	宁夏
Niucun	牛村
Northern Miaopu	苗圃北地
Northern Xiaotun	小屯北地
nu	奴
Pengzhu Ning	彭祖宁
Pingling	平陵
Pingyang	平阳
Pingyin Commendary	冯翊郡
Pingzhun ling	平准令
Pu Pass (*guan*)	蒲关
Puguan pathway	蒲关道
Qi Commandery	齐郡
Qi state (Warring States period)	齐国
qian	茜
Qian River	汧水
qian (currency unit)	钱
qiandan zhi xian	千石(担)之县
Qianwei zhihui	汧渭之会
Qijia	齐家
Qin Shihuang	秦始皇
Qin state (Warring States period)	秦国
Qin	秦
Qinling Mountains	秦岭山脉
Qinyi	秦邑
"Qu jie"(*Zhuangzi*)	《庄子·胠箧》
quan	甽
Rong	戎
Rui River	汭河
sanfu	三辅
Sang Hongyang	桑弘羊
Sangong	三公
Sanyangzhuang	三杨庄
Shaanbei	陕北
Shaanxi	陕西

Shandong	山东
Shang era	商代
Shangcunling	上村岭
Shanglin yuan	上林苑
Shanglin Zhongguan	上林钟官
Shangmonao	上磨垴
Shangshu	尚书
Shanxi	山西
Shanyang Commandery	山阳郡
Shaofu	少府
shetai	赊贷
Shi (elite class of Zhou Dynasty)	士
shi (food for the people)	食
shi (market)	市
shi (unit of capacity)	石
shi (unit of weight)	石
Shifotang	石佛堂
shihuo	食货
Shiji Zhengyi	《史記正義》
Shizuo	师佐
shoutian	授田
Shu Commandery	蜀郡
Shu	蜀
Shujun Xigong	蜀郡西工
Shuiheng duwei	水衡都尉
Shuihudi	睡虎地
"Shuikan" (*Yantielun*)	《盐铁论·水旱》
Sima Chang	司马昌
Sima Qian	司马迁
"Sitie" (*The Book of Poetry*)	《诗经·驷驖》
Siwa Culture	寺洼文化
Solid-state decarburization of cast iron	铸铁脱碳钢
Songshan Mountain	嵩山
Su Ling	苏令
su (millet)	粟
suanfu	算赋
"Suanshushu" (*Zhangjiashan hanjian*)	《张家山汉简.算数书》
Suiyang	睢阳
Suizhou	随州
Sunjianantou	孙家南头
Ta'erpo	塔儿坡
Tai'an	泰安
Taicang ling	太仓令
Taicang	太仓
Taichang	太常

Taicheng	邰城
Tailai basin	泰莱盆地
Taipu	太仆
Taishan Commandery	泰山郡
Taishan mountain	泰山
Taishen	台神
Taiwei	太尉
Taixi site in Hebei	河北台西遗址
Taixian (in Han time)	邰县
taiyi	太一
Tanghu	唐户
Tangyi yuanshou ernian yaojubu	堂邑元寿二年要具簿
Teng (a tribe of Qiang)	腾
Tengguo Gucheng	滕国故城
Tengzhou	滕州
Tianma-Qucun	天马-曲村
Tianxingguan	天星观
Tieguan	铁官
Tieguancheng	铁官丞
Tieshenggou	铁生沟
Tieshi	铁市
Tingwei	廷尉
tong (slave)	僮
Tongbai mountain	桐柏山
Tongchuan	铜川
tu	徒
Tuntian	屯田
Tushantun	土山屯
Wafangzhuang	瓦房庄
wai cangguo	外藏椁
Wan city	宛城
Wang Mang	王莽
Wangchenggang	望城岗
Wayaotou	瓦窑头
Wei (a lineage in the Chu state)	蒍氏
Wei River	渭河
Wei (Warring States period)	魏国
Weibei pathway	渭北道
Weiling	渭陵
Weiwei	卫尉
Weiyang Palace (*gong*)	未央宫
Wendi (Emperor Wen of Han)	汉文帝
Wenxue	文学
Western Chu	西楚
Western Han	西汉

Wrought iron	熟铁
Wu pass (*guan*)	武关
Wu state (kingdom of Western Han)	吴国
Wu state (Warring States period)	吴国
Wudi (Emperor Wu of Han)	汉武帝
Wugang	舞钢
Wugong	武功
Wuguan pathway	武关道
wujun	五均
Wuku	武库
Wuyangtai	武阳台
Wuyi Guangchang	五一广场
Xi'an	西安
Xia County	夏县
Xiahewan	下河湾
Xiang Yu	项羽
Xianglinggang	响岭岗
Xiangzikou	巷子口
Xianliang	贤良
Xianling (a tribe of Qiang)	先零
Xianling	县令
Xianrentai	仙人台
Xianyang	咸阳
Xiaomintun	孝民屯
Xiaotieguan	小铁官
Xiaotun	小屯
Xiasi	下寺
xie	灺
Xiliucang	细柳仓
Xin Mang period	新莽时期
Xin River	新河
Xinfeng	新丰
Xingyang	荥阳
Xinjiang	新疆
Xinzheng	新郑
Xiongnu	匈奴
Xiping	西平
Xiquanqiu	西犬丘
Xishi	西市
Xiyu	西域
Xuechi	血池
Xuzhou	徐州
Yan	燕
Yangcheng	阳城
Yangjiashan (Changsha)	杨家山

Yangling (District of Xianyang)	阳陵
Yangling	杨凌
Yangling Mausoleum	阳陵
Yangshao	仰韶
Yangying	杨营
Yanling	延陵
Yanmen	雁门
Yanxiadu	燕下都
Yaoshan Mountains	崤山
Yaoshang	尧上
"Yibing" (*Xunzi*)	《荀子·议兵》
Yiling	义陵
Yimencun	益门村
Yingchuan Commandery	颍(潁)川郡
Yinxu	殷墟
Yiyang	益阳
Yong River	雍水
yong (waged laborers)	庸(傭)
Yongcheng	雍城
You caitie	右采铁
Youjiazhuang	尤家庄
Yuandi (Emperor Yuan of Han)	汉元帝
Yuan River	沅水
Yuanshou	元狩
Yunxi	郧西
Yuchi	鱼池
yue (axe)	钺
Yuelu Qinjian	岳麓秦简
Yueyang	栎阳
Yunmeng	云梦
Yunnan	云南
Yunyang	云阳
Yushi dafu	御史大夫
Yutaishan	雨台山
Yuwangcheng	禹王城
zao (stove)	灶
Zhang Anshi	张安世
Zhang Shoujie	张守节
Zhang Tang	张汤
Zhangdi (Emperor Zhang of Han)	章帝
Zhanghe	章和
Zhangjiajie	张家界
Zhangjiaping	张家坪
Zhangli	长吏
Zhangqiu	章丘

Zhao (Warring States period)	赵国
Zhao Chongguo	趙充国
Zhaodi (Emperor Zhao of Han)	汉昭帝
Zhaolun	兆伦
Zhengguo Canal	郑国渠
Zheng-Han Gucheng	郑韩故城
Zhengzhou	郑州
"Zhilü" (*Zhangjiashan hanjian*)	《张家山汉简.秩律》
Zhicheng gate	直城门
Zhidao highway network	直道
zhong **(unit of volume)**	钟
Zhonghang	中行
Zhongnan Mountains	终南山
Zhou era	周代
Zhou Yafu	周亚夫
Zhouyuan	周原
Zhouzhi	周至
zhugangjian	铸钢剑
Zi River	淄河
Ziwu pass (*guan*)	子午关
Ziwu pathway	子午道
Zongzheng	宗正
Zoumalou	走马楼
zu	卒
Zuo caitie	左采铁

Bibliography

Allard, Francis
2006   Frontiers and Boundaries: The Han Empire from Its Southern Periphery. In, *Archaeology of Asia*. Miriam T. Stark (ed.), Pp. 233–254. Malden, MA: Blackwell Publishing Inc.

Appadurai, Arjun
1986   Introduction: Commodities and the Polities of Value. In, *The Social Life of Things*. Arjun Appadurai (ed.), Pp. 3–63. Cambridge: Cambridge University Press.

Arnold, Dean E.
2014   *The Evolution of Ceramic Production Organization in a Maya Community*. Boulder: University Press of Colorado.

Bai, Yunxiang 白云翔
2005   先秦两汉铁器的考古学研究 [*Archaeological Study on Iron Works before 3rd Century A.D. in China*]. 北京 Beijing: 科学出版社 Science Press.
2011   汉长安城手工业生产遗存的考古学研究 (Archaeological Research on Craft Production Remains in Han Chang'an City). In, 汉长安城考古与汉文化 [*Archaeology of Han Chang'an City and Han Culture*]. Zhongguo Shehui Kexueyuan Kaogu Yanjiusuo 中国社会科学院考古研究所 et al. (eds.), Pp. 97–161. 北京 Beijing: 科学出版社 Science Press.
2014   汉代"蜀郡西工造"的考古学论述 (Archaeological Study of Inscriptions of Shujun Xigongzao in the Han Period). 四川文物 [*Sichuan Cultural Relics*] 2014(6):39–51.
2020   东周秦汉时期齐都临淄的金属冶铸业综合考察 (A Synthetic Investigation of Metal Industries in Linzi City of the Qi State during the Eastern Zhou and Qin-Han Periods). In, 临淄齐故城冶铸业考古 [*Archaeology of Metallurgy and Foundry Industry in the Linzi City Site of Qi State*]. Zhongguo Shehui Kexueyuan Kaogu Yanjiusuo 中国社会科学院考古研究所 et al. (eds.), Pp. 1131–1152. 北京 Beijing：科学出版社 Science Press.

Bai, Yunxiang 白云翔, and Yasuji, Shimizu 清水康二 (eds.)
2007   山东省临淄齐国故城汉代镜范的考古学研究 [*Research on Mirror Casting Molds from the Qi Capital City in Linzi, Shandong*]. 北京 Beijing: 科学出版社 Science Press.

Bagley, Robert W.
1993   Replication Techniques in Eastern Zhou Bronze Casting. In, *History from Things: Essays on Material Culture*. Steven Lubar and David W. Kingery (eds.), Pp. 231–241. Washington, D.C. and London: Smithsonian Institution Press.

1995   What the Bronzes from Hunyuan Tell Us about the Foundry at Houma. *Orientations* 26(1):46–54.

1996   Debris from the Houma Foundry. *Orientations* 27(9):50–58.

2009   Anyang Mold-making and the Decorated Model. *Artibus Asiae* 69(1):39–90.

Bang, Peter F.

2006   Imperial Bazaar: Towards a Comparative Understanding of Markets in the Roman Empire. In, *Ancient Economies Modern Methodologies: Archaeology, Comparative History, Models and Institutions.* Peter F. Bang, Mamoru Ikeguchi and Harmut Ziche (eds.), Pp. 51–88. Bari: Edipuglia.

2008   *The Roman Bazaar: A Comparative Study of Trade and Markets in a Tributary Empire.* Cambridge: Cambridge University Press.

2009   Commanding and Consuming the World: Empire, Tribute, and Trade in Roman and Chinese History. In, *Rome and China: Comparative Perspectives on Ancient World Empires.* Walter Scheidel (ed.), Pp. 100–120. Oxford: Oxford University Press.

Baojishi [Baojishi Kaogu Gongzuodui 宝鸡市考古工作队]

1991   宝鸡市谭家村春秋及唐代墓 (Excavation of Spring-and-Autumn and Tang Tombs at Tanjiacun). 考古 [*Archaeology*] 1991(5):392–399.

2002   陕西陇县原子头汉墓发掘简报 (Preliminary Report on the Excavation of Han Tombs at Yuanzitou in Long County, Shaanxi). 文博 [*Relics and Museology*] 2002(2):4–11.

Baojishi, and Baojishi [Baojishi Bowuguan 宝鸡市博物馆, and Baojishi Weibinqu Wenhuaguan 宝鸡市渭滨区文化馆]

1979   陕西宝鸡市茹家庄东周墓 (Excavation on Eastern Zhou Tombs at Rujiazhuang in Baoji, Shaanxi). 考古 [*Archaeology*] 1979(5):408–411.

Baojishi, and Baojixian [Baojishi Bowuguan 宝鸡市博物馆, and Baojixian Tushuguan 宝鸡县图书馆]

1980   宝鸡县西高泉村春秋秦墓发掘记 (Excavation on Qin Spring-and-Autumn Tombs at Xigaoquncun in Baoji). 考古与文物 [*Archaeology and Cultural Relics*] 1980(9):1–9.

Baojishi, and Longxian [Baojishi Kaogudui 宝鸡市考古队, and Longxian Bowuguan 陇县博物馆]

2001   陕西陇县韦家庄秦墓发掘简报 (Preliminary Report on the Excavation of Qin Tombs at Weijiazhuang in Long County, Shaanxi). 考古与文物 [*Archaeology and Cultural Relics*] 2001(4):9–19.

Barbieri-Low, Anthony J.

2007   *Artisans in Early Imperial China.* Seattle and London: University of Washington Press.

2011   Craftsman's Literacy: Uses of Writing by Male and Female Artisans in Qin and Han China. In, *Writing and Literacy in Early China: Studies from the Columbia Early China Seminar.* Feng Li and David P. Branner (eds.), Pp. 370–400. Washington, D.C.: University of Washington Press.

2021   Coerced Migration and Resettlement in the Qin Imperial Expansion. *Journal of Chinese History* 2021(5):181–202.

Barbieri-Low, Anthony J., and Yates, Robin D. S.

2015   *Law, State, and Society in Early Imperial China: A Study with Critical Edition and Translation of the Legal Texts from Zhangjiashan Tomb No. 247.* Leiden: Brill.

Barnard, Noel
1978–1979 Did the Swords Exist? Rejoinder. *Early China* 4:60–65.

Barnard, Noel, and Satō, Tamotsu
1975 *Metallurgical Remains of Ancient China*. Tokyo: Nichiōsha.

Beida Shangzhou, and Shanxi [Beijing Daxue Kaogu Xuexi Shang Zhou Zu 北京大学考古学系商周组, and Shanxisheng Kaogu Yanjiusuo 山西省考古研究所]
2000 天马 – 曲村 [The Tianma Qucun Site]. 北京 Beijing: 科学出版社 Science Press.
Beijing Gangtie [Beijing Gangtie Xueyuan Yali Jiagong Zhuanye 北京钢铁学院压力加工专业]
1975 易县燕下都44号墓葬铁器金相考察初步报告 (Preliminary Report on the Metallurgical Analysis of Iron Objects from Tomb No. 44 at Yanxiadu in Yi County). 考古 [*Archaeology*] 1975(4):241–243.

Beijing Keji [Beijing Keji Daxue Yajinshi Yanjiushi 北京科技大学冶金史研究室]
1996 角楼建筑遗址出土铁器金相鉴定报告 (Metallurgical Report on the Analysis of Iron Objects from the Jiaolou Architectural Site). In, 汉长安城未央宫:1980–1989年考古发掘报告 [*Weiyang Palace in Han Chang'an City: 1980–1989 Excavation Report*]. Zhongguo Shehui Kexueyuan Kaogu Yanjiusuo 中国社会科学院考古研究所 (ed.), P. 269. 北京 Beijing: 中国大百科全书出版社 Encyclopedia of China Publishing House.

Beijingshi et al. [Beijingshi Wenwu Yanjiusuo 北京市文物研究所, Beijing Keji Daxue Kejishi yu Wenhua Yichan Yanjiuyuan 北京科技大学科技史与文化遗产研究院, Beijing Daxue Kaogu Wenbo Xueyuan 北京大学考古文博学院, and Yanqingqu Wenhua Weiyuanhui 延庆区文化委员会]
2018 北京市延庆区大庄科辽代矿冶遗址群水泉沟冶铁遗址 (The Excavation of the Shuiquangou Iron Smelting Site of the Dazhuangke Mining and Metallurgical Sites of the Liao Dynasty in Yanqing District, Beijing). 考古 [*Archaeology*] 2018(6):38–50.

Beikeda, and Xuzhou [Beijing Keji Daxue Yajinshi Yanjiusuo 北京科技大学冶金史研究所, and Xuzhou Hanbingmayong Bowuguan 徐州汉兵马俑博物馆]
1997 徐州狮子山楚王陵出土铁器的金相实验研究 (Metallurgical Report on the Analysis of Iron Objects from the Mausoleum of the Chu State at Shizishan in Xuzhou). 文物 [*Cultural Relics*] 1997(7):146–156.

Betts, Alison, Jia, Peter W., and Dodson, John
2014 The Origins of Wheat in China and Potential Pathways for Its Introduction: A Review. *Quaternary International* 348:158–168.

Bi, Yajing 毕雅静
2010 回中道考 (A Study on Huizhongdao). In, 秦汉研究(第四辑) [*Qin and Han Studies* (vol. 4)]. Liang Anhe 梁安和 and Xu Weimin 徐卫民 (eds.), Pp. 230–233. 西安 Xi'an: 陕西人民出版社 Shaanxi People's Publishing House.

Bielenstein, Hans
1980 *The Bureaucracy of Han Times*. Cambridge: Cambridge University Press.

Binford, Lewis R.
1980 Willow Smoke and Dogs' Tails: Hunter-gatherer Settlement Systems and Archaeological Site Formation. *American Anthiquity* 45:4–20.
1981 *Bones: Ancient Men and Modern Myths*. New York: Academic Press.

Blanton, Richard E.

1996   The Basin of Mexico Market Systems and the Growth of Empire. In, *Aztec Imperial Strategies*. Francis F. Berdan (ed.), Pp. 47–84. Washington, D.C.: Dumbarton Oaks Research Library and Collection.

Bowen, Joanne

1992   Faunal Remains and Urban Household Subsistence in New England. In, *The Art and Mystery of Historical Archaeology: Essays in Honor of James Deetz*. Anne Elizabeth Yentsch and Mary C. Beaudry (eds.), Pp. 267–281. Boca Raton, FL: CRC Press.

1994   A Comparative Analysis of the New England and Chesapeake Herding Systems. In, *Historical Archaeology of the Chesapeake*. Paul Shackel and Barbara Littler (eds.), Pp. 155–167. Washington, D.C.: Smithsonian Institution Press.

1998   To Market, to Market: Animal Husbandry in New England. *Historical Archaeology* 32(3):137–152.

Bowman, Alan, and Wilson, Andrew

2009   Quantifying the Roman Economy: Integration, Growth, Decline? In, *Quantifying the Roman Economy: Methods and Problems*. Alan Bowman and Andrew Wilson (eds.), Pp. 3–84. Oxford: Oxford University Press.

Braswell, Geoffrey E.

2010   The Rise and Fall of Market Exchange: A Dynamic Approach to Ancient Maya Economy. In, *Archaeological Approaches to Market Exchange in Ancient Societies*. Christopher P. Garraty and Barbara L. Stark (eds.), Pp. 127–140. Boulder: University Press of Colorado.

Bronson, Bennet

1999   The Transition to Iron in Ancient China. In, *The Archaeometallurgy of the Asian Old World*. Vincent C. Pigott (ed.), Pp. 178–198. Philadelphia: The University Museum and University of Pennsylvania.

Brughmans, Tom

2013   Thinking through Networks: A Review of Formal Network Methods in Archaeology. *Journal of Archaeological Method and Theory* 20:623–662.

Brumfiel, Elizabeth M.

1980   Specialization, Market Exchange, and the Aztec State: A View from Huexotla. *Current Anthropology* 21(4):459–478.

Brunson, Katherine, He, Nu, and Dai, Xiangming

2016   Sheep, Cattle, and Specialization: New Zooarchaeological Perspectives on the Taosi Longshan. *International Journal of Osteoarchaeology* 26:460–475.

Bu, Xianqun 卜宪群

2018   谈我国历史上的"大一统"思想与国家治理   (On the "Great Unification" Thought and State Governance in My Country's History). 中国史研究 [*Chinese History Studies*] 2018(2):14–20.

Cao, Fazhan 曹发展

1989   陕西户县南关春秋秦墓清理记   (Excavation of the Spring-and-Autumn Qin Tombs at Nanguan in Hu County, Shaanxi). 文博 [*Relics and Museology*] 1989(2):3–12.

Cao, Long 曹龙

2012   西汉帝陵陪葬制度初探 (Initial Investigation of the Systems of Accessory Tombs). 考古与文物 [*Archaeology and Cultural Relics*] 2012(5):82–85.

Carr, Christopher
1984　The Nature of Organization of Intrasite Archaeological Records and Spatial Analytic Approaches to Their Investigation. *Advances in Archaeological Method and Theory* 7:103–222.

Carrier, James G.
1995　*Gifts and Commodities: Exchange and Western Capitalism since 1700.* London: Routledge.

Chai, Yi 柴怡
2017　西安地区汉代人物俑的发现与分析研究 (Discovery and Analysis of Human Figurines of the Han Period in Xi'an). 文博 [*Relics and Museology*] 2017(4):42–52.

Chang, Chun-shu
2007　*The Rise of the Chinese Empire* (2 vols.). Ann Arbor: University of Michigan Press.

Changsha [Changsha Tielu Chezhan Jianzao Gongcheng Wenwu Fajuedui 长沙铁路车站建造工程文物发掘队]
1978　长沙新发现春秋晚期的钢剑和铁器 (The New Discoveries of Spring-and-Autumn Steel Swords and Iron Products in Changsha). 文物 [*Cultural Relics*] 1978(10):44–48.

Chen, Bo 陈博
2007　两汉京畿地区城址研究 [*The Study on the City Sites of Han Dynasty Surrounding the Capitals*], 吉林大学 Master thesis, Jilin University.
2016　从中心到边疆——汉帝国城市与城市体系的考古学研究 [*From Center to Peripheries: An Archaeological Investigation of the Urban Systems of the Han Empire*]. 北京 Beijing: 科学出版社 Science Press.

Chen, Jianli 陈建立
2007　山东临淄出土战国铁器实验研究 (Metallurgical Analysis of Iron Implements in Warring States Tombs in Linzi, Shandong). In, 临淄齐墓(第一集) [*Tomb of the Qi state in Linzi* (vol. 1)]. Shandongsheng Wenwu Kaogu Yanjiusuo 山东省文物考古研究所 (ed.), Pp. 489–491. 北京 Beijing: 文物出版社 Cultural Relics Press.
2014　中国古代金属冶铸文明新探 [*Exploration of the Metal Smelting and Casting Civilization in Ancient China*]. 北京 Beijing: 科学出版社 Science Press.
2020　新疆早期铁器的制作技术及年代学研究 (Manufacturing Technology and Chronological Study of Early Iron Objects in Xinjiang). In, 考古学研究（十一）[*Archaeological Study* (vol. 11)]. Beijing Daxue Kaoguwenbo Xueyuan 北京大学考古文博学院 and Beijing Daxue Zhongguo Kaoguxue Yanjiuzhongxin 北京大学中国考古学研究中心 (eds.), Pp. 39–55. 北京 Beijing: 科学出版社 Science Press.

Chen, Jianli 陈建立, and Han, Rubin 韩汝玢
2000　汉诸侯王陵墓出土铁器的比较 (Comparative Studies on Iron and Steel Artifacts Unearthed from the Tombs of Han Princes). 文物保护与考古科学 [*Sciences of Conservation and Archaeology*] 12(1):1–8.
2007　汉晋中原及北方地区钢铁技术研究 [*Iron and Steel Technology in Central Plains and Northern Region during the Han and Jin Dynasties*]. 北京Beijing: 北京大学出版社 Peking University Press.

Chen, Jianli 陈建立, and Ma, Qinglin 马清林
2009　甘肃出土早期铁器的金相组织及AMS-14C年代测定 (The Metallurgical Study and AMS-14C Dating of Early Iron Products from Gansu). 文物科技研究 [*Research on Technologies for Ancient Relics*] 6:1–13.

Chen, Jianli 陈建立, Mao, Ruilin 毛瑞林, Wang, Hui 王辉, Chen, Honghai 陈洪海, Xie, Yan 谢焱, and Qian, Yaopeng 钱耀鹏

2012　甘肃临潭磨沟寺洼文化墓葬出土铁器与中国冶铁技术起源 (Iron Artifacts Unearthed from Burials of the Siwa Culture at the Mogou Site in Lintan, Gansu, and the Origin of Iron Smelting Technology in China). 文物 [*Cultural Relics*] 2012(8):45–53.

Chen, Jianli 陈建立, Yang, Junchang 杨军昌, Sun, Binjun 孙秉君, and Pan, Yan 潘岩

2009　梁带村遗址M27出土铜铁复合器的制作技术 (Manufacture Technique of Bronze-iron Bimetallic Objects Found in M27 of Liangdaicun Site, Hancheng, Shaanxi). 中国科学E辑 [*Science in China Series E-Technological Science*] 52(10):3038–3045.

Chen, Kunlong 陈坤龙, Mei, Jianjun 梅建军, and Qian, Wei 潜伟

2018　丝绸之路与早期铜铁技术的交流 (Silk Road and the Exchange of Early Bronze and Iron Techniques). 西域研究 [*The Western Regions Studies*] 2018(2):127–137, 150.

Chen, Kunlong 陈坤龙, Mei, Jianjun 梅建军, and Wang, Lu 王璐

2019　中国早期冶金的本土化与区域互动 (Localisation and Regional Exchange of Metallurgical Technology in Early China). 考古与文物 [*Archaeology and Cultural Relics*] 2019(3):114–121.

Chen, Liang 陈靓, and Deng, Puying 邓普迎

2017　临潼新丰秦墓人骨鉴定研究 (Osteological Research of Human Remains from Qin Tombs in Xinfeng, Lintong). In, 临潼新丰——战国秦汉墓葬考古发掘报告 [*Lintong Xinfeng—Archaeological Excavation Report of Tombs in the Warring States, Qin and Han Dynasties*]. Shaanxisheng Kaogu Yanjiuyuan 陕西省考古研究院 (ed.), Pp. 1927–1966. 北京 Beijing: 科学出版社 Science Press.

Chen, Wenhao 陈文豪

2018　汉代大司农研究 [*Research on Dasinong*]. 新北市 New Taipei city: 花木兰文化出版社 Huamulan Press.

Chen, Xingcan 陈星灿, Liu, Li 刘莉, and Zhou, Chunyan 赵春燕

2010　解盐与中国早期国家的形成 (Salt in Jiecheng and Formation of States in Early China). In, 中国盐业考古2：国际视野下的比较观察 [*Salt Archaeology in China Volume 2: Global Comparative Perspectives*]. Li Shuicheng 李水城 and Lothar von Falkenhausen 罗泰 (eds.), Pp. 42–65. 北京 Beijing: 科学出版社 Science Press.

Chen, Xingyu 陈星宇

2020　战国秦汉粮食亩产问题再探 (Rediscovery of per *mu* Yield of Grain in Warring States, Qin and Han Dynasties). 中国农史 [*Agricultural History of China*] 2020(1):63–72, 62.

Chen, Xuexiang 陈雪香, Ma, Fangqing 马方青, Xu, Longguo 徐龙国, Bai, Yunxiang 白云翔, and Wang, Qi 王祁

2020　临淄齐故城阚家寨遗址B区第I地点植物浮选结果及分析 (Plant Remains from the Locality of Area BI at Kanjiazhai Site, Linzi City Site of the Qi State, Shandong Province). In, 临淄齐故城冶铸业考古 [*Archaeology of Metallurgy and Foundry Industry in the Linzi City Site of Qi State*], Zhongguo Shehui Kexueyuan Kaogu Yanjiusuo 中国社会科学院考古研究所 et al. (eds.), Pp. 748–771. 北京 Beijing: 科学出版社 Science Press.

Chen, Yexin 陈业新

2002　两汉时期气候状况的历史学再考察 (A Historical Re-investigation of Climatic Conditions during the Han Periods). 历史研究 [*History Research*] 2002(4):76–95.

Chen, Zhi 陈直

1980 两汉经济史料论丛 [*Collection of Textual Records Regarding the Economic History in the Han Periods*]. 西安 Xi'an: 陕西人民出版社 Shaanxi People's Publishing House.

1986 居延汉简研究 [*Research on Juyan Bamboo Slips*]. 天津 Tianjin: 天津古籍出版社 Tianjin Guji Press.

Cheng, Lin, and Zhang, Shen

2019 From Contention to Unification: Transformation of Economic Thought in the Han Dynasty and Its Heritage. In, *The Political Economy of the Han Dynasty and Its Legacy*. Cheng Lin, Terry Peach and Wang Fang (eds.), Pp. 31–50. London and New York: Routledge.

Cheng, Linquan 程林泉, Han, Guohe 韩国河, Yang, Junkai 杨军凯, and Wu, Chun 吴春

1992a 西安市未央区房地产开发公司汉墓发掘简报 (Preliminary Report on the Excavation of Han Tombs at the Weiyang Real Estate Company in Xi'an). 考古与文物 [*Archaeology and Cultural Relics*] 5:32–45.

1992b 西汉陈请士墓发掘简报 (Preliminary Report on the Excavation of Chen Qingshi Tomb in the Western Han Period). 考古与文物 [*Archaeology and Cultural Relics*] 6:5–12.

Childe, Gordon V.

1944 Archaeological Ages as Technological Stages. *The Journal of the Royal Anthropological Institute of Great Britain and Ireland* 74(1/2):7–24.

Chin, Tamara T.

2015 *Savage Exchange: Han Imperialism, Chinese Literary Style, and the Economic Imagination*. Cambridge, MA: Harvard University Asia Center.

Choi, Jae-Yong 崔在容

1998 西汉初关中地区官营冶铁业探讨 (Research on the State-owned Iron Industry in the Guanzhong Region during the Early Western Han Period). 史学集刊 [*Collected Papers of History Studies*] 1998(4):7–12.

Christaller, Walter

1966 *Central Places in Southern Germany*. Englewood: Prentice-Hall.

Clark, John E., and Parry, William J.

1990 Craft Specialization and Cultural Complexity. *Research in Economic Anthropology* 12:289–346.

Costin, Cathy L.

1991 Craft Specialization: Issues in Defining, Documenting, and Explaining the Organization of Production. In, *Archaeological Method and Theory Volume 3*. Michael Schiffer (ed.), Pp. 1–56. Tuscon: University of Arizona Press.

2005 Craft Production. In, *Handbook of Archaeological Methods*. Herbert Maschner and Christopher Chippindale (eds.), Pp. 1032–1105. Lanham, MD: AltaMira Press.

2007 Thinking about Production: Phenomenological Classification and Lexical Semantics. In, *Rethinking Craft Specialization in Complex Societies: Archeological Analyses of the Social Meaning of Production*. Zachary X. Hruby and Rowan K. Flad (eds.), Pp. 143–162. Archeological papers of the American Anthropological Association. Arlington, VA: American Anthropological Association and the University of California Press.

Crader, Diana C.

1989   Faunal Remains from Slave Quarter Sites at Monticello, Charlottesville, Virginia. *Archaeozoologia* 3:1–12.

1990   Slave Diet at Monticello. *American Antiquity* 55(4):690–717.

Crump, James

1996   Chan-kuo Ts'e. Ann Arbor: Center for Chinese Studies, University of Michigan.

Cui, Jingxian 崔景贤

1992   渭南市郊古墓葬清理简报 (Preliminary Report on the Excavation of Ancient Tombs on the Suburbs of Weinan City). 文博 [*Relics and Museology*] 6:3–12.

Cui, Jingxian 崔景贤, and Wang, Wenxue 王文学

1998   渭南市区战国、汉墓清理简报 (Preliminary Report on the Excavation of Warring States and Han Tombs in the City District of Weinan). 考古与文物 [*Archaeology and Cultural Relics*] 2:14–24, 13.

Dahlin, Bruce H., Daniel, Bair, Beach, Timothy, Moriarty, Matthew, and Terry, Richard E.

2010   The Dirt on Food: Ancient Feasts and Markets among the Lowland Maya. In, *Pre-Columbian Foodways: Interdisciplinary Approaches to Food, Culture, and Markets in Ancient Mesoamerica.* John E. Staller and Michael Carrasco (eds.), Pp. 191–234, New York: Springer.

Dahlin, Bruce H., Jensen, Christopher T., Terry, Richard E., Wright, David R., and Beach, Timothy

2007   In Search of an Ancient Maya Market. *Latin American Antiquity* 18(4):363–384.

de Haas, Tymon C. A., and Tol, Gijs W.

2017   *The Economic Integration of Roman Italy: Rural Communities in a Globalizing World.* Leiden and Boston, MA: Brill.

Deng, Fuqiu 邓福秋

1994   西汉前期的市场经济和我国历史上的资本主义萌芽问题——读《史记货殖列传》札记之二 (The Initial Development of Capitalism in Ancient China and the Market Economy of the Early Western Han: Notes on the Merchant Biography of Shiji). 中国经济史研究 [*Journal of Chinese Economic History Research*] 1994(4):41–53.

Di Cosmo, Nicola

2009   Han Frontiers: Toward an Integrated View. *Journal of the American Oriental Society* 129(2):199–214.

Ding, Bangyou 丁邦友, and Wei, Xiaoming 魏晓明

2016   秦汉物价史料汇释 [*Collection of Textual Records about Prices during the Qin and Han Periods*]. 北京 Beijing: 中国社会科学出版社 China Social Sciences Press.

Du, Fuyuan 杜弗远, and Han, Rubin 韩汝玢

2005   汉长安城武库遗址出土部分铁器的鉴定 (Indentification of Iron Objects from the Arsenal Site in Han Chang'an). In, 汉长安城武库 [*The Arsenal Site at Han Chang'an*]. Zhongguo Shehui Kexueyuan Kaogu Yanjiusuo 中国社会科学院考古研究所 (ed.), Pp. 132–133. 北京 Beijing: 文物出版社 Cultural Relics Press.

Du, Ning 杜宁, Li, Jianxi 李建西, Zhang, Guangming 张光明, Wang, Xiaolian 王晓莲, and Li, Yangxiang 李延祥

2011   山东临淄齐国故城东北部冶铁遗址的调查与研究 (Survey and Research on Iron Produdction Sites in Northeastern Capital City of the Qi State in Linzi,

Shandong). 江西理工大学学报 [*Journal of Jiangxi University of Science and Technology*] 32(6):12–15.

Du, Ning 杜宁, Li, Yangxiang 李延祥, Zhang, Guangming 张光明, Wang, Xiaolian 王晓莲, and Li, Jianxi 李建西
2012 临淄故城南部炼铁遗物研究 [Studying on Ancient Iron Smelting Relics in the South of the Capital City Linzi]. 中国矿业 [*China Mining Magazine*] 21(12):115–120.

Duan, Hongzhen 段宏振
2009 赵都邯郸城研究 [*Research of Handan City, the Capital of the Zhao Site*]. 北京 Beijing: 文物出版社 Cultural Relics Press.

Duan, Qingbo 段清波
2017 汉长安城轴线变化与南向理念的确立 ——考古学上所见汉文化之一 (The Change of Han Chang'an City Axis and the Establishment of Idea of Facing the South——One of the Han Culture Viewed in Archaeology). 中原文化研究 [*The Central Plains Culture Research*] 2017(2):25–33.

Düring, Bleda S.
2020 *The Imperialisation of Assyria: An Archaeological Approach*. Cambridge: Cambridge University Press.

Earle, Timothy K.
2011 Redistribution and the Political Economy: The Evolution of an Idea. *American Journal of Archaeology* 115(2):237–244.

Emura, Haruki 江村治树
1995 战国时代的城市和城市统治 (Chinese translation) (City and City Rulership in the Warring States Period). In, 日本中青年学者论中国史：上古秦汉卷 [*A Collection of Studies on Chinese History by Young and Senior Japanese Scholars: The Volume of Prehistory and Qin-Han*]. Liu Junwen 刘俊文 (ed.), Pp. 170–211. 上海 Shanghai: 上海古籍出版社 Shanghai Guji Press.
2000 春秋戦国秦漢時代出土文字資料の研究 [*Study on Excavated Texts during the Spring-and-Autumn, Warring States, and Qin-Han Periods*]. 東京 Tōkyō: 汲古書院 Kyūko Shoin.
2011 春秋戦国時代青銅貨幣の生成と展開[*Formation and Development of Bronze Coinage in the Spring-and-Autumn and Warring States Period*]. 東京 Tōkyō: 汲古書院 Kyūko Shoin.

Erb-Satullo, Nathaniel L.
2019 The Innovation and Adoption of Iron in the Ancient Near East. *Journal of Archaeological Research* 27(4):557–607.

Erdkamp, Paul
2005 *The Grain Market in the Roman Empire*. Cambridge: Cambridge University Press.

Fargher, Lane F.
2009 A Comparison of the Spatial Distribution of Agriculture and Craft Specialization in Five State-Level Societies. *Journal of Anthropological Research* 65(3):353–387.

Feinman, Gary M.
1999 Rethinking Our Assumptions: Economic Specialization at the Household Scale in Ancient Ejutla, Oaxaca, Mexico. In, *Pottery and People: A Dynamic Interaction*. James M. Skibo and Gary M. Feinman (eds.), Pp. 81–105. Salt Lake City: The University of Utan Press.

Feinman, Gary M., and Garraty, Christopher P.
2010   Preindustrial Markets and Marketing: Archaeological Perspectives. *Annual Review of Anthropology* 39(1):167–191.

Feinman, Gary M., and Nicholas, Linda M.
2012   The Late Prehispanic Economy of the Valley of Oaxaca, Mexico: Weaving Threads from Data, Theory, and Subsequent History. In, *Political Economy, Neoliberalism, and the Prehistoric Economies of Latin America*. Ty Matejowsky and Donald Wood (eds.), Pp. 225–258. Bingley: Emerald Group Publishing.

Feng, Shi 冯时
2015   《保训》故事与地中之变迁 (The Precedent of Baoxun and the Changes of the Center of the Realm). 考古学报 [*Acta Archaeologica Sinica*] 2015(2):129–156.

Fine, Ben
1997   Review of Gifts and Commodities: Exchange and Western Capitalism since 1700. By James G. Carrier. London: Routledge, 1995. Pp. xvi, 240. £45.00. *The Journal of Economic History* 57(3):772–773.

Finley, Moses I.
1999[1973] *The Ancient Economy*. Berkeley: University of California Press.

Fish, Suzanne K., and Kowalewski, Stephen A. (eds.)
1990   *The Archaeology of Regions: A Case for Full-coverage Survey*. Washington, D.C.: Smithsonian Institution Press.

Flad, Rowan
2011   *Salt Production and Social Hierarchy in Ancient China*. Cambridge: Cambridge University Press.
2018   Where Did the Silk Road Come from? In, *The China Questions: Critical Insights into a Rising Power*. Jennifer Rudolph and Michael Szonyi (eds.), Pp. 237–243. Cambridge, MA and London: Harvard University Press.

Franklin, Ursula M.
1999   *The Real World of Technology*. Toronto: Anansi.

Fu, Zhufu 傅筑夫
1982   中国封建社会经济史 [*Economic History of Chinese Feudal Society*]. 北京 Beijing: 人民出版社 People's Publishing House.

Fujita, Masakatsu 藤田勝久
2016   中国古代国家と情報伝達: 秦漢簡牘の研究 [*Information System in Ancient Chinese States: A Study of Bamboo and Wooden Slips during the Qin and Han Periods*]. 東京 Tōkyō: 汲古書院 Kyūko Shoin.

Gale, Esson M.
1967   *Discourses on Salt and Iron: A Debate on State Control of Commerce and Industry in Ancient China (chapters I-XXVIII translated from the Chinese of Huan K'uan with introduction and notes)*. Taipei: Ch'eng-wen Publishing Company.

Gao, Jie 高杰
2019   汉代地方工官研究: 以出土骨签与漆器铭文为中心 [*Research on the Regional Gongguan of the Han Period: Case Studies of Inscriptions on Bone Tags and Lacquerware*]. 南京 Nanjing: 凤凰出版社 Fenghuang Press.

Gao, Min 高敏
1986   东汉盐、铁官制度辨疑 (A Discrimination of the Salt and Iron Official System in the Eastern Han Dynasty). 中州学刊 [*Academic Journal of Zhongzhou*] 1986(4):90–93, 89.

Gao, Ruoci 高若次, and Wang, Guizhi 王桂枝
1988   宝鸡县甘峪发现一座春秋早期墓葬 (An Early Spring-and-Autumn Tomb in Ganyu, Baoji). 文博 [*Relics and Museology*] 1988(4):21.

Gao, Weigang 高维刚
2008   秦汉市场研究 [*Research on the Qin and Han Market*]. 成都 Chengdu: 四川大学出版社 Sichuan University Press.

Gao, Zhixi 高至喜
2012   湖南楚墓与楚文化 [*Chu Tombs in Hunan and Chu Culture*]. 长沙 Changsha: 岳麓书社 Yuelu Press.

Gao, Zhongyu 高忠玉, and Zhao, Caixiu 赵彩秀
1996   西北林学院基建中发现的古墓 (Ancient Tombs Discovered during the Construction Project in Northwest Forestry University). 文博 [*Relics and Museology*] 1996(5):65–73.

Gardner, Andrew
2012   Time and Empire in the Roman World. *Journal of Social Archaeology* 12(2):145–166.

Garraty, Christopher P.
2009   Evaluating the Distributional Approach to Inferring Market Exchange: A Test Case from the Mexican Gulf Lowlands. *Latin American Antiquity* 20(1):157–174.
2010   Investigating Market Exchange in Ancient Societies: A Theoretical Review. In, *Archaeological Approaches to Market Exchange in Ancient Societies.* Christopher P. Garraty and Barbara L. Stark (eds.), Pp. 3–32. Boulder: University Press of Colorado.

Ge, Jianxiong 葛剑雄
1986   西汉人口地理 [*Demographic Geology in the Western Han Dynasty*]. 北京 Beijing: 人民出版社 People's Publishing House.
1990   西汉长安——陵县中国最早的城市群 (The Earliest Cluster of Urban Centers in China: Xi'an and Mausoleum Towns in the Western Han Period). In, 纪念顾颉刚学术论文集 [*Festschrift for Gu Jiegang*]. Yin Da 尹达 (ed.), Pp. 676–680. 成都 Chengdu: 巴蜀出版社 Bashu Press.

Ge, Quansheng 葛全胜
2011   中国历朝气候变化 [*Climatic Changes in Chinese Historical Periods*]. 北京 Beijing: 科学出版社 Science Press.

Ge, Quansheng 葛全胜, Wang, Shunbing 王顺兵, and Zheng, Jingyun 郑景云
2006   过去5000年中国气温变化序列重建 (Reconstruciton of the Sequence of Temperature Changes in the Past 5,000 Years). 自然科学进展 [*Progress in Natural Science*] 16(6):689–696.

Gettens, Rutherford J., Clarke Jr., Roy S., and Chase, William T.
1971   *Two Early Chinese Bronze Weapons with Meteoritic Iron Blades.* Freer Gallery of Art Occasional Paper.

Gidney, Louisa
2000   Economic Trends, Craft Specialisation and Social Status: Bone Assemblages from Leicester. In, *Animal Bones, Human Societies.* Peter Rowley-Conwy (ed.), Pp. 170–178. Oxford: Oxbow Books.

Gordon, Robert B.
1996   *American Iron: 1607–1900.* Baltimore, MD and London: The Johns Hopkins University Press.

Grant, Annie
1982   The Use of Tooth Wear as a Guide to the Age of Domestic Animals. In, *Ageing and Sexing Animal Bones from Archaeological Sites*. Bob Wilson, Caroline Grigson and Sebastian Payne (eds.), Pp. 91–108. Oxford: BAR.

Greenfield, Haskel J., and Miller, Duncan
2004   Spatial Patterning of Early Iron Age Metal Production at Ndondondwane, South Africa: The Question of Cultural Continuity between the Early and Late Iron Age. *Journal of Archaeological Science* 31:1511–1532.

Gregory, Christopher A.
1982   *Gifts and Commodities*. London: Academic Press Inc.
1997   *Savage Money: The Anthropology and Politics of Commodity Exchange*. Amsterdam: Harwood Academic Publishers.

Guanzi jiaozhu
2009   管子校注 [Guanzi jiaozhu], annotated by Li Xiangfeng 黎翔凤. Beijing 北京: 中华书局 Zhonghua Press.

Guo, Hao 郭浩
2011   汉代地方财政研究 [*Research on the Han Local Finance*]. 济南 Jinan: 山东大学出版社 Shandong University Press.

Guo, Meiling 郭美玲, Chen, Kunlong 陈坤龙, Mei, Jianjun 梅建军, Sun, Zhanwei 孙占伟, and Shao, Jin 邵晶
2014   陕西黄陵寨头河战国墓地出土铁器的初步科学分析研究 (Scientific Analysis of Iron Objects from the Zhaitouhe Cemetery in Huangling, Shaanxi). 考古与文物 [*Archaeology and Cultural Relics*] 2014(2):121–127.

Guo, Wu
2009   From Western Asia to the Tianshan Mountains: On the Early Iron Artefacts Found in Xinjiang. In, *Metallurgy and Civilisation: Eurasia and Beyond (Proceedings of the 6th International Conference on the Beginnings of the Use of Metals and Alloys)*. Mei Jianjun and Thilo Rehren (eds.), Pp. 107–115. London: Archetype.

Guo, Yanlong
2016   *Affordable Luxury: The Entanglements of Metal Mirrors in Han China (202 BCE-220 CE)*, Ph.D dissertation, University of British Columbia.
2018   The Monetary Value of Bronze Mirrors in the Han Dynasty. *T'oung Pao* 104(1–2):66–115.

Guojia [Guojia Wenwuju 国家文物局 (ed.)]
1998   中国文物地图集·陕西分册 [*Atlas of Cultural Relics. Shaanxi Volume*]. 西安 Xi'an: 西安地图出版社 Xi'an Ditu Press.

Guowuyuan, and Guojia [Guowuyuan Sanxia Gongcheng Jianshe Weiyuanhui Bangongshi 国务院三峡工程建设委员会办公室, and Guojia Wenwuju 国家文物局]
2003   秭归柳林溪 [*The Liulinxi Site in Zigui*]. 北京 Beijing: 科学出版社 Science Press.

Han, Baoquan 韩保全, and Cheng, Linquan 程林泉
1991   西安北郊枣园村汉墓发掘简报 (Preliminary Report on the Excavation of Han Tombs at Zaoyuancun on the Northern Suburbs of Xi'an). 考古与文物 [*Archaeology and Cultural Relics*] 1991(4):34–41.
1992   西安北郊枣园汉墓第二次发掘简报 (Preliminary Report on the Second Excavation of Han Tombs at Zaoyuancun on the Northern Suburbs of Xi'an). 考古与文物 [*Archaeology and Cultural Relics*] 1992(5):23–34.

Han, Guohe 韩国河, and Zhang, Jihua 张继华

2015 汉代聚落考古的几个问题 (Several Issues Related to the Settlement Archaeology of the Han Period). 中原文物 [*Cultural Relics of Central China*] 2015(6):22–26.

Han, Guohe 韩国河, and Zhang, Xiangyu 张翔宇

2011 西安地区中小型西汉墓的分期与年代研究 (Research on the Chronology and Date of Medium and Small Western Han Tombs in Xi'an Area). 考古学报 [*Acta Archaeologica Sinica*] 2011(2):213–244.

Han, Maoli 韩茂莉

2017 近代山西乡村集市的地理空间与社会环境 (Geographical Space and Social Environment of Village Fair in Modern Shanxi Province). 中国经济史研究 [*Researches in Chinese Economic History*] 2017(1):115–125.

Han, Rubin 韩汝玢

1987 吉林榆树老河深鲜卑墓葬出土金属文物的研究 (Reseach on the Metal Objects from Xianbei Tombs at the Laoheshen Site in Yushu, Jilin). In, 榆树老河深 [*The Laoheshen Site in Yushu*]. Jilinsheng Wenwu Yanjiusuo 吉林省文物研究所 (ed.), Pp. 146–156. 北京 Beijing: 文物出版社 Cultural Relics Press.

1998 中国早期铁器(公元前5世纪以前)的金相学研究 (A Metallographic Study on Early Iron Objects of China). 文物 [*Cultural Relics*] 1998(2):87–96.

Han, Rubin, and Chen, Jianli

2013 Casting Iron in Ancient China. In, *The World of Iron*. Jane Humphris and Thilo Rehren (eds.), Pp. 168–77. London: Archetype.

Han, Rubin, and Duan, Hongmei

2009 An Early Iron-using Center in the Ancient Jin State Region (8th-3rd Century BC). In, *Metallurgy and Civilisation: Eurasia and Beyond*. Mei Jianjun and Thilo Rehren (eds.), Pp. 99–106. London: Archetype.

Han, Rubin 韩汝玢, and Ke, Jun 柯俊

2007 中国科学技术史(矿冶卷) [*China Science and Technology History*] *(Volume of Mining and Smelting)*. 北京 Beijing: 科学出版社 Science Press.

Han, Wei 韩伟, and Jiao, Nanfeng 焦南峰

1988 秦都雍城考古发掘研究综述 (A Summary of the Excavation and Research on the Qin Capital Yongcheng). 考古与文物 [*Archaeology and Cultural Relics*] 1988(5&6):111–126.

Han, Yiliang 韩宜良, Luo, Wugan 罗武干, Liu, Jian 刘剑, Bai, Yunxiang 白云翔, and Wang, Changsui 王昌燧

2012 济南运署街汉代铁工场遗址的相关问题探讨 (Disscussion of Han Dynasty Smelting Relics of the Yunshujie Site, Jinan City). 文物保护与考古科学 [*Sciences of Conservation and Archaeology*] 2012(4):25–32.

Hanshu 汉书

1997[1962] 汉书 [*Hanshu*], by Ban Gu 班固 and others, annotated by Yan Shigu 颜师古. 北京Beijing: 中华书局 Zhonghua Press.

Hayashi, Minao 林巳奈夫

1975 漢代の飲食 (Food and Drink in Han Times). 東方學報 [*Journal of Oriental Studies*] 48:1–98.

He, Tangkun 何堂坤, Wang, Jihong 王继红, and Jin, Fengyi 靳枫毅

2004 延庆山戎文化铜柄铁刀及其科学分析 (Scientific Analysis of the Bimetallic Dagger from the Yanqing Site). 中原文物 [*Cultural Relics of Central China*] 2004(2):71–75.

He, Xi 贺喜
2012   明末至清中期湘东南矿区的秩序与采矿者的身份 (Order in Mining Regions of Southeast China and Identities of Miners in Mining Regions of Southeast Hunan, from Late Ming to Middle Qing Periods). 中国社会经济史研究 [*The Journal of Chinese Social and Economic History*] 2012(2):19–20.

Hebei [Hebeisheng Wenwu Yanjiusuo 河北省文物研究所]
1985   藁城台西商代遗址 [*The Shang Site of Taixi in Gaocheng*]. 北京 Beijing: 文物出版社 Cultural Relics Press.
1996   燕下都 [*Lower Capital of the Yan State*]. 北京 Beijing: 文物出版社 Cultural Relics Press.

Henan [Henansheng Wenwu Kaogu Yanjiusuo 河南省文物考古研究所]
1993   河南新发现"扶戈当析"陶范 (Molds with Fujiandangxi Inscriptions Recently Discovered in Xinzheng, Henan). 中国钱币 [*China Coins*] 1993(2):53–55, 63.
1994   新郑新发现的战国钱范 (Warring-States Coin Molds Recently Discovered in Xinzheng). 华夏考古 [*Huaxia Archaeology*] 1994(4):14–20.
2006   新郑郑国祭祀遗址 [*The Sacrificial Site of the Zheng State in Xinzheng*]. 郑州 Zhengzhou: 大象出版社 Elephant Press.
2009   河南泌阳县下河湾冶铁遗址调查报告 (Report on the Survey of Iron Smelitng Site at Xiahewan, Biyang, Henan). 中原文物 [*Cultural Relics of Central China*] 2009(4):16–28.

Henan bianxiezu [Henansheng Bowuguan *Zhongguo Yejinshi* Bianxiezu 河南省博物馆《中国冶金史》编写组]
1978   汉代叠铸: 温县烘范窑的发掘和研究 [*The Excavation and Research of Moulds-firing Kilns in Wen County*]. 北京 Beijing: 文物出版社 Cultural Relics Press.

Henan, and Lushan [Henansheng Wenwu Kaogu Yanjiusuo 河南省文物考古研究所, and Lushanxian Wenwu Guanli Weiyuanhui 鲁山县文物管理委员会]
2002   河南鲁山望城岗汉代冶铁遗址一号炉发掘简报 (Preliminary Report on the Excavation of No. 1 Furnace at the Han Dynasty Iron Smelting Site in Wangchenggang, Lushan, Henan). 华夏考古 [*Huaxia Archaeology*] 2002(1):3–11.

Henan et al. [Henansheng Wenwu Kaogu Yanjiuyuan 河南省文物考古研究院, Lushanxian Wenwu Baohu Guanlisuo 鲁山县文物保护管理所, and Chengshi Kaogu Yu Baohu Guojia Wenwuju Zhongdian Keyan Jidi 城市考古与保护国家文物局重点科研基地]
2021   鲁山望城岗冶铁遗址2018年度调查发掘简报 (Preliminary Report on Investigation and Excavation of the Iron Smelting Site at Wangchenggang, Lushan in 2018). 华夏考古 [*Huaxia Archaeology*] 2021(1):14–39.

Henan, and Sanmenxia [Henansheng Wenwu Kaogu Yanjiusuo 河南省文物考古研究所, and Sanmenxiashi Wenwu Gongzuodui 三门峡市文物工作队]
1999   三门峡虢国墓 [*Guo State Tombs at Sanmenxia*]. 北京 Beijing: 文物出版社 Cultural Relics Press.

Henan Wenhuaju [Henansheng wenhuaju wenwu gongzuodui 河南省文化局文物工作队]
1959   郑州二里冈 [*Erligang in Zhengzhou*]. 北京 Beijing: 科学出版社 Science Press.
1962   巩县铁生沟 [*Iron Workshop at Tieshengou, Gongxian*]. 北京 Beijing: 文物出版社 Cultural Relics Press.

Henan Wenwu [Henansheng Wenwu Yanjiusuo 河南省文物研究所]
1991a   南阳北关瓦房庄汉代冶铁遗址发掘报告 (The Site Report of Ironworks at Wafangzhuang, Beiguan, Nanyang). 华夏考古 [*Huaxia Archaeology*] 1991(1):1–110.

1991b 河南新郑郑韩故城制陶作坊遗迹发掘简报 (Preliminary Report on the Excavation of Remains at the Ceramic Workshop in the Zheng-Han Capitals, Xinzheng, Henan). 华夏考古 [*Huaxia Archaeology*] 1991(3):33–54.

1994 南阳瓦房庄汉代制陶、铸铜遗址的发掘 (Preliminary Report on the Excavation of the Ceramic Workshop and Bronze Foundry of the Han Period at the Wafangzhuang Site]). 华夏考古 [*Huaxia Archaeology*] 1994(1):31–44.

Henan Wenwu, and Zhongguo [Henansheng Wenwu Yanjiusuo 河南省文物研究所, and Zhongguo Lishi Bowuguan Kaogubu 中国历史博物馆考古部]

1992 登封王城岗与阳城 [*The Wangchenggang Site at Dengfeng and the Ancient Cities of Yangcheng*]. 北京 Beijing: 文物出版社 Cultural Relics Press.

Henan Wenwu et al. [Henansheng Wenwu Yanjiusuo 河南省文物研究所, Henansheng Danjiang Kuqu Kaogu Fajuedui 河南省丹江库区考古发掘队, and Xichuanxian Bowuguan 淅川县博物馆]

1991 淅川下寺春秋楚墓 [*The Spring-and-Autumn Period Chu Tombs at Xiasi, Xichuan*]. 北京 Beijing: 文物出版社 Cultural Relic Press.

Henn, Roselle E.

1985 Reconstructing the Urban Foodchain: Advances and Problems in Interpreting Faunal Remains Recovered from Household Deposits. *American Archaeology* (5):202–209.

Henry, Susan L.

1987a A Chicken in Every Pot: The Urban Subsistence Pattern in Turn-of-the-century Phoenix, Arizona. In, *Living in Cities: Current Research in Urban Archaeology*. Edward Staski (ed.), Pp. 19–28. Pleasant Hill: CA Society for Historical Archaeology.

1987b Factors Influencing Consumer Behavior in Turn-of-the-century Phoenix, Arizona. In, *Consumer Choice in Historical Archaeology*. Suzanne Spence-Wood (ed.), Pp. 359–381. Plenum: New York.

Hietala, Harold J.

1984 Intrasite Spatial Analysis: A Brief Overview. In, *Intrasite Spatial Analysis in Archaeology*. Harold J. Hietala (ed.), Pp. 1–3. Cambridge: Cambridge University Press.

Hingley, Richard

2005 *Globalizing Roman Culture: Unity, Diversity, and Empire*. London: Routledge.

Hirth, Kenneth G.

1998 The Distributional Approach: A New Way to Identify Marketplace Exchange in the Archaeological Record. *Current Anthropology* 39(4):451–476.

2009 Housework and Domestic Craft Production: An Introduction. In, *Housework: Craft Production and Domestic Economy in Ancient Mesoamerica*. Kenneth G. Hirth (ed.), Pp. 1–12. Archaeological Papers of the American Anthropological Association. Hoboken, NJ: Wiley-Blackwell.

Hirth, Kenneth G., and Pillsbury, Joanne (eds.)

2013 *Merchants, Markets, and Exchange in the Pre-Columbian World*. Washington, D.C.: Dumbarton Oaks Research Library and Collection.

Hitchner, Bruce R.

2005 "The Advantage of Wealth and Luxury": The Case for Economic Growth in the Roman Empire. In, *The Ancient Economy: Evidence and Models.* Ian Morris and Joseph G. Manning (eds.), Pp. 207–222. Stanford, CA: Stanford University Press.

2012   Roads, Integration, Connectivity and Economic Performance in the Roman Empire. In, *Highways, Byways, and Road Systems in the Pre-modern World*. Susan Alcock, John Bodel and Richard J. A. Talbert (eds.), Pp. 222–234. Hoboken, NJ: Wiley-Blackwell.

Hong, Shi 洪石
2006   战国秦汉漆器研究 [*Research on Lacquerware in the Warring States and Qin-Han Periods*]. 北京 Beijing: 文物出版社 Cultural Relics Press.

Horden, Peregrine, and Purcell, Nicholas
2000   *The Corrupting Sea: A Study of Mediterranean History*. Oxford: Blackwell.

Hou Hanshu 后汉书
2018[1965] 后汉书 [*Hou Hanshu*], by Fan Ye 范晔, annotated by Li Xian 李贤 and others. 北京 Beijing: 中华书局 Zhonghua Press.

Hou, Ningbin 侯宁彬
2004   西安地区汉代墓葬的分布 (Distribution of Han Tombs in Xi'an District). 考古与文物 [*Archaeology and Cultural Relics*] 2004(5):50–57.

Hou, Xiaorong 后晓荣
2009   秦代政区地理 [*Geography of the Political Division of the Qin Period*]. 北京 Beijing: 社会科学文献出版社 Social Sciences Academic Press.

Hsing, I-tien 邢义田
2009   从出土数据看秦汉聚落形态和乡里 (Research on the Han Settlement Pattern and Xiangli Based on Excavated Materials). In, 中国史新论-基层社会分册 [*New Perspective on Chinese History: Grassroots Society*]. Huang Kuanzhong 黄宽重 (ed.), Pp. 13–126. 台北 Taipei: 中央研究院 Academia Sinica.
2011[1983] 试释汉代的关东、关西与山东、山西 (Explanation of the Terminology Guandong and Guanxi as Well as Shandong and Shanxi). In, 治国安邦:法制、行政与军事 [*Zhiguo Anbang: Political, Adminstrative, and Military System of the Han Dynasty*], Pp. 180–210. 北京 Beijing: 中华书局 Zhonghua Press.
2011[1989] 汉代案比在县或在乡? (Did *Anbi* Occur in County or *Xiang* Village?). In, 治国安邦: 法制、行政与军事 [*Zhiguo Anbang: Political, Adminstrative, and Military System of the Han Dynasty*], Pp. 211–248. 北京 Beijing: 中华书局 Zhonghua Press.
2020   有待发掘的汉武帝「外长城」—边塞汉简研究的未来 (The Pending Excavation of Emperor Wu's "Outer Great Wall" and the Prospects for the Study of Wooden Slips Unearthed along the Han Northern Frontier). 古今论衡 [*Disquisitions on the Past & Present*] 34:4–52.

Hsu, Cho-yun 许倬云
1980   *Han Agriculture: The Formation of Early Chinese Agrarian Economy (206 B.C.-A.D. 220)*. Jack L. Dull (ed.). Seattle: University of Washington Press.
2006[1965] 中国古代社会史论: 春秋战国时期的社会流动 [*Ancient China in Transition: An Analysis of Social Mobility, 722-222 B.C*]. 桂林 Guilin: 广西师范大学出版社 Guangxi Normal University Press.

Hu, Feng 胡方
2015   汉武帝"广关"措置与西汉地缘政策的变化——以长安、洛阳之间地域结构为视角 ("Expanding the Pass" Policy and the Change in Geopolitical Strategy in the Western Han Dynasty from the Perspective of the Regional Space between Chang'an and Luoyang). 中国历史地理论丛 [*Journal of Chinese Historical Geography*] 2015(3):40–46.

Hu, Hongqiong 胡洪琼
2012   殷墟时期牛的相关问题探讨 (Research on Issues Related to Cattle in the Yinxu Period), 华夏考古 [*Huaxia Archaeology*] 2012(3):47–54.

Hu, Songmei 胡松梅, Liu, Zhendong 刘振东, and Zhang, Jianfeng 张建锋
2006   西安汉长安城城墙西南角遗址出土动物骨骼研究报告 (Report on Faunal Remains from the North-Western Corner of the Enclosing Walls of Han Chang'an). 文博 [*Relics and Museology*] 2006(5):59–60.

Hua, Jueming
1983   The Mass Production of Iron Castings in Ancient China. *Scientific American* 248(1):121–124.

Huang, Jinyan 黄今言
2003   论秦汉商品市场发育水平的几个问题 (Issues of the Developmental Degree of the Qin-Han Commodity Economy). 中国经济史研究 [*Journal of Chinese Economic History Research*] 2003(3):93–102.
2005   秦汉商品经济研究 [*Research on the Commodity Economy in the Qin and Han Period*]. 北京 Beijing: 人民出版社 People's Publishing House.

Huang, Yongmei 黄永美
2013   西汉长城若干问题研究 [*Research on Several Issues Related to the Great Wall of the Western Han Dynasty*], 西北大学博士论文 Ph.D dissertation, Northwest University.

Huang, Zhanyue 黄展岳
1976   关于中国开始冶铁和使用铁器的问题 (The Origin of Iron-metallurgy and Earliest Use of Iron-tools). 文物 [*Cultural Relics*] 1976(8):62–70.

Hubei [Hubeisheng Wenwu Kaogu Yanjiusuo 湖北省文物考古研究所]
1995   江陵九店东周墓 [*Eastern Zhou Tombs at Jidian, Jiangling*]. 北京 Beijing: 科学出版社 Science Press.
2000   湖北宜昌县上磨垴周代遗址的发掘 (The Excavation of the Zhou-era Site at Shangmonao in Yichang County, Hubei). 考古 [*Archaeology*] 2000(9):22–35, 99.
2011   湖北丹江口市薄家湾遗址发掘简报 (An Excavation Report of the Bojiawan Site in Danjiangkou City, Hubei Province). 江汉考古 [*Jianghan Archaeology*] 2011(1):42–58.

Hubei, and Hubei [Hubeisheng Wenwu Kaogu Yanjiusuo 湖北省文物考古研究所, and Hubeisheng Wenwuju Nanshui Beidiao Bangongshi 湖北省文物局南水北调办公室]
2010   湖北郧西张家坪遗址发掘简报 (An Excavation Report of Zhangjiaping Site in Yunxi County). 江汉考古 [*Jianghan Archaeology*] 2010(3):3–19.

Hubei, and Guangshui [Hubeisheng Wenwu Kaogu Yanjiusuo 湖北省文物考古研究所, and Guangshuishi Bowuguan 广水市博物馆]
2008   湖北广水巷子口遗址发掘简报 (Preliminary Report of the Excavation at the Xiangzikou Site in Guangshui, Hubei). 江汉考古 [*Jianghan Archaeology*] 2008(1):15–36.

Hubei, and Laohekou [Hubeisheng Wenwu Kaogu Yanjiusuo 湖北省文物考古研究所, and Laohekoushi Bowuguan 老河口市博物馆]
2003   湖北老河口杨营春秋遗址发掘简报 (Brief Report on Excavation of Spring-and-Autumn Period Site in Yangying, Laohekou, Hubei). 江汉考古 [*Jianghan Archaeology*] 2003(3):16–31.

Hubei, and Xiaogan [Hubeisheng Wenwu Kaogu Yanjiusuo 湖北省文物考古研究所, and Hubeisheng Xiaoganshi Bowuguan 湖北省孝感市博物馆]
2006　孝感大家园东周遗址发掘简报 (Brief Report on the Excavation of Eastern Zhou Dynasty Site at Dajiayuan, Xiaogan). 江汉考古 [*Jianghan Archaeology*] 2006(2):12–16.

Hubei et al. [Hubeisheng Wenwu Kaogu Yanjiusuo 湖北省文物考古研究所, Jingmenshi Bowuguan 荆门市博物馆, and Xiangjing Gaosu Gonglu Kaogudui 襄荆高速公路考古队]
2006　荆门左冢楚墓 [*The Chu Tomb in Zuozhong*]. 北京 Beijing: 文物出版社 Cultural Relics Press.

Hubei Bowuguan [Hubeisheng Bowuguan 湖北省博物馆]
1982a 楚都纪南城的勘察与发掘(上) (The Survey and Excavation of Jinancheng, the Chu Capital). 考古学报 [*Acta Archaeologica Sinica*] 1982(3):323–350.
1982b 楚都纪南城的勘察与发掘(下) (The Survey and Excavation of Jinancheng, the Chu Capital). 考古学报 [*Acta Archaeologica Sinica*] 1982(4):477–507.

Hubei Jingdi [Hubeisheng Jingzhou Diqu Bowuguan 湖北省荆州地区博物馆]
1982　江陵天星观1号楚墓 (Excavation of the No. 1 Chu Tomb at Tianxingguan in Jianling). 考古学报 [*Acta Archaeologica Sinica*] 1982(1):82–103.
1984　江陵雨台山楚墓 [*Chu State Tombs at Yutaishan of Jiangling*]. 北京 Beijing: 文物出版社 Cultural Relics Press.

Hubei Jingsha [Hubeisheng Jingsha Tielu Kaogudui 湖北省荆沙铁路考古队]
1991　包山楚墓 [*Chu Tombs at Baoshan*]. 北京 Beijing: 文物出版社 Cultural Relics Press.

Hubei Jingzhou [Hubeisheng Jingzhou Bowuguan 湖北省荆州博物馆]
2003　荆州天星观二号楚墓 [*No. 2 Chu Tomb at Tianxingguan in Jingzhou*]. 北京 Beijing: 文物出版社 Culutral Relics Press.

Hubei Wenwuju, and Hubei Nanshuibeidao [Hubeisheng Wenwuju 湖北省文物局, and Hubeisheng Nashuibeitiao Guanliju 湖北省南水北调管理局]
2018　荆州张家台遗址 [*The Zhangjiatai Site in Jingzhou*]. 北京 Beijing: 科学出版社 Science Press.

Huelsbeck, David R.
1991　Faunal Remains and Consumer Behavior: What Is Being Measured? *Historical Archaeology* 25(2):62–76.

Hulsewé, Anthony F. P.
1985　*Remants of Ch'in Law*. Leiden: Brill.

Hunansheng et al. [Hunansheng Wenwu Kaogu Yanjiusuo 湖南省文物考古研究所, Hunan Zhangjiajieshi Wenwuju 湖南张家界市文物局, Hunan Sangzhixian Wenwuju 湖南桑植县文物局, and Department of Anthropology/History, The Chinese University of Hong Kong 香港中文大学人类学系/历史系]
2019　湖南桑植官田冶炼遗址发掘简报及冶金分析研究 (Preliminary Report of the Smelting Site of the Guantian Site in Sangzhi and Metallurgical Analysis of Manufacturing Remains). 南方文物 [*Southern Cultural Relics*] 2019(3):69–92.

Ikeda, Yūichi 池田雄一(translated by Zheng, Wei 郑威)
2017　中国古代的聚落与地方行政 [*Ancient Settlements and Local Administration in China*]. 上海 Shanghai: 复旦大学出版社 Fudan University Press.

Jaang, Li
2015   The Landscape of China's Participation in the Bronze Age Eurasian Network. *Journal of World Prehistory* 28(3):179–213.

Jennings, Justin
2011   *Globalizations and the Ancient World*. Cambridge: Cambridge University Press.

Ji, Chaoding 冀朝鼎
1981[1930]   中国历史上的基本经济区与水利事业的发展 [*Key Economics Areas in China History and Development of Water Conservancy*]. 北京 Beijing: 中国社会科学出版社 China Social Sciences Press.

Jia, Lajiang 贾腊江
2011   秦早期青铜器科技考古学研究 [*Scientific Research of Bronzes from the Early Qin State*]. 北京 Beijing: 科学出版社 Science Press.

Jiang, Lu 蒋璐
2016   北方地区汉墓的考古学研究 [*Archaeological Research on the Tombs of Han Dynasty in the Northern China*]. 杭州 Hangzhou: 浙江大学出版社 Zhejiang University Press.

Jiangsu, and Nanjing [Jiangsusheng Wenwu Guanli Weiyuanhui 江苏省文物管理委员会, and Nanjing Bowuyuan 南京博物院]
1965   江苏六合程桥东周墓 (The Eastern Zhou Tomb at Chengqiao, Liuhe, Jiangsu). 考古 [*Archaeology*] 1965(3):105–115.

Jiao, Nanfeng 焦南峰
2006   汉阳陵从葬坑初探 (Initial Explanation of the External Chambers in the Yangling Mausoleum of the Western Han Period). 文物 [*Cultural Relics*] 2006(7):51–57.
2013   西汉帝陵形制要素的分析与推定 (Analysis and Identification of Major Structural Elements in Western Han Mausoleums). 考古与文物 [*Archaeology and Cultural Relics*] 2013(5):72–81.

Jiao, Nanfeng 焦南峰, and Ma, Yongying 马永嬴
2011   西汉帝陵选址研究 (Location Selection of Imperial Mausoluems in the Western Han Period). 考古 [*Archaeology*] 2011(11):76–82, 113.

Jin, Wen 晋文
2011   桑弘羊评传 [*Biography of Sang Hongyang*]. 南京 Nanjing: 南京大学出版社 Nanjing University Press.
2021   秦汉土地制度研究 [*Research on the Land System in the Qin-Han Periods*]. 北京 Beijing: 社会科学文献出版社 Social Sciences Academic Press.

Jin, Xueshan 金学山
1957   西安半坡的战国墓葬 (Warring States Tombs at Banpo in Xi'an). 考古学报 [*Acta Archaeologica Sinica*] 1957(3):63–92.

Jingmen [Jingmen Shi Bowuguan 荆门市博物馆]
1990   荆门市响岭岗东周遗址与墓地发掘简报 (A Brief Report on the Excavation of Residential Area and Cemetery at Xianglinggang, Jingmen City). 江汉考古 [*Jianghan Archaeology*] 1990(4):12–55.

Kageyama, Tsuyoshi 影山刚
1984   中国古代の制铁手工業と専売制 (Iron Handicraft and Monopoly in the Ancient China). In, 中国古代の商工業と専売制 [*Industry, Business, and Monopoly in the Ancient China*], Pp. 271–309. 东京 Tokyo: 東京大学出版会 Tōkyō daigaku shuppankai.

akinuma, Yōhei 柿沼陽平
_)11   中国古代货幣経済史研究 [*Research on the History of Coinage Economy in Ancient China*]. 東京 Tōkyō: 汲古書院 Kyūko Shoin.

Kamiya, Masakazu 紙屋正和
1994   両漢時代の商業と市 (Commerce and Market during the Han Periods). 東洋史研究 [*The Journal of Oriental Researches*] 52(4):655–682.

Kato, Shigeru 加藤繁
1993[1918]   汉代的国家财政和帝室财政区别及帝室财政一斑 (Difference of the State Finance and Royal-house Finance in the Han Dynasty and Details of the Royal-house Finance). In, 日本学者研究中国史论著选译 (vol. 3) [*Translation of Selected Articles of Japanese Scholars Working on Chinese History*]. Liu Junwen 刘俊文 (ed.), Pp. 294–388. 北京 Beijing: 中华书局 Zhonghua Press.

Ke, Jun 柯俊, Wu, Kunyi 吴坤仪, Han, Rubin 韩汝玢, and Miao, Changxing 苗长兴
1993   河南古代一批铁器的初步研究 (Research on Ancient Iron Artifacts from Henan). 中原文物 [*Cultural Relics of Central China*] 1993(1):95–104, 87.

Keightley, David N.
1976   Where Have All the Sword Gone? Reflections on the Unification of China. *Early China* 2:31–34.

Kelley, Klara B.
1976   Dendritic Central-Place Systems and the Regional Organization of Navajo Trading Posts. In, *Regional Analysis (Volume I): Economic System.* Carol A. Smith (ed.), Pp. 219–254. New York: Academic Press.

Kidder, Tristram R., Liu, Haiwang, and Li, Minglin
2012   Sanyangzhuang: Early Farming and a Han Settlement Preserved Beneath Yellow River Flood Deposits. *Antiquity* 86(331):30–47.

Kim, Kyung-ho, and Lai, Mingchiu
2018   An Overview of the Qin-Han Legal System from the Perspective of Recently Unearthed Documents. In, *Routledge Handbook of Early Chinese History.* Paul R. Goldin (ed.), Pp. 386–404. Abingdon: Routledge.

Kim, Nam
2018   Sinicization and Barbarization: Ancient State Formation at the Southern Edge of Sinitic Civilization. In, *Imperial China and Its Southern Neighbours.* Victor H. Mair and Liam Kelley (eds.), Pp. 43–79. Cambridge: Cambridge University Press.

König, Horst Erich, and Liebich, Hans Georg
2020   *Veterinary Anatomy of Domestic Mammals* (7th Edition). Stuttgart: Thieme Medical Publishers.

Korolkov, Maxim
2021   *The Imperial Network in Ancient China: The Foundation of Sinitic Empire in Southern East Asia.* New York and London: Routledge.

Korolkov, Maxim, and Hein, Anke
2020   State-Induced Migration and the Creation of State Spaces in Early Chinese Empires: Perspectives from History and Archaeology. *Journal of Chinese History* 5(2):1–23.

Lai, Mingchiu 黎明钊

2013　辐辏与秩序:汉帝国地方社会研究 [*Power Convergence and Social Order: The Study of Local Society of the Han Empire*]. 香港 Hong Kong: 香港中文大学出版社 The Chinese University of Hong Kong Press.

Landon, David B.

1996　Feeding Colonial Boston: A Zooarchaeological Study. *Journal of the Society for Historical Archaeology* 30(1):1–153.

1997　Interpreting Urban Food Supply and Distribution Systems from Faunal Assemblages: An Example from Colonial Massachusetts. *International Journal of Osteoarchaeology* 7(1):51–64.

Lam, Wengcheong 林永昌

2014　Everything Old Is New Again? Rethinking the Transition to the Cast Iron Production in the Central Plains of China. *Journal of Anthropological Research* 70:511–542.

2019　秦汉陶文性质所见行政与手工业制度演变: 以关中为中心 (Ceramic Inscriptions during the Qin-Han Periods and Changes of Craft-production System: A Case Study of Guanzhong). In, 中国古代政治制度与历史地理——严耕望先生百龄纪念论文集 [*Political System and Historiography in Ancient China: A Collection of Papers to Commemorate Yan Gengwang*]. Centre for Chinese History CUHK et al. (eds.), Pp. 99–126. 济南 Jinan: 齐鲁书社 Qilu Press.

2020　Integration and the Regional Market System in the Early Chinese Empires: A Case Study of the Distribution of Iron and Bronze Objects in the Wei River Valley. *Asian Perspectives* 59(1):117–158.

2021　Iron Technology and Its Regional Development during the Eastern Zhou Period of Ancient China. In, *The Oxford Handbook of Early China*. Elizabeth Childs-Johnson (ed.), Pp. 595-614. Oxford: Oxford University Press.

Lam, Wengcheong 林永昌, and Chen, Jianli 陈建立

2017　东周时期铁器技术与工业的地域性差异 (On the Regional Variation of Iron Technology and Iron Industry during the Eastern Zhou Period). 南方文物 [*Southern Cultural Relics*] 2017(3):98–106.

Lam, Wengcheong 林永昌, Chen, Jianli 陈建立, Chong, Jianrong 种建荣, and Lei, Xingshan 雷兴山

2017a　论秦国铁器普及化与关中地区战国时期铁器流通模式 (The Spread of Iron Industry in the Qin State and Distribution Network of Iron in the Guanzhong Basin during the Warring States Period). 中国国家博物馆馆刊 [*Journal of National Museum of China*] 3:36–53.

Lam, Wengcheong, Chen, Jianli, Chong, Jianrong, Lei, Xingshan, and Tam, Wai-lun

2018　An Iron Production and Exchange System at the Center of the Western Han Empire: Scientific Study of Iron Products and Manufacturing Remains from the Taicheng Site Complex. *Journal of Archaeological Science* 100:88–101.

Lam, Wengcheong 林永昌, Cheng, Jing 郑婧, and Chen, Jianli 陈建立

2017b　西汉地方铸铁作坊的技术选择: 以关中邰城作坊冶金陶瓷科技分析为例 (Technological Choice of Local Iron Foundries in the Western Han Period: Scientific Analysis of Metallurgical Ceramic from Taicheng in the Guanzhong Basin). 南方文物 [*Southern Cultural Relics*] 2017(2):121–130.

Lam, Wengcheong, Chong, Jianrong, Lei, Xingshan, and Chen, Jianli
2019 Economic Embeddedness and Small-scale Iron Production in the Capital Region of the Han Empire: The Perspective from Faunal Remains. *Archaeological Research in Asia* 17:117–132.

Lam, Wengcheong, Zhang, Qianglu, Chen, Jianli, and Wu, Sumyi
2020 Provision of Iron Objects in the Southern Borderlands of the Han Empire: A Metallurgical Study of Iron objects from Han Tombs in Guangzhou. *Archaeological and Anthropological Sciences* 12:230.

Lao, Kan 劳榦
1947 论汉代之陆运与水运 (On Land and Water Transportation of the Han Period). 中央研究院历史语言研究所集刊 [*Bulletin of the Institute of History and Philology Academia Sinica*] 16:69–91.
1971 汉代黄金及铜钱的使用问题 (The Problem of the Uses of Copper Coins and Gold Pieces in Han Time). 历史语言研究所集刊 [*Bulletin of the Institute of History and Philology Academia Sinica*] 42:341–390.
1986 居延汉简考释(考释之部) [*Documents of the Han Dynasty on Wooden Slips from Edsen Gol (Part 2: Transliterations and Commentaries)*]. 台北 Taipei: 中央研究院历史语言研究所 Institute of History and Philology, Academia Sinica.
1993 汉简人物眼中的世界 (The World Portraited in Han Bamboo Slips). In, 汉简研究的现状与展望 [*The Current Stage and Perspective of the Research of Han Bamboo Slips*]. Osamu Ōba 大庭修 (ed.), Pp. 16–21. 吹田 Suita: 关西大学出版社 Kansai University Press.

Larreina, David, Li, Yanxiang, Liu, Yaxiong, and Martinón-Torres, Marcos
2018 Bloomery Iron Smelting in the Daye County (Hubei): Technological Traditions in Qing China. *Archaeological Research in Asia* 16:148–165.

Legge, James D. D.
1876 *The She King (The Book of Ancient Poetry): Translated in English Verse, with Essays and Notes*. London: Trubner & Co., 57 & 59, Ludgate Hill.

Lei, Congyun 雷从云
1980 战国铁农具的考古发现及其意义 (Discovery and Its Significance of Iron Agricultural Tools in the Warring States Period). 考古 [*Archaoelogy*] 1980(3):259–260.

Leng, Pengfei 冷鹏飞
2002a 战国秦汉时期农业领域商品经济的发展 (Development of the Commodity Economy in the Agricultural Domain during the Warring States and Qin-Han Periods). 湖南师范大学社会科学学报 [*Journal of Social Science of Hunan Normal University*] 31(1):122–128.
2002b 中国古代社会商品经济形态研究 [*Research on the Pattern of Commodity Economies in Ancient Chinese Society*]. 北京 Beijing: 中华书局 Zhonghua Press.

Lewis, Mark Edward
1999 Warring States Political History. In, *The Cambridge History of Ancient China: From the Origins of Civilization to 221 BC*. Michael Loewe and Edward Shaughnessy (eds.), Pp. 587–650. Cambridge: Cambridge University Press.

Li, Feng
2006 *Landscape and Power in Early China: The Crisis and Fall of the Western Zhou, 1045–771 BC*. Cambridge: Cambridge University Press.

Li, Genpan 李根蟠
2001　汉魏之际社会变迁论略 (On the Social Change during the Transition between the Han and Wei Periods). In, 中国社会历史评论(第3辑) [*Review on Chinese Social History* (vol. 3)], Pp. 1–27. 北京 Beijing: 中华书局 Zhonghua Press.

Li, Jian 李健
2009　新泰单家庄矿冶遗址综合研究 [*Synthetic Analysis of the Shanjiazhuang Mining and Smelting Site in Xintai*], 山东大学硕士论文 Master thesis, Shandong University.

Li, Jiannong 李剑农
1957　先秦两汉经济史稿 [*Economic History of Pre-Qin and Han Dynasties*]. 北京 Beijing: 三联书店 Joint Publishing Company.

Li, Jinghua 李京华
1994[1985] 秦汉铁范铸造工艺探讨 (On the Casting Techniques of Iron Molds during the Qin-Han Periods). In, 中原古代冶金技术研究 [*A Study of Ancient Central Plains Metallurgical Technology*], Pp. 107–119. 郑州 Zhengzhou: 中州古籍出版社 Zhongzhou Guji Press.
1994[1993] 中国秦汉冶铁技术与周围地区的关系 (The Iron Technology during the Qin-Han China and Its Relationship with Neighboring Regions). In, 中原古代冶金技术研究 [*A Study of Ancient Central Plains Metallurgical Technology*], Pp. 190–204. 郑州 Zhengzhou: 中州古籍出版社 Zhongzhou Guji Press.
2000　汉代大铁官职官管理体系的再研究 (Restudy on the Management System of Datieguan in the Han Dynasty). 中原文物 [*Cultural Relics of Central China*] 2000(4):27–32.

Li, Jinghua 李京华, and Chen, Changshan 陈长山
1995　南阳汉代冶铁 [*Iron Production during the Han Period in Nanyang*]. 郑州 Zhengzhou: 中州古籍出版社 Zhongzhou Guji Press.

Li, Lingfu 李令福
2004　关中水利开发与环境 [*The Development of Irrigation System and Environment in Guanzhong*]. 北京 Beijing: 人民出版社 People's Publishing House.
2012　论西汉关中平原的水运交通 (On Water Transportation in the Guanzhong Plain in the Western Han Dynasty). 唐都学刊 [*Tangdu Journal*] 28(2):5–14.

Li, Xinwei 李新伟
2020a 第一个"怪圈"——苏秉琦"大一统"思想束缚论述的新思考 (The First "Magic Circle" – New Thinking on Ideological Bondage of "Great Unification" by Su Bingqi). 南方文物 [*Southern Cultural Relics*] 2020(3):1–13.

Li, Xiuzhen
2020b *Bronze Weapons of the Qin Terracotta Warriors: Standardisation, Craft Specialisation and Labour Organisation*. Oxford: BAR Publishing.

Li, Xiuhui 李秀辉
2006　郑国祭祀遗址出土部分铁器的金相实验研究 (Metallographical Report of Irons from the Xinzheng Sacrificial Site). In, 新郑郑国祭祀遗址 [*The Sacrificial Site of Zheng State in XinZheng*]. Henansheng Wenwu Kaogu Yanjiusuo 河南省文物考古研究所 (ed.), Pp. 1050–1057. 郑州 Zhengzhou: 大象出版社 Elephant Press.

Li, Yung-Ti
2007　Co-craft and Multicraft: Section-mold Casting and the Organization of Craft Production at the Shang Capital of Anyang. In, *Craft Production in Complex*

Societies: Multicraft and Producer Perspective. Shimada Izumi (ed.), Pp. 184–223. Salty Lake City: University of Utah Press.

Li, Yung-Ti 李永迪, Yue, Zhanwei 岳占伟, and Liu, Yu 刘煜
2007   从孝民屯东南地出土陶范谈对殷墟青铜器的几点新认识 (New Understanding of Yinxu Bronzes Based on the Analysis of Casting Molds from Xiaomintun Southeast). 考古 [*Archaeology*] 2007(3):52–63.

Li, Zhipeng 李志鹏
2011   殷墟孝民屯遗址出土家猪的死亡年龄与相关问题研究 (A Study on Death Age of Domestic Pigs Excavated from Xiaomintun Site of Yinxu and Related Issues). 江汉考古 [*Jianghan Archaeology*] 2011(4):89–96.
2020   临淄齐故城阚家寨遗址出土动物遗存的鉴定与分析 (Faunal Remains from the Locality of Area BII and BIII at Kanjiazhai Site, Linzi City Site of the Qi State, Shandong Province). In, 临淄齐故城冶铸业考古 [Archaeology of Metallurgy and Foundry Industry in the Linzi City Site of Qi State]. Zhongguo Shehui Kexueyuan Kaogu Yanjiusuo 中国社会科学院考古研究所 et al. (eds.), Pp. 730–741. 北京 Beijing: 科学出版社 Science Press.

Li, Zhipeng 李志鹏, Campbell, Roderick 江雨德, He, Yuling 何毓灵, and Yuan, Jing 袁靖
2010   殷墟铁三路制骨作坊遗址出土制骨遗存的分析与初步认识 (Analysis and New Understanding on the Bone Manufacturing Waste from the Tiesanlu Bone Workshop at Yinxu). In, 中国文物报 [*Chinese Cultural Relics News*], 2010/09/25, p. 7.

Li, Zhipeng 李志鹏, He, Yuling 何毓灵, and Campbell, Roderick 江雨德
2011   殷墟晚商制骨作坊与制骨手工业的研究回顾与探讨 (Research on Late Shang Bone Workshops and the Bone Working Industry at Yinxu). In, 三代考古(四) [*Archaeology of the Three Dynasties* (vol. 4)], Pp. 471–480. 北京Beijing: 科学出版社 Science Press.

Li, Zhong 李众
1975   中国封建社会前期钢铁冶炼技术发展的探讨 (The Development of Iron and Steel Technology in Ancient China). 考古学报 [*Acta Archaeologica Sinica*] 1975(2):1–21.
1976   关于藁城商代铜钺铁刃的分析 (Analysis of the Iron-Edged Bronze Yue-Axe from Gaocheng in the Shang Period). 考古学报 [*Acta Archaeologica Sinica*] 1976(2):17–34.

Liang, Wanbin 梁万斌
2013   从长安到洛阳: 汉代的关中本位政治地理 [*From Chang'an to Luoyang: The Guanzhong-based Political Geography in the Han Period*], 复旦大学博士学位论文 Ph.D dissertation, Fudan University.
2016   《津关令》与汉初之政治地理建构 (The Decrees for Ferries and Passes and the Construction of the Early Western Han Dynasty's Political Geography). 复旦学报(社会科学版) [*Fudan Journal (Social Sciences)*] 2016(2):46–53.

Liang, Yun 梁云
2008   战国时代的东西差别——考古学的视野 [*Differences between the Qin and the Eastern Six States from Archaeological Survey*]. 北京 Beijing: 文物出版社 Cultural Relics Press.
2020   西垂有声:《史记·秦本纪》的考古学解读 [*Xichui Yousheng: The Archaeological Interpretation of the Qin Basic Annual in Shiji*]. 北京 Beijing: 生活·读书·新知三联书店 SDX Joint Publishing Company.

Lie, John
1997   Sociology of Markets. *Annual Review of Sociology* 23:341–360.

Lin, Sen 林森
2014   商周时期"百工"研究 (A Study on Baigong of Shang and Zhou Dynasties). 史学集刊 [*Collected Papers of History Studies*] 2014(1):105–112.

Lin, Tsung-shun 林聪舜
2018   盐铁会议的政治义涵新探——霍光的意图与桑弘羊在处境认知上的盲点 (New Interpretation on the Discussion on Salt and Iron: The Political Intention of Huo Guang and the Unperceived Situation of Sang Hongyang). 台大文史哲学报 [*NTU Humanitas Taiwanica*] 89:1–40.

Lin, Yide 林益德
2008   论前汉山海池泽业务与少府之关系 (Management of Resources in Mountains, Sea, Ponds, and Forest during the Western Han Period and Its Relationship with Shaofu). 中兴史学 [*Historical Journal of NCHU*] 14:1–38.

Liu, Cheng 刘成
1999   龙首原西汉早期墓出土金属器件的能谱及金相显微组织分析 (Spectrum and Microstructure Analysis of Metal Objects from Early Western Han Tombs in Longshouyuan). In, 西安龙首原汉墓 [*Western Han Tombs in Longshouyuan, Xi'an*]. Xi'anshi Wenwu Baohu Kaogusuo 西安市文物保护考古所 (ed.), Pp. 262–270. 西安 Xi'an: 西北大学出版社 Northwest University Press.

Liu, Dezhen 刘得祯, and Zhu, Jiantang 朱建唐
1981   甘肃灵台县景家庄春秋墓 (The Spring-and-Autumn Tomb at Jingjiazhuang in Lingtai, Ganshu). 考古 [*Archaeology*] 1981(4):298–301.

Liu, Dongya 刘东亚
1962   河南新郑仓城发现战国铸铁器泥范 (Discovery of Clay Molds for Casting Iron Implements of the Warring States Period at Cangcheng, Xinzheng). 考古 [*Archaeology*] 1962(3):165–166.

Liu, Guanghua 刘光华
1988   汉代西北屯田研究 [*Studies on the Tuntian System in North-West Regions of Han Period*]. 兰州 Lanzhou: 兰州大学出版社 Lanzhou University Press.

Liu, Haifeng 刘海峰, Qian, Wei 潜伟, and Chen, Jianli 陈建立
2020   临淄齐故城冶铸遗址出土冶铁遗物分析报告 (Analytical Report on Iron Manufacturing Remains from the Ironworks in Qigucheng, Linzi). In, 临淄齐故城冶铸业考古 [*Archaeology of Metallurgy and Foundry Industry in the Linzi City Site of Qi State*]. Zhongguo Shehui Kexueyuan Kaogu Yanjiusuo 中国社会科学院考古研究所 et al. (eds.), Pp. 966–984. 北京 Beijing: 科学出版社 Science Press.

Liu, Jiangwei 刘江卫, Xia, Yin 夏寅, Zhao, Kun 赵昆, Wang, Weifeng 王伟峰, Du, An 杜安, and Zhou, Tie 周铁
2010   郑庄秦石料加工场遗址出土铁器的初步研究 (Preliminary Report on the Analysis of Iron Objects from the Stone Workshop at Zhengzhuang). 中原文物 [*Cultural Relics of Central China*] 2010(5):100–103.

Liu, Qingzhu 刘庆柱
1990   论秦咸阳城布局形制及其相关问题 (On the Layout of the Xianyang Capital City and Related Issues). 文博 [*Relics and Museology*] 1990(5):200–211.
1995   汉长安城未央宫布局形制初论 (Preliminary Discussion on the Structure and Layout of the Weiyang Palace in Han Chang'an City). 考古 [*Archaeology*] 1995(12):1115–1124.

2000   古代都城与帝陵考古研究 [*Archaeological Research on Ancient Capital Cities and Mausolea*]. 北京 Beijing: 科学出版社 Science Press.

Liu, Qingzhu 刘庆柱, and Li, Yufang 李毓芳
1985   秦汉栎阳城遗址的勘探和试掘 (Investigation and Preliminary Excavation of the Yueyang Walled Town in the Qin and Han Periods). 考古学报 [*Acta Archaeologica Sinica*] 1985(3):353–381, 411–418.
2006   汉长安城考古的回顾与瞻望——纪念汉长安城考古半个世纪 (Retrospect and Prospect of the Archaeology of Han Chang'an City: In Commemoration of the 50th Anniversary of the Archaeology of Han Chang'an City). 考古 [*Archaeology*] 2006(10):12–21, 2.

Liu, Rui 刘瑞
2011   汉长安城的朝向、轴线与南郊礼制建筑 [*Orientation, Axis of Chang'an City in the Han Dynasty and Etiquette Architecture in Its Southern Suburbs*]. 北京 Beijing: 中国社会科学出版社 China Social Sciences Press.

Liu, Rui 刘瑞, Li, Yufan 李毓芳, Zhang, Xiangyu 张翔宇, and Gao, Bo 高博
2020a[2018] 西安阎良秦汉栎阳城遗址 (The Yueyang City of the Qin-Han Periods in Yanliang, Xi'an). In, 栎阳考古发现与研究 [*Archaeological Discoveries and Research of Yueyang*]. Zhongguo Shehui Kexueyuan Kaogu Yanjiusuo 中国社会科学院考古研究所 and Xi'anshi Wenwu Baohu Kaogu Yanjiuyuan 西安市文物保护考古研究院 (eds.), Pp. 72–78. 北京 Beijing: 科学出版社 Science Press.
2020b   [2018]陕西西安秦汉栎阳城遗址考古取得重要收获-发现三座古城，确定三号古城遗址为秦汉栎阳所在 (Important Archaeological Achievements at the Yueyang City Site in Xi'an, Shaanxi: The Confirmation of the No. 3 Walled Town as the Location of the Yueyang City during the Qin-Han Periods). In, 栎阳考古发现与研究 [*Archaeological Discoveries and Research of Yueyang*]. Zhongguo Shehui Kexueyuan Kaogu Yanjiusuo 中国社会科学院考古研究所 and Xi'anshi Wenwu Baohu Kaogu Yanjiuyuan 西安市文物保护考古研究院 (eds.), Pp. 79–81. 北京 Beijing: 科学出版社 Science Press.

Liu, Tseng-kuei 刘增贵
1999   居延汉简所见汉代边境饮食生活 (Daily Food Subsistence of the Han Dynasty in Bamboo Slips from Juyan). 古今论衡 [*Gujin Lunheng*] 1999(12):2–18.

Liu, Hui 刘慧
1989   山东省莱芜市古铁矿冶遗址调查 (Investigation of Ancient Mining and Smelting Sites in Laiwu, Shandong). 考古 [*Archaeology*] 1989(2):149–154.

Liu, Xinglin 刘兴林
2017   先秦两汉农业与乡村聚落的考古学研究 [*Archaeological Research on the Agriculture and Village Settlement of the Pre-Qin and Han Periods*]. 北京 Beijing: 文物出版社 Cultural Relics Press.

Liu, Xinyi, Lister, Diane L., Zhao, Zhijun et al.
2017   Journey to the East: Diverse Routes and Variable Flowering Times for Wheat and Barley en Route to Prehistoric China. *PLOS ONE* 13(12):e0187405.

Liu, Yan
2018   Emblems of Power and Glory: The Han-period Chinese Lacquer Wares Discovered in the Borderlands. In, *Production, Distribution and Appreciation: New Aspects of East Asian Lacquer Ware*. Patricia Frick and Annette Kieser (eds.), Pp. 30–63. Leiden: Brill.

Liu, Yaxiong, Martinón-Torres, Marcos, Chen, Jianli, Sun, Weigang, and Chen, Kunlong

2019 Iron Decarburisation Techniques in the Eastern Guanzhong Plain, China, during Late Warring States Period: An Investigation Based on Slag Inclusion Analyses. *Archaeological and Anthropological Sciences* 11:6537–6549.

Liu, Yinming 刘殿茗, Lan, Wanli 蓝万里, and Wang, Ruixue 王瑞雪

2021 鲁山望城岗冶铁遗址汉代植物大遗存浮选分析 (Floatation Analysis of Plant Macro-remains of Han Dynasty Excavated from Iron Smelting and Casting Site, Wangchenggang Site, in Lushan County). 华夏考古 [*Huaxia Archaeology*] 2021(1):88–89, 105.

Liu, Zhendong 刘振东

2016 简论汉长安城之郊 (On the Suburbs of Han Chang'an). 考古与文物 [*Archaeology and Cultural Relics*] 2016(5):117–121.

2017 汉长安城综论——纪念汉长安城遗址考古六十年 (On the Synthesis of Discoveries in Chang'an: A Memorial Essay Celebrating the 60-year Anniversary of Archaeological Work in Chang'an). 考古 [*Archaeology*] 2017(1):9–16.

2018 汉长安城城门遗址考古发现与研究 (Archaeological Findings and Research on the City Gate Location of Han Chang'an City). 华夏考古 [*Huaxia Archaeology*] 2018(6):3–8, 99.

Liu, Zhendong 刘振东, and Zhang, Jianfeng 张建锋

2006 西汉骨签的几个问题 (Issues Related to Bone Tags of the Western Han). 考古与文物 [*Archaeology and Cultural Relics*] 2006(3):58–62.

Liu, Zhiwei 刘志伟

2019 代序: 中国王朝的贡赋体制与经济史——在云南大学"中国经济史研究的理论方法与发展趋势"课程上的演讲 (Preface: The Tribute System and Economic History of the Chinese Dynasty: A Lecture on the Course "Theoretical Methods and Development Trends of Chinese Economic History Research" at Yunnan University). In, 贡赋体制与市场: 明清社会经济史论稿 [*Tribute System and Market: An Essay on the Social and Economic History of the Ming and Qing Dynasties*], Pp. 1–30. 北京 Beijing: 中华书局 Zhonghua Press.

Liu, Zhiyuan 刘志远

1973 汉代市井考:说东汉市井画像砖 [On the Market and Market-wells of the Han Period: A New Discovery of Pictorial Bricks Showing Scenes of Markets and Market-wells in the Eastern Han Period]. 文物 [*Cultural Relics*] 1973(3):52–57.

Liye qinjiandu jiaoshi

2018 里耶秦简牍校释(第二卷) [*Commentaries of Liye Qin Bamboo Slips* (vol. 2)], Chen Wei 陈伟 (ed.). 武汉 Wuhan: 武汉大学出版社 Wuhan University Press.

Loewe, Michael

1974 *Crisis and Conflict in Han China, 104 BC to AD 9*. London: George Allen and Unwin.

1985 Attempts at Economic Co-ordination during the Western Han Dynasty. In, *The Scope of State Power in China*. Stuart R. Schram (ed.), Pp. 237–267. New York: Chinese University Press and St. Martin's Press.

2000 *A Biographical Dictionary of the Qin, Former Han and Xin Periods (221 BC-AD 24)*. Leiden: Brill.

2004 *The Men Who Governed Han China: Companion to a Biographical Dictionary of the Qin, Former Han and Xin Periods*. Leiden: Brill.

2006   *The Government of the Qin and Han Empires 221BCE-220CE*. Indianapolis, IN and Cambridge, MA: Hackett Publishing Company, Inc.

Lu, Defu 陆德富
2018   战国时代官私手工业的经营形态 [*Management of Private and Official Craft Industries during the Warring States Period*]. 上海 Shanghai: 上海古籍出版社 Shanghai Guji Press.

Lunyu jishi
1990   论语集释 [*Lunyu jishi*], annotated by Cheng Shude 程树德. 北京 Beijing: 中华书局 Zhonghua Press.

Luo, Qingkang 罗庆康, and Luo, Wei 罗威
1995a 汉代盐制研究 (A Study of the Salt System in the Han Dynasty). 盐业史研究 [*Salt Industry History Research*] 1995(1):54–63.
1995b 汉代盐制研究续 (A Study of the Salt System in the Han Dynasty 2). 盐业史研究 [*Salt Industry History Research*] 1995(4):30–35.
1996   汉代盐制研究续 (A Study of the Salt System in the Han Dynasty 3). 盐业史研究 [*Salt Industry History Research*] 1996(1):73–80.

Luoyangshi [Luoyangshi Di'er Wenwu Gongzuodui 洛阳市第二文物工作队]
2000   黄河小浪底盐东村汉函谷关仓库建筑遗址发掘简报 (Excavation of a Storehouse of the Hangu Pass of the Han Dynasty in Yandongcun, Yellow River Xiaolangdi). 文物 [*Cultural Relics*] 2000(10):12–25.

Luo, Yunbing 罗运兵, Yang, Mengfei 杨梦菲, and Yuan, Jing 袁靖
2006   郑国祭祀遗址动物骨骼研究报告 (Report of Faunal Reamins from the Xinzheng Sacrificial Site). In, 郑国祭祀遗址 [*The Sacrificial Site of Zheng State in Xinzheng*]. Henansheng Wenwu Kaogu Yanjiusuo 河南省文物考古研究所 (ed.), Pp. 1063–1152. 郑州 Zhengzhou: 大象出版社 Elephant Press.

Lyman, Lee R.
1984   Bone Density and Differential Survivorship of Fossil Classes. *Journal of Anthropological Archaeology* 3:259–299.
1987   On Zooarchaeological Measures of Socioecnomic Position and Cost-efficient Meat Purchases. *Historical Archaeology* 21(1):58–66.
2004   The Concept of Equifinality in Taphonomy. *Journal of Taphonomy* 2(1):15–26.

Ma, Daying 马大英
1983   汉代财政史 [*The Financial History of the Han Dynasty*]. 北京 Beijing: 中国财政经济出版社 Zhongguo Caizheng Jingji Press.

Ma, Daizhong 马代忠
2013   长沙走马楼西汉简〈都乡七年垦田租簿〉初步考察 (Preliminary Study of the "Duxiang Qinian Kentian Zubu" from the Western Han Zoumaluo Collection, Changsha). In, 出土文献研究（第12辑） [*Research on Unearthed Documents*]. Zhongguo Wenhua Yichan Yanjiuyuan 中国文化遗产研究院 (ed.), Pp. 213–222. 北京 Beijing: 中西书局 Zhongxi Press.

Ma, Jianxi 马建熙
1959   陕西耀县战国、西汉墓葬清理简报 (Preliminary Report on the Excavation of Warring States and Western Han Tombs in Yao County, Shaanxi). 考古 [*Archaeology*] 1959(3):147–149.

Ma, Juncai 马俊才
1999   郑、韩两都平面布局初论 (A Preliminary Analysis on the Spatial Layout of Capital of the Zheng and Han States). 中国历史地理论丛 [*Journal of Chinese Historical Geography*] 1999(2):115–129.

Ma, Menglong 马孟龙
2012   汉武帝"广关"与河东地区侯国迁徙 ("Expanding the Pass" Policy of Western Han Dynasty and the Migration of Marquisates in the Areas to the East of the Yellow River). 中华文史论丛 [*Journal of Chinese Literature and History*] 1:210–231.

Ma, Tsangwing 马增荣
2012   秦汉时期的雇佣活动与人口流动 (Hired Activities and Movement of Population in Qin-Han Periods). 中国文化研究所学报 [*Journal of Chinese Studies*] 54:1–27.

Ma, Xiao 马啸, Lei, Xinghe 雷兴鹤, and Wu, Hongqi 吴宏岐
2018   秦直道线路与沿线遗存 [*Routes of Qin Zhidao and Remains alongside the Routes*]. 西安 Xi'an: 陕西师范大学出版 Shaanxi Normal University Publishing House.

Ma, Xiaolin 马萧林
2008   Pig Husbandry Strategies in an Emergent Complex Society in Central China. *Journal of Indo-Pacific Archaeology* 24:91–102.
2010   周原遗址齐家制玦作坊出土动物骨骼研究报告 (Report on Faunal Remains from the Lithic Workshop at Zhouyuan). In, 周原—2002年度齐家制玦作坊和礼村遗址考古发掘报告 [*Zhouyuan: The 2002 Excavation Report on the Jue Workshop at Qijia and the Licun Site*]. Zhouyuan Kaogudui 周原考古队 (ed.), Pp. 724–751. 北京 Beijing: 科学出版社 Science Press.

Ma, Xueqin 马雪芹
2000   东汉长安与关中平原 (Chang'an in the Eastern Han Period and the Guanzhong Plain). 中国历史地理论丛 [*Journal of Chinese Historical Geography*] 2000(2):187–197.

Ma, Yongying 马永赢
2011   汉武帝茂陵陵园布局的几点认识 (Issues Related to the Layout of the Maoling Mausoleum of Emperor Wu). 考古与文物 [*Archaeology and Cultural Relics*] 2011(2):70–75.

Maddin, Robert, Muhly, James D., and Wheeler, Tamara S.
1977   How the Iron Age Began. *Scientific American* 237(4):122–131.

Manning, G. Joseph, and Morris, Ian
2005   Introduction. In, *The Ancient Economy: Evidence and Models.* Joseph Manning and Ian Morris (eds.), Pp. 1–46. Stanford, CA: Stanford University Press.

Maoshi zhengyi
1999   毛诗正义 [*Maoshi zhengyi*], annotated by Zheng Xuan 郑玄 and Kong Yingda 孔颖达, compiled by Ruan Yuan 阮元. 北京 Beijing: 北京大学出版社 Peking University Press.

Martinón-Torres, Marcos, Li, Janice Xiuzhen, Bevan, Andrew, Xia, Yin, Zhao, Kun, and Rehren, Thilo
2014   Forty Thousand Arms for a Single Emperor: From Chemical Data to the Labor Organization Behind the Bronze Arrows of the Terracotta Army. *Journal of Archaeological Method and Theory* 21:534–562.

Mattingly, David J.
2006   The Imperial Economy. In, *A Companion to the Roman Empire.* David S. Potter (ed.), Pp. 283–297. Oxford: Blackwell Publishing.
2011   *Imperialism, Power, and Identity: Experiencing the Roman Empire.* Princeton, NJ: Princeton University Press.

268   *Bibliography*

Mauss, Marcel; translated by W. D. Halls
1990[1954] *The Gift: The Form and Reason for Exchange in Archaic Societies.* London: Routledge.

McKee, Larry W.
1987   Delineating Ethnicity from the Garbage of Early Virginians: Faunal Remains from the Kingsmill Plantation Slave Quarter. *American Archaeology* 6(1):31–39.

Millett, Paul
2001   Productive to Some Purpose? The Problem of Ancient Economic Growth. In, *Economies beyond Agriculture in the Classical World.* David Mattingly and John Salmon (eds.), Pp. 17–48. London: Routledge.

Minc, Leah D.
2006   Monitoring Regional Market Systems in Prehistory: Models, Methods, and Metrics. *Journal of Anthropological Archaeology* 25:82–116.

Morley, Neville
2010   *The Roman Empire: Roots of Imperialism.* London: Pluto Press.
2014   Globalisation and the Roman Economy. In, *Globalisation and the Roman World: World History, Connectivity and Material Culture.* Martin Pitts and Miguel J. Versluys (eds.), Pp. 49–67. Cambridge: Cambridge University Press.

Mustchler, Fritz-Heiner, and Mittag, Achim (eds.)
2008   *Conceiving the Empire: China and Rome Compared.* Oxford: Oxford University Press.

Nan, Puheng 南普恒, Wang, Xiaoyi 王晓毅, and Qian, Wei 潜伟
2019   山西隰县瓦窑坡墓地M23出土铜器的技术特征及相关问题   (Manufacturing Techniqes of Bronzes from Tomb M23 in the Wayaopo Cemetery in Xi County, Shanxi, and Related Questions). 中原文物 [*Central Cultural Relics*] 2019(1):114–119.

Naerebout, Frederick G.
2013   Convergence and Divergence: One Empire, Many Cultures. In, *Integration in Rome and in the Roman World.* Gerda de Kleijn and Stéphane Benoist (eds.), Pp. 263–281. Leiden and Boston, MA: Brill.

Nanjing [Nanjing Bowuyuan 南京博物院]
1974   江苏六合程桥二号东周墓 (The Eastern Zhou Tomb at Chengqiao, Liuhe, Jiangsu). 考古 [*Archaeology*] 1974(2):116–120.

Nichols, Deborah L., Brumfiel, Elizabeth M., Neff, Hector, Hodge, Mary, Charlton, Thomas H., and Glascock, Michael D.
2002   Neutrons, Markets, Cities, and Empires: A 1000-Year Perspective on Ceramic Production and Distribution in the Postclassic Basin of Mexico. *Journal of Anthropological Archaeology* 21:25–82.

Nickel, Lukas
2006   Imperfect Symmetry: Re-thinking Bronze Casting Technology in Ancient China. *Artibus Asiae* 66(1):5–39.

Nishijima, Sadao
1986   The Economic and Social History of Former Han. In, *The Cambridge History of China, Vol. 1: The Chin and Han Empires, 221 B.C-A.D.220*, Michael Loewe (ed.), Pp. 545–607. Cambridge: Cambridge University Press.

Nylan, Michael

2012 The Power of Highway Networks during China's Classical Era (323 BCE-316 CE): Regulations, Metaphors, Rituals, and Deities. In, *Highways, Byways, and Road Systems in the Pre-modern World*. Susan Alcock, John Bodel and Richard J. A. Talbert (eds.), Pp. 33–65. Hoboken, NJ: Wiley-Blackwell.

2015 Supplying the Capital with Water and Food. In, *Chang'an 26 BCE: An Augustan Age in China*. Michael Nylan and Griet Vankeerberghen (eds.), Pp. 99–130. Seattle: University of Washington Press.

Patterson, John R.

2006 *Landscapes and Cities: Rural Settlement and Civic Transformation in Early Imperial Italy*. Oxford: Oxford University Press.

Peacock, David P. S.

1982 *Pottery in the Roman World: An Ethnoarchaeological Approach*. London and New York: Longman.

Peng, Wei 彭卫

2010 关于小麦在汉代推广的再探讨 (Reconsideration of the Promotion of Wheat during the Han Periods). 中国经济史研究 [*Journal of Chinese Economic History Research*] 2010(4):63–71.

Percy, John

1864 *Metallurgy: The Art of Extracting Metals from Their Ores, and Adapting Them to Various Purposes of Manufacture, Volume 2, Iron; Steel*. London: John Murray.

Pines, Yuri

2000 "The One That Pervades the All" in Ancient Chinese Political Thought: The Origins of "The Great Unity" Paradigm. *T'oung Pao* 86(4/5):280–324.

2017 *The Book of Lord Shang: Apologetics of State Power in Early China*. New York: Columbia University Press.

Pirazzoli-t'Serstevens, Michele

2010 Urbanism. In, *China's Early Empires: A Re-appraisal*. Michael Nylan and Michael Loewe (eds.), Pp. 169–185. Cambridge: Cambridge University Press.

Pitts, Martin

2017 Gallo-Belgic Wares: Objects in Motion in the Early Roman Northwest. In, *Materialising Roman Histories*. Astrid van Oyen and Martin Pitts (eds.), Pp. 47–64. Oxford: Oxbow Books.

Pitts, Martin, and Versluys, Miguel John

2014 Globalisation and the Roman World: Perspectives and Opportunities. In, *Globalisation and the Roman World: World History, Connectivity and Material Culture*. Martin Pitts and Miguel J. Versluys (eds.), Pp. 3–31. Cambridge: Cambridge University Press.

Plattner, Stuart

1989 Markets and Marketplaces. In, *Economic Anthropology*. Stuart Plattner (ed.), Pp. 171–208. Stanford, CA: Stanford University Press.

Polanyi, Karl

1957 The Economy as Instituted Process. In, *Trade and Market of Early Empire*. Karl Polanyi, Conrad M. Arensberg and Harry W. Pearson (eds.), Pp. 243–270. Glencoe: Free Press.

2001[1944] *The Great Transformation: The Political and Economic Origins of Our Time*. Boston, MA: Beacon Press.

Poo, Mu-chou
2018   *Daily Life in Ancient China*. Cambridge: Cambridge University Press.

Psarras, Sophia-Karin
2015   *Han Material Culture: An Archaeological Analysis and Vessel Typology*. New York: Cambridge University Press

Qian, Yanhui 钱彦惠
2020   西汉长安城市场研究——兼论汉魏洛阳城的市场 (A Study on the Markets of the Western Han Dynasty Chang'an City: Inspired by the Market Remains in the Han-Wei Period Luoyang City Site). 考古学报 [*Acta Archaeologica Sinica*] 2020(2):161–176.

Qin, Jianming 秦建明, Zhang, Zhaiming 张在明, and Yang, Zhen 杨政
1995   陕西发现以汉长安城为中心的西汉南北向超长建筑基线 (Discovery of the Extended North-South Central Axial Line Centered on Chang'an). 文物 [*Cultural Relics*] 1995(3):4–15.

Qin, Jin 秦晋
1980   凤翔南古城遗址的钻探和试掘 (Augering and Preliminary Excavation of the Nangucheng Site in Fengxiang). 考古与文物 [*Archaeology and Cultural Relics*] 1980(4):48–54.

Qin, Zhen 秦臻, Chen, Jianli 陈建立, and Zhang, Hai 张海
2016   河南舞钢、西平地区战国秦汉冶铁遗址群的钢铁生产体系研究 (The Prodcution System of the Cluster of Iron Smelting Sites in the Wugang and Xiping Areas of Henan during the Warring-States and Qin-Han Periods). 中原文物 [*Cultural Relics of Central China*] 2016(1):109–117.

Qinjiandu heji
2014   秦简牍合集 [*Collection of Qin Bamboo Slips*], Chen Wei 陈伟 (ed.). 武汉 Wuhan: 武汉大学出版社 Wuhan University Press.

Qingdaoshi, and Huangdaoqu [Qingdaoshi Wenwu Baohu Kaogu Yanjiusuo 青岛市文物保护考古研究所, and Huangdaoqu Bowuguan 黄岛区博物馆]
2019   山东青岛土山屯墓群四号封土与墓葬的发掘 (The Excavation of Mound No. 4 and Burials of the Tushantun Cemetery in Qingdao, Shandong). 考古学报 [*Acta Archaeologica Sinica*] 2019(3):405–459.

Qinyong [Qinyong Kaogudui 秦俑考古队]
1980   临潼上焦村秦墓清理简报 (Preliminary Report on the Excavation of Qin Tombs at Shangjiaocun in Lintong). 考古与文物 [*Archaeology and Cultural Relics*] 1980(2):42–50.

Redding, Richard
2010   Status and Diet at the Workers' Town, Giza, Egypt. In, *Anthropological Approaches to Zooarchaeology: Colonialism, Complexity and Animal Transformations*. Douglas V. Campana, Pamela Crabtree, Susan D. deFrance, Justin Lev-Tov, and Alice M. Choyke (eds.), Pp. 65–75. Oxford: Oxbow Books.

Rehren, Thilo, Belgya, Tamás, and Jambon, Albert et al.
2013   5,000 Years Old Egyptian Iron Beads Made from Hammered Meteoritic Iron. *Journal of Archaeological Scienc*e 40(12):4785–4792.

Reitz, Elizabeth J.
1986 Urban/Rural Contrasts in Vertebrate Fauna from the Southern Atlantic Coastal Plain. *Historical Archaeology* 20(2):47–58.

Reitz, Elizabeth J., and Zierden, Martha A.
2014 Wildlife in Urban Charleston, South Carolina, USA. *Anthropozoologica* 49(1):33–46.

Ren, Jie 任洁, Li, Yan 李严, and Zhang, Yukun 张玉坤
2017 阴山-河套平原地区西汉长城防御体系分布结构研究 (Research on the Distribution and Structure of the Fortification System of the Western Han Great Wall in the Yinshan-Hetao Plain). 中国文化遗产 [*China Cultural Heritage*] 2007(3):100–106.

Renfrew, Colin
1975 Trade as Action at a Distance. In, *Ancient Civilization and Trade.* Jeremy A. Sabloff and Clifford C. Lamberg-Karlovsky (eds.), Pp. 3–59. Albuquerque: University of New Mexico Press.
1977 Alternative Models for Exchange and Spatial Distribution. In, *Exchange Systems in Prehistory.* Timothy K. Earle and Jonathon E. Ericson (eds.), Pp. 71–90. New York: Academic Press.

Robbins, Lionel
1945[1932] *An Essay on the Nature and Significance of Economic Science* (second edition, revised and extended). London: Macmillan and Co., Limited.

Rong, Yan 戎岩, Luo, Wugan 罗武干, Wei, Guofeng 魏国锋, Song, Guoding 宋国定, and Wang, Changsui 王昌燧
2013 申明铺遗址出土铁器的工艺考察 (Study on Manufacturing Technique for Iron Artifacts Unearthed from the Shenmingpu Site). 文物保护与考古科学 [*Sciences of Conservation and Archaeology*] 2013(3):64–70.

Rothschild, Nan A.
1989 The Effect of Urbanization on Faunal Diversity: A Comparison between New York City and St Augustine, Florida, in the Sixteenth to Eighteenth Centuries. In, *Quantifying Diversity in Archaeology.* Robert D. Leonard and George T. Jones (eds.), Pp. 92–99. Cambridge: Cambridge University Presss.

Rothschild, Nan A., and Balkwill, Darlene
1993 The Meaning of Change in Urban Faunal Deposits. *Historical Archaeology* 27(2):71–89.

Sahara, Yasuo 佐原康夫
2002[1985] 漢代の市 (On the Market of the Han Period). In, 漢代都市機構の研究[*Research on Urban Institutes in the Han Period*], Pp. 281–323. 東京 Tōkyō: 汲古書院 Kyūko Shoin.
2002[1994] 漢代鉄専売制の再検討 (Re-analysis of the Iron Monopoly Policy in the Han Period). In, 漢代都市機構の研究 [*Research on Urban Institutes in the Han Period*], Pp. 350–392. 東京 Tōkyō: 汲古書院 Kyūko Shoin.

Sanft, Charles
2014 *Communication and Cooperation in Early Imperial China: Publicizing the Qin Dynasty.* Albany, NY: State University of New York Press.

Sanfu Huangtu Jiaoshi 三辅黄图校释
2005 三辅黄图校释 [*Sanfu Huangtu Jiaoshi*], annotated by He Qinggu 何清谷. 北京 Beijing: 中华书局 Zhonghua Press.

Santley, Robert S., and Kneebone, Ronald R.

1993 Craft Specialization, Refuse Disposal, and the Creation of Spatial Archaeological Records in Prehispanic Mesoamerica. In, *Prehispanic Domestic Units in Western Mesoamericas: Studies of the Household, Compound, and Residence.* Robert S. Santley and Kenneth G. Hirth (eds.), pp. 37–63. Boca Raton, FL: CRC Press.

Santley, Robert S., Arnold III, Philip, and Pool, Christopher

1989 The Ceramics Production System at Matacapan, Veracruz, Mexico. *Journal of Field Archaeology* 16(1):107–132.

Satō, Taketoshi 佐藤武敏

1962 中国古代工業史の研究 [*Research on the History of Craft Industries in Ancient China*]. 東京 Tokyo: 吉川弘文館 Yoshikawa koubunkan.

Schefold, Bertram

2019 A Western Perspective on the Yantie Lun. In, *The Political Economy of the Han Dynasty and Its Legacy.* Cheng Lin, Terry Peach and Wang Fang (eds.), Pp. 153–174. London and New York: Routledge.

Scheidel, Walter

2009 The Monetary System of the Han and Roman Empires. In, *Rome and China: Comparative Perspectives on Ancient World Empires.* Walter Scheidel (ed.), Pp. 137–208. New York: Oxford University Press.

2011 The Roman Slave Supply. In, *The Cambridge World History of Slavery 1: The Ancient Mediterranean World.* Keith Bradley and Paul Cartledge (eds.), Pp. 287–310. Cambridge: Cambridge University Press.

2012 Slavery. In, *The Cambridge Companion to the Roman Economy.* Walter Scheidel (ed.), Pp. 321–333. Cambridge: Cambridge University Press.

2014 The Shape of the Roman World: Modelling Imperial Connectivity. *Journal of Roman Archaeology* 27:7–32.

2015 State Revenue and Expenditure in the Han and Roman Empires. In, *State Power in Ancient China and Rome.* Walter Scheidel (ed.), Pp. 150–180. New York: Oxford University Press.

Schiffer, Michael B.

1987 *Formation Processes of the Archaeological Record.* Albuquerque: University of New Mexico Press.

Schmitt, Dave N., and Zeier, Charles D.

1993 Not by Bones Alone: Exploring Household Composition and Socioeconomic Status in an Isolated Historic Mining Community. *Historical Archaeology* 27(4):20–38.

Schulz, Peter D., and Gust, Sherri M.

1983 Faunal Remains and Social Status in 19th Century Sacramento. *Historical Archaeology* 17(1):44–53.

Shaanxi Difangzhi [Shaanxisheng Difangzhi Bianzuan Weiyuanhui 陕西省地方志编纂委员会] (ed.)

1993 陕西省志(第四卷):地质矿产志 [*Shaanxi Provincial Chronograph (Vol. 4): Geology and Minerals Chronograph*]. 西安 Xi'an: 陕西人民出版社 Shaanxi People's Publishing House.

Shaanxi Fengxiang [Shaanxisheng Kaogusuo Fengxiang Fajuedui 陕西省考古所凤翔发掘队]

1962 陕西凤翔南古城村遗址试掘记 (Preliminary Excavation of the Nangucheng Site in Fengxiang, Shaanxi). 考古 [*Archaeology*] 1962(9):493–495, 408.

Shaanxi Huacang [Shaanxisheng Kaogusuo Huacangdui 陕西省考古所华仓队]
1983 韩城芝川镇汉代冶铁遗址调查简报 (Preliminary Report on the Ironworks Site in Zhichuan County, Hancheng). 考古与文物 [*Archaeology and Cultural Relics*] 1983(4):27–29.

Shaanxi Yanjiusuo [Shaanxisheng Kaogu Yanjiusuo 陕西省考古研究所]
1984 陕西长武上孟村秦国墓葬发掘简报 (Preliminary Report on the Excavation of Qin Tombs at Shangmengcun in Changwu, Shaanxi). 考古与文物 [*Archaeology and Cultural Relics*] 1984(3):8–17.
1986 陕西铜川枣庙秦墓发掘简报 (Preliminary Report on the Excavation of Qin Tombs at Zaomiao in Tongcun, Shaanxi). 考古与文物 [*Archaeology and Cultural Relics*] 1986(2):7–17.
1987 西安北郊大白杨秦汉墓葬清理简报 (Preliminary Report on the Excavation of Qin and Han Tombs at Dabaiyang, Northern Suburbs of Xi'an). 考古与文物 [*Archaeology and Cultural Relics*] 1987(2):43–51.
1990 西汉京师仓 [*Jingshi Warehouse of the Western Han Period*]. 北京 Beijing: 文物出版社 Cultural Relics Press.
1998a 陇县店子秦墓 [Qin Tombs at Dianzi in Long County]. 西安 Xi'an: 三秦出版社 Sanqin Press.
1998b 陕西临潼零口战国墓葬发掘简报 (Preliminary Report on the Excavation of Warring States Tombs at Lingkou in Lintong, Shaanxi). 考古与文物 [*Archaeology and Cultural Relics*] 1998(3):15–21.
2001 西安南郊三爻村汉唐墓葬清理发掘简报 (Preliminary Report on the Excavation of Han and Tang Tombs at Sanyaocun on the Southern Suburbs of Xi'an). 考古与文物 [*Archaeology and Cultural Relics*] 2001(3):3–26.
2003a 白鹿原汉墓 [*Han Tombs at Bailuyuan*]. 西安 Xi'an: 三秦出版社 Sanqin Press.
2003b 陕西高陵县益尔公司秦墓发掘简报 (Preliminary Report on the Excavation of Qin Tombs at the Site of Yi'er Company in Gaoling, Shaanxi). 考古与文物 [*Archaeology and Cultural Relics*] 2003(6):3–15.
2003c 西安北郊汉代积沙墓发掘简报 (Preliminary Report on the Han Tomb Refilled with Sand on the Northern Suburbs of Xi'an). 考古与文物 [*Archaeology and Cultural Relics*] 2003(5):25–33.
2004a 高陵张卜秦汉唐墓 [*Excavation of Han and Tang Tombs at Zhangbu in Gaoling*]. 西安 Xi'an: 三秦出版社 Sanqin Press.
2004b 秦都咸阳考古报告 [*Archaeological Report on the Investigations and Excavations at the Ancient Qin Capital Xianyang*]. 北京 Beijing: 科学出版社 Science Press.
2004c 陕西临潼零口汉墓清理简报 (Preliminary Report on the Excavation of Han Tombs at Lingkou in Lintong, Shaanxi). 文博 [*Relics and Museology*] 2004(1):68–78.
2006a 宝鸡建河墓地 [*Jianhe Cemetery in Baoji*]. 西安 Xi'an: 陕西科学技术出版社 Shaanxi Science and Technology Press.
2006b 陕西投资策划服务公司汉墓清理简报 (Preliminary Report on the Excavation of Han Tombs at the Site of Shaanxi Investment and Consultant Company). 考古与文物 [*Archaeology and Cultural Relics*] 2006(4):10–22.
2006c 西安北郊秦墓 [*Qin Tombs in Northern Suburbs of Xi'an*]. 西安 Xi'an: 三秦出版社 Sanqin Press.
2006d 西北农林科大战国秦墓发掘简报 (Preliminary Report on the Excavation of Qin Tombs during the Warring States Period at Northwest A&F University). 考古与文物 [*Archaeology and Cultural Relics*] 2006(5):37–47.

2007   西安南郊缪家寨汉代厕所遗址发掘简报 [Preliminary Report on the Excavation of a Toilet Site of the Han Period at Miaojiazhai in Southern Suburb of Xi'an]. 考古与文物 [*Archaeology and Cultural Relics*] 2007(2):15–20.

2008   西安北郊郑王村西汉墓 [*Western Han Tombs at Zhengwangcun in the Northern Suburbs of Xi'an*]. Xi'an 西安: Sanqin Press 三秦出版社.

Shaanxi Yanjiusuo, and Baojishi [Shaanxisheng Kaogu Yanjiusuo Baoji Gong-zuozhan 陕西省考古研究所宝鸡工作站, and Baojishi Kaogu Gongzuodui 宝鸡市考古工作队]

1988   陕西陇县边家庄五号春秋墓发掘简报 (Preliminary Report on the Excavation of the No. 5 Spring-and-Autumn Tomb at Bianjiazhuang in Long County, Shaanxi). 文物 [*Cultural Relics*] 1988(11):14–23, 54.

1989   陕西眉县常兴汉墓发掘报告 (Report on the Excavation of Han Tombs at Changxing in Mei County, Shaanxi). 文博 [*Relics and Museology*] 1989(10):43–51.

Shaanxi Yanjiusuo, and Beijing [Shaanxisheng Kaogu Yanjiusuo 陕西省考古研究所, and Beijing Daxue Kaogu Shixidui 北京大学考古实习队]

1987   铜川市王家河墓地发掘简报 (Preliminary Report on the Excavation at Wang-jiahe in Tongchuan). 考古与文物 [*Archaeology and Cultural Relics*] 1987(2):1–8.

Shaanxi Yanjiusuo, and Qinshihuang [Shaanxisheng Kaogu Yanjiusuo 陕西省考古研究所, and Qinshihuang Bingayong Bowuguan 秦始皇兵马俑博物馆]

2006   华县东阳 [*Excavation of the Dongyang Site in Hua County*]. 北京 Beijing: 科学出版社 Science Press.

2007   秦始皇帝陵园考古报告2001～2003 [*Report on Archaelogicl Researches of the Qin Shihuang Mausoleum Precinct (2001–2003)*]. 北京 Beijing: 文物出版社 Cultural Relics Press.

Shaanxi Yanjiusuo et al. [Shaanxisheng Kaogu Yanjiusuo 陕西省考古研究所, Baojishi Kaogu Gongzuodui 宝鸡市考古工作队, and Fengxiangxian Bowuguan 凤翔县博物馆]

2005   陕西凤翔县长青西汉汧河码头仓储建筑遗址 (Storage Facility and the Docking Site of the Qian River in Changqing, Fengxiang, Shaanxi). 考古 [*Archaeology*] 2005(7):21–28.

Shaanxi Yanjiuyuan [Shaanxisheng Kaogu Yanjiuyuan 陕西省考古研究院]

2008a 西安尤家庄秦墓 [*Qin Tombs at Youjiazhuang, Xi'an*]. 西安 Xi'an: 陕西科学技术出版社 Shaanxi Science and Technology Press.

2008b 汉阳陵帝陵东侧11～21号外藏坑发掘简报 (Preliminary Report on the Excavation of External Chambers No. 11–21 in the Eastern Part of the Yangling Mausoleum). 考古与文物 [*Archaeology and Cultural Relics*] 2008(3):3–32.

2009   西安凤栖原西汉墓地田野考古发掘收获 (The Fieldwork Excavation and Discovery of the Western Han Cemetery at Fengqiyuan in Xi'an). 考古与文物 [*Archaeology and Cultural Relics*] 2009(5):111–112.

2010   陕西扶风纸白西汉墓发掘简报 (Preliminary Report on the Western Han Tombs at Zhibai, Fufeng). 文物 [*Cultural Relics*] 2010(10):43–51.

2011   陕西眉县尧上遗址为秦汉中小型聚落遗址研究提供重要实物资料 (The Yaoshang Site Provided New Piece of Information for the Study of Medium and Small Settlements in the Qin and Han Periods). In, 中国文物报 [*Chinese Cultural Relics News*], 2011/03/11, p. 4.

2016   临潼新丰——战国秦汉墓葬考古发掘报告 [*Lintong Xinfeng—Archaeological Excavation Report of Tombs in the Warring States, Qin and Han Dynasties*]. 北京 Beijing: 科学出版社 Science Press.

2017a 陕西西安富力赛高城市广场汉墓发掘简报 (Preliminary Report on the Excavation of Han Tombs at the Fulisaigao City Plaza in Xi'an, Shaanxi). 考古与文物 [*Archaeology and Cultural Relics*] 2017(3):3–13.

2017b 西安北郊枣园南岭西汉墓发掘简报 (Preliminary Report on the Excavation of Western Han Tombs at Zaoyuannanling in the Northern Suburbs of Xi'an). 考古与文物 [*Archaeology and Cultural Relics*] 2017(6):17–33.

2018a 邰城铸铁：陕西杨凌汉代铸铁遗址发掘与研究 [*Taicheng Ironworks: Report on the Excavation and Research of a Cast Iron Foundry of the Han Period in Yangling, Shaanxi*]. 上海 Shanghai: 上海古籍出版社 Shanghai Guji Press.

2018b 西安张家堡秦墓 [*Qin Tombs at Zhangjiabao in Xi'an*]. 西安 Xi'an: 陕西科学技术出版社 Shaanxi Science and Technology Press.

2018c 咸阳东郊秦墓 [*Cemeteries of Qin Tombs on the Eastern Suburbs of Xianyang*]. 北京 Beijing: 科学出版社 Science Press.

2020 陕西西安咸新区坡刘村秦墓发掘简报 (Preliminary Report on the Excavation of Qin Tombs at the Poliu Cemetery in Qin-Han Xincheng of Xi-Xian New District, Shaanxi). 考古与文物 [*Archaeology and Cultural Relics*] 2020(4):12–35.

Shaanxi Yanjiuyuan, and Baojishi [Shaanxisheng Kaogu Yanjiuyuan 陕西省考古研究院, and Baojishi Kaogu Yanjiusuo 宝鸡市考古研究所]

2012 陕西宝鸡苟家岭西汉墓葬发掘简报 (Preliminary Report on the Excavation of Western Han Tombs at Goujialing in Baoji, Shaanxi). 考古与文物 [*Archaeology and Cultural Relics*] 2012(1):3–11.

2013 陕西宝鸡凉泉汉墓发掘简报 (Preliminary Report on the Excavation of Han Tombs at Liangquan in Baoji, Shaanxi). 考古与文物 [*Archaeology and Cultural Relics*] 6:3–19.

Shaanxi Yanjiuyuan, and Beida [Shaanxisheng kaogu yanjiusuo 陕西省考古研究所, and Beijing Daxue Kaogu Wenbo Xueyuan 北京大学考古文博学院]

2019 陕西岐山孔头沟遗址铸铜作坊发掘简报 (Preliminary Report on the Bronze Foundry at Kongtougou Site in Qishan, Shaanxi). 南方文物 [*Southern Cultural Relics*] 2019(3):59–68.

Shaanxi Yanjiuyuan, and Xianyangshi Wenwu [Shaanxisheng Kaogu Yanjiuyuan 陕西省考古研究院, and Xianyangshi Wenwu Kaogu Yanjiusuo 咸阳市文物考古研究所]

2012 汉哀帝义陵考古调查、勘探简报 (Preliminary Report on the Investigation and Augering of Yiling Mausoleum of Emperor Ai in the Western Han Period). 考古与文物 [*Archaeology and Cultural Relics*] 2012(5):18–27.

2013 汉元帝渭陵考古调查、勘探简报 (Preliminary Report on the Investigation and Augering of the Weiling Mausoleum of Emperor Yuan in the Western Han Period). 考古 [*Archaeology*] 2013(11):23–34.

2014 汉平帝康陵考古调查、勘探简报 (The Survey and Detection of the Kangling Museum of Emperor Ping of the Western Han Dynasty). 考古 [*Archaeology*] 2014(6):50–63.

Shaanxi Yanjiuyuan, and Weinanshi [Shaaxisheng Kaogu Yanjiuyuan 陕西省考古研究院, and Weinanshi Kaogu Yanjiusuo 渭南市考古研究所]

2011 陕西渭南阳郭庙湾战国秦墓发掘简报 (Preliminary Report on the Excavation of the Warring States and Qin Tombs at Yangguomiaowan in Weinan, Shaanxi). 文博 [*Relics and Museology*] 2011(5):3–14.

Shaanxi Yanjiuyuan, and Yanglingqu [Shaaxisheng Kaogu Yanjiuyuan 陕西省考古研究院, and Yanglingqu Wenwu Guanlisuo 杨凌区文物管理所]

2018　邰城汉墓 [*The Han Cemetery at Taicheng*]. 上海 Shanghai: 上海古籍出版社 Shanghai Guji Press.

Shaanxi Yanjiuyuan et al. [Shaanxisheng Kaogu Yanjiuyuan 陕西省考古研究院, Baojishi Kaogu Yanjiusuo 宝鸡市考古研究所, and Fengxianxian Bowuguan 凤翔县博物馆]

2013　秦雍城豆腐村战国制陶作坊遗址 [*Ceramic Workshop of the Warring States Period at Doufucun Site in Qin Yongcheng*]. 北京 Beijing: 科学出版社 Science Press.

2015　凤翔孙家南头：周秦墓葬与西汉仓储建筑遗址发掘报告 [*Fengxiang Sunjia Nantou: Excavation Report of Zhou-Qin Tombs and Storage Building Sites in Western Han Dynasty*]. 北京 Beijing: 科学出版社 Science Press.

Shaanxi Yanjiuyuan et al. [Shaanxisheng Kaogu Yanjiuyuan 陕西省考古研究院, Xianyangshi Kaogu Yanjiusuo 咸阳市考古研究所, and Maoling Bowuguan 茂陵博物馆]

2011　汉武帝茂陵考古调查、勘探简报 (A Preliminary Report on the Archaeological Surveys of the Maoling of Emperor Wu, Western Han Dynasty). 考古与文物 [*Archaeology and Cultural Relics*] 2011(2):3–13.

Shaanxi Yanjiuyuan et al. [Shaanxisheng Kaogu Yanjiuyuan 陕西省考古研究院, Xianyangshi Kaogu Yanjiusuo 咸阳市考古研究所, and Weichengqu Qin Xianyanggong Yizhi Bowuguan 渭城区秦咸阳宫遗址博物馆]

2019　陕西咸阳聂家沟秦代制骨作坊清理简报 (Preliminary Report on the Excavation of the Bone Workshop of the Qin Period at the Niejiagou Site). 考古与文物 [*Archaeology and Cultural Relics*] 2019(3):50–62.

Shaanxi Yanjiuyuan et al. [Shaanxisheng Kaogu Yanjiuyuan 陕西省考古研究院, Yananshi Wenwu Yanjiusuo 延安市文物研究所, and Huanglingxian Luyou Wenwuju 黄陵县旅游文物局]

2018　寨头河：陕西黄陵战国戎人墓地考古发掘报告 [*Zhaitouhe: The Excavation of the Warring-States-Period Rong-Barbarian Cemetery at Huangling, Shaanxi*]. 上海 Shanghai: 上海古籍出版社 Shanghai Guji Press.

Shaanxi Yanjiuyuan et al. [Shaanxisheng Kaogu Yanjiuyuan 陕西省考古研究院, Zhongguo Guojia Bowuguan 中国国家博物馆, Baojishi Kaogu Yanjiusuo 宝鸡市考古研究所, Fengxiangxian Bowuguan 凤翔县博物馆, Baoji Xianqin Lingyuan Bowuguan 宝鸡先秦陵园博物馆, and Xibei Daxue 西北大学]

2020　陕西凤翔雍山血池秦汉祭祀遗址考古调查与发掘简报 (The Preliminary Report on the Excavation and Survey of the Xuechi Sacrifice Site of Qin-Han Periods). 考古与文物 [*Archaeology and Cultural Relics*] 2020(6):3–24.

Shaanxi Yanjiuyuan et al. [Shaanxisheng Kaogu Yanjiuyuan 陕西省考古研究院, Zhongguo Shehui Kexueyuan Kaogu Yanjiusuo 中国社会科学院考古研究所, and Xi'anshi Wenwu Baohu Kaogu Yanjiuyuan 西安市西安市文物保护考古研究院]

2014　西安市汉长安城北渭桥遗址 (Remains of Bei Weiqiao Associated with the Han Chang'an City in Xi'an). 考古 [*Archaeology*] 2014(7):34–47.

2021　汉宣帝杜陵考古调查勘探简报 (Preliminary Report on the Archaeological Survey and Reconnaissance of the Du Mausoleum of Emperor Xuan of the Han Period). 考古与文物 [*Archaeology and Cultural Relics*] 2021(1):40–52.

Shaanxisheng, and Chengcheng [Shaanxisheng Wenguanhui 陕西省文管会, and Chengchengxian Wenhuaguan Lianhe Fajuedui 澄城县文化馆联合发掘队]
1982　陕西坡头村西汉铸钱遗址发掘简报 (Preliminary Report on the Excavation of Western Han Coin Mint Site in Potou Village, Shaanxi). 考古 [*Archaeology*] 1982(1):23–30.

Shaanxisheng, and Dalixian [Shaanxisheng Wenguanhui 陕西省文管会, and Dalixian Wenhuaguan 大荔县文化馆]
1978　朝邑战国墓葬发掘简报 (Preliminary Report on the Excavation on Warring States Tombs in Chaoyi). In, 文物资料丛刊(2) [*Collected Articles on Cultural Relics Data (2)*], Wenwu Bianji Weiyuanhui 文物编辑委员会 (ed.), Pp. 75–91. 北京 Beijing: 文物出版社 Cultural Relics Press.

Shaanxisheng Baozhong [Shaanxisheng Kaogu Yanjiusuo Baozhong Tielu Kaogudui 陕西省考古研究所宝中铁路考古队]
1999　陕西陇县店子村汉唐墓葬 (Han and Tang Tombs at Dianzi in Long County, Shaanxi). 考古与文物 [*Archaeology and Cultural Relics*] 1999(4):3–29.

Shaanxisheng Gongzuozhan [Shaanxisheng Kaogu Yanjiusuo Yongcheng Gongzuozhan 陕西省考古研究所雍城工作站]
1991　凤翔邓家崖秦墓发掘简报 (Preliminary Report on the Excavation of Qin Tombs at Dengjiaya in Fengxiang). 考古与文物 [*Archaeology and Cultural Relics*] 1991(2):14–19.

Shaanxisheng Peihe [Shaanxisheng Kaogusuo Peihe Jijian Kaogudui 陕西省考古所配合基建考古队]
1989　陕西临潼骊山床单厂基建工地古墓清理简报 (Preliminary Report on the Excavation of Tombs at the Lishan Bedsheet Factory Construction Site in Lintong, Shaanxi). 考古与文物 [*Archaeology and Cultural Relics*] 1989(5):2–11.

Shaanxisheng Wenguanhui [Shaanxisheng Wenguanhui Qinmu Fajuezu 陕西省文管会秦墓发掘组]
1975　陕西省户县宋村春秋秦墓发掘简报 (Preliminary Report on the Excavation of Spring-and-Autumn Qin Tombs at Songcun in Hu County, Shaanxi). 文物 [*Cultural Relics*] 1975(10):13–20.

Shaanxisheng Wenwu [Shaanxisheng Wenwu Guanli Weiyuanhui 陕西省文物管理委员会]
1960　西安东郊韩森寨汉墓清理简报 (Preliminary Report on the Han Tomb at Hansenzhai, Eastern Suburbs of Xi'an). 文物 [*Cultural Relics*] 1960(5):72, 91.
1965　陕西宝鸡阳平镇秦家沟村秦墓发掘记 (Excavation of Qin Tombs at the Qinjiagoucun in Yangping Town, Baoji, Shaanxi). 考古 [*Archaeology*] 1965(7):330–346.
1966　秦都栎阳遗址初步勘探记 (Preliminary Investigation of the Yueyang Site of the Qin Captial). 文物 [*Cultural Relics*] 1966(1):10–16.

Shaanxisheng Yongcheng [Shaanxisheng Yongcheng Kaogudui 陕西省雍城考古队]
1980　陕西凤翔八旗屯秦国墓葬发掘简报 (A Brief Report on the Qin Tombs at Baqitun in Fengxiang, Shaanxi). In, 文物资料丛刊(3) [*Collected Articles on Cultural Relics Data (3)*]. Wenwu bianji weiyuanhui 文物编辑委员会 (ed.), Pp. 67–85. 北京 Beijing: 文物出版社 Cultural Relics Press.
1986　一九八一年凤翔八旗屯墓地发掘简报 (A Brief Report on the Excavation of the Cemetery at Baqitun in Fengxiang, 1981). 考古与文物 [*Archaeology and Cultural Relics*] 1986(5):23–40.

Shandong Daxue [Shandong Daxue Kaogudui 山东大学考古队]
1998   长清仙人台周代墓地 (Excavation of Zhou Dynasty Cemetery at Xianrentai in Changqing Country, Shangdong). 考古 [*Archaeology*] 1998(9):11–25.

Shandong Jiningshi [Shandongsheng Jiningshi Wenwu Guanliju 山东省济宁市文物管理局]
1991   薛国故城勘查和墓葬发掘报告 (Report on the Investigation of Xue State's Ancient City and the Excavation of Tombs). 考古学报 [*Acta Archaeologica Sinica*] 1991(4):449–495, 521–534.

Shandong et al. [Shandongsheng Wenwu Kaogu Yanjiuyuan 山东省文物考古研究院, Beijing Daxue Kaogu Wenbo Xueyuan 北京大学考古文博学院, and Jinanshi Kaogu Yanjiusuo 济南市考古研究所]
2019   济南市章丘区东平陵城遗址铸造区2009年发掘简报 (Preliminary Report on the 2009 Excavation in the Casting Area of the Dongpingling Site in Zhangqiu, Jinan). 考古 [*Archaeology*] 2019(11):49–66.
2020   济南市章丘区东平陵城遗址铸造区2012年发掘简报 (Preliminary Report on the 2012 Excavation in the Casting Area of the Dongpingling Site in Zhangqiu, Jinan). 考古 [*Archaeology*] 2020(12):41–52.

Shangjunshu zhuyi 商君书注译
2011   商君书注译 [*Shangjunshu zhuyi*], annotated by Gao Heng 高亨. 北京 Beijing: 清华大学出版社 Tsinghua University Press.

Shang, Xinli 尚新丽
2008   西汉人口问题研究 [*Research on the Demograph of the Western Han*]. 北京 Beijing: 线装书局 Xianzhuang Press.

Shang, Zhiru 尚志儒, and Zhao, Congcang 赵丛苍
1986   陕西凤翔八旗屯西沟道秦墓发掘简报 (Preliminary Report on the Excavation of Qin Tombs at Xigoudao in Baqitun, Fengxiang, Shaanxi). 文博 [*Relics and Museology*] 1986(3):19–25.

Shanxi [Shanxisheng Kaogu Yanjiusuo 山西省考古研究所]
1993   侯马铸铜遗址 [*Bronze Foundry Sites at Houma*]. 北京 Beijing: 文物出版社 Cultural Relics Press.
1994   山西夏县禹王城汉代铸铁遗址试掘简报 (Preliminary Excavation Report on the Han Dynasty Casting Iron Site in Yuwangcheng, Xia County, Shanxi). 考古 [*Archaeology*] 1994(8):685–691.
1996   侯马陶范艺术 [*Art of Houma Foundry*]. Princeton, NJ: Princeton University Press.
2012   侯马白店铸铜遗址 [*The Bronze Foundry Site at Baidian, Houma*]. 北京 Beijing: 科学出版社 Science Press.

Shanxi et al. [Shanxisheng Kaogu Yanjiusuo 山西省考古研究所, Shanxi Bowuyuan 山西博物院, and Changzhishi Bowuguan 长治市博物馆]
2010   长治分水岭东周墓地 [*The Eastern Zhou Cemetery at Fenshuiling in Changzhi*]. 北京 Beijing: 文物出版社 Cultural Relic Press.

Shanxi et al. [Shanxisheng Kaogu Yanjiushuo 山西省考古研究所, Yunchengshi Wenwuju 運城市文物局, Lingyixiang Wenwu Luyouju 臨猗縣文物旅游局, and Yinxuxiang Bowuguan 臨猗縣博物館]
2012   临猗铁匠营古城南汉代遗址发掘报告 (Preliminary Report on the Excavation of the Tiejiangying Walled-town of the Han Period in Linyi). In, 三晉考古(第四輯)

[*Sanjin Kaogu* (vol. 4)], Pp. 457–467. 上海 Shanghai: 上海古籍出版社 Shanghai Guji Press.

Shanxi Houma [Shanxisheng Kaogu Yanjiusuo Houma Gongzuozhan 山西省考古研究所侯马工作站]

1995 1992年侯马铸铜遗址发掘简报 (Excavation of a Bronze Casting Site at Houma, Shanxi). 文物 [*Cultural Relics*] 1995(2):29–53.

1996 晋都新田 [*The New Capital Xintian of the Jin State*]. 太原 Tainyuan: 山西人民出版社 Shanxi People's Press.

Shaw, Leslie C.

2012 The Elusive Maya Marketplace: An Archaeological Consideration of the Evidence. *Journal of Archaeological Research* 20:117–155.

Shelach-Lavi, Gideon

2016 East Asia as laboratory for Early Globalization. In, *The Routledge Handbook of Archaeology and Globalization*. Tamar Hodos (ed.), Pp. 389–393. London and New York: Routledge.

Shelach-Lavi, Gideon, and Pines, Yuri

2006 Secondary State Formation and the Development of Local Identity: Change and Continuity in the State of Qin (770-221 B.C.). In, *Archaeology of Asia*. Mirlam T. Stark (ed.), Pp. 202–230. Malden, MA: Blackwell Publishing.

Shen, Ruiwen 沈睿文

2001 西汉帝陵陵地秩序 (The Order in the Layout of Western Han Mausoleums). 文博 [*Relics and Museology*] 2001(3):17–23.

Shen, Ruiwen 沈睿文, and Yi, Shufeng 易曙峰

2021 安溪青洋下草埔冶铁遗址的几点初步认识 (Preliminary Understanding of Xiacaopu Iron Smelting Site in Qingyang, Anxi). 自然与文化遗产研究 [*Study on Natural and Cultural Heritage*] 2021(3):48–58.

Shi, Jingjing 石晶晶, Zhao, Fengyan 赵凤燕, and Li, Xiuhui 李秀辉

2019 西安古桥遗址出土汉代大型铸铁件的分析研究 (Analysis of the Large Cast Iron Components of the Han Period Yielded from the Ancient Bridge Site in Xi'an). 文博 [*Relics and Museology*] 2019(6):91–97.

Shi, Nianhai 史念海

1963 古代的关中 (On the Ancient Guanzhong). In, 河山集(一) [*Heshanji* (vol. 1)], Pp. 26–66. 北京 Beijing: 三联书店 Joint Publishing Company.

1991 娄敬和汉朝的建都 (Lou Jing and the Establishment of the Han Capital). In, 河山集(四) [*Heshanji* (vol. 4)], Pp. 368–380. 西安 Xi'an: Shaanxi Normal University Press 陕西师范大学出版社.

Shih, Changju 石璋如

1955 殷代的铸铜工艺 (Bronze Casting Techniques of the Shang Dynasty). 中央研究院历史语言研究所集刊 [*Bulletin of the Institute of History and Philology*] 26:95–130.

Shihuangling [Shihuangling Qinyong Kaogudui 始皇陵秦俑坑考古队]

1983 陕西省临潼鱼池遗址调查简报 [Preliminary Report on the Survey of the Yuchi Site in Lintong, Shaanxi]. 考古与文物 [*Archaeology and Cultural Relics*] 1983(4):14–26.

Shiji 史记

1997 史记 [*Shiji*], by Sima Qian 司马迁 and others, annotated by Zhang Shoujie 张守节, Sima Zhen 司马贞, and Pei Yin 裴骃. 北京 Beijing: 中华书局 Zhonghua Press.

Silver, Ian A.

1969   The Ageing of Domestic Animals. In, *Archaeology: A Survey of Progress and Research*. Don Brothwell and Eric Higgs (eds.), Pp. 283–302. London: Science Thames and Hudson.

Simek, Jan F.

1989   Structure and Diversity in Intrasite Spatial Analysis. In, *Quantifying Diversity in Archaeology*. Robert D. Leonard and George T. Jones (eds.), Pp. 59–68. Cambridge: Cambridge University Press.

Sinopoli, Carla M.

1988   The Organization of Craft Production at Vijayanagara, South India. *American Anthropologist* 90(3):580–597.

2003   *The Political Economy of Craft Production: Crafting Empire in South India. C. 1350–1650.* New York: Cambridge University Press.

Skinner, William

1964   Marketing and Social Structure in Rural China: Part I. *Journal of Asian Studies* 24(1):3–43.

1965a Marketing and Social Structure in Rural China: Part II. *Journal of Asian Studies* 24(2):195–228.

1965b Marketing and Social Structure in Rural China: Part III. *Journal of Asian Studies* 24(3):363–399.

Smith, Carol A.

1976a Regional Economic Systems: Linking Geological Models and Socioeconomic Problems. In, *Regional Analysis (Volume I): Economic System*. Carol A. Smith (ed.), Pp. 3–68. New York: Academic Press.

1976b Analyzing Regional Social Systems. In, *Regional Analysis (Volume II): Social Systems*. Carol A. Smith (ed.), Pp. 3–20. New York: Academic Press.

Smith, Cyril Stanley

1970   Art, Technology, Science: Notes on Their Historical Interaction. *Technology and Culture* 11:493–549.

Smith, Michael E.

1978   The Aztec Marketing System and Settlement Pattern in the Valley of Mexico: A Central Place Analysis. *American Antiquity* 44:110–125.

1999   On Hirth's "Distributional Approach". *Current Anthropology* 40(4):528–530.

2004   The Archaeology of Ancient State Economies. *Annual Review of Anthropology* 33:73–102.

2010   Regional and Local Market Systems in Aztec-period Morelos. In, *Archaeological Approaches to Market Exchange in Ancient Societies*. Christopher P. Garraty and Barbara L. Stark (eds.), Pp. 151–184. Boulder: University Press of Colorado.

Song, Jie 宋杰

1994   《九章算术》与汉代社会经济 [*The Nine Chapters on the Mathematical Art and Social Economy in the Han Dynasty*]. 北京 Beijing: 首都师范大学出版社 Capital Normal University Press.

Song, Rong 宋蓉

2016   汉代郡国分治的考古学观察: 以关东地区汉代墓葬为中心 [The Archaeeological View of the System of Counties Coexisting with Kingdoms in Han Dynasty: Centering the Graves in Guandong Area]. 上海 Shanghai: 上海古籍出版社 Shanghai Guji Press.

Sterckx, Roel

2011   *Food, Sacrifice, and Sagehood in Early China.* Cambridge: Cambridge University Press.

2015   Ideologies of the Peasant and Merchant in Warring States China. In, *Ideology of Power and Power of Ideology in Early China.* Yuri Pines, Paul R. Goldin and Martin Kern (eds.), Pp. 211–248. Leiden: Brill.

2020   Agrarian and Mercantile Ideologies in Western Han. *Journal of the Economic and Social History of the Orient* 63:465–504.

Su, Bingqi 苏秉琦

1984   斗鸡台东区墓葬(节选) [Tombs in the Eastern Part of the Doujitai Site: Selection]. In, 苏秉琦考古学论术选集 [*Collected Archaeological Studies of Su Bingqi*], Pp. 3–58. 北京 Beijing: 文物出版社 Cultural Relics Press.

Sun, Tieshan 孙铁山, and Chong, Jianrong 种建荣

2001   西安北郊永济电机厂秦汉墓发掘简报 (Site Report of Qin and Western Han Tombs in Yongji Motormaker Factory, North Suburb of Xi'an). 文博 [*Relics and Museology*] 2001(5):3–8.

Sun, Zhouyong

2008   *Craft Production in the Western Zhou Dynasty (1046–771BC): A Case Study of a Jue-Earrings Workshop at the Predynastic Capital Site, Zhouyuan, China.* Oxford: Archaeo Press.

Swann, Nancy Lee

1950   *Food and Money in Ancient China: The Earliest Economist History of China to A.D. 25 (Han shu 24, with related texts, Han shu 91 and Shih-chi 129).* New York: Octagon Books.

Swedberg, Richard

1994   Markets as Social Structure. In, *The Handbook of Economic Sociology.* Neil L. Smelser and Richard Swedberg (eds.), Pp. 255–282. Princeton, NJ: Princeton University Press.

Tan, Chongyee 谭宗义

1967   汉代国内陆路交通考 [*A Study on the Land Communications of Han Dynasty*]. 香港 Hong Kong: 香港新亚研究所 The Research Institute of New Asia College.

Tang, Chao 汤超

2019   秦铁官体系与冶铁业新识 (A New Study of the Bureaucratic System of Qin State Iron Administrations). 江汉考古 [*Jianghan Archaeology*] 2019(2):75–80.

Tang, Jigen 唐际根

1993   中国冶铁术的起源问题 (The Origin of Chinese Iron Metallurgy). 考古 [*Archaeology*] 1993(6):563–564.

Teng, Mingyu 滕铭予

1993   论关中秦墓中洞室墓的年代 (On the Date of Qin Catacombs in the Guanzhong Basin). 华夏考古 [*Huaxia Archaeology*] 1993(2):90–97.

1995   论秦釜 (On Qin Fu Cauldrons). 考古 [*Archaeology*] 1995(8):731–736.

2002   秦文化: 从封国到帝国的考古学观察 [*Qin Culture in Archaeological Perspective: From a Feudal State to a Great Empire*]. 北京 Beijing: 学苑出版社 Xueyuan Press.

2013   From Vassal State to Empire: An Archaeological Examination of Qin Culture (trans. Susanna Lam). In, *Birth of an Empire: The State of Qin Revisited.* Yuri Pines, Gideon Shelach, Lothar von Falkenhausen and Robin D. S. Yates (eds.), Pp. 113–140, Berkeley: University of California Press.

Temin, Peter
2013   *The Roman Market Economy*. Princeton, NJ and Oxford: Princeton University Press.

Tian, Renxiao 田仁孝, and Lei, Xingshan 雷兴山
1993   宝鸡市益门村二号春秋墓发掘简报 (Preliminary Report on the Excavation of the No. 2 Tomb in the Spring-and-Autumn Period in Yimencun, Baoji). 文物 [*Cultural Relics*] 1993(10):1–14.

Tian, Tian
2015   The Suburban Sacrifice Reforms and the Evolution of the Imperial Sacrifices. In, *Chang'an 26 BCE: An Augustan Age in China*. Michael Nylan and Griet Vankeerberghen (eds.), Pp. 263–292. Seattle: University of Washington Press.

Tian, Yaqi 田亚岐
2013   秦都雍城布局研究 (Research on the Layout of the Yong Capital of the Qin State). 考古与文物 [*Archaeology and Cultural Relics*] 2013(5):63–71.
2018   雍城：东周秦都与秦汉"圣城"布局沿革之考古材料新解读 (Yongcheng: The Qin Capital during the Eastern Zhou Period and the New Interpretation of Archaeological Materials about the Transformation of the Layout of the "Holy" City of the Qin-Han Periods). In, 新果集(二)：纪念林沄先生八十华诞论文集 [*Xinguoji (Vol. 2): Collection of Papers Celebrating the 80th Birthday of Lin Yun*]. Jilin Daxue Bianjiang Kaogu Yanjiu Zhongxin 吉林大学边疆考古研究中心 (ed.), Pp. 328–341. 北京 Beijing: 科学出版社 Science Press.

Tian, Yaqi 田亚岐, and Yang, Yachang 杨亚长
1998   陇县温水乡汉墓清理简报 (Preliminary Report on the Excavation of Han Tombs at Wenshuixiang, Long County). 文博 [*Relics and Museology*] 1998(2):44–49.

Tong, Enzheng 童恩正
1990   试论我国从东北至西南的遍地半月形传播带 (On the Crescent-shaped Cultural Communication Belt). In, 中国西南民族考古论文集 [*Collection of Articles on Archaeology and Ethnology in Southwest China*], Pp. 252–278. 北京 Beijing: 文物出版社 Cultural Relics Press.

Tong, Chunfung 唐俊峰
2014   秦汉的地方都官与地方行政 (The Administrative Relationships between Regional Duguan and Local Administrations during the Qin and Han Dynasties). 新史学 [*New Historiography*] 25(3):1–63.

Trousdale, William
1977   Where All the Swords Have Gone. Reflections on Some Questions Raised by Professor Keightley. *Early China* 3:65–66.

Vaiglova, Petra, Reid, Rachel E. B., and Lightfoot, Emma et al.
2021   Localized Management of Non-indigenous Animal Domesticates in Northwestern China during the Bronze Age. *Scientific Reports* 11:15764.

van der Leeuw, Sander E.
1977   Towards a Study of the Economics of Pottery Making. In, *Ex Horreo*. van Ben L. Beek, Roel W. Brandt and Willy Groenman-van Watteringe (eds.), Pp. 68–76. Amsterdam: University of Amsterdam.

van Oyen, Astrid
2015   Actor-Network Theory's Take on Archaeological Types: Becoming, Material Agency, and Historical Explanation. *Cambridge Archaeological Journal* 25(1):63–78.

Vogel, Hans Ulrich
1993   *Salt Production Techniques in Ancient China: The Aobo Tu*. Translated and revised by Hans Ulrich Vogel. Leiden: Brill.

von Falkenhausen, Lothar
2004   Mortuary Behavior in Pre-imperial Qin: A Religious Interpretation. In, *Religion and Chinese Society. Volume 1: Ancient and Medieval China*. John Lagerwey (ed.), Pp. 109–172. Hong Kong: Chinese University of Hong Kong Press.
2006   *Chinese Society in the Age of Confucius (1000–250 BC): The Archaeological Evidence*. Los Angeles, CA: The Costen Institute of Archaeology at UCLA.

von Glahn, Richard
2016   *An Economic History of China: From Antiquity to the Nineteenth Century*. New York: Cambridge University Press.

Wagner, Donald B.
1993   *Iron and Steel in Ancient China*. Leiden: Brill.
2001   *The State and the Iron Industry in Han China*. Copenhagen: NIAS.
2008   *Science and Civilisation in China. Vol 5. Chemistry and Chemical Technology. Part 11, Ferrous Metallurgy*. Cambridge: Cambridge University Press.

Waldbaum, Jane C.
1999   The Coming of Iron in the Eastern Mediterranean: Thirty Years of Archaeological and Technological Work. In, *The Archaeometallurgy of the Asian Old World*. Vincent C. Pigott (ed.), Pp. 27–57. Philadelphia: University of Pennsylvania Museum.

Wan, Chiapao 万家保
1975   A Comparative Study of the Casting of Bronze *Ting*-cauldrons from Anyang and Hui-Hsien. In, *Ancient Chinese Bronzes and Southeast Asian Metal and Other Archaeological Artifacts*. Barnard Noel (ed.), Pp. 17–46. Melbourne: National Gallery of Victoria.

Wang, Changqi 王长启, and Kong, Haoqun 孔浩群
1987   西安北郊发现汉代墓葬 (Han Tombs Discovered on the Northern Suburbs of Xi'an). 考古与文物 [*Archaeology and Cultural Relics*] 1987(4):3–14.

Wang, Guangyong 王光永
1975   陕西省千阳县汉墓发掘简报 (Preliminary Report on the Excavation of Han Tombs in Qianyang County, Shaanxi). 考古 [*Archaeology*] 1975(3):178–181.

Wang, Jiugang 王久刚
1994   西安南郊山门口战国秦墓清理简报 (Preliminary Report on the Excavation of Qin Tombs at the Shanmenkou Site on the Southern Suburbs of Xi'an). 考古与文物 [*Archaeology and Cultural Relics*] 1994(1):27–31.

Wang, Kai 王凯
2010   郑韩故城手工业遗存的考古学研究 [*Archaeological Studies on Handicraft Industry Sites of the Zheng and Han States' Capital*], 郑州大学硕士学位论文 Master thesis, Zhengzhou University.

Wang, Peihua 王培华
2009   汉唐长安粮食供应与关中天地人关系 (Food Supply of Chang'an City in the Han and Tang Dynasties and the Relationship between Heaven, Nature and Human in Guanzhong). 陕西师范大学学报(哲学社会科学版) [*Journal of Shaanxi Normal University (Philosophy and Social Sciences Edition)*] 38(3):60–66.

Wang, Renxiang 王仁湘
1985 带钩概论 (A General Survey of Ancient Chinese Belt Hooks). 考古学报 [*Acta Archaeologica Sinica*] 1985(3):267–312.
2012 善自约束：古代带钩与带扣 [*Shanzi Yueshu: Belt Hooks and Buckles in Ancient China*]. 上海 Shanghai: 上海古籍出版社 Shanghai Guji Press.

Wang, Shejiao 王社教
1999 论西汉定都长安与关中经济发展的新格局 (On the Establishment of Chang'an Capital during the Western Han Period and the New Pattern of Economic Development in the Guanzhong Region). 中国历史地理论丛 [*Journal of Chinese Historical Geography*] 1999(3):46–63.

Wang, Xiaokun 王晓琨
2014 战国至秦汉时期河套地区古代城址研究 [*Archaeological Research on the Ancient Walled Sites in Hetao Area from Warring States to Qin and Han Dynasties*]. 北京 Beijing: 社会科学文献出版社 Social Sciences Academic Press.

Wang, Xiaoqing 王晓青, Tian, Qiqiong 田奇瑰, and Liu, Zuyi 刘祖彝
1934 湖南铁矿志 [*The Iron Ores of Huna (no. 1)*]. 湖南 Hunan: 湖南地质调查所 Hunan Geological Survey Institute.

Wang, Xueli 王学理
1999 咸阳帝都记 [*Research on the Capital Xianyang*]. 西安 Xi'an: 三秦出版社 Sanqin Press.
2004 秦始皇陵园汉墓清理简报 (Excavation Report on Han Tombs at Qinshihuang Mausoleum). 文物 [*Cultural Relics*] 2004(5):31–37.

Wang, Xueli 王学理, and Liang, Yun 梁云
2000 秦文化 [*Qin Culture*]. 北京 Beijing: 文物出版社 Cultural Relics Press.

Wang, Yingchen 王颖琛, Liu, Yaxiong 刘亚雄, Jiang, Tiao 姜涛, and Chen, Kunlong 陈坤龙
2019 三门峡虢国墓地M2009出土铁刃铜器的科学分析及其相关问题 (Scientific Research of Bimetallic Objects Unearthed from M2009 in the Guo State Cemetery at Sanmenxia). 光谱学与光谱分析 [*Spectroscopy and Spectral Analysis*] 39(10):3154–3158.

Wang, Yong 王勇
2004 东周秦汉关中农业变迁研究 [*Research on the Change of Agriculture in Guanzhong from the Eastern Zhou to the Qin-Han Periods*]. 长沙 Changsha: 岳麓书社 Yuelu Press.
2008 大司农的演变与汉代的农业经营 (Changes of Dasinong and the Management of Agriculture during the Han Periods). 南京农业大学学报：社会科学版 [*Journal of Nanjing Agricultural University (Social Sciences Edition)*] 2008(3):101–106.

Wang, Zijin 王子今
2007 西汉长安居民的生存空间 (Habitation Space of Residents in Chang'an during the Western Han Period). 人文杂志 [*The Journal of Humanities*] 2007(2):150–158.
2018 秦直道：秦始皇直道考察与研究 [*Qin Zhidao: The Investigation and Research on the Zhidao Established by Qinshihuang*]. 西安 Xi'an: 陕西师范大学出版社 Shaanxi Normal University Press.
2019 宛珠·齐纨·穰橙邓橘：战国秦汉商品地方品牌的经济史考察 (Wan Zhu, Qi Wan, Rangcheng Dengju: A Study on the Local Brands of Goods in the Warring States and Qin-Han Dynasties from the Perspective of Economic History). 中国经济史研究 [*Researches in Chinese Economic History*] 2019(3):5–17.

2021 秦汉边政的方位形势: "北边""南边""西边""西北边" (Position and Situation of Frontier Politics in Qin and Han Dynasties: In "North", "South", "West", and "Northwest" Respectively). 中央民族大学学报(哲学社会科学版) [*Journal of Minzu University of China (Philosophy and Social Sciences Edition)*] 2021(3):144–151.

Watanabe, Shinichirō 渡边信一郎
1989 漢代の財政運営と国家的物流(Operation of Han Finance and State-controlled Transportation). 京都府立大学学術報告. 人文 [*Bulletin of Kyoto Prefectual University: Humanity*] 41:1–20.

Watson, Burton
1993[1961] *Records of the Grand Historian of China: Translations from the Shiji of the Sima Chien* (Han Dynasty I). Hong Kong and New York: A Renditions-Columbia University Press.
2007 *The Analects of Confucius*. New York: Columbia University Press.
2013 *The Complete Works of Zhuangzi*. New York: Columbia University Press.

Wei, Jian 魏坚
2020 河套地区战国秦汉塞防研究 (A Study of Qin and Han Periods Defenses in the Hetao Region). In, 大漠朔风: 魏坚北方考古文选 (历史卷) [*Damo Shuofeng: Collection of Archaeological Papers on Northern China by Wei Jian (Volume of Historical Periods)*], Pp. 52–65. 北京 Beijing: 科学出版社 Science Press.

Wertime, Theodore A., and Muhly, James D. (eds.)
1980 *The Coming of the Age of Iron*. New Haven, CT: Yale University Press.

Wilbur, Martin C.
1943a Industrial Slavery in China during the Former Han Dynasty (206 B.C.-A.D. 25). *The Journal of Economic History* 3(1):56–69.
1943b *Slavery in China during the Former Han Dynasty, 206 B.C.-A.D. 25*. Chicago, IL: Museum of Natural History.

Witcher, Robert
2017 The Globalized Roman World. In, *The Routledge Handbook of Archaeology and Globalization*. Tamar Hodos (ed.), Pp. 634–651. New York: Routledge.

Woolf, Greg
1998 *Becoming Roman: The Origins of Provincial Civilization in Gaul*. Cambridge: Cambridge University Press.

Wu, Hsiao-yun 吴晓筠
2011 马车在早期东西交流中的地位与交流模式: 公元前2000-1200年 (The Role of the Transmission of Chariots in the Early East-West Interaction: 2,000–1,200 BCE). 故宫学术季刊 [*The National Palace Museum Research Quarterly*] 28(4):95–119.

Wu, Hui 吴辉
2008 长沙楚墓年代学研究述评 (Review of the Research of the Date of Chu Tombs in Changsha). 江汉考古 [*Jianghan Archaeology*] 2008(1):90–95.

Wu, Naixiang 吴礽骧
2005 河西汉塞调查与研究 [*Investigation and Research on the Fortification System in Hexi*]. 北京 Beijing: 文物出版社 Cultural Relics Press.

Wu, Rongzeng 吴荣曾
2012 隶臣姜制度探讨 (The Systme of Lichengqie). In, 简牍与古代史研究 [*Bambool Wooden Slips and the Research on Ancient History*]. Wu Rongzeng 吴荣曾 and Wang Guihai 汪桂海 (eds.), Pp. 21–32. 北京 Beijing: 北京大学出版社 Peking University Press.

Wu, Xiaoping 吴小平
2007   从铭文看两汉铜器皿的生产经营方式及其变化 (Discussion on Management of Production and Its Chronological Change of Han Bronze Vessels According to Inscriptions). 故宫博物院院刊 [*Journal of National Museum of China*] 2007(4):100–107.

Wu, Zhaoyang 吴朝阳, and Jin, Wen 晋文
2013   秦亩产新考——兼析传世文献中的相关亩产记载 (A New Investigation on per mu Yield of Millet of Qin Dynasty and an Analysis of per mu Yield of Millet Appeared in Historical Literature). 中国经济史研究 [*Researches in Chinese Economic History*] 2013(4):38–44, 64.

Xi'an Zhongxin [Xi'an Wenwu Baohu Xiufu Zhongxin 西安文物保护修复中心]
2004   汉锺官铸钱遗址 [*The Zhongguan Bronze Mint Site of the Western Han Period*]. 北京 Beijing: 科学出版社 Science Press.

Xi'anshi [Xi'anshi Wenwu Baohu Kaogusuo 西安市文物保护考古所]
1997a 西安北郊二府庄汉墓发掘简报 (Preliminary Report on the Excavation of Han Tombs at Erfuzhuang on the Northern Suburbs of Xi'an). 文博 [*Relics and Museology*] 1997(5):15–25.
1997b 西安财政干部培训中心汉、后赵墓发掘简报 (Report on the Excavation of Han and Later Zhao Tombs at the Financial Civil Servants Training Center Site in Xi'an). 文博 [*Relics and Museology*] 1997(6):19–25.
1998a 西安北郊方新村汉墓第二次发掘简报 (Preliminary Report on the Second Excavation of Han Tombs at Fangxin Village in Northern Suburbs of Xi'an). 文博 [*Relics and Museology*] 1998(2):3–11.
1998b 西安北郊青门汉墓发掘简报 (Preliminary Report on the Excavation of Han Tombs at Qingmen on the Northern Suburbs of Xi'an). 文博 [*Relics and Museology*] 1998(4):16–31.
1999   西安龙首原汉墓(甲编) [*Western Han Tombs in Longshouyuan, Xi'an*]. 西安 Xi'an: 西北大学出版社 Northwest University Press.
2003   西安北郊枣园大型西汉墓发掘简报 (Preliminary Report on the Excavation of the Large Scale Western Han Tomb at Zaoyuan on the Northern Suburbs of Xi'an). 文物 [*Cultural Relics*] 2003(12):29–38.
2004a 西安东郊西汉窦氏墓(M3)发掘报告 (Excavation of Dou's Tomb of the Western Han in the Eastern Suburbs of Xi'an). 文物 [*Cultural Relics*] 2004(6):4–21.
2004b 西安南郊秦墓 [*Qin Tombs in Southern Suburb of Xi'an*]. 西安 Xi'an: 陕西人民出版社 Shaanxi People's Publishing House.
2004c 西安市长安区西北政法学院西汉张汤墓发掘简报 (Excavation of Zhang Tang's Tomb of the Western Han Dynasty in Xi'an). 考古 [*Archaeology*] 2004(6):22–28.
2009a 西安南郊荆寺二村西汉墓发掘简报 (Preliminary Report on the Excavation of Western Han Tombs at Jinsi Ercun on the Southern Suburbs of Xi'an). 考古与文物 [*Archaeology and Cultural Relics*] 2009(4):3–12.
2009b 西安张家堡新莽墓发掘简报 (Excavation of a Tomb of Xin Dynasty in Zhangjiapu Xi'an). 文物 [*Cultural Relics*] 2009(5):4–20.

Xi'anshi, and Zhengzhou [Xi'anshi Wenwu Baohu Kaogusuo 西安市文物保护考古所, and Zhengzhou Daxue Kaogu Zhuanye 郑州大学考古专业]
2004   长安汉墓 [*Han Tombs in Chang'an*]. 西安 Xi'an: 陕西人民出版社 Shaanxi People's Publishing House.

Xi'anshi Yanjiuyuan [Xi'anshi Wenwu Baohu Kaogu Yanjiuyuan 西安市文物保护考古研究院]

2012　西安南郊西汉墓发掘简报 (Preliminary Report on the Excavation of Western Han Tombs in the Southern Suburbs of Xi'an). 文物 [*Cultural Relics*] 2012(10):4–24.

2013　西安南郊曲江羊头镇西汉墓发掘简报 (Preliminary Report on the Excavation of Western Han Tombs in Yangtou Town, Qujian District, Southern Xi'an). 文博 [*Relics and Museology*] 2013(6):3–17.

2017　西安未央印象城汉墓发掘简报 (Preliminary Report on the Excavation of the Burials of the Han Dynasty at the Xi'an Incity Construction Site in Weiyang District, Xi'an). 文博 [*Relics and Museology*] 2017(2):3–12.

2018　西安北郊两座汉墓发掘简报 (Preliminary Report on the Excavation of Two Burials of the Han Dynasty in Northern Suburb of Xi'an). 文博 [*Relics and Museology*] 2018(2):13–24.

2019a 西安市张家堡两座西汉墓葬的发掘 (Preliminary Report on the Excavation of Two Western Han Tombs at Zhangjiapu, Xi'an). 考古 [*Archaeology*] 2019(2):23–37.

2019b 陕西高陵坡底战国秦汉墓地发掘报告 (Preliminary Report on the Exavation of the Tombs Dating from the Warring States to Qin-Han Periods at Podi in Gaoling, Shaanxi). 黄河.黄土.黄种人(華夏文明) [*Huanghe. Huangtu. Huangzhongren (Huaxia Wenmin)*] 2019(24):6–14.

Xi'anshi Yanjiuyuan, and Beijing Lianhe [Xi'anshi Wenwu Baohu Kaogu Yanjiuyuan 西安市文物保护考古研究院, and Beijing Lianhe Daxue 北京联合大学]

2020　陕西西安曲江春临村汉代窑址发掘简报 (Preliminary Report on the Excavatoin of Han Kilns at Chunlincun in Qujiang, Xi'an, Shaanxi). 文博 [*Relics and Museology*] 2020(2):3–11.

Xianyang Qindu [Xianyang Qindu Kaogu Gongzuozhan 咸阳秦都考古工作站]

1986　陕西秦都咸阳汉墓清理简报 (Preliminary Report on the Excavation of Han Tombs in Xianyang, the Qin Capital). 考古与文物 [*Archaeology and Cultural Relics*] 1986(5):10–15.

Xianyangshi Wenguanhui 咸阳市文管会

1992　西北林学院古墓清理简报 (A Brief Report on the Excavation of Ancient Tombs in Northwest Forestry University). 考古与文物 [*Archaeology and Cultural Relics*] 1992(3):21–35.

Xianyangshi Wenwu [Xianyangshi Wenwu Kaogu Yanjiusuo 咸阳市文物考古研究所]

1996　咸阳市杨凌区秦, 汉墓葬清理简报 (Preliminary Report on the Excavation of Qin and Han Tombs in Yangling District, Xianyang City). 考古与文物 [*Archaeology and Cultural Relics*] 1996(2):23–27.

1998　塔儿坡秦墓 [*Qin Tombs in Ta'erpo*]. 西安 Xi'an: 三秦出版社 Sanqin Press.

1999　陕西第二针织厂空心砖汉墓 (Excavation of Brick-chamber Han Tombs at the Shaanxi Second Fabric Factory). 文博 [*Relics and Museology*] 1999(3):11–15.

2000　咸阳马泉镇西汉空心砖墓清理报告 (Report on the Excavation of Brick-chamber Tombs in the Western Han Period in Maquan Town, Xianyang). 文博 [*Relics and Museology*] 2000(6):10–20.

2004　陕西咸阳市北郊杜家堡新莽墓发掘简报 (Preliminary Report on the Excavation of Han Tombs in the Xing Dynasty at Dujiabao on the Northern Suburbs of Xianyang, Shaanxi). 考古与文物 [*Archaeology and Cultural Relics*] 2004(3):23–27.

2005　任家咀秦墓 [*Qin Tombs at Renjiazui*]. 北京 Beijing: 科学出版社 Science Press.

2006　陕西咸阳202所西汉墓葬发掘简报 (Preliminary Report on the Excavation of Western Han Tombs at the 202 Suo Site in Xianyang, Shaanxi). 考古与文物 [*Archaeology and Cultural Relics*] 2006(1):5–14.

2007　西汉昭帝平陵钻探调查简报 (Preliminary Report on the Augering of the Pingling Mausoleum of Emperor Zhao in the Western Han Period). 考古与文物 [*Archaeology and Cultural Relics*] 2007(5):3–5.

2010　西汉帝陵钻探调查报告 [*Augering Survey Report on the Mausoleums of the Western Han Dynasty*]. 北京 Beijing: 文物出版社 Cultural Relics Press.

2017　咸阳花杨战国秦墓群发掘简报 (Preliminary Report on the Excavation of Qin Tombs during the Warring States Period at Huayang, Xianyang). 文博 [*Relics and Museology*] 2017(1):10–18.

Xianyangshi Wenwu, and Shaanxi Yanjiuyuan [Xianyangshi Wenwu Kaogu Yanjiusuo 咸阳市文物考古研究所, and Shaanxisheng Kaogu Yanjiuyuan 陕西省考古研究院]

2019　汉成帝延陵考古调查勘探报告 [*The Site Report of the Archaeological Reconnaissance of the Yanling Mausoleum of Chengdi*]. 北京 Beijing: 文物出版社 Cultural Relics Press.

Xiao, Ailing 肖爱玲

2007　西汉初年汉郡区城市等级及空间分布特征探析——张家山汉简研究 (An Analysis of City Grading and Spatial Distribution Features of County Areas in the Early Western Han Dynasty—A Study of Bamboo Slips Unearthed from Han Tomb in Zhangjiashan). 中国历史地理论丛 [*Journal of Chinese Historical Geography*] 22(4):60–70.

Xiao, Jianyi 肖健一

2007　长安城郊中小型西汉墓葬的研究现状及存在问题 (Analysis on the Research about the Middle and Small-sized Tombs of the Western Han Dynasty in the Suburbs of Chang'an City). 西北大学学报(哲学社会科学版) [*Journal of Northwest University (Philosophy and Social Science Edition)*] 37(1):48–52.

Xiao, Jianyi 肖健一, Shi, Ruiling 师瑞玲, and Zhang, Xiaojuan 张小涓

2017　咸阳周边秦墓的时空范围 (Establishing a Time-space Range for Qin Tombs around Capital City Xianyang). 西安电子科技大学学报(社会科学版) [*Journal of Xidian University(Social Science Edition)*] 27(4):123–126.

Xibei [Xibei Daxue Lishixi Kaogu Zhuanye 77ji Shixidui 西北大学历史系考古专业77级实习队]

1989　陕西华县梓里村汉墓清理记 (Excavation of Han Tombs at Zilicun in Hua County, Shaanxi). 文博 [*Relics and Museology*] 1989(2):13–21.

Xin, Deyong 辛德勇

1988　西汉至北周时期长安附近的陆路交通—汉唐长安交通地理研究之一　　(Land Transportation Nearby Chang'an from the Western Han to the Northern Zhou Dynaties: The Transportaion Geology of Chang'an during the Han and Tang Periods). 中国历史地理论丛 [*Journal of Chinese Historical Geograph*] 1988(3):85–113.

1989a 汉唐期间长安附近的水路交通— 汉唐长安交通地理研究之三 (River Transportation Nearby Chang'an from the Western Han to the Northern Zhou Dynaties: The Transportaion Geology of Chang'an during the Han and Tang Periods). 中国历史地理论丛 [*Journal of Chinese Historical Geography*] 1989(1):33–44.

1989b 长安城兴起与发展的交通基础—汉唐长安交通地理研究之四 (Rise of Chang'an and the Transporation Foundation of Development: The Transportaion Geology of Chang'an during the Han and Tang Periods). 中国历史地理论丛 [*Journal of Chinese Historical Geography*] 1989(2):131–140.

2008　汉武帝"广关"与西汉前期地域控制的变迁 (Emperor Wu's "Broadering the Area of Pass" Policy and the Change of the Geographic Control of the Early Western Han). 中国历史地理论丛 [*Journal of Chinese Historical Geography*] 2008(2):76–82.

2010　论细柳仓与澄邑仓 (On Xiliu Warehouse and Chengyi Warehouse). 陕西师范大学学报(哲学社会科学版) [*Journal of Shaanxi Normal University (Philosophy and Social Sciences Edition)*] 39(2):118–124.

Xin, Yihua 辛怡华

2018　血池遗址与雍地五畤及相关问题 (Xuechi Sacrificial Site and Related Issue of the Wuzhi in Yong). 湖南省博物馆馆刊第十四辑 [*Journal of Hunan Provincial Museum*] 14:19–25.

Xu, Hong 许宏

2017　先秦城邑考古 [*Archaeology of the Yi and Walled Settlements during the Pre-Qin Period*]. 北京 Beijing: 西苑出版社 Xiyuan Press.

Xu, Longguo 徐龙国

2003　秦都咸阳的手工业和商业遗存初探 (Investigation of Remains Associated with Craft Industries and Commerce in Xianyang, Qin Capital City). 文博 [*Relics and Museology*] 2003(4):11–16.

2013　秦汉城邑考古学研究 [*Archaeological Study of Qin-Han Walled Towns*]. 北京 Beijing: 中国社会科学出版社 Social Science Academic Press.

2020　汉长安城地区铸钱遗址与上林铸钱三官 (Minting Locations in the Chang'an Region and the Minting Site at Shanglin Sanguan). 考古 [*Archaeology*] 2020(10):97–107.

2021　汉长安城手工业遗存的发现与研究 (Discoveries and Research of Craft Production Remains Inside the Han Chang'an City). 南方文物 [*Southern Cultural Relics*] 2021(2):175–182.

Xu, Weihong 许卫红

2021　从手工业遗存看秦都咸阳城北区布局 (On the Distribution of the Northern Part of Xianyang, the Qin Capital, Based on Craft Production Remains). 南方文物 [*Southern Cultural Relics*] 2021(2):168–174.

Xu, Weihong 许卫红, and Su, Qingyuan 苏庆元

2016　秦都咸阳城(北区)西界点的分析 (Analysis of the Western Boundary of Xianyang, the Qin Capital). 北方文物 [*Northern Cultural Relics*] 2016(1):37–43.

Xu, Weimin 徐卫民

2000　秦都城研究 [*Research on Qin Capitals*]. 西安 Xi'an: 陕西人民教育出版社 Shaanxi People's Education Press.

2011　秦汉都城与自然环境关系研究 [*Research on Qin-Han Capitals and Relationship with Natural Environment*]. 北京 Beijing: 科学出版社 Science Press.

Yahalom-Mack, Naama, and Eliyahu-Behar, Adi

2015　The Transition from Bronze to Iron in Canaan: Chronology, Technology, and Context. *Radiocarbon* 57(2):285–305.

Yamada, Katsuyoshi 山田勝芳

1993　秦漢財政収入の研究[*Research on the Financial Revenues of the Qin and Han Periods*]. 東京 Tokyo: 汲古書院 Kyūko Shoin.

1998　秦漢代手工業の展開: 秦漢代工官の変遷から考える(The Development of Manual Industries and the Vicissitudes of Government Workshops (Gong Guan) in the Qin and Han Dynasties). 東洋史研究 [*The Journal of Oriental Researches*] 56:701–732.

Yang, Jian 杨建
2010   西汉初期津关制度研究：附《津关令》简释 [*The Passes and Fords System of the Early Western Han Period: With Commentaries of the Statutes of Fords and Passes*]. 上海 Shanghai: 上海古籍出版社 Shanghai Guji Press.

Yang, Kuan 杨宽
2003   战国史 [*History of Warring-States*]. 上海 Shanghai: 上海人民出版社 Shanghai People's Publishing House.
2004   中国古代冶铁技术发展史 [*History of Ferrous-metallurgy Development in Ancient China*]. 上海 Shanghai: 上海人民出版社 Shanghai People's Publishing House.

Yang, Quanxi 杨权喜
2004   试论楚国铁器的使用和发展 (The Utilization and Development of Iron Tools and Wares in the Chu State). 江汉考古 [*Jianghan Archaeology*] 2004(2):70–77.

Yang, Ruidong 杨瑞栋, and Li, Xiaocen 李晓岑
2011   云南曲靖市董家村石范制作技术的调查及相关问题 (The Investigation of the Production Techniques of Stone Casting Molds at Dongjiacun in Qujing, Yunnan, and Their Related Issues). 四川文物 [*Sichuan Culutral Relics*] 2011(6):84–92.

Yang, Ruidong 杨瑞栋, Li, Xiaocen 李晓岑, Li, Jinsong 李劲松, and Hua, Jueming 华觉明
2010   云南会泽石范铸铁的调查 (An Investigation on the Craft of Iron Casting by Stone Mould in Huize County, Yunnan Province). 中国科技史杂志 [*The Chinese Journal for the History of Science and Technology*] 2010(10):94–113.

Yang, Wuzhan 杨武站, and Wang, Dong 王东
2014   西汉陵邑营建相关问题研究 (Research of Questions Related to the Construction of Mausoleum Towns in the Western Han Period). 文博 [*Cultural Relics and Museology*] 2014(6):39–43.

Yang, Yishi, Ren, Lele, Dong, Guanghui, Cui, Yifu, Liu, Ruiliang, Chen, Guoke, Wang Hui, Shevan, Wilkin, Chen, Fahu
2019   Economic Change in the Prehistoric Hexi Corridor (4800–2200BP), North-West China. *Archaeometry* 61(4):957–976.

Yang, Yong 杨勇
2021   临淄齐故城冶铸业考古的收获与进展 (Archaeological Research of Metallurgy and Foundry Industry in the Linzi City of Qi State). 南方文物 [*Southern Cultural Relics*] 2021(2):154–161.

Yang, Yong 杨勇, Wei, Chengmin 魏成敏, Xu, Longguo 徐龙国, Qin, Yihui 钱益汇, and Wang, Xiaolian 王晓莲
2013   山东临淄齐故城冶铸遗存考古调查与发掘取得重要收获 (Important Results of the Survey and Excavation of the Smelting and Melting Sites at the Qi Capital City in Linzi, Shandong). 中国文物报 [*Chinese Cultural Relics News*], 2013/07/19, p. 8.

Yang, Yuan 杨远
1978   西汉盐、铁、工官的地理分布 (The Geographical Distribution of the Yen-Kuan, Tieh-Kuan, and Kung-Kuan in the Former Han Dynasty). 中国文化研究所学报 [*Journal of Chinese Studies*] 9:219–244.

Yang, Zhefeng 杨哲峰
2009   渭北西汉帝陵布局设计之观察 (Layout of Western Han Mausoleums in the North Bank of the Wei River). 文物 [*Cultural Relics*] 2009(4):61–68.

Yantielun Jiaozhu 盐铁论校注
1992   盐铁论校注 [*Yantielun Jiaozhu*], by Huan Kuan 桓宽, annotated by Wang Liqi 王利器. 北京 Beijing: 中华书局 Zhonghua Press.

Yao, Alice
2016   *The Ancient Highlands of Southwest China: From the Bronze Age to the Han Empire*. Oxford: Oxford University Press.
2020   The Great Wall as Destination? Archaeology of Migration and Settlers under the Han Empire. In, *Archaeologies of Empire: Local Participants and Imperial Trajectories*. Anna L. Boozer, Bleda Düring and Bradley J. Parker (eds.), Pp. 57–88. Albuquerque: University of New Mexico Press.

Yates, Robin D. S.
2002   Slavery in Early China: A Socio-cultural Approach. *Journal of East Asian Archaeology* 3(1–2):283–331.

Yin, Hongbing 尹弘兵
2019   楚都纪南城探析: 基于考古与出土文献新资料的考察 (Investigation of the Chu Capital Jinancheng: A Synthetical Study of Archaeological and New Unearthed Documents). 历史地理研究 [*The Chinese Historical Geography*] 2019(2):46–57.

Yinxu [Yinxu Xiaomintun Kaogudui 殷墟孝民屯考古队]
2007   河南安阳市孝民屯商代铸铜遗址 2003~2004 年的发掘 (A Report on the Excavation of a Shang Bronze Casting Workshop in Xiaomintun, Anyang). 考古 [*Archaeology*] 2007(1):14–25.

Yiyang, and Yiyangshi [Yiyangshi Wenwu Guanlichu 益阳市文物管理处, and Yiyangshi Bowuguan 益阳市博物馆]
2008   益阳楚墓 [*Yiyang Chu Tombs*]. Beijing 北京: Cultural Relics Press 文物出版社.

Yongcheng [Yongcheng Kaogudui 雍城考古队]
1980   凤翔县高庄战国秦墓发掘简报 (A Brief Report on the Excavation of Qin Tombs at Gaozhuang, Fengxiang). 文物 [*Cultural Relics*] 1980(9):10–14, 31.
1985   陕西凤翔县大辛村遗址发掘简报 (Preliminary Report on the Excavation of the Daxincun Site in Fengxiang County, Shaanxi). 考古与文物 [*Archaeology and Cultural Relics*] 1985(1):38–44.
1986   陕西凤翔西村战国秦墓发掘简报 (Report on the Excavation of Qin Tombs in the Warring States Period at Xicun in Fengxiang, Shaanxi). 考古与文物 [*Archaeology and Cultural Relics*] 1986(1):52–64.

Yu, Xi 喻曦, and Li, Lingfu 李令福
2012   浅析秦汉上林苑农业的多功能性 (Study on the Multifunctional Agriculture of Shanglin Garden of the Western Han Dynasty). 中国农史 [*Agricultural History of China*] 2012(3):3–10.

Yu, Ying-shih
1977   The Han Period. In, *Food in Chinese Culture: Anthropological and Historical Pespectives*, Chang Kwang-chih (ed.), Pp. 23–53. New Heaven, CT: Yale University Press.

Yu, Weichao 俞伟超, and Gao, Ming 高明
1985[1978, 1979] 周代用鼎制度 (The Ritual System of Ding in the Zhou Dynasty). In, 先秦两汉考古学论文集 [*A Collection of Papers Related to the Pre-Qin and Han*

Dynasties Archaeology]. Yu Weichao 俞伟超 (ed.), Pp. 62–114. 北京 Beijing: 文物出版社 Cultural Relics Press.

Yu, Zhenbo 于振波
2006   走马楼吴简师佐籍蠡测 (The Registers of Shi and Zuo as Seen in the Wu Slips Unearthed at Zoumalou, Changsha). 汉学研究 [*Sinology Research*] 24(2):41–69.

Yuan, Jing, and Flad, Rowan K.
2005   New Zooarchaeological Evidence for Changes in Shang Dynasty Animal Sacrifice. *Journal of Anthropologcial Archaeology* 24(3):252–270.

Yuan, Yansheng 袁延胜
2018   秦汉简牍户籍资料研究 [*Research on the Household Census Information in Bamboo Slips and Wooden Tablets during the Qin and Han Periods*]. 北京 Beijing: 人民出版社 People's Publishing House.

Yuan, Zhongyi 袁仲一, and Liu, Yu 刘钰
2009   秦陶文新编 [*New Edited Volume of Qin Pottery Inscriptions*]. 北京 Beijing: 文物出版社 Cultural Relics Press.

Zaccagnini, Carlo
1990   The Transition from Bronze to Iron in the Near East and in the Levant: Marginal Notes. *Journal of the American Oriental Society* 110(3):493–502.

Zang, Zhifei 臧知非
2012   秦汉赋役与社会控制 [*The Tax and Corvée System in the Qin-Han Period and Social Management*]. 西安 Xi'an: 三秦出版社 Sanqin Press.
2017   秦汉土地赋役制度研究 [*Research on the Land and Tax System of the Qin-Han Periods*]. 北京 Beijing: 中央编译出版社 Central Compilation & Translation Press.

Zeder, Melinda A.
1988   Understanding Urban Process through the Study of Specialized Subsistence Economy in the Near East. *Journal of Anthropological Archaeology* 7:1–55.

Zeder, Melinda A., Lemoine, Ximena, and Payne, Sebastian
2015   A New System for Computing Long-bone Fusion Age Profiles in Sus Scrofa. *Journal of Archaeolical Science* 55:135–150.

Zhang, Guoshuo 张国硕, and Tang, Jieyuan 汤洁娟
2017   中原地区早期冶铁问题分析 (On Issues Related to Early Smelted Iron in the Central Plains). 中原文物 [*Cultural Relics of Central China*] 2017(2):64–69.

Zhang, Hong 张弘
2003   战国秦汉时期商人和商业资本研究 [*Research on Merchants and Commercial Capital in the Warring States and Qin-Han Periods*]. 济南 Jinan: 齐鲁书社 Qilu Press.

Zhang, Jianfeng 张建锋
2016   汉长安城地区城市水利设施和水利系统的考古学研究 [*Archaeological Research about the Urban Water Conservancy Facilities and System of Han Chang'an Area*]. 北京 Beijing: 科学出版社 Science Press.

Zhang, Jihai 张继海
2006   汉代城市社会 [*A Study of the Urban Society in Han China*]. 北京 Beijing: 社会科学文献出版社 Social Science Academic Press.
2015   The Residential Wards of Western Han Chang'an. In, *Chang'an 26 BCE: An Augustan Age in China*. Michael Nylan and Griet Vankeerberghen (eds.), Pp. 175–200. Seattle: University of Washington Press.

Zhang, Jinguang 张金光
2013   战国秦社会经济形态新探 [*New Exploration of Socio-economic Formation in the Warring States and Qin Dynasty*]. 北京 Beijing: 商务印书馆 The Commercial Press.

Zhang, Junmin 张俊民
2007   简牍文书所见"长安"资料辑考 (Records about Chang'an in Excavated Bamboo Slips), 武汉大学简帛研究中心 (Center of Bamboo Silk Manuscript of Wuhan University), 简帛网 [*Jianbowang*], 2007.12.8, http://www.bsm.org.cn/show_article.php?id=757.

Zhang, Mengyi, Li, Yingfu, Xiong, Zhaoming, Li, Shijia, and Li, Yuniu
2020   Iron Production and Trading in Lingnan during the Qin and Han Dynasties. *Antiquity* 94(373)e4:1–6.

Zhang, Tianen 张天恩
1987   宝鸡市谭家村四号汉墓 (Han Tomb No. 4 at Tanjiacun in Baoji City). 考古 [*Archaeology*] 1987(12):1086–1090, 1158.

Zhang, Tianyu 张天宇, Zhang, Ji 张吉, Huang, Fengchun 黄风春, and Chen, Jianli 陈建立
2020   叶家山 M111 出土的商代铁援铜戈 (Discovery of Bronze Ge-dagger with Iron Yuan-blade of the Shang Dynasty in Tomb M111 at the Yejiashan Cemetery). 南方文物 [*Southern Cultural Relics*] 2020(2):110–115.

Zhang, Tongxin 张童心, and Huang, Yongjiu 黄永久
1993   夏县禹王城庙后辛庄战国手工业作坊遗址调查简报 (A Brief Report on the Warring States Handicraft Workshops at Miaohou Xinzhuang in Yuwangcheng, Xia County). 文物季刊 [*Journal of Chinese Antiquity*] 1993(2):11–16.

Zhang, Wanzhong 张万钟
1997   从侯马出土的工具范试论青铜农具的铸造与使用 (Study on Bronze Agricultural Tools Casting and Utilization Based on the Tools Molds from Houma). 中国历史博物馆馆刊 [*Bulletin of The National Museum*] 1997(1):57–64.

Zhang, Xiande 张先得, and Zhang, Xianlu 张先禄
1990   北京平谷刘家河商代铜钺铁刃的分析鉴定 (Metallurgical Analysis of the Iron-edged Bronze Yue-Axe from Liujiahe, Pinggu, Beijing). 文物 [*Cultural Relics*] 1990(7):66–71.

Zhang, Xinrui 张昕瑞
2017   汉阳陵出土铁器制作工艺与保存现状研究 [*Study on the Manufacturing Technique and Preservation of the Iron Objects Unearthed from Han Yangling*], 西北大学硕士论文 Master thesis, Northwest University.

Zhang, Zhaoyang 张朝阳
2019   东汉临湘县交址来客案例详考——兼论早期南方贸易网络 (A Detailed Study on the Case of Jiaozhi Visitors to Linxiang County in Eastern Han Dynasty: Early Trade Networks in the South). 中山大学学报(社会科学版) [*Journal of Sun Yat-sen University(Social Science Edition)*] 2019(1):78–84.

Zhang, Zhenming 张振明 (ed.)
2009   古荥镇汉代冶铁遗址 [*A Han Iron Production Site at Guxingzhen*]. 扬州 Yangzhou: 广陵书社 Guangling Shushe.

Zhang, Zhongyi 张中一
1959   陕西长安洪庆村秦汉墓第二次发掘简记 (Preliminary Report on the Second Excavation of Qin and Han Tombs at Hongqincun in Chang'an County, Shaanxi). 考古 [*Archaeology*] 1959(12):662–667.

Zhangjiashan [张家山二四七号汉墓竹简整理小组 Zhangjiashan 247 hao Hanmu zhujian zhenglixiaozu] (ed.)
2001   张家山汉墓竹简(二四七号墓) [*Bamboo Slips from the Zhangjiashan Han Tomb (No. 247)*]. 北京 Beijing: 文物出版社 Cultural Relics Press.

Zhangsun, Yingzi, Liu, Ruiliang, and Jin, Zhengyao et al.
2017   Lead Isotope Analyses Revealed the Key Role of Chang'an in the Mirror Production and Distribution Network during the Han Dynasty. *Archaeometry* 59(4):685–713.

Zhao, Chunyan 赵春燕, Li, Zhipeng 李志鹏, and Yuan, Jing 袁靖
2015   河南省安阳市殷墟遗址出土马与猪牙釉质的锶同位素比值分析 (Strontium Isotopic Analysis of Horse and Pig Teeth in the Yinxu Site, Anyang, Henan). 南方文物 [*Southern Cultural Relics*] 2015(3):77–80, 112.

Zhao, Fengyan, Sun, Manli, Li, Xiuhui, Guo, Fei, and Li, Mengyu
2020   The Manufacturing Technology of Iron Swords from the Capital of the Han Empire in China. *SN Applied Science* 2, 1510.

Zhao, Huacheng 赵化成
1997   宝鸡市益门村二号春秋墓族属管见 (Analysis of the Ethnicity of the Spring-and-Autumn Tomb No. 2 at Yimencun, Baoji). 考古与文物 [*Archaeology and Cultural Relics*] 1997(1):31–34.
2006   从商周"集中公墓制"到秦汉"独立陵园制"的演化轨迹   (The Development Trail from Collective Cemetery to Individual Mausoleum). 文物 [*Cultural Relics*] 2006(7):41–48.
2012   The Application and Production of Iron. In, *The History of Chinese Civilization* (vol. 1). Yuan Xingpei, Yan Wenming, Zhang Chuanxi and Lou Yulie (eds.), Pp. 312–46. Cambridge: Cambridge University Press.

Zhao, Qingyun 赵青云, Li, Jinghua 李京华, Han, Rubin 韩汝玢, Qiu, Lianghui 丘亮辉, and Ke, Jun 柯俊
1985   巩县铁生沟汉代冶铁遗址再探讨 (A Re-investigation of the Remains of the Iron and Steel Works of the Han Dynasty at Tieshenggou, Henan). 考古学报 [*Acta Archaeologica Sinica*] 1985(2):157–183.

Zhao, Xueqian 赵学谦, and Liu, Suisheng 刘随盛
1963   陕西宝鸡福临堡东周墓葬发掘记 (Excavation of Eastern Zhou Tombs at Fulingbao Site in Baoji, Shaanxi). 考古 [*Archaeology*] 1963(10):536–543.

Zhao, Yipeng 赵艺蓬, Chong, Jianrong 种建荣, and Chen, Gang 陈钢
2012   陕西杨凌邰城汉代铸铁作坊遗址 (The Han Iron Foundry at Taicheng in Yangling, Shaanxi). In, 中国文物报 [*China Cultural Relics News*], 2012/3/16, p. 8.

Zhao, Zhijun 赵志军
2010   植物考古学: 理论、方法和实践 [*Paleoethnobotany: Theories, Methods and Practice*]. 北京 Beijing: 科学出版社 Science Press.
2020   临淄齐故城阚家寨遗址B区第Ⅱ和第Ⅲ地点植物浮选结果及分析   (Plant Remains from the Locality of Area BII and BIII at Kanjiazhai Site, Linzi City Site of the Qi State, Shandong Province). In, 临淄齐故城冶铸业考古 [*Archaeology of Metallurgy and Foundry Industry in the Linzi City Site of Qi State*]. Zhongguo Shehui Kexueyuan Kaogu Yanjiusuo 中国社会科学院考古研究所 et al. (eds.), Pp. 772–794. 北京 Beijing: 科学出版社 Science Press.

Zhejiang [Zhejiangsheng Wenwu Kaogu Yanjiusuo 浙江省文物考古研究所]
2009   浙江越墓 [*Yue Tombs in Zhejiang*]. 北京 Beijing: 科学出版社 Science Press.

Zhejiang, and Deqing [Zhejiangsheng Wenwu Kaogu Yanjiusuo 浙江省文物考古研究所, and Deqingxian Bowuguan 德清县博物馆]

2011   德清亭子桥: 战国原始瓷窑址发掘报告 [*Deqing Tingziqiao: Excavation Report on the Proto-porcelain Kilns*]. 北京 Beijing: 文物出版社 Cultural Relics Press.

Zhengzhou [Zhengzhoushi Bowuguan 郑州市博物馆]

1978   郑州古荥镇汉代冶铁遗址发掘简报 (*Preliminary Report on the Excavatoin of the Ironworks in Guxingzhen, Zhengzhou*). 文物 [*Cultural Relics*] 1978(2): 28–43.

Zhongguo Kexueyuan [Zhongguo Kexueyuan Kaogu Yanjiusuo 中国科学院考古研究所]

1962   沣西发掘报告: 1955–1957年陕西长安县沣西乡考古发掘资料 [*Excavation Report on Fengxi: Excavation at Fengxi Village, Chang'an County, Shaanxi 1955–1957*]. 北京 Beijing: 文物出版社 Cultural Relics Press.

Zhongguo Kuangcang [Zhongguo Kuangcang Faxianshi. Shaanxijuan Bianweihui 中国矿藏发现史. 陕西卷编委会] (ed.)

1996   中国矿藏发现史: 陕西卷 [*Discovery History of Mineral Ores in China – Shaanxi Volume*]. 北京 Beijing: 地质出版社 Geology Press.

Zhongguo Shehui [Zhongguo Shehui Kexueyuan Kaogu Yanjiusuo 中国社会科学院考古研究所]

1987   殷墟发掘报告, 1958–1961 [*A Report of the Excavation of Yinxu*, 1958–1961]. 北京 Beijing: 文物出版社 Cultural Relics Press.

1995   1992年汉长安冶铸遗址发掘简报 (Excavation of an Iron Foundry Site at Han Chang'an City, 1992). 考古 [*Archaeology*] 1995(9):792–798.

1996a 汉长安城未央宫:1980–1989年考古发掘报告 [*Site Report on the Excavation of the Weiyang Palace: 1980–1989*]. 北京 Beijing: 中国大百科全书出版社 Encyclopedia of China Publishing House.

1996b 宣帝杜陵陵园遗址 [*Excavation of Duling Mausolueum of Empeor Xuan*]. 北京 Beijing: 科学出版社 Science Press.

1997   1996年汉长安冶铸遗址发掘简报 (Excavation of an Iron Foundry Site at Han Chang'an City, 1996). 考古 [*Archaeology*] 1997(7):5–12.

2003   西汉礼制建筑遗址 [*The Site of Ritual Buildings of the Western Han period*]. 北京 Beijing: 文物出版社 Cultural Relics Press.

2004   安阳小屯 [*Xiaotung in Anyang*]. 北京 Beijing: 世界图书出版公司 World Publishing Cooperation.

2005   汉长安城武库 [*The Arsenal Site in Han Chang'an*]. 北京 Beijing: 文物出版社 Cultural Relics Press.

2007   南邠州.碾子坡 [*The Nianzipo Site in Nanbinzhou*]. 北京 Beijing: 世界图书出版公司 World Publishing Corporation.

2010   中国考古学 (秦汉卷) [*Chinese Archaeology: Qin and Han*]. 北京 Beijing: 中国社会科学出版社 China Social Science Press.

2020   安阳孝民屯三 (殷商遗存·铸铜遗物) [*Anyang Xiaomintun III: Late Shang Bronze Foundry Remains*]. 北京 Beijing: 文物出版社 Cultural Relics Press.

Zhongguo Shehui, and Jinan [Zhongguo Shehui Kexueyuan Kaogu Yanjiusuo中国社会科学院考古研究所, and Jinanshi Kaogu Yanjiusuo 济南市考古研究所]

2018   山东济南魏家庄墓地出土铁器的保护修复 [*Conservation and Restoration of Iron Objects Unearthed from Weijiazhuang Cemetery in Jinan, Shandong*]. 北京 Beijing: 故宫出版社 Gugong Press.

Zhongguo Shehui, and Riben [Zhongguo Shehui Kexueyuan Kaogu Yanjiusuo 中国社会科学院考古研究所, and Riben Nailiang Guoli Wenhuacai Yanjiusuo 日本奈良国立文化财研究所]

2007 汉长安城桂宫:1996–2001年考古发掘报告 [*Gui Palace in Han Chang'an City: Report on the Excavation from 1996–2001*]. 北京 Beijing: 文物出版社 Cultural Relics Press.

Zhongguo Shehui, and Xi'anshi Yanjiuyuan [Zhongguo Shehui Kexueyuan Kaogu Yanjiusuo 中国社会科学院考古研究所, and Xi'anshi Wenwu Baohu Kaogu Yanjiuyuan 西安市文物保护考古研究院]

2018 秦汉上林苑——2004–2012年考古报告 [*Shanglinyuan in the Qin and Han Dynasties: Archaeological Report 2004–2012*]. 北京 Beijing: 文物出版社 Cultural Relics Press.

Zhongguo Shehui et al. [Zhongguo Shehui Kexueyuan Kaogu Yanjiusuo 中国社会科学院考古研究所, Shandonsheng Wenwu Kaogu Yanjiuyuan 山东省文物考古研究院, and Ziboshi Linziqu Qiwenhua Fazhan Yanjiu Zhongxin 淄博市临淄区齐文化发展研究中心]

2020 临淄齐故城冶铸业考古 [*Archaeology of Metallurgy and Foundry Industry in the Linzi City Site of Qi State*]. 北京 Beijing: 科学出版社 Science Press.

Zhongguo Shehui Anyang [Zhongguo Shehuikexueyuan Kaogu Yanjiusuo Anyang Gongzuodui中国社会科学院考古研究所安阳工作队]

2006 2000–2001年安阳孝民屯东南地段铸铜遗址发掘报告 (A Brief Report on the Excavation of a Bronze Casting Workshop in Southeastern Xiaomintun, Anyang). 考古学报 [*Acta Archaeologica Sinica*] 2006(3):351–381.

Zhongguo Shehui Chang'an [Zhongguo Shehui Kexueyuan Kaogu Yanjiusuo Han Chang'ancheng Gongzuodui 中国社会科学院考古研究所汉长安城工作队]

2018 西安市汉长安城遗址直城门大街试掘简报 (Preliminary Report on the Zhichengmen Road in the Han Chang'an City, Xi'an). 考古 [*Archaeology*] 2018(11):34–49.

Zhongguo Shehui Chang'an, and Xi'anshi Yanjiuyuan [Zhongguo Shehui Kexueyuan Kaogu Yanjiusuo Han Chang'ancheng Gongzuodui 中国社会科学院考古研究所汉长安城工作队, and Xi'anshi Wenwu Baohu Kaogu Yanjiuyuan 西安市文物保护考古研究院]

2014 西安市大白杨村汉墓发掘简报 (The Excavation of the Tombs of the Han Dynasty in Dabaiyang Village, Xi'an City). 考古 [*Archaeology*] 2014(10):16–28.

2017 西安市莲湖区三民村西汉大型建筑遗址发掘简报 (The Excavation of a Large-scale Architectural Foundation of the Western Han Dynasty at Sanmin Village in Lianhu District, Xi'an City). 考古 [*Archaeology*] 2017(1):17–28.

Zhongguo Shehui Hancheng [Zhongguo Shehui Kexueyuan Kaogu Yanjiusuo Hanchengdui 中国社会科学院考古研究所汉城队]

1994 汉长安城窑址发掘报告 (Excavation of Kiln Sites at Han Chang'an City). 考古学报 [*Acta Archaeologica Sinica*] 1994(10):99–129.

Zhongguo Shehui Hanchenggongzuo [Zhongguo Shehui Kexueyuan Kaogu Yanjiusuo Hancheng Gongzuodui 中国社会科学院考古研究所汉城工作队]

1994 汉长安城23—27号窑址发掘简报 (Preliminary Report on the Excavation of Kilns No. 23–27 at Han Chang'an City). 考古 [*Archaeology*] 1994(11):986–996.

Zhongguo Shehui Shaanxi [Zhongguo Shehui Kexueyuan Kaogu Yanjiusou Shaanxi Liudui 中国社会科学院考古研究所陕西六队]

1988 陕西兰田泄湖战国墓发掘简报 (Preliminary Report on the Warring States Tombs at Xiehu in Lantian, Shaanxi). 考古 [*Archaeology*] 1988(12):1084–1089.

Zhongguo Shehui Tangchengdui [Zhongguo Shehui Kexueyuan Kaogusuo Tangchengdui 中国社会科学院考古所唐城队]

1991　西安北郊汉墓发掘报告 (Report on the Excavation of Han Tombs on the Northern Suburbs of Xi'an). 考古学报 [*Acta Archaeologica Sinica*] 1991(2):240–267.

Zhongguo Shehui Wugong [Zhongguo Shehui Kexueyuan Kaogu Yanjiusuo Wugong Fajuedui 中国社会科学院考古研究所武功发掘队]

1996　陕西武功县赵家来东周时期的秦墓 (Excavation of Qin Tombs in the Eastern Zhou Period at Zhaojialai in Wugong, Shaanxi). 考古 [*Archaeology*] 1996(12):44–48.

Zhongguo Yejin [Zhongguo Yejinshi Bianxiezu 中国冶金史编写组]

1978　从古荥遗址看汉代生铁冶炼技术 (Ancient Cast Iron Technology during the Han Peroid Based upon Evidence from Guxing). 文物 [*Cultural Relics*] 1978(2):27, 44–47.

Zhouyuan [Zhouyuan Kaogudui 周原考古队]

2007　周原庄李西周铸铜遗址2003 与2004 年春季发掘报告 (The Excavation of the Bronze Casting Remains in Locus West of Zhuangli Village at Zhouyuan Site in the Springs of 2003 and 2004). 考古学报 [*Acta Archaeologica Sinica*] 2011(2):246–300.

Zhouyuan, Bowuguan 周原博物馆

2001　陕西扶风县官务汉墓清理发掘简报 (Preliminary Report on the Excavation of Han Tombs at Guanwu in Fufeng, Shaanxi). 考古与文物 [*Archaeology and Cultural Relics*] 2001(5):17–29.

Zhou, Zhenhe 周振鹤

1999　西汉县城特殊职能探讨 (Research on the Special Functions and Duties of the Xian Local Government in the Western Han Period). In, 周振鹤自选集 [*Collection of Zhou Zhenhe Academic Works*], Pp. 15–35. 桂林 Guilin: 广西师范大学出版社 Guangxi Normal University Press.

Zhou, Zhenhe 周振鹤, Li, Xiaojie 李晓杰, and Zhang, Li 张莉

2016　中国行政区划通史 (秦汉卷) [*General History of the Administrative Division in China (Vol. Qin-Han)*]. 上海 Shanghai: 复旦大学出版社 Fudan University Press.

Zhu, Chenlu 朱晨露, and Zhao, Juntao 赵钧陶

2018　西汉帝陵朝向新探 (A New Exploration of the Mausoleums of Western Han Dynasty). 西北大学学报(哲学社会科学版) [*Journal of Northwest University (Philosophy and Social Sciences Edition*] 48(2):96–104.

Zhu, Shiguang 朱士光, Wang, Yuanlin 王元林, and Huling, Gui 呼林贵

1998　历史时期关中地区气候变化的初步研究 (Study of Climate Variations in the Region of Guanzhong in the Historical Period). 第四纪研究 [*Quaternary Sciences*] 1998(1):1–10.

Zhuang, Huaizhi 庄蕙芷

2016　论汉代车马出行图的形式与墓室结构的关系 (On the Relationship between the Chariot-parade Murals and the Burial Structure). 中国美术研究 [*Research of Chinese Fine Arts*] 2016(3):13–24.

Zhuangzi jishi 庄子集释

2013　庄子集释 [*Zhuangzi jishi*], annotated by Guo Qingfan 郭庆藩. 北京 Beijing: 中华书局 Zhonghua Press.

Zhuo, Zhenxi 禚振西

1980　陕西户县两座汉墓 (Two Han Tombs in Huxian, Shaanxi). 考古与文物 [*Archaeology and Cultural Relics*] 1:46–52.

Zierden, Martha A., and Reitz, Elizabeth J.
2009   Animal Use and the Urban Landscape in Colonial Charleston, South Caro-
    lina, USA. *International Journal of Historical Archaeology* 13:327–365.

Zou, Shuijie 邹水杰
2008   两汉县行政研究 [*Research of the County Administration of the Han Periods*].
    长沙 Changsha: 湖南人民出版社 Hunan People's Publishing House.

Index

agricultural production: capital region 70; Han period 66, 106; Warring States period 32

Analects (*lunyu*): 223–224

assembly-line production 16, 126, 131

axe: Chu state 42; Jin states 40–41; Niucun 130–133; Taicheng 110; *yue* 34; Zhonghang 135–137

belt hook: Han period 205, 208; Jin states 40–41, 131; Meixian 79; Qin 48–49, 192, 197–200

bimetallic weapons: Shang bimetallic *yue* 34; in southern China 36; in Spring-and-Autumn period 34–35

bloomery iron 13, 24, 32–38, 51, 89, 93

Book of Poetry (*Shijing*): 29

bronze: bells 200, 208; belt-hooks 79, 131, 192, 198–199, 208, 214; bracelets 198, 201, 208; chariot 54, 192, 198, 208 (*see also* copper); knives 198–201; mirrors (*lianhu jin*) 4, 24, 78, 86, 104–105, 186, 192–193, 197–202, 207–209; pattern block 130; vessels 36, 70, 78, 130, 139, 149, 208; weaponry 41–42, 127, 137

bronze foundry: Dawuliu 135 (*see also* Houma (Niucun)); Kanjiazhai 105 (*see also* Zhonghang)

canal: Bai canal 66; Cao canal 67, 70, 193; Chenggou canal 68; Liufu canal 67; Longshou canal 66; transportation 193

capital region (Guanzhong): analysis of iron objects in 87; bronze mint 78 (*see also* canal; Chang'an); ceramic production 82; craft industry in 77, 82; food production 60; Guanzhong-central policies 8; Huizhongdao 207; iron production 82, 110–114; irrigation network 60, 66; Jingshicang 68; land route 70; manufacturing luxury products 78 (*see also* mausoleum); Meixiang 79; Nangucheng 79–80, 82; ore deposits 68 (*see also* Passes); population density 61; *sanfu* 58, 78, 82; Taicang 68 (*see also* Taicheng); topo-geography 59–60; transformation 58; transportation system 61, 66–69; Xiliu 68; Yaoshang 78 (*see also* Yongcheng and Yueyang); Zhaolun village 78 (*see also* agricultural production)

cast iron production: grey cast iron 93, 110, 114 (*see also* iron (steel)); labor force 30, 33, 39, 52, 89–92; mottled cast iron 99; technique 32–33, 217; transition 30–32, 39 (*see also* decarburization)

casting molds: in Chang'an 77, 78; in Dongpingling 103; in Houma 130–131; in Kanjiazhai 105; mother-molds in Wafangzhuang 101, 115; pattern block 130; plowshare molds in Wafangzhuang 101; in Taicheng 108; in Zhonghang 135

Central Plains 112, 159

ceramic inscription 47, 52, 98, 141

Cha spade 37, 110, 209

Chang'an: Bacheng gate 62; Changle palace 62–63; coin minting 73, 78; Dongdi 62; Dongshi 63–64; Gui palace 63; Jianzhang palace 62; kilns 77; layout 62; Luli 63–64; luxury good workshop 68; marketplace 63; Mingguang palace 63; north-south axis 62–63 (*see also* population;

Shanglin yuan); transportation hub of the entire Guanzhong 9, 61, 69; Weiyang palace 63; Wuku 62; Xishi 63–64, 193; Zhicheng gate 62

Changlong (Longdong): 30, 44, 198

Changsha: Chu tombs 55; crop yield 179; iron in 41–42; Yangjiashan 39; Zoumalou 85

Chengqiao 38

chidao 9, 61

Chu state: Baoshan 42; capital (Jinancheng) 41–42 (*see also* Changsha); iron technology 31, 38–39, 41–43; Jiudian 42; Tianxingguan 42; Xiashi 36; Yangying 38–39; Yiyang area 42; Zuozhong 42

commodities: alienable objects 14; coinage system 51, 185; gift and 14–17; in Han period 16, 25, 182

connectivity: circulation of goods 17, 225; definition 6–7, 11–12, 148, 176, 216; integration 183, 186, 188–192; network-based approached 5–6; periphery perspective of 7; relationship between the core and various parts 7, 222; represented by changes in iron production 13, 16, 107, 216, 225; social relationship 15–17; transformation of social lives 10

copper price 208–209; transmission via the Silk Road 30, 53; *see also* bronze

Costin, C. 120–124, 155–157, 176

daitian 57, 61, 83

decarburization: decarburized cast iron in Changsha 39; decarburized steel in Jiudian 42; kilns (furnaces) for 99, 104; malleable iron 89, 93–95, 114; steel made of solid-state cast iron 89, 94, 96 (*see also* Taicheng (analysis of iron)); Tanghu 39

Dongpingling: aligning pattern of features 141; cupola furnaces 92; iron ingots 103 (*see also* ironworks (Dongpingling)); *taiyi* 103

duhui 101–102

embeddedness: deep economic 156; ▓▓mic 21, 154–155, 238; faunal ▓▓6–159; Polanyi 154; ▓▓c economic 156

Erligang 41, 48

Eurasian steppes: early iron technology 29; interaction with Central or West Asia 33; technology transmission 32, 36, 54 (*see also* Xiongnu)

food: body-part assemblage 164–166, 171–173; intensity of craft specialization 152, 155 (*see also* Kanjiazhai (faunal remains and palaeobotanical remains)); kill-off pattern 166–168, 173–175; market supply 156, 158–159, 161, 169, 171–172, 175, 177; pattern of independent household production 158, 161, 176; pattern of nucleated and retainer workshop 155–158; price 160–161; procurement 152–154; Qijia stone earring workshop 165 (*see also* Taicheng (faunal remains and palaeobotanical remains)); urban food-chain 155–156, 177 (*see also* Zhonghang (faunal assemblage))

Franklin, Ursula 126–127

frontier: northern 9, 22, 24, 62, 68; northwestern 3,8–10, 22, 160, 180; southern (Linxiang) 3, 43, 52, 71, 115

Funiu mountain 102

furnace: blast furnace at Guxingzhen 99; blast furnaces at Minguo ironworks 91–92; blast furnace at Wanchenggang 91; cupola furnace at Dongpinglin 92, 103

globalization 4–5, 10

Gong Yu 140, 150; *see also* Han government (Yushi dafu)

Great Unity 3–4, 23

Guandong: definition 8; ironworks 96–107; relocation 51, 61, 66, 84

Guanghan 70

Guxingzhen: aligning pattern of features 141 (*see also* furnace (Blast furnace at Guxingzhen)); iron office 99, 106; Songshan Mountain cluster 99

Han government: Dasinong 71–75, 85; expansion 3–5; Gongguan 85, 139, 150, 208, 213; Jiuqing 70; Sangong 70; Shanglin Zhongguan 78; Shaofu 70, 74, 85; Shuiheng Duwei 78; Xianling 73, 79; Xiaotieguan 75, 98; Yushi dafu 14, 140, 150; Zuo/You caitie 71

Han state (Warring state) 55, 102, 134

Han tombs: Han-style artifacts in 3–4; structure 204

Hedong commandery 105

Henan commandery: bronze weapon production 193; ironworks 99

Hexi: corridor 8, 34, 60–61, 160, 207, 222; Dunhuang 2; Juyan 1–2; transportation of grain 68, 83; Xiyu 2

hoe-head: from Erligang 41; molds from Dongpinglin 103; molds from Nangucheng 80; molds from Taicheng 80, 108, 143–146; molds from Zhonghang 135, 137

Houma: distribution of remains 130–134; Niucun foundry 128–130

imperialism: definition 5, 23; imperial process 7, 12, 14, 183

integration: connection 36, 53, 147 (*see also* connectivity); of market system 5; network 17, 19, 33, 148, 183, 193, 206, 211, 220; regional 22, 184–188, 190, 206–210, 212, 220; transportation of iron 73, 106, 210, 220

iron implements: cauldrons 112, 197, 205, 211; digging tools 48, 192, 197, 205 (*see also* hoe-head); ingot 103 (*see also jue* axe); knives 4, 40–41, 48–49, 50, 107, 110–112, 197, 199, 201, 205, 211; lamps 107–108, 112, 197, 205; pickaxe 40 (*see also* plowshare); price 208–209; sword 38–39, 42–43, 48, 94–95, 107, 110–111, 197–198, 205, 211; vessels 108, 110, 197, 205, 207, 218; weapons 32, 34, 39, 41–43, 48, 50, 55, 73, 102–103, 197–198, 217; *see also* bimetallic weapons

iron (steel) making technique: annealing 93–94; bloomery iron 34, 89 (*see also* cast iron production); direct process 94; facilities 33; fined iron (*chaogang*) 94; fuel 91 (*see also* furnace); Lingnan 107; meteoric iron 34; mining 90–91; regional development 40–53; smelting and casting 91–92; solid-state decarburization 94, 96; underdeveloped pattern 52–53; welding 94

iron management: economies 14 (*see also* iron office); office merchant (Kong Jing) 74–75, 84; merchant (Mr. Zhuo) 71, 74, 85; system 71

iron office: administration 106 (*see also* Han government (xiaotieguan)); *heyi* and *hesan* 99; labor 140; location 97–99; Nanyang commandery 101–102; *taiyi* 103; tieguan in Liye 71

ironworks: broader Central Plains 97; Cangcheng 135; clustering pattern 105, 107; Dawuliu 135; Dongpinglin 103; Guxingzhen 99–100; Handan 105; Huize 124–125; labor force 138; Linzi (Kanjiazhai) 103–105, 141; Minguo period 91–92; Nanyang basin cluster 101–102; Nanzhao 101–102; regional labor division 106, 112–113, 218, 220; Songshan cluster 99 (*see also* Taicheng); Taishan cluster 102–105; Tengguo Guchen 105; Tieshengguo 99–100; Wafangzhuang 101; Wanchenggang 102; Xiahewan 101; Xiping-Wugang area 102; Yuwangcheng 105 (*see also* Zhonghang)

Jin states: Changzi 40; Fengshuiling 40–41; iron development 41; Tianma-Qucun 37

Jing and Luo river 60

Jingdi 42, 60, 160

jue axe: Erligang 41; Zhonghang 135–136

Jundushan 35

Jun-xian (commandery-county): 3, 6

Kanjiazhai: aligning pattern 141; bronze foundry 104–105; faunal remains 163, 170; iron industry 104; palaeobotanical remains 176

Korean peninsula 4

labor: food ration for *tu* 139, 150; *gong* 139; *nu* slave 140; rebellion 90, 114, 140; *tu* convict labor 138–140; *yong* waged laborers 138–139, 148, 160; *zu* conscript laborers 138–140

lacquerware: black-and-red designs 4; *gong* or slave production 139–140; industry 24, 75; long distance trade 185–186

Lao Kan 1

Li wards 3, 47, 62, 113

Liangdaicun 35

Linzi: aligning pattern of features 141; animal consumption 163–164, 170;

botanical records 176; bronze mirror production 104, 193; iron production 104–105 (*see also* Kanjiazhai); production system 105
Liu Bang 59
Liu Jing 59
Liu Zhiwei 223–225, 227
Liye 52, 71, 226
long-distance trade 5, 18, 22, 107, 185–186
Luoyang 24, 39, 59, 83, 105

market: administration 184; administrative-integrated model 191, 210; dendritic model 190, 202, 209–210; economic rationality 224; equifinality 192, 214; fall-off distribution 187; fully-integrated model 191, 211–212; household distribution approach 187; marketplace exchange 183; multi-layer process 186; normal and abnormal 188; regional scale mechanism of 210; scene of marketplaces 185; *shihuo* system 224–225 (*see also* commodities)
mass production 17, 101, 127, 132, 147, 223–225
mausoleum: craft production 66; parks 65; population 65–66; satellite cities 66, 82, 217; storage pits 65; structure 83; town 57, 61, 64–66, 70, 78–79
Mauss, M.: 14
meteoric iron 34, 36, 54
middle Yangtze river valley: Bojiawang 54; Dajiayuan 38; iron production 38; Liulinxi 38; Shangmonao 38; Xianglinggang 38; Xiangzikou 54; Yangying 38–39, 43, 55; Zhangjiaping 54
Mogou cemetery 33
monopoly: criticism of the state monopoly 14; economic benefit 75 (*see also* Han government (xiaotieguan)); implementation 74; lifting 76; state-owned industry 75

Nangucheng 79–80, 82, 108
Nanyang 74, 101–102; *see also* Wafangzhuang
Niucun: bronze foundry 128–129; division of labor 136; intra-site distribution 132–134; pattern block 130

northern Vietnam 4, 23

operational chain 20, 87, 96
organization: cellular production 126–127, 146–148, 152, 154; centralized coordination 148; concentration 121, 154; context (independent/attached) 121–123, 139, 155–159, 162, 178; food pattern 161; holistic specialization 126, 148; horizontal collaboration 143, 178, 219; intensity (full-time/part-time) 121–123, 148, 152, 155, 189; large scale factories 119–121; prescribed specialization 126–127; scale 121; single flow line production 126–127; small-scale household production 119–121, 151

Pass: Dasanguan 59; Guanzhong 59; Hanguguan 8, 24, 46, 59, 83; Wuguan 59, 61; Ziwuguan 61
plowshare: Hexi 222; Huize 124; lending farming tools 73; Meixian 79; Nangucheng 80; Taicheng 81, 108–109, 143–146; Tieshenggou 100; Wafangzhuang 101; Yueyang 79
population: access to iron 197, 205; capital region 57, 61, 65–67, 78, 83, 217; Chang'an 64, 69–70; growth 16, 32, 95; relocation 3, 5, 24, 61; Rome 10

Qian river 68
Qijia stone workshop 162
Qin: Bianjiazhuang 34; ceramic inscription 47, 52; Dabuzishan 34; Duke Xian 51; Duke Xiao 46; early iron 34–35; iron production 45–50, 53; iron weapon 51–52; Jingjiazhuang 34; labor mobilization 95; land system 32; Lord Shang 51, 56; Majiazhuang 37, 45; market development 51 (*see also* Qin Shihuang); Ta'erpo 49; tombs 194–195; Yimencun 35, 37 (*see also* Yongcheng)
Qin Shihuang: bronzes 126–127; *chidao* 9, 61; ironware 95; mausoleum 50, 52 (*see also* organization (cellular production)); unification 8, 21, 23, 31, 48, 53; workshop 95; Yuchi 52; *zhidao* 9, 61–62

rebellion: of Seven states 59; Su Ling 90, 114
region: definition 7; multi-layer process 186; transportation system 82, 106, 113, 147
relational approach 12, 15
Rome: changes of settlement patterns 10–11; coins 12; economy 186; globalization 5; imperial network 5, 226; imperialism 6, 23; Romanization 5, 7, 23; slave labor 140; tributary empire 227
rong: Non-sinitic ethnic group 35, 37; Zhaihetou 94

Sang Hongyang 14, 25, 140
Shangcunling 35
Shanglin yuan: bronze manufacturing (mint) 81, 193 (*see also* Han government (Shangli Zhongguan)); royal garden 62, 78
Shanyang commandery 90
shihuo 223–226
shovel 40, 132
Shu commandery 85, 193, 214
Shuihudi bamboo slips: caitie 71; food rations 150; statues on currencies 73, 85; statutes on stables and parks 85, 171, 181
sickle: Chu state 42; Jin states 40; Wafangzhuang 101
Silk road 30, 36, 54
Sima Chang 71
Sinicization 4, 23
Siwa culture 33
Songshan mountain: cluster of ironworks 99 (*see also* ironworks (Tieshenguo and Guxingzhen))
spade: Chu state 42; Erligang 41; Fenshuiling 41; Guxingzhen 100; Hexi Corridor 222; Jinan commandery 103; Qin state 37, 48, 197; price 209; Taicheng 110
Stack-casting 77, 86
Su Ling 90, 114, 140

Taicheng: analysis of iron 110–111; casting mold 108–109; distribution of remains 143–147; faunal remains 169–175; interregional exchange 112–113; joining signs 143–144; palaeobotanical remains 175; production procedures 110–111; recycling of scrap iron

112; slag 109–110; solid-state decarburization of cast iron 110; spacer 145–146
Taishan mountains: cluster of ironworks 102–105; Tailai basin 103
Taixi site 34
Tongbai mountain 101
transportation: Jingshicang 68; network 3, 9, 17, 19, 33, 148, 183, 193; Sunjianantou 68; Xiliu 68

Vijayanagara 151, 153

Wafangzhuang 101–102, 106, 108, 119, 138, 192, 218, 222
Wagner, D.: Han economy 225; innovation of cast iron 31, 42–43, 51, 53–54; iron monopoly 85, 97; production organization/form 119; steel making techniques 89, 94, 96, 114–115; transmission of iron 32–33, 36
Wangchenggang: furnace 91, 102; palaeobotanical remains 175
Wei river 24, 44, 55, 59–60, 65, 66–68, 70
Wu state (Eastern Zhou period): 38–39
Wudi: construction 66–67; crop yield 179; Dasinong 71; environment 61; expansion 6, 207; Gongguan 85; *junshu* 74; minting 78; monopoly of iron and salt 73–76; relocation of Hangu 83; state-owned enterprise/industry 13, 75, 178

Xianrentai 35
Xianyang: bone workshop 50; capital 46–47; ceramic production 47; Niejiaguo 46
Xinfeng: cemetery 95; fined iron techniques 95
Xinjiang: communication 2; early worked iron 30, 36; transmission of iron technology 34; Xiyu 2
Xiongnu 2, 8, 60, 74

Yang state: bloomery iron 51; Wuyangtai 56
Yantielun: market economy 185; state monopoly and criticism 14, 222
Yanxiadu 56

Yingchuan commandery 70, 90
Yong River 7
Yongcheng (Baoji): bronze
    manufacturing remains 193; capital
    of the Qin state 37, 44–45; Doufucun
    workshop 45–46, 50; Duke Jing's
    mausoleum of the Qin state 37
    (*see also* Nangucheng); as a ritual
    center 196; Sunjinantou 68; Xuechi
    44, 55
Yueyang: as capital 45–46, 59, 86;
    production remains 79; 1000-shi-
    grank magistrate-county 203
Yunyang 9

Zhang Anshi's family 204
Zhangdi 76

Zhangjiashan (Ernian lülling): food price
    180; Statutes on Forts and Passes 85;
    tax collection 73; Zhi lü 202
Zheng-Han Gucheng: Cangcheng 135;
    Dawuliu 135; iron tools 41; layout 134
    (*see also* Zhonghang)
zhidao 9, 62
Zhonghang: body part assemblage 164–
    166; decarburization 94; estimation of
    slaughtering ages of animals 166–168;
    faunal assemblage 162–163; ironworks
    41, 134; production organization
    136–137
Zhuangzi 200
Zhugangjian 45; *see also* Iron (steel)
    making technique (solid-state
    decarburization)